CHRIS CUNNEEN
ROB WHITE

JUVENILE JUSTICE

YOUTH AND CRIME IN AUSTRALIA

THIRD EDITION

OXFORD

UNIVERSITY PRESS

OXFORD
UNIVERSITY PRESS

253 Normanby Road, South Melbourne, Victoria 3205, Australia

Oxford University Press is a department of the University of Oxford.
It furthers the University's objective of excellence in research,
scholarship, and education by publishing worldwide in

Oxford New York

Auckland Cape Town Dar es Salaam Hong Kong Karachi
Kuala Lumpur Madrid Melbourne Mexico City Nairobi
New Delhi Shanghai Taipei Toronto

With offices in

Argentina Austria Brazil Chile Czech Republic France Greece
Guatemala Hungary Italy Japan Poland Portugal Singapore
South Korea Switzerland Thailand Turkey Ukraine Vietnam

OXFORD is a trade mark of Oxford University Press
in the UK and in certain other countries

First published 1995
Second edition published 2002
Reprinted 2003, 2004, 2005
Third edition 2007

National Library of Australia Cataloguing-in-Publication data:

Cunneen, Chris, 1953– .
Juvenile Justice: Youth and Crime in Australia.

3rd ed.
Bibliography.
Includes index.
For 2nd and 3rd year criminology, sociology and social science tertiary students.

ISBN 9780195550504.
ISBN 0 19 555050 1.

1. Juvenile delinquency - Australia - Textbooks.
2. Juvenile justice, Administration of - Australia - Textbooks.
3. Juvenile detention - Australia - Textbooks. I. White,
R. D. (Robert Douglas), 1956- . II. Title.

364.360994

Edited by Roy Garner
Text and cover design by Jenny Pace Walter
Proofread by Sandra Goldbloom Zurbo
Indexed by Neale Towart
Typeset in India by diacriTech, Chennai
Printed in Hong Kong by Sheck Wah Tong Printing Press Ltd

CONTENTS

TABLES, BOXES, AND FIGURES

INTRODUCTION

Depictions of young offenders and juvenile justice agencies are all too often based upon exaggeration, stereotype, and conjecture. Politicians and the media constantly bemoan the present youth generation's lack of discipline and respect. We are frequently told that many of these young people, especially certain 'ethnic' youth, are beyond redemption. For every story about a youth gang, there is a simultaneous demand for an even bigger stick to keep young people in line.

Young people, it seems, should not be seen or heard. They should not be allowed in the street or be visible in city centres or local neighbourhoods. To grow up 'good', they need to be restricted in where they can go and what they can do. To protect society, young people need to be under control and under surveillance.

When young people act up, when they commit crimes or engage in anti-social behaviour, then they must be held accountable. Here, we are told, the solution is to make them responsible for their actions. They must pay for their transgressions. They must make amends for the harm they have caused. They must be made to change their ways.

This book is about youth and crime in Australia, and the institutions and agencies associated with the administration of juvenile justice. It provides an overview and introduction to the main concepts and issues of juvenile justice in a way that is simple and descriptive, yet critical. The intention is to provide basic information across a broad range of areas, and in so doing raise a number of questions about the institutions of juvenile justice and, indeed, how we think about juvenile justice issues.

The distorted outlooks on and punitive approaches to youth behaviour that are so prominent in the media and in the political arena are made manifest in many different ways in the juvenile justice system. Simultaneously, however, non-coercive alternatives are also being developed, as many practitioners and theorists in the field of juvenile justice appreciate more fully than others in the community the complexities and difficulties of life for young people in the twenty-first century. Ongoing debate and discussion surround how people think about the problems of 'youth crime' and also how best to respond to it. Competing opinions indicate both the highly political nature of juvenile justice and important differences in basic philosophies.

The last decade has seen heightened public concern and moral panics about ethnic minority youth; imposition of mandatory sentences on juvenile offenders; adoption of zero-tolerance policing, especially in public spaces; persistent overrepresentation of Indigenous young people within the juvenile justice system; and intensification of intervention in the lives of young offenders and non-offenders alike. Inequality and social polarisation are growing, accompanied by the racialisation of criminal justice and the criminalisation of the poor. With the demise of the welfare state and the rise of the repressive state, discussion has often centred on how best to control, manage, and contain those youth suffering most from the disadvantages of social, economic, and political exclusion.

On the positive side, greater attention is now being given to the basic rights and well-being of young people. In particular, there has been a growth in the human rights perspective as a critical perspective by which to evaluate policing practices, the operation of courts and youth conferences, and the conditions under which young people are detained or sentenced to community work. Renewed emphasis on crime prevention has likewise been used to challenge explicitly the coercive 'law and order' approaches. Meanwhile, the increasing popularity of 'restorative justice', with an emphasis on repairing social harm, can serve as an important counterweight to traditional retributive methods that emphasise punishment.

Analysis of the principles, policies, and practices of juvenile justice is never a politically neutral exercise: that is, it always involves value judgments of some kind. In our view, such review and evaluation ought to be guided by a vision of society, and of young people, in which human rights and dignity are respected, and social equality and human liberation are the goals. This means that issues of class division, racism, sexism, homophobia, and colonialism can never be far from the centre of analysis. The marginalisation of specific groups of young people (and their families and communities), and their criminalisation by the mainstream criminal justice system, reflect substantive inequalities and the oppressive structures that shape everyday life in Australian society.

This book is divided into three parts. Part I, 'History, Theory, and Institutions', provides a historical and theoretical overview of the development of juvenile justice, its main institutions, and the nature of contemporary juvenile crime as determined by the actions of official state agencies. Part II, 'The Social Dynamics of Juvenile Justice', provides an analysis of how class, ethnicity, race, and gender impinge upon the processes and institutions of juvenile justice, and how particular groups of young people are dealt with by the system in ways that reflect their specific social location and status in society.

Part III, 'The State, Punishment, and Community', examines the operation of various parts of the juvenile justice system, from police and courts through to detention, crime prevention, and juvenile conferencing. Each section of the book attempts to provide a wide-ranging survey of relevant facts and figures, literature, and concepts, while raising issues and perspectives necessary to a critical appraisal of key questions in the juvenile justice area.

If we are to comprehend the situation of young people adequately, and to interpret their position within the field of criminal justice, then analysis must be informed theoretically as well as validated empirically. A critical criminology is one that builds upon the knowledge and conceptual contributions of socially progressive perspectives and approaches. In so doing, the objective is to provide a clear, unambiguous picture of the existing field, while retaining a critical edge.

The misrepresentation of youth on the one hand, and the intrusiveness of the state on the other, demand that issues of young people and crime be considered carefully and in a wider social and political context. We hope that, in its own modest way, this book will assist those who wish to create a more humane and socially just system of juvenile justice in Australia.

PART I
HISTORY, THEORY,
AND INSTITUTIONS

1 | The development of juvenile justice

CHAPTER HIGHLIGHTS

Introduction
Early nineteenth-century developments
Poor or criminal?
Reformatories and industrial schools
The reality of life in the schools
The juvenile court
Judicial therapists
Gendered approaches
Police, law, and juvenile delinquency
Explaining change
Conclusion

INTRODUCTION

To understand the contemporary debates about juvenile justice and the nature of juvenile crime, it is important to think about issues relating to history and theory. Have juveniles always been involved in crime, or is it a modern phenomenon? How have our thoughts about young people and crime changed? Has the place of young people in society changed? The aim of this chapter is to consider these questions in more detail through an understanding of the historical development of a separate juvenile justice system. To begin with, it is worth considering the terms we use. First, it is necessary to realise that the categories 'youth', 'adolescent', and 'juvenile' are not universal, nor are they necessarily used consistently within a society. It is important to know where particular ideas about young people came from and how these developed. The social construction of youth is neither a natural nor a neutral process, nor is it divorced from wider social, political, and economic developments.

Second, notions of juvenile delinquency depend on and recreate particular ideas about young people as a separate and socially definable group. Put simply, there can be no theory of juvenile offending without a concept of 'juvenile'. For example, in public usage and academic study, the word 'youth' has often implicitly (if not explicitly) been used to refer primarily to young men. Much of the concern with youth questions has consistently ignored the experiences of young women, or relegated these to secondary importance because of sexist definitions and conceptions of the 'real world' (see McRobbie & Garber 1976; Brake 1985; Alder 1998).

Third, the systems developed for dealing with juvenile delinquency and crime are created and developed in particular historical contexts. A considered understanding of the historical development of juvenile justice is important because of the level of mythology surrounding juvenile offending. Pearson (1983) in particular has analysed the way notions of 'hooliganism' have taken on a symbolic and mythological quality. He has analysed the way in which 'causes' of juvenile crime constantly find their way into public rhetoric, reappear at particular historical moments, and usually involve the presumed loss of authority and order. Pearson (1983:3) summarises the stereotype as follows:

> The family no longer holds its proper place and parents have abandoned their responsibilities. In the classroom where once the tidy scholars applied themselves diligently in their neat rows of desks, there is a carnival of disrespect. The police and magistrates have had their hands tied by the interference of sentimentalists and do-gooders.

The common themes of loss of authority in the key institutions—the family, education, and law enforcement—constantly re-emerge, along with claims that permissiveness has increased levels of juvenile violence and lowered standards of public behaviour. Within this scenario, the solutions proposed are often equally simple: greater levels of intervention by state agencies armed with more punitive powers.

The concept of juvenile delinquency dates from the early nineteenth century. According to Bernard (1992), one of the first uses of the term was in the *Report of the Committee for Investigating the Causes of the Alarming Increase of Juvenile Delinquency in the Metropolis*, published in London in 1816. The concept of juvenile delinquency is historically contingent (that is, the concept developed at a particular moment in history). Several commentators have also argued that the *phenomenon* of juvenile crime is also contingent. Indeed, Ferdinand (1989) provocatively asks: 'Which came first: juvenile delinquency or juvenile justice?' In other words, what are the origins of and relationship between the behaviours that are characterised as juvenile offending, and the institutions and practices of the criminal justice system developed specifically to deal with youth? In our view, both arise simultaneously. The phenomenon of juvenile delinquency appears to be specifically modern. Some commentators have argued that it occurs with the transition from rural to urban societies and is associated with five factors, these being the breakdown of traditional mechanisms of social control, urbanisation, industrialisation, population growth, and juvenile justice mechanisms that systematically detect juvenile offending (Bernard 1992:43–4). While these five factors are important, it is our view that the class-based nature of juvenile justice needs to be recognised. The transformations to which Bernard refers occurred with the development of industrial capitalism, which created an urbanised working class. New systems of dealing with young people targeted the youth of this newly formed class. In addition, the systems of control that were introduced into colonies such as Australia were imposed in a society that was also in the process of dispossessing an Indigenous minority. The treatment of Indigenous young people became an important component in the development of juvenile justice in Australia.

The key period in understanding the development of a separate system for dealing with juvenile offenders is the second half of the nineteenth century. This was an important period in the construction of other age-based differences involving young people, including restrictions on child labour and the introduction of compulsory schooling. The state began to intervene actively in the provision of 'welfare' for the children of the 'perishing classes'. In practice, these various measures were linked closely. For example, in the same year that the *Public Schools Act 1866* (NSW) was passed the Reformatory Schools Act (for young people convicted of criminal offences) and the Industrial Schools Act and Workhouse Act (for vagrant children) were passed in the United Kingdom. Specifically, in Australia the first moves to identify and recognise the category of 'young offenders' occurred with the development of institutions for dealing with neglected and destitute children. The major legal change in Australia during the period was the modification of court procedures to allow for juveniles to be dealt with summarily (that is, to have their less serious charges determined by a magistrate) (Seymour 1988:3). More broadly, juvenile justice was an element in the expansion of state control and regulation that occurred during the later part of the nineteenth and the early twentieth centuries.

EARLY NINETEENTH-CENTURY DEVELOPMENTS

There are a number of similarities in the methods that were developed for dealing with juveniles across various nations, including Australia, the USA, Canada, and the United Kingdom. One reason for these similarities was the economic, social, and political transformations already mentioned that were occurring at the time.

Until the early nineteenth century, children were expected to enter the adult world at a young age. Child labour was still regarded as universal. For example, in the early part of the nineteenth century, some 80 per cent of workers in English cotton mills were children (Morris & Giller 1987:4). Similarly, the criminal justice system did little to formally separate children from adults. There was no separate legal category of 'juvenile offender'. At common law, the age of criminal responsibility was 7 years old. For children between the ages of 7 and 14 years, there was a presumption that they were incapable of committing an offence (*doli incapax*). However, this presumption could be rebutted in court by showing that the child knew the difference between right and wrong, and knew the act in question to be wrong. It is not clear whether rules relating to the age of criminal responsibility were effective in practice: accurate knowledge of children's ages might not have been available, or magistrates might have been ignorant of the law. In any case, children under the age of 7 were incarcerated, and in Victoria in the mid-1860s, children as young as 6 could be found in Pentridge Gaol (Seymour 1988:6).

In terms of punishment, adults and juveniles were treated the same: deterrence was the main object. An English judge, after sentencing a 10 year old to death, stated that the child was a 'proper subject for capital punishment and ought to suffer'. On one day in 1815, five children between 8 and 12 years old were hanged in England for petty larceny (theft) (Morris & Giller 1987:6). Similarly, in Australia, youths were executed, flogged, and sentenced to road gangs, transportation, and imprisonment (Seymour 1988:8–9).

There is some argument, however, over the extent to which children were treated the same as adults. The age of the offender was sometimes held to be a mitigating factor in sentencing. Platt (1977) suggests that in cases relating to capital punishment, the prosecution refused to charge, juries refused to convict, and pardons were given more frequently than for adults. Notions of 'contamination' were also important in arguments concerning the separation of juveniles from adult offenders in prison. In 1836 in England, the report of the Inspector of Prisons noted that: 'the boy [sic] is thrown among veterans in guilt ... and his vicious propensities cherished and inflamed ... He enters the prison a child in years, and not infrequently also in crime; but he leaves it with a knowledge in the ways of wickedness' (cited in Morris & Giller 1987:8). In Australia, there were attempts to keep children separate from adults, even where they were held in the same jail. Some magistrates attempted to avoid imprisoning young people by discharging first offenders; using conditional discharges by placing children in the care of parents or institutions, or using conditional pardons (Seymour 1988:9). These practices modified an otherwise draconian code. The increasing prison population in the United Kingdom during the mid-nineteenth century also prompted reform (May 1981).

In the USA, the first juvenile institutions were houses of refuge such as the New York House of Refuge. This refuge was established in 1825 after numerous reports drew attention to the fact that penitentiaries contained no separate facilities for juveniles. However, it appears that few of the youth sent to the refuge would have gone to the penitentiary in any case. Many were there for vagrancy (that is, being penniless and unemployed in a public place). The 'placing out' system for juveniles, whereby youth were sent to work on farms (Bernard 1992), developed at about the same time.

There was a sense of crisis in the early nineteenth century concerning social issues such as urbanisation, industrialisation, and the growth of trade unions and working-class militancy, along with concerns about pauperism, vagrancy, and juvenile crime. There were also changes in the way crime was being conceptualised. As we discuss in chapter 2, classical criminology saw crime as an outcome of free will, and the role of punishment as deterrence. However, by the early nineteenth century there was a growth in classificatory systems of criminal causation related to the rise of positivist criminology. For example, the 1816 report into juvenile delinquency in London, mentioned earlier, states the main causes of juvenile delinquency to be the improper conduct of parents, the want of education, and the want of suitable employment. The same report also identifies problems with the severity of the criminal code, and the poor and deficient state of policing. In other words, the responsibility for juvenile offending was not necessarily seen as solely that of the young person (Morris & Giller 1987:16).

Growth in the collection of criminal statistics facilitated a focus on juveniles. By the mid-nineteenth century, criminal statistics in England and Wales were showing that the 15–20 year old age group was overrepresented in offending figures (Morris & Giller 1987:7). Thus, the development of statistics, combined with that of other disciplines, allowed for the discovery of a 'new problem'.

Contemporary religious views also fitted well with the notion that delinquency was the result of social and moral conditions rather than innate depravity. The focus on the physical conditions of the poor increased, as did the view that working-class families were ineffective and unreliable in their parenting.

POOR OR CRIMINAL?

In Australia, the first steps towards creating a separate system for juveniles occurred as a result of the problem of dealing with young people who were arriving as transported convicts. From the late eighteenth century, various schemes involving apprenticeships were utilised: indeed the first 'special institution' for juveniles was a barracks for the training of convict boys under 16 years old.

Orphan schools were also established from the early 1800s to deal with destitute children. The origins of the child welfare system in Australia include the establishment of the Female Orphan School (1801); the Male Orphan School (1819); the Benevolent Asylum (1821) for 'destitute, unfortunate, needy families'; the Female School of Industry (1826); the Roman Catholic

Orphan School (1837); and the Destitute Children's Asylum (1852). Both the female and male orphan schools adopted the policy of apprenticing children out to work. Legislative changes in New South Wales beginning in 1828 and 1834 enabled magistrates to place orphans as apprentices. Further legislative changes occurred until the late 1850s that expanded the category of children who could be bound over as apprentices (Seymour 1988:21–3). There was overlap between the processes of criminalisation and the development of specific welfare institutions. A child in poverty could be dealt with under vagrancy laws and potentially imprisoned, or the child could be treated as destitute and kept in a welfare institution. Thus, it is possible to see the development of different strategies for dealing with issues essentially related to poverty and young people, which raises important questions about discretion and decision-making powers. Certainly, part of the method of dealing with poverty was reflected in middle- and upper-class notions of the 'deserving' and 'undeserving' poor. Although all poor people shared similar material conditions, a distinction was made between the deserving and undeserving on the basis of their behaviour, attitudes, and respectability. Welfare and charitable institutions were there to assist those defined as the deserving poor, while the 'others' were treated as criminal. It appears that many children sent to jail in Australia were there as a result of vagrancy charges. A large proportion of the 230 children under 14 years of age sent to prison in Victoria during 1860 and 1861 had been sentenced for vagrancy (Seymour 1988:18–19). Thus, they were imprisoned for the crime of poverty rather than for committing any substantive offence.

REFORMATORIES AND INDUSTRIAL SCHOOLS

During the mid-nineteenth century, there were two fundamental moves towards establishing a separate system for dealing with juveniles. One was to change the role of the magistrate's court in relation to hearing offences against juveniles; the other was to establish reformatories and industrial schools.

In the United Kingdom, the first parliamentary bills to alter procedures for dealing with juveniles were debated in 1821, 1829, and 1837. However, it was not until 1847 that the Juvenile Offenders Act was passed. This legislation increased the powers of magistrates to hear summarily larceny and theft offences committed by those under 14 years of age. In Australia, the method of dealing with 'young offenders' began to change in 1849 with the introduction of an 'Act to provide for the care and education of infants who may be convicted of felony or misdemeanour' (13 Vict. No. 21). The legislation dealt with young people up to 19 years old, and allowed the court to apprentice young offenders. A more significant legislative change was the introduction of an 'Act for the more speedy trial and punishment of Juvenile Offenders' (14 Vict. No. 2) in 1850. The Act extended the summary jurisdiction to young people under 14 years old who were charged with larceny and associated offences. The legislation also allowed for different and lesser penalties to be applied to juveniles convicted of larceny than were applied to adults for the same crimes, and began the process of development of children's courts in Australia. It created not only different procedures for dealing with young people than for dealing with adults who had committed the same crimes, but also different penalties for different offences.

The establishment of reformatories (now known as juvenile detention centres) represented a major change in dealing with young people. In the United Kingdom, the statutory recognition of reformatory and industrial schools for the 'dangerous' and 'perishing' classes occurred with the *Youthful Offenders Act 1854* and the *Industrial Schools Act 1857*. Similarly, reformatories appeared in the USA in the mid-nineteenth century. In Australia, industrial and reformatory school Acts were passed in most states between 1863 and 1874 amid concern about destitute children and criticism of the lack of alternatives to imprisonment for young offenders.

English reformers such as Mary Carpenter were influential in developing new methods of dealing with young people. They saw discipline through punishment as ineffective: rather, they sought fundamental and lasting rehabilitation through change within the young person. The issue of training and reform was essentially one of effectiveness rather than benevolence. It demonstrated a fundamental shift away from deterrence as a rationale for punishment. Carpenter noted that reform occurred 'only when the child's soul is touched, when he yields from the heart'. Carpenter played a leading role in the reform movement, particularly with her book *Reformatory Schools for the Children of the Perishing and Dangerous Classes and for Juvenile Offenders*, published in 1851. Carpenter's work made a distinction between the establishment of reformatory schools for delinquents (of the 'dangerous classes') and industrial schools for the poor (the pre-delinquents of the 'perishing classes'). However, both regimes stressed religious instruction, elementary education, and industrial training.

The Australian legislation contained definitions of the situations in which 'neglected' children could be placed in institutions. For example, the *Neglected and Criminal Children's Act 1864* (Vic.), s. 13, defined a neglected child as any child found begging or receiving alms; 'wandering about', or having no home or visible means of subsistence; or any child 'whose parent represents that he is unable to control such child'. In some cases, the legislation simply recast the existing vagrancy definitions as being applicable to children, but it also added new definitions that were the forerunner of modern notions of 'uncontrollability'. The legislation in Victoria, Queensland, and New South Wales also provided for the establishment of industrial schools for those young people defined as neglected (Seymour 1988:37–43).

In addition, the new legislation provided for special procedures for dealing with young offenders. In Victoria, Queensland, and South Australia, a child convicted of an offence could be sent to a reformatory school regardless of the seriousness of the offence. In New South Wales, a young person who had been convicted of an offence that was punishable by 14 or more days imprisonment could be committed to a reformatory. These changes represented an important shift in the sentencing of young people through the separation of the nature of the offence from the penalty imposed, and a new focus on the offender rather than the offence.

Although the system established two groups—neglected children and young offenders—in reality there was a blurring of distinctions. In most Australian states, young offenders could be sent to industrial schools by the court under certain circumstances. Amendments to legislation during the 1870s further blurred the distinction between the two groups, when courts were empowered to send neglected children to reformatories if they had been leading an 'immoral or depraved life'. In addition, neglected children could be transferred administratively to the reformatory system if they proved difficult to manage.

The new legislation also empowered courts to commit young people for extended periods. This power expressed the notion that young people were being committed for training and education. Offenders were to be committed for lengthy periods, regardless of whether the crime was serious. As a result, the normal sentencing consideration that a punishment should be proportional to the seriousness of the crime was not seen as part of the law governing juveniles (Seymour 1988:48–9).

A further factor that was important in the development of the juvenile justice system was that release was determined by the institution's administration rather than by the court. Additionally, the conditions of release (on 'licence', for example) were also determined by the institution's administration. This administrative discretion was legitimated by an ideology that assumed the state was acting in the best interests of the child.

The use of reformatories and industrial schools in the United Kingdom was similar to that in Australia. The offence was often irrelevant to committal. Reformatories encouraged early intervention unrelated to the nature of the juvenile's offence, and about half the juveniles sent to reformatories were sent there on their first conviction. In addition, reform was based on discipline through work. Yet the 'work' was not training or skills acquisition, but laborious and monotonous work designed to produce individuals who would be suitable for any menial job (Morris & Giller 1987:24–7).

In the USA, there were important legal challenges concerning the placement of young people in houses of refuge, reformatories, and industrial schools. The Pennsylvania Supreme Court determined the Crouse case in 1838, in which Mary Anne Crouse had not committed a criminal offence but was seen to be in danger of growing up to be a pauper. She was committed to a house of refuge, the court deciding that holding her there was legal because she was being helped and not punished. The state assumed the role of *parens patriae*, whereby it acted in the role of the child's parents, who were seen as incapable of fulfilling the task. Further, because Crouse was being helped and not punished, there was seen to be no need for the protection of formal due process (such as presumption of innocence, or guilt proven beyond reasonable doubt) (for more details, see Bernard 1992:68–70). The Crouse case was important as the first US legal challenge to the practice of committing young people to houses of refuge and reformatories even where they had committed no criminal offence.

The O'Connell case (for details, see Bernard 1992), which was determined in the Illinois Supreme Court in 1870, saw the court reject the *parens patriae* argument (the court acting in the best interests of the child and protecting the child) and order the release of O'Connell from the Chicago Reform School. The court heard of the harsh conditions in the school, and found that O'Connell was being punished, not helped. The court was of the view that O'Connell was being imprisoned, although he had not committed a criminal offence. The O'Connell decision influenced the establishment of the juvenile court in Chicago in 1899, and led to such challenges being circumvented by new definitions of delinquency (Bernard 1992:70–3).

The rationale for the establishment of reformatories was that they would provide a special form of prison discipline for young people and transform delinquents into law-abiding citizens. According to Platt (1977), reformatory life was designed to teach the value of adjustment, private enterprise, thrift, and self-reliance. Like Mary Carpenter's aim to 'touch the soul', the reformatory masters sought to 'revolutionise … the entire being' (Platt, 1977:52). This transformation involved a different mode of punishment, and can be contextualised within broader changes occurring in punishment during the second half of the nineteenth century. By the end of that century, the focus had shifted from the belief that a criminal should be punished according to the severity of the offence to a view that the offender should receive treatment. Treatment was to be based on the diagnosis of the person's pathological condition, and also enabled the expansion and diversification of penal sanctions. According to Garland, this development marked the beginning of a new mode of sentencing that claimed to treat offenders according to their specific characteristics or needs, and not equally on the basis of the seriousness or nature of the offence (Garland 1985:28, Foucault 1977).

THE REALITY OF LIFE IN THE SCHOOLS

If so much faith was placed in the development of the new methods of control and reformation, it is fair to ask what the outcomes were. Although a separate penal system had been established for young people, in some areas children were still imprisoned with adults. In the USA, the reformatories were described as 'overcrowded, poorly equipped, badly situated and more like a prison than a school' (Platt 1977:146). In the United Kingdom, the reality of the schools was similarly far from the rhetoric. According to Harris and Webb (1987:14), there were serious problems in the recruitment of suitable staff, and punishments were severe, including solitary confinement, whipping, and diets of bread and water. Such punishments mirrored those in the adult system. In addition, early attempts to separate juvenile offenders from adult offenders were not successful. The prison hulks (boats) used for young people were in worse condition than those used for adults.

In Australia, hulks were used as reformatories in Victoria, South Australia, Queensland, and New South Wales during the latter part of the nineteenth century. There was a series of official investigations into conditions in the reformatories and industrial schools during the 1870s and 1880s. The inquiries in South Australia, New South Wales, Victoria, and Tasmania painted a picture of the institutions as brutal jails (Seymour 1988:58–61).

Reformatories and industrial schools were often combined, thus further undermining the distinction between 'neglected' young people and young offenders. Indeed, the criteria for referral to reformatory and industrial schools were vague:

- *The perishing classes:* Regarded as pre-delinquent, they were seen as the legitimate object of the state's intervention. The so-called perishing classes consisted of young people who had 'not yet fallen' into crime, but who were likely to do so because of poverty.
- *The dangerous classes:* These consisted of young people who had already committed offences and who had received the 'prison brand'.

The mixing of welfare and criminal cases within the systems of detention became a hallmark of dealing with young people in the juvenile justice system until well into the contemporary period. Many young people were sent to reformatories for minor offences. Seymour provides examples of young people being given long committals, such as a 9-year-old boy in South Australia being sent to a reformatory for six years for stealing six apples (Seymour 1988:56). One outcome was that such institutions provided for the detention of young people who would not previously have been imprisoned.

It has been suggested that in the United Kingdom the 'institutions constituted a major extension of control over the young, while simultaneously offering the apparent possibility of mass reformation and the near elimination of juvenile crime' (Harris & Webb 1987:11). Certainly, it appears the reformatories attracted a new clientele. More juveniles were brought into the juvenile justice system and were sent to reformatories. In England between 1865 and 1873, some 26,326 juveniles were sent to reformatories or industrial schools. In addition, juveniles were incarcerated longer than their adult counterparts: instead of an average three months imprisonment, they spent 2 to 5 years in reformatories (Morris & Giller 1987:24–7).

We can summarise the effects of changes brought about by the introduction of reformatories and industrial schools as:

- separate procedures for dealing with young people for some offences
- different penalties for some offences for juveniles when compared to penalties for adults
- a different and separate penal regime for juveniles
- different criteria for intervention between juveniles and adults
- overlap between welfare and criminal intervention
- high levels of administrative discretion over those young people within the juvenile penal regime
- extended and indeterminate periods of detention
- adult sentencing tariffs were no longer seen as relevant to juveniles
- earlier committal to detention for minor offences
- more young people incarcerated than previously.

It was within the context of these changes that the development of specialist children's courts took place. We deal with this issue in the following section.

THE JUVENILE COURT

The new juvenile courts that developed at the end of the nineteenth century were based on the notion of *parens patriae*. The concept had originally referred to the protection of property rights of juveniles and others who were legally incompetent; however, it came to refer to the responsibility of the juvenile courts and the state to act in the best interests of the child.

As one early twentieth-century British commentator put it, the doctrine of *parens patriae* allowed the court 'to get away from the notion that the child is to be dealt with as a criminal; to save it from the brand of criminality, the brand that sticks to it for life' (cited in Morris & Giller 1987:12).

Children's courts were established at roughly the same time in the United Kingdom, the USA, Canada, and Australia, this being during the last decades of the nineteenth century and the early years of the twentieth century. The powers of the court varied from state to state and country to country.

In the USA, the *Illinois Juvenile Court Act 1899* established the juvenile court with the power to determine the legal status of 'troublesome' or 'pre-delinquent' children. Such courts were able to investigate a variety of behaviour. Statutory definitions of delinquency included acts that would be criminal if committed by adults; acts that violated country, town, or municipal ordinances; and violations of vaguely defined catch-alls, such as vicious or immoral behaviour, incorrigibility, truancy, profane or indecent language, growing up in idleness, or living with any vicious or disreputable person (Platt 1977:138).

The concept of *parens patriae* authorised the courts to use wide discretion in resolving the problems of young people. A child was not accused of a crime, but offered assistance and guidance. Intervention was not supposed to carry the stigma of a criminal record, and hearings were conducted in relative privacy with informal proceedings.

The legislation introduced in Illinois was well received by the judiciary and legal profession, and became the foundation for other US states. Juvenile courts were established in Wisconsin and New York in 1901, and in Ohio and Maryland in 1902. By 1928, all but two US states had adopted a juvenile court system. Canada adopted legislation in 1908.

The first annual reports from the Cook County juvenile court in Chicago indicated that public-order offences and school truancy made up the majority of charges that led to the 'delinquency' cases dealt with by the court (Platt 1977:140). Failure to conform to new forms of social control (such as compulsory education) was clearly an important source of delinquency classifications.

In England by the end of the nineteenth century, some towns, such as Manchester and Birmingham, had begun to operate separate juvenile courts. Separate courts were established throughout England and Wales after the *Children Act 1908* was introduced. The legislation gave the courts criminal jurisdiction over criminal matters and civil jurisdiction in relation to welfare matters. According to Harris and Webb, 'it made the juvenile court itself a locus for conflict and confusion, a vehicle for the simultaneous welfarization of delinquency and the juridicization of need' (1987:9). The legislation also contained a variety of provisions, of which those dealing with a separate juvenile court were only a part. Other sections dealt with the prevention of cruelty to children, and prohibitions on begging and prostitution. At around the same time, the statutory creation of probation and preventive detention occurred.

In Australia, the major reason given for establishing children's courts was that they ensured that young people were tried separately from adults and were not subject to the harmful effects of contamination and stigma—particularly where the young person was before the court on neglect matters. Australian legislation establishing separate children's courts was introduced as follows:

- South Australia—*State Children Act 1895*
- New South Wales—*Neglected Children and Juvenile Offenders Act 1905*
- Victoria—*Children's Court Act 1906*
- Queensland—*Children's Court Act 1907*
- Western Australia—*State Children Act 1907*
- Tasmania—*Children's Charter 1918.*

The Australian legislation was based on child-saving rhetoric similar to that used in the USA. The courts were to be parental and informal, with correction administered in a 'fatherly manner' (Seymour 1988:70–1).

Magistrates were to be specially selected, trained, and qualified to deal with young people; probation officers were to play a special role in supervising young people and preparing background reports.

The legislation establishing children's courts in Australia gave jurisdiction to the courts over criminal matters (juvenile offending) and welfare matters (neglected children and young people). The children's courts also had exclusive jurisdiction, which meant that other, lower courts could not hear cases involving children. The legislation also stipulated that the children's court had to sit separately to the other courts, and that special magistrates had to be appointed. In practice, most magistrates were simply designated as children's magistrates, and only in the major cities did anything like special courts exist (Seymour 1988:96).

There were important variations between jurisdictions concerning the extent to which the juvenile court differed from the adult criminal courts. For instance, the children's court in Australia was not as different from the adult courts as it was in the USA. In the USA, the young person appeared in the court as a result of a delinquency petition, and the court had to determine whether the child was delinquent, not whether they had committed a particular offence. In contrast, in Australia the court had to determine whether the young person had committed an offence, at least in regard to criminal matters. In relation to welfare matters, the court had to be shown that the child or young person was neglected within the terms of the legislation (although this was not the case in relation to Indigenous children).

The development of probation was also an important adjunct to the new children's courts. Probation predated the courts and had arisen from voluntary charitable and religious work. In the USA, members of the Board of State Charities had attended court hearings involving children, and as a result about one-third of such children were placed on probation under the members' supervision. In the United Kingdom, the First Offenders Act, passed in 1887, had allowed the supervision of minor first offenders by 'missionaries' and voluntary workers. Similarly, in Australia, the courts had offered conditional discharges to offenders, and this had been referred to as probation. The development of separate courts for young people led to a more systematic use of probation, and in various parts of Australia the children's court legislation allowed for juvenile offenders to be released on probation.

Initially, honorary probation officers were attached to the children's courts, with the function of preparing background reports and conducting supervision. The use of probation became an important sentencing option for the children's courts. By 1908, there were 211 honorary officers appointed to the children's courts in Victoria, and by 1909, there were 250 officers in New South Wales (Seymour 1988:100–101). Outcomes for the Sydney Children's Court for a 12-month period ending in April 1911 revealed that 873 children had been found guilty of an offence, of whom 46 per cent were released on probation (Seymour 1988:104).

JUDICIAL THERAPISTS

The children's courts encouraged minimum procedural formality and greater dependency on new personnel such as probation officers. Judges were encouraged to look at the character and social background of the 'delinquents'. In this sense, the movement has been described as anti-legal (Platt 1977:141). Furthermore, the court's intervention was justified where no offence had actually been committed but where the young person was causing problems for someone in authority, be that a parent, teacher, or social worker. In Australian jurisdictions, such matters could come before the courts in the form of a range of welfare complaints or status offences, such as uncontrollability, exposure to moral danger, or truancy.

One way of conceptualising the relationship between the children's court, its ancillary staff, and the young person has been through notions of the 'therapeutic' state. Some commentators have argued that the 'role model for juvenile court judges was doctor-counselor rather than lawyer. Judicial therapists were expected to establish a one-to-one relationship with delinquents' (Platt 1977:142). Donzelot (1979) has also argued that the advent of the juvenile court changed the relationship of the family to outside agencies. He argues that the family became subject to a 'tutelary complex', whereby a number of agencies, including juvenile justice, reduced the family's autonomy and instead established the family as a site of intervention. In Donzelot's terms, the transition has been from government of the family, to government through the family. The term 'government' in this context refers to the process of social and legal regulation. With the development of a separate system for dealing with young people, families can be more closely policed (in the broadest sense of the term), and recalcitrant children removed.

During the late nineteenth century, there were specific intellectual developments that had an impact on the construction of juvenile delinquency and that facilitated specific forms of intervention. These new forms of knowledge gave the promise of scientific neutrality, which also provided legitimacy to the benevolent intentions of the court. The discourse of reformation included a range of new disciplines, such as child psychiatry, psychology, and paediatrics. The forms of intervention were also connected to the new categorisation of young people as 'adolescent'—a term thought to have been created by G. Stanley Hall in his book *Adolescence*, published in the late nineteenth century (Morris & Giller 1987:4). Developing social and psychological theories began to identify the developmental stages of children and adolescents. These intellectual developments saw children and youth as vulnerable, and were linked to—and justified the introduction of—'a deluge of protective legislation' in areas such as child welfare, education, and labour (Gillis 1981:133).

There was also a shift in attitudes towards penality. The 'scientific' discourses on behaviour supported the move to impose long-term 'training' through indeterminate (open-ended, with no fixed term) sentences for young people. The growth of positivist criminology in the later part of the nineteenth century also provided an intellectual framework that facilitated separate treatment for juveniles, with the emphasis on classification by age and the psychological attributes of each offender (Morris & Giller 1987:18).

Views on the therapeutic nature of intervention are also reflected in the development of the notion that justice is to be personalised in terms of its style as well as its outcomes. At the time the new juvenile court buildings were opened in Chicago in 1907, it was claimed that 'the hearings will be held in a room fitted up as a parlour rather than a court, around a table instead of a bench ... The hearings will be in the nature of a family conference, in which the endeavour will be to impress the child with the fact that his own good is sought alone' (cited in Platt 1977:143).

Similar arguments were put forward in Australia for the construction of separate facilities for children's court hearings. In reality, though, most matters were determined in the physical surroundings of the local magistrate's court.

GENDERED APPROACHES

Because in its development juvenile justice was concerned with questions of youth behaviour, it is not surprising that this interest had a special meaning for young women. From the earliest developments of separate systems for dealing with youth, there appear to have been specific gender-based differences in the treatment of young people. Schlossman and Wallace (1978) note that, in the USA young women were focused upon because of their sexuality. The 'immoral conduct' of girls was broadly defined, and they were subjected to physical examinations to determine whether they had been sexually active. Schlossman and Wallace also found that girls were given longer reformatory sentences. In Canada, it has also been noted that, historically, females received more severe forms of intervention from the juvenile courts than males (Schissel 1993:11).

Similar issues have been raised in Australia. Jaggs (1986:62) noted that, in Victoria, 'girls' larceny and other offences gave cause for concern, but general "wildness" and sexual misbehaviour gave more, since they breached strongly held views on female purity'. Girls who misbehaved were thought to be worse than boys and more difficult to reform. As a result, longer periods of incarceration seemed appropriate for young women.

A study of Parramatta Industrial School for Girls also argued that the school's focus was on moral reconstruction of the young women sent there. Training focused on domestic skills and moral purity, and at least until the early twentieth century the regime was harsh, with no personal possessions allowed, no privacy, two outside visits per year, and no outside authority to whom the girls could appeal. Punishments included caning ('thrashing' or 'whipping'), head shaving, 'standing out' (standing outside perfectly still for a number of hours), and isolation (Willis 1980:184–8).

By the early twentieth century, legislation also began to refer specifically to young women and their behaviour. Thus, the *Neglected Children and Juvenile Offenders Act 1905* (NSW) neglect category had specific provisions that related to girls and young women. Girls and young women could be charged with being neglected if they were found soliciting men or otherwise behaving in an indecent manner (Willis 1980:185). There were no equivalent provisions relating to males.

Young women were also punished when they were the victims of serious crime. As Van Krieken (1991:93) has noted, the entry books to Parramatta Industrial School for Girls showed that girls who were raped or the victims of incest often found themselves committed to the institution, while the perpetrators remained free. Parramatta was to remain the main institution for girls in New South Wales until the late 1970s. A recent senate inquiry into institutional care in Australia noted that:

> Parramatta Girls' Industrial School ... became renowned for extreme cruelty, was the subject of many inquiries which were scathing of its activities and achieved notoriety in the 1960s when many of the girls rioted against its conditions (Senate Community Affairs References Committee 2004:55).

The inquiry received many submissions from women who had been in the Parramatta institution, such as the following.

> When I got to Parramatta I was told that they would break my spirit at that time I didn't know what they meant. A Mr Gordon punched me in the face several times, my nose bled. (Sub 39)
>
> I did not know what cruelty was like until I went into Parramatta Girls Home ... no child should have endured the neglect, the cruelty, the brutality, malice and immorality that were shown by many of the staff to many of the girls in the home. (Sub 110)
>
> I was involved in the Parramatta riots. Myself and other girls were the first to get on the roof at Parramatta which was to escape the brutal bashing we knew we would get for leaving the laundry. Mr Johnson was then in charge, he was a brutal man and within that week I had seen him bash and kick a girl that he had been molesting to try and induce a miscarriage. (Sub 250) (Senate Community Affairs References Committee 2004:56).

POLICE, LAW, AND JUVENILE DELINQUENCY

The development of new methods of dealing with young people went hand in hand with developments in the recorded incidence of essentially new categories of minor juvenile crime. An analysis by Gillis (1975) of Oxford Police Court records between 1895 and 1914 shows that juvenile crime was apparently increasing at a faster rate than adult crime in this period. These figures would seem to support fears at that time about rising juvenile crime, but a closer examination of the pattern of offending shows uneven distribution across various offences. The major increases were in minor summary and public-order offences such as drunkenness, gambling, malicious mischief, loitering, wilful damage, begging, dangerous play, and discharge of fireworks. The analysis of a more serious offence, theft, shows that this was associated with minor items (fruit, vegetables, toys, sweets, cigarettes, and so on).

It would appear that two broad categories of offences were important. Young people were brought before the courts for public-order offences related to leisure activities in public, and for property offences associated with economic need. Humphries (1981) has argued, on the basis of oral histories, that many offences can be viewed as expressions of 'social crime'. The concept of social crime encompasses 'the innumerable minor crimes against property committed by working class children and youth that were condoned by large sections of both the youth and parent cultures as legitimate despite their illegality' (Humphries 1981:151). Many property crimes were necessitated and justified by extreme poverty and the struggle for survival. The most common form of property theft, which was seen as a customary right among working-class communities, involved supplementing the family's food and fuel supplies. In England, the single most important category of juvenile crime during the early twentieth century was 'simple and minor larceny', which 'comprised taking coal from pitheads, chumps of wood from timber yards and vegetables from farmer's fields, poaching rabbits and so on' (Humphries 1981:151). The actual nature of social crime was complex, and varied significantly between different areas, depending on opportunities offered by the local economy and the nature of local traditions.

Various government studies at the time suggested that petty crime was most common among unskilled, unemployed, and sole-parent families, and that older children in the family were more likely to be delinquent. The dominant criminological classifications of juvenile delinquency during the late nineteenth and early twentieth centuries saw juvenile crime as associated with weakness of character, ignorance, irrationality, or some other form of pathology. The associated explanations relied on biological and psychological interpretations such as 'primitive impulses'. However, Humphries has argued that such explanations ignored the significance of poverty, inequality, and class conflict as significant factors in crime. The domestic economy of the working-class household provided a rational set of motives, whereby the eldest children committed offences to help support the family. In other words, there was a moral economy operating that valued family support more than compliance with the law.

Offences related to public order tended to involve arrests of young people in groups of two or more, and sometimes in groups of as many as ten or fifteen. Charges relating to property damage, mischief, and dangerous play could involve many young people and derive from particular policing activities. Gillis states: 'Sliding on bridges, throwing rocks and playing street football were typical activities which led to the arrest of large groups. This would seem to suggest that there was a tendency on the part of the public and the police to attribute antisocial intents to boys collectively, thus raising the rate of recorded offences ...' (1975:103).

The surveillance of public space and the ability of police to arrest young people raise the issue of developments in policing—particularly with a focus on the economic and leisure activities of working-class young people. Gillis (1975) argues that, ironically, the collective behaviour of youth had actually improved by the later part of the nineteenth century. Thus, increased arrest rates were likely to have been a function of a number of factors, including law-enforcement practices, new legislation, and the growth of a range of organisations (such as the Boy Scouts) whose intent was to modify young people's behaviour.

Police functions and practices were altering. The late nineteenth century saw expanded, reorganised, and increasingly professional police forces. Police had responsibilities in relation to young people that extended beyond the notion of criminality to one of monitoring young people's social life. Police were involved as welfare agents, truant officers, and moral guardians (Finnane 1994:7). In New South Wales in the 1890s, the police took on the role of regulating truants. Official arrest figures from the nineteenth century in Australia show a primary concern with petty crime and public order; however, welfare complaints such as neglect or uncontrollability were also important. Girls were increasingly represented in welfare complaints such as of uncontrollability (Finnane 1994).

The different sentencing regimes for juveniles convicted of larceny, and the extension of the magistrates' jurisdiction, resulted in more juveniles being prosecuted by police. In other words, the net was made wider because more juveniles were brought before the courts as a result of the seemingly beneficial reforms (Seymour 1988:33). Special laws were developed during the 1870s and 1880s that were aimed specifically at young people's behaviour. In legislation such as the *Juvenile Offenders Act 1875* (Tas.), specific juvenile behaviour, such as indecent exposure, assault, obscene language, throwing stones, obstructing a railway, and vandalism, could be dealt with in the magistrate's court.

There was also a move away from the old police practice of dealing with juvenile offenders on the spot. Corporal punishment by police was viewed as inappropriate, particularly by organisations such as the National Society for the Prevention of Cruelty to Children. One effect of reducing the use of arbitrary punishment was that the police made more use of the courts (Gillis 1975). Indeed, in New South Wales the establishment of the children's court and legislation relating to neglected children was recognised by its architects as facilitating police intervention (Finnane 1994:17). Information available from the Sydney Children's Court was seen to support greater intervention, particularly in relation to public behaviour. In 1911, about one-third of all the offences determined in the Sydney Children's Court related to riotous behaviour, throwing stones, playing games, 'boarding or quitting tram in motion', and 'bathing in view' (Seymour 1988:104). Similar evidence from Western Australia also suggests prosecutions for very minor offences, such as breaking branches from trees and kicking footballs in a park. Seymour argues that minor incidents such as these would probably not have been brought before magistrates prior to the advent of the children's court, and it seems likely that the net was widened, with greater level of prosecutions for minor offences (Seymour 1988:109).

Schools and youth organisations also had the indirect effect of causing more young people to appear before the courts as they defined and attempted to control the public behaviour, work activities, and leisure of young people. Such organisations' influence was extended through social changes, such as the provision of compulsory education; and legislation, such as the *English Prevention of Cruelty and Protection of Children Act 1889*. There was also a range of reformative organisations, such as the Salvation Army, Boy Scouts, Boys' Brigades, Young Men's Christian Associations (YMCA), and Young Women's Christian Associations (YWCA), which were engaged in activities aimed at altering young people's public and private behaviour. 'Keeping them off the streets' became a shorthand way of describing this function (Maunders 1984; Gillis 1975). The school itself also became a site of discipline and the law. One school's punishment book for 1905 showed that almost one-third of the punishments related to extracurricular activities (Gillis 1975:118).

One outcome of the changes in legislation and of the spread of schooling and youth organisations was that clearer distinctions between 'rough' and 'respectable' working-class youth were established. Certainly, police perceptions of male youth were defined in terms of class and sex. 'Such perceptions did not necessarily mean that police would deferentially side with the wishes of social elites against the alleged depredations of working class youth. But they did work with social distinctions which pitted the respectable against the rough' (Finnane 1994:13).

The new and expanding jurisdiction dealing specifically with young people allowed greater regulation. New offences were created and welfare provisions were developed. There were new methods of surveillance and new bureaucratic structures for enforcing social regulation. There is widespread empirical evidence to suggest that increased numbers of young people were dealt with formally by the juvenile justice system.

EXPLAINING CHANGE

Historians and criminologists have debated how to conceptualise the effects of the establishment of a separate legal regime for dealing with young people. These debates are not of purely academic interest because they also illuminate current issues relevant to juvenile justice. Different conceptual approaches can be seen in box 1.1.

As can be seen in box 1.1, one way of conceptualising the period of changing policy is to view it in terms of progress. A separate children's court and separate penal system can be seen as a humanitarian advance on former methods of dealing with young people. They can be seen as necessarily good. Liberal (or 'Whig') histories are often criticised for their teleological or evolutionary view of the past: that is, for seeing the past as inevitably and progressively leading to the present. An implicit assumption is that because the present is the outcome of progressive steps in the past, then the present system is the best and most advanced. This view of history sees the main source of change as deriving from enlightened and humane individuals who care about the plight and welfare of working-class children. The state is seen as a neutral institution towards which reform activity can be directed.

In the 1960s and early 1970s, these views of the past were subjected to intense criticism. The institutions of juvenile justice were seen as a mechanism of social control, and criticised for being inefficient, brutal, mismanaged, and corrupt. A key component of the critique was that the new systems of regulation increased levels of surveillance and 'subjected more and more juveniles to arbitrary and degrading punishments' (Platt 1977:xvii). In some of these 'social control' approaches, the issue of class is seen as important. Social control mechanisms are seen as extending control over the working class, particularly young people. Implicit in these approaches is the view that state institutions are a form of regulation by one class over another.

Some writers have stressed the incorporation of a political economy approach, which argues that the nineteenth and early twentieth century developments in juvenile justice were neither isolated nor autonomous, since broader economic and social reforms were occurring that were opposed to *laissez-faire* capitalism, and there was an increased role for state institutions in economic regulation. The new political economy at this time was characterised by long-range planning and bureaucratic routine (Platt 1977:xix). Conceptual changes related to scientific management in industry, intelligence testing in education, and classifications and treatment in criminal justice. Developments within industrial capitalism demanded a greater role for the state in preparing potential workers for the labour market while ensuring the maintenance of public order and protection of property.

BOX 1.1 HISTORICAL INTERPRETATIONS

THE LIBERAL ANALYSIS (PROGRESS AND HUMANITARIANISM)
Focus: Individual moral reformation and training for respectable work and life

CENTRAL IDEAS	KEY PLAYERS	SOURCE OF CHANGE
Progress	Middle-class reformers	Humane individuals
Humanitarianism	Child-savers' movement	Neutral state
Benevolent intentions according to bourgeois ideals	Charities	Enlightenment ideals
Salvation of children		

CRITICAL ANALYSIS (SOCIAL CONTROL AND POLITICAL ECONOMY)

Focus: The policing and regulation of the lives of working-class families and children to ensure social order and capitalist economic relations

CENTRAL IDEAS	KEY PLAYERS	SOURCE OF CHANGE
Social divisions	State	Structural changes associated with capitalist development
Maintenance of bourgeois social order	Ruling class	
	New professions	Resocialisation of working class
Structural need for disciplined and hard-working labour	Police	
	Juvenile courts and institutions	Increased state intervention
Effects of policies on working-class children		

SITUATIONAL ANALYSIS (SOCIAL ACTORS AND DIVERSE INTERESTS)

Focus: The complexity of change reflects active responses from diverse actors with different interests

CENTRAL IDEAS	KEY PLAYERS	SOURCE OF CHANGE
Power is dispersed throughout social interactions	Middle-class reformers	Self-conscious actions and attitudes of people
	Working-class parents and organisations who used the system to their advantage	Unintended effects
Emphasis on how reforms translated into practical situations		Institutional dynamics shape activity/policy
	Police and institutional staff	
Actual processes of implementation in relation to child's circumstances versus seriousness of offences		
Agency or role of working class, as well as middle class, in reform period		

Australian historians of child welfare and juvenile justice, such as Van Krieken (1991), have argued that it is important to understand how the working class used the new institutions to their own advantage. Depending on their situation, different social actors had different interests in how the juvenile justice system developed and was used. Class was important, but the new institutions were not merely repressive of working-class youth. Complaints about young people might arise from family members, neighbours, or the public, and not simply derive from police or institutional surveillance (see also Finnane 1994).

Van Krieken (1991) argues that there was a division between the 'respectable' and 'non-respectable' sections of the working class. The respectable working class and sections of the labour movement supported some aspects of the new institutions, such as compulsory education. They might well have supported new standards of public propriety and morality against what they saw to be the behaviour of the non-respectable urban poor. Indeed, Finnane (1994:10–15) notes that police used distinctions between the respectable and the 'rough' working class when deciding whether to enforce particular public-order laws. According to Van Krieken, we need to consider how working-class people accepted certain standards in their own interests and were not simply passive victims of new levels of state intervention.

CONCLUSION

The changes that occurred in the last half of the nineteenth and early part of the twentieth centuries with the introduction of specific measures to deal with young people brought before the courts can be understood within the context of broad changes occurring in the forms of state intervention. Education Acts compelled children between certain ages to attend school. Legislation regulating labour prohibited children of certain ages from working. The period of dependency of children was extended. In relation to welfare, reliance on private philanthropic organisations was transformed so that the state assumed responsibility for welfare provision.

State intervention changed the overall position of young people in Australia during this time. New forms of regulation related to education, work, and leisure. Increased police surveillance, the development of the children's court, alterations to the penal regime for young people, and the growth of new professions were all part of this broader change. There was also greater regulation of family relations, including guardianship laws. It is clear that the law was used to enforce standards and obligations on parents. Compulsory education is one example. In England, there were 86,149 prosecutions of parents under the 1870 Education Act in one year alone (Morris & Giller 1987:22).

However we conceptualise the changes, it is clear there were fundamental shifts during the late nineteenth and early twentieth centuries in the relationship between young people and the law. There was a separate method of punishment for young people, including new penal institutions and greater surveillance at home and in the community through probation officers. Separate sentencing regimes were established, including the use of indeterminate sentencing. Separate children's courts were established, not only to determine criminal matters but also to assess neglect and welfare matters. Particular practices were also seen as appropriate in dealing with young people who came before the courts, particularly the use of social-background reports. Partly as a response to changes in legislation and developments in policing, and partly as a result of the existence of separate children's courts, there was an increase in the number of young people prosecuted and brought formally into the justice system. Finally, there were gendered approaches to the application of the new forms of controlling young people.

These changes in policy need to be contextualised within the theoretical developments in criminology. We have referred on a number of occasions in this chapter to developments in classification, new disciplines, and changes in thinking about young people. In the following chapters, we explore the developments of criminological theory and various explanations for juvenile offending.

2 | Theories of juvenile offending

INTRODUCTION

The aim of this chapter is to explore theories and explanations for why young people commit crime. The chapter outlines the main theories of juvenile offending, and provides a brief overview of key concepts and ideas pertaining specifically to young offenders. As will be seen, there are many different explanations put forward to explain juvenile offending. These range from perspectives that emphasise individual offender choice in whether to offend, through to those that emphasise social factors such as poverty, limited employment opportunities, and school performance in shaping juvenile criminal careers. The chapter concludes with a discussion of the different levels of analysis evident in general accounts of youth offending.

The focus of the many different theories of juvenile offending varies considerably. Some concentrate on examining the criminal act; some, the offender. Others see crime as a social process; still others look at it in terms of power relations. The manner in which causes are represented has major implications for strategies of crime prevention and crime control. Again, depending upon the theory adopted, the 'solution' may be seen in terms of punishment, treatment, or rehabilitation of offenders, restitution involving victims and offenders, or major structural change requiring transformations in the nature of basic social institutions. Specific theories therefore arise from specific ways of viewing crime, the role of criminal justice institutions, and the appropriate strategies for grappling with criminal and deviant behaviour.

Differences in the broad level of analysis, and in specific discipline-related perspectives, can be linked to some extent to differences in the political framework of the writer. It is a truism that any particular criminological theory does not exist in a political vacuum: each is tied to a wider social and philosophical view of society. The motivation, conceptual development, methodological tools, and social values associated with a specific approach are usually intertwined with one of the three broad political perspectives: conservative, liberal, or radical (see White & Haines 2004). If we acknowledge the centrality of 'politics' in criminological analysis, then we must accept that there is no such thing as value-free criminology. Values of the Right (conservative), Left (radical) and Centre (liberal) are embedded in the criminological enterprise. Criminological theory is always related to specific historical contexts, material conditions, and political struggles.

The objectives and methods of analysis used in criminology reflect certain underlying ideas and concerns of the writer. In reading criminological material, then, it is important to examine the assumptions of the writers, the key concepts they use, and the methods or arguments used to support their theories, in order to identify their conceptions of society and of human nature, and the kinds of reforms or institutions they ultimately support. It is also important to identify the silences in a particular theory or tradition: that is, which questions are not being asked, and why not? Finally, it is crucial to consider the social relevance of the theory or perspective. What does it tell us about our society and the direction our society is or ought to be taking? Fundamentally, the study of crime involves the values and opinions of the criminologist, and this is no less true of juvenile justice than of any other area of criminology.

CLASSICAL THEORY AND INDIVIDUAL CHOICE

In the classical tradition, the purpose of punishment within the law is to deter individuals from impinging upon and violating others' rights and interests. All of us as individuals are seen to have an equal capacity to reason, and hence are deemed responsible for our own actions. The classical view is that there is a consensus among members of a society regarding the desirability of a social contract that denotes the relationship between the state and the individual. Since individuals are viewed as having equal power to reason and to support a rational system based upon reason, then any laws and rules developed under such a system are seen to be reasonable and binding for all (known as the social contract). Thus, rule is by consensus, which in turn is rationally established. An individual who engages in crime either acts irrationally or makes a bad choice.

Classicism locates the source of criminality within the rational, reasoning individual, and sees it as a matter of choice and intent on the part of the offender. Related to this is the notion that each individual should be made familiar with the law, and with its punishments, in order to make a correct choice in terms of behaviour. Punishment is intended to deter individuals from choosing wrongly in their immediate and future activities, through the threat of possible pain (penalty). Individuals are held responsible for their actions.

Classical criminal policy focuses primarily on the criminal act and suggests equal punishments for equal crimes. Again, the emphasis is on equal treatment because of the presumption of equal rationality and the necessity for equality in legal proceedings. The punishment is meant to fit the crime. It is assumed that, through punishment, the offending individual will come to see obeying the law as the most rational of choices. For the sake of equality, it is thought that penalties should be fixed prior to sentencing, and be administered in accordance with the actual offence that has been committed, rather than with any prior offences, or as a result of speculation regarding of the offender's possible future offences.

The classical school of criminology emphasises choice, responsibility, and intent. This is a *voluntaristic* conception of crime, which locates the reasons for crime within the individual social actor. It stresses equality before the law, and equality in people's capacity to reason and make choices. Crime is seen as a violation of the legal consensus, which itself is seen to reflect the social contract. The law is seen as needing to be codified, neutral, and impartial, and punishment is seen as intended to deter individuals according to pleasure—pain principles. The main stress is on the criminal act, and the equal and systematic application of laws in relation to this act.

The *right-wing libertarian* perspective is a modern version of the classical approach. It is based upon a moral philosophy of egoism (selfishness), in which the only constraint on behaviour is the duty not to initiate force over others. The notion of a competitive ethos pervades this perspective. This is usually tied to the idea of rights to private property as being the first virtue of the legal and criminal justice system. Accordingly, crime is defined in terms of the infringement of private property, including infringements of one's physical self. Since this perspective conceives of human nature as being possessive and individualistic—and conceives of crime mainly in terms of private property—the role of the state is seen as being restricted to those instances where other people actually come to harm through one's social actions (see Tame 1991). So-called 'victimless crimes' are therefore seen as needing to be decriminalised insofar as they do not directly affect those beyond oneself. In other words, 'anything goes' in this perspective: people should have complete liberty to do as they will, as long as they do not infringe upon the property of others in an illegal way.

From the point of view of *rational choice theory*, we need to assume that most 'criminals' are rational agents who can be deterred from committing additional crimes by an increase in the punishment they might expect to receive (Buchanan & Hartley 1992). According to the advocates of this approach, the most economically efficient way to manage the crime problem is to privatise institutions such as prisons, and to increase the probability of detection and conviction of offenders. The broad philosophical orientation of rational choice theory is also closely related to the adoption of prevention techniques directed primarily at reducing opportunities for crime (see Felson 1994), rather than at the structural reasons for offending behaviour or the criminalisation process itself.

The *traditional conservative* perspective takes a broader view than the right-wing libertarian of what constitutes a crime. The conservative view of crime includes not only that activity which endangers property or the person, but also includes morality. Hence, attacks on certain traditional values and people's respect for authority generally may be linked to criminality. From this point of view, crime is not only a matter of free choice: it is also linked to certain intrinsic aspects of humanity. In particular, people are seen as possessing certain 'natural urges' that go against the more civilised or divine purposes of society. In order to constrain these urges, it is felt necessary to establish a strong order based upon personal sacrifice, self-discipline, and submission to authority (Tame 1991). Order must take precedence over all else, including justice. Crime is said to be caused by the unwillingness of people to accept discipline, by the undermining of traditional loyalties such as to the (patriarchal) family, and by the pursuit of immediate individual gratification without appropriate hard work.

According to this approach, punishment is an essential part of deterrence not only because it establishes personal responsibility for one's actions, but also because punishment has an important symbolic impact on society as a whole. That is, punishment is seen in terms of its effect on the establishment of moral solidarity through stigmatisation. Strong emphasis is placed upon the importance of morality in the maintenance of social authority: thus, someone who does something deemed to be wrong or harmful must be punished swiftly and appropriately in order to set the moral standard. Unlike the libertarian perspective, the conservative point of view often favours increased state intervention in everyday social life because it is felt that only strong coercive measures will ultimately keep people in line and teach them the discipline they require to live as members of a civilised community.

The overriding message of these theories is that there is a need to 'get tough on criminals', to hold them responsible for their actions, and to punish wrongdoers in a consistent manner so they get their 'just deserts'. People make choices, and according to these theories they must pay for these choices. In a nutshell, the argument is that if you 'do the crime', then you must 'do the time'. But should these principles also apply to juvenile offenders?

The main problem of classical theory and its variants is that they tend to ignore individual differences between criminal actors. They assume that everyone is a rational actor capable of exercising free choice. Practically speaking, however, it has long been recognised that some categories of people—the aged, the young, people with mental illness or intellectual disability—do not have the same capacities as others. Thus, they are singled out as possessing diminished responsibility for their actions. Within the juvenile justice area, these considerations are evident, for example in legal doctrine pertaining to the age of criminal responsibility, and *doli incapax*, both of which relate to competency and responsibility (see chapter 10). A key tension within the classical tradition is whether to emphasise full criminal responsibility on the part of juveniles, or whether to acknowledge different capacities depending upon age.

More generally, classicism has been criticised for assuming equality for all when this is clearly not the case in a society riven by deep social divisions and inequalities (Young 1981). Locating crime causation within the individual (by way of their supposed exercise of free will or choice) has also been criticised by another school of criminology, namely, the positivists.

POSITIVISM AND INDIVIDUAL CRIMINAL BEHAVIOUR

In contrast to classical thinking, the hallmark of positivism is that behaviour is *determined*, in the sense that individual behaviour is shaped by factors such as physiology, personality, social upbringing, and so on. Positivism further asserts that offenders vary, that individual differences exist between offenders, and that these in turn must be acknowledged and classified or measured in some way. The focus is on individuals, who are seen to require treatment, since they are not necessarily responsible for their criminality. Thus, positivists concentrate on the offender and the offender's characteristics.

The practitioner's role is seen to be to identify specific determining factors with regard to a particular offender, and then to treat the offender or correct the problem in some way. This type of reasoning places a lot of power in the hands of the 'expert' whose job it is to diagnose, classify, and ultimately prescribe treatment for the individual. A central idea of positivism is that when a person is sentenced, they are sentenced to receive help. The idea is to treat the criminal, not the crime.

When it comes to the operation of the criminal justice system, the positivist concept of treatment differs from the classical emphasis on punishment. For example, positivism translates into an argument in favour of indeterminate sentences; the criminal act is downplayed in favour of concentration on the offender. Since each offender is an individual, and different from all other offenders, treatment must be individualised. The length of sentence in custody therefore depends upon the diagnosis and classification (severe or minor problem, dangerous or not dangerous) rather than simply the content of the criminal act that was committed. As we saw in chapter 1, these ideas have had particular application to young people.

Positivism is an overarching perspective, and thus within this general orientation there are numerous different studies and explanations (see White & Haines 2004). The three main strands of positivism include the biological, the psychological, and the sociological. Although positivism embraces a diverse range of ideas, techniques, and concepts specific to particular disciplines, a central proposition is that a moral consensus exists in society in relation to what constitutes 'deviant' and 'normal' behaviour.

Our initial concern is with positivist approaches that see behavioural problems in terms of an individual pathology or deficiency. These approaches can be summarised in terms of three main tendencies in research:

- those that focus on biological factors
- those that concentrate on psychological factors
- those that present biosocial explanations for crime.

There are two broad strands within the *biological* explanatory framework. One argues that, in essence, the criminal is 'born'. Criminality and criminal behaviour are thus seen as primarily attributable to inherited predispositions. Some writers argue that our genetic makeup directly affects things such as our intellect and our temperamental traits, putting us at risk of engaging in criminal behaviour (see Fishbein 1990). Different genetic factors are thus seen as being linked to particular behavioural patterns.

The other strand in the biological explanatory framework argues that biological factors are crucial in determining behaviour, but that they may stem from the environment rather than simply be inherited. In this framework, criminals are *made* as a result of environmental factors that affect their biological functioning. For example, much work has been done on how psychopharmacological inducements such as cocaine, alcohol, PCP, and amphetamines influence behaviour, with suggestions that these kinds of external factors propel or facilitate those under their influence to commit crimes (see Fishbein 1990). In such cases, it is seen as broadly possible for some kind of biological 'corrective' to be developed to prevent criminal behaviour occurring, this corrective taking the form of removing the source of the problem (such as removing lead from one's living environment, banning alcohol sales), or regulating the biochemical and physiological operations of the body through appropriate treatment (such as drugs that restore hormonal equilibrium or ensure a regular heart rate).

Psychological explanations of crime are based upon analyses of various personality or behavioural traits that propel some people into committing crime. This approach sees such people as perhaps lacking some kind of internal regulatory self-control, or posits that patterns of early socialisation may have negatively affected social development. Psychological approaches include those that focus on 'personality types' (see Farrington 1996), and that present typologies of abnormalities in the psychological structure of individuals (for example 'over-aggressive', 'highly strung'). Such approaches often see the formation of particular personality types as linked to certain biological predispositions as well as developmental experiences. Another kind of approach, the *psychoanalytic*, turns attention to the unconscious mind and the way in which experience shapes and is shaped by processes beyond those consciously apparent to the subject (see Gibbons 1977).

The *psychiatric theory of deviant behaviour* is based on the assumption that certain childhood experiences have an effect that transcends all other social and cultural experiences (Clinard 1974). Such explanations adopt a medical model in which deviancy or criminality is seen to reside within the maladjusted individual. All human beings are seen as having inherited universal needs, such as the need for emotional security. It is thought that if such needs are unmet during childhood, then particular personality patterns form in later life, resulting especially in those personality types associated with deviant or criminal behaviour. Family experiences are thus seen as determining later behaviour, with the development of certain behaviours being viewed as an individual's means of dealing with particular personal traits such as aggressiveness, emotional insecurity, or feelings of inadequacy (these having been generated by unmet needs in childhood).

More sophisticated biological and psychological accounts of criminality accept that behaviour is subject to biological *and* environmental influences. These are referred to as *biosocial* approaches, and they characteristically view behaviour as the product of nature plus nurture, rather than one or the other. Proponents of this perspective argue that human beings have a 'conditional free will', that is, individual choice within a set, yet to some degree changeable, range of possibilities (Fishbein 1990). For example, Eysenck (1984) put forward the argument that behaviour can be explained as resulting from a combination of biological and environmental influences. His study analysed crime in terms of two broad processes of development:

- The *differential ability to be conditioned*, wherein genetic inheritance affects one's ability to be conditioned—that is, the sensitivity of the autonomic nervous system individuals inherit determines whether each individual is an extrovert or an introvert, and thus how well each is able to be conditioned in society.
- The *differential quality of conditioning*, whereby family conditioning makes use of a range of techniques, some of which are more efficacious than others. The way in which a child is reared therefore has an impact on the child's subsequent behaviour.

The biosocial argument is that a combination of biological potentials set through inheritance and interacting with environmental potentials shaped by parenting practices determine the overall propensity to commit crime. Human behaviour thus contains a biological and a social element (see, for example, Moffitt 1996).

In summary, the positivist perspective in criminology emphasises the role of external and internal determinants of crime and criminality. People, it is argued, do not choose to engage in deviant or criminal behaviour; they are locked into such behaviour by a wide range of biological and/or psychological influences beyond their immediate control. The positivist position stresses 'individual differences' among people, as well as the necessity to pinpoint the main factor or factors that have given rise to the criminality. Pinpointing of such factors is done through testing, diagnosis, classification, and treatment, all of which centre upon individual traits and needs as perceived by the 'expert professional'.

One problem with individual-focused positivism is that it puts an inordinate amount of power into the hands of a few 'experts' who may argue for ever-greater levels of intervention in the lives of citizens generally. For example, in order to deal adequately with the 'predisposition' to crime (based upon biological or psychological indicators), ideally intervention should take place before the crime or deviant act is actually committed. How early are we to intervene to 'change' someone? Who is going to do this? Should we 'treat' people when in fact no crime or law breaking has occurred? Further questions can be asked regarding whose 'norms' and 'values' we are to measure people's behaviour against, the social impact of attempting to mould each individual into passive conformity, and the way in which racist and sexist assumptions have been built into the 'scientific' study of biological differences, intelligence, and social behaviour. As seen in chapter 1, many of these concerns and questions have been central to the history of juvenile justice institutions and the development of the idea of juvenile delinquency.

Both the classical and the positivist approaches locate crime in terms of individual attributes, whether with respect to 'rationality' or 'pathology'. The 'remedy' in each case is to deal with the individual directly—either to coerce the individual back into rational decision-making, or to cure the individual of a predisposing tendency to commit deviant acts. In the end, the objective is to reintegrate the offender into the consensus. This can be achieved either through the threat and experience of punishment, or by the intervention of expert assistance to resocialise and rehabilitate the individual.

SOCIOLOGICAL THEORIES

Rather than reduce deviant or criminal behaviour solely to the individual level, a *sociological perspective* argues that, in order to understand the nature and occurrence of crime, we need to look at the structure of the society that moulds and shapes culture and behaviour. Individual action is thus attributable to social causes, and crime can be seen as a matter of social pathology. Sociologists and criminologists are both concerned with connecting wider situational factors (for example, immediate opportunities, specific peer groups) and social structural factors (for example, employment and educational patterns) with criminal activity. Crime is seen as essentially a social phenomenon that cannot be reduced to personal psychology or individual biology. In one sense, then, the impulse to commit crime is seen as 'normal' and is socially induced. The 'criminal' or 'delinquent' is thus a product of a specific kind of social order.

The underlying theme of many sociological theories is that crime is due to social disjunctures or *social strains* within a society. The strains or sources of tension are thought to be generated by the society itself: they do not reside within the individual (as in the case, for example, of a person feeling strained or pressured by circumstance). The cause of crime is seen as being located in social structures and/or social values that in some way are unfair or socially pathological. To deal with crime, therefore, requires strategies and policies that are pitched at institutional reform rather than solely at changing or modifying the individual in some way.

By and large, strain theories see crime as something linked to strains between 'structural opportunities' and 'cultural processes'. Decisions are made by people in the context of whether or not they have the means or opportunities to achieve their goals relative to other people in society, and whether through social circumstance they associate with others who share their ideas and cultural understandings regarding acceptable and unacceptable behaviour. The key social conflict in this perspective is that arising from a disjuncture between social means and cultural ends. Deviant behaviour is viewed as a meaningful attempt to solve problems faced by groups of individuals who are located in particular disadvantaged positions within the social structure.

There are several different strands of thought within strain theory. Some of these focus on opportunity structures relating to education and paid work; others concentrate on peer networks and the learning of particular norms and values. One of the earliest formulations of strain theory is that which examined crime in terms of *social disorganisation*. Also known as a 'social ecology' perspective, this kind of approach attempts to link the nature and extent of crime with specific social processes associated with urban life. Shaw and McKay (1942), for example, examined the ways in which successive waves of immigrants moved into inner-city neighbourhoods of the urban spatial grid, and then gradually moved to the outer areas. This process of urban settlement and transition was seen to produce tensions and chaos; it was characterised by a high degree of social disorganisation. Against this backdrop, Shaw and McKay examined the life histories of juvenile offenders, coming to the conclusion that juvenile offending is intimately linked to the transitional processes of social change. They argued that delinquency can be viewed as part of the natural social process of settling in experienced by new immigrants. Specifically, these communities were seen to exhibit a high degree of social disorganisation. Customary social norms that usually produce conforming behaviour were often inapplicable or in apparent conflict with the norms of the new society. The new immigrants were rarely integrated into the wider social, economic, and political systems. Questions of language, education, work skills, and social networks all came into play in shaping the life affairs of individuals and immigrant communities.

The importance of analysing social values and social structures is a particularly strong feature of *opportunity theories*. According to Merton (1957), for example, malintegration occurs where there is a disproportionate balance or disjuncture between the culturally defined goals of a society and the institutionalised means whereby these goals can be achieved. He argued that all individuals share the same cultural goal (in this case, the 'American Dream' of financial success, fame, and status), but that they have different opportunities to achieve success through the established institutionalised means (such as education). That is, in a society where emphasis has been placed upon certain valued goals, but the universal provision of appropriate means to attain these goals has been neglected, malintegration is inevitable.

Depending upon one's location in the social structure, one chooses whether to accept or reject culturally defined goals, and whether to accept or reject the institutional means to attain these goals. The importance of youth employment opportunities is stressed time and again as being a crucial variable in the conditions that give rise to varying forms of youth criminality (Wilson & Lincoln 1992; Braithwaite & Chappell 1994; Polk & White 1999). The issue of the lack of individual opportunity for economic and social advancement is particularly pertinent in a period of generalised high unemployment. From the point of view of policy, the opportunity approach places great emphasis on enhancing and developing more opportunities for young people in the labour market so as to reduce incentives to commit crime. The key point of this perspective is that, ultimately, 'strain' or conflict is not seen to reside within the individual, but within the structure of society and its institutions. It is thus the tensions existing between cultural goals and available means that provide the impetus for different types of individual adaptation.

The notion of opportunity also partially underlies *control theory*. Here, however, the issue is not so much the presence or absence of opportunity, but the actual use of opportunity by young people. Control theory is premised upon the idea that it is an individual's 'bond' to society that makes the difference in terms of whether or not they abide by society's general rules and values. From this perspective, all people are inherently antisocial: thus, all young people would commit crime if they dared. It is the nature of the bond that children have with their society that ultimately determines their behaviour (Empey 1982; Nettler 1984). Hirschi (1969) theorised that the social bond is made up of the following four major elements:

- *Attachment*—the ties of affection and respect to significant others in one's life, and more generally a sensitivity to the opinion of others.
- *Commitment*—the investment of time and energy in activities such as school and various conventional and unconventional means and goals.

- *Involvement*—the patterns of living that shape immediate and long-term opportunities, for example the idea that keeping busy doing conventional things will reduce the exposure of young people to illegal opportunities.
- *Belief*—the degree to which young people agree with the rightness of legal rules, which are in turn seen to reflect a general moral consensus in society.

It is the combination of attachment, commitment, involvement, and belief that shapes the life world of the young person, and that essentially dictates whether they will take advantage of conventional means and goals of social advancement, or whether they will pursue illegal pathways to self-gratification.

In related work, Gottfredson and Hirschi (1990) argue that the central issue in explaining crime is that of *self-control*, that is, people differ in the extent to which they are restrained from criminal acts. This in turn is linked to the question of social bonding, and especially the problem of ineffective child-rearing. Control theory incorporates elements of classical theory (in its acceptance of the idea that people are basically self-seeking), biosocial positivism (in its focus on the importance of proper 'conditioning' or training of the young), and sociological perspectives (which look to the nature of the family as a key variable in the development of self-control). The theory does not analyse specific social divisions such as class, gender, and ethnicity, but rests upon a conception of human nature that sees all people as essentially driven by the same universal tendency to enhance their own pleasure. Given this, the crucial issue becomes how best to socialise all people to conform to society's values and to engage in conventional law-abiding behaviour. In policy terms, the approach's answer to juvenile crime lies in redressing the defective social training that characterises offenders who have in some way 'lost control'. In other words, the emphasis from a practitioner's perspective is to reattach the young people to some kind of family, to recommit them to long-range conventional goals, to involve them in school and other constructive activities, and to have them acquire belief in the morality of law (Empey 1982:269).

Writers have explored the impact of social strains as manifested in youth subcultures and individual learning processes. Sutherland and Cressy (1974) for example, argue, that crime is essentially cultural in nature, in the sense that it is learnt behaviour. Crime is not simply determined by biological factors or youthful experiences of lack of opportunity. Over a period of years, Sutherland and Cressy developed a theory of *differential association* as a means to explain how criminal behaviour is learnt in interactions between people. What is differentially associated is the behaviour, in that some individuals will associate with the holders of criminal norms, while others will not.

The theory argues that people learn to define a situation and to define their conduct in relation to the law, and that this learning takes place within specific group contexts. One learns to associate certain classes of conduct, either legal or illegal, with the group's approval or disapproval. If we are to intervene in young people's lives to stop them from offending, then, according to this theory, we must attempt to change the way in which certain groups define their immediate situations and their relationship to law-abiding or law-breaking behaviour.

The idea that decisions to engage in deviant or criminal behaviour are collective in nature has been the subject of those who look to youth subcultures as the source of the problem. Various writers, for instance, have argued that the strain between ends and means is reflected in specific class cultures. Cohen (1955), and Cloward and Ohlin (1960) point to the existence of working-class ways of doing things, and working-class concepts of the social world. Rather than focusing on the disappointed individual who adapts in varying ways to the strain between opportunities and means to attain desired ends, these perspectives emphasise that crime is collective behaviour. Whether it be a conflict between middle-class values and working-class values, or the adoption of illegitimate opportunity structures specifically related to one's class background, delinquency and crime are seen to be collective phenomena. Related to this type of analysis is the literature on youth gangs, again with an emphasis on the group nature of youth offending and antisocial behaviour (see chapter 7, pp. 130–5 for an extended discussion).

The specific reasons for certain types of collective response to a general situation of blocked opportunity have been seen to include lack of self-esteem (Cohen 1955) and a sense of injustice (Cloward & Ohlin 1960). But others (Matza 1964; Downes 1966) have argued that working-class boys neither reject nor invert the dominant culturally prescribed values of society. Rather, youth subcultures often simply accentuate particular 'subterranean values' that are a part of normal society (for example, risk, adventure, fun), but sometimes take them too far. In the face of restricted access to opportunity, the response of young people is to resort to a form of 'manufactured excitement' of their own (Matza 1964; see also Hayward 2002; Presdee 2001). From a sociological perspective, the answer to the crime being learnt behaviour that often takes place in a subcultural context is to dismantle delinquent subcultures and replace them with something more positive.

In summary, sociological theories examine the nature of social constraints as they relate to behaviour, that is, the disjuncture between aspirations and opportunities, and between dominant values and subcultures. These kinds of disjunctures produce friction, frustration, and strain, which result in criminal behaviour. The focus of such perspectives tends to be on working-class crime, particularly street crime, and various other forms of antisocial behaviour. Sociological theories signal a major shift away from attempts to locate the causes of youth crime within the individual, and towards an examination of the social structure. It is claimed that crime is not a matter of disturbed people acting out their personal pathologies; rather, crime is a case of normal people coping with abnormal or unequal situations. The policy options of sociological theories include such things as enhancing opportunities in order to overcome the disparity between ends and means, and encouraging the development of 'healthy' peer networks and relationships. On a personal level, this translates into the provision of training, and educational, vocational, and rehabilitation programs.

LABELLING PERSPECTIVES

Labelling theories are closely associated with the *interactionist* theories, which argue that the social world is actively made by human beings in their everyday interactions (see Berger & Luckmann 1971). Such perspectives challenge the notion that the world and crime are objectively given, instead arguing that crime should be viewed as a social process. That is, human beings do not simply respond passively to external stimuli: they possess choice, they are creative, and they bring to bear their own meanings upon situations. The meanings that people attach to situations and the manner in which they define situations in turn have an impact on behaviour. Labelling perspectives therefore focus on subjectivity, seeing our perceptions of ourselves as arrived at through a process of interactions with others and through negotiating the multiple possible definitions of a situation or event.

From this perspective, deviance or criminality is not something that is objectively given; it is subjectively problematic (Plummer 1979). The labelling perspective therefore attempts to provide a processual account of deviancy and criminality. The broad interactionist perspective focuses on how people typify one another (that is, see each other as a particular type of person, such as 'mentally ill' or 'young offender'), how people relate to one another on the basis of these typifications, and what the consequences are of these social processes (Rubington & Weinberg 1978:1). Essentially, it argues that deviancy itself can be the result of the interactive process between individual juveniles and the criminal justice system; that, for example, police intervention can actually produce deviancy.

In early versions of labelling theories, it was asserted that deviancy is not an inherent property of behaviour, but something that is conferred upon the individual by society. In other words, deviance is created by social reaction. According to Becker (1963:9), the impact of social reaction on certain types of behaviour or on particular categories of people is crucial to explaining the criminalisation process, in that:

> Social groups create deviance by making the rules whose infraction constitutes deviance, and by applying those rules to particular people and labeling them as outsiders. From this point of view, deviance is not a quality of the act the person commits, but rather a consequence of the application by others of rules and sanctions to an 'offender'. The deviant is one to whom the label has successfully been applied; deviant behavior is behavior that people so label.

The argument here is that we need to look at the impact of the application of certain labels (for example 'bad', 'criminal', 'delinquent') in fostering deviant behaviour. Public labelling, it is argued, may affect an individual's self-identity and transform them so that they see themselves in the light of the label. The process of labelling is tied up with the idea of the self-fulfilling prophecy. That is, if you tell someone sufficiently often that they are 'bad' or 'stupid', or 'crazy', that person may start to believe the label and to act out the stereotypical behaviour associated with it.

A further aspect of the public labelling process is that *stigmatisation* may occur. This involves the application of a negative label that becomes the 'master' (or dominant) definition of the person concerned. Regardless of current behaviour or past experiences, a person may become known to the wider community mainly or solely in terms of the label applied to them. A negative label such as 'criminal' or 'delinquent' can colour the perceptions of people with whom the individual interacts, and influence how the community in general treats that person. Where such stigma exists, it may lead to a situation where the 'deviant' begins to live up to the dictates of the label, and to change their identity and behaviour accordingly.

Labelling theories in criminology have had their greatest impact in the specific area of juvenile justice. This is not surprising, given the general view that young people and children are more impressionable than older people, and therefore more likely to respond to any labelling that might occur. It is argued that if a young person comes to court and is labelled as an offender, this process of public labelling and stigmatisation creates a new identity for the young person and, as a consequence, that individual will become committed to the roles and behaviour of the 'delinquent'.

Whether they are good or bad, positive or negative, constructive or destructive, it is argued that labels do affect and have consequences for subsequent behaviour. Matza (1964) investigated the question of 'delinquency' on the basis of the proposition that crime itself is ubiquitous—that is, most people at some stage engage in some form of criminal, deviant, or antisocial behaviour. In studying youth subcultures and delinquents, a 'naturalistic' approach was adopted, one that was committed to providing an account describing youth experiences from the point of view of the young people. This not only enabled the researcher to reconsider the question of values and to challenge the idea that only working-class young people experience strain, but also to explore the motivational accounts provided by the actors themselves as to why they engage in certain types of activity. Sykes and Matza (1957) and Matza (1964) described the ways in which young people use certain techniques of 'neutralisation' as a way of denying the moral bind of law (for example 'They started it', 'No one got hurt'). Furthermore, Matza argued that the actions of the juvenile justice system, and especially youth perceptions of the competence of officials and the application of sanctions, also affect the 'will to crime' of young people and form part of the ways in which they neutralise their moral restraint.

In studying young people, Matza found that juveniles eagerly explore all aspects of social life. He found that in this process they tend to drift between the two poles of conventional and unconventional behaviour (including crime), without being fully committed to either. In the end, most juveniles drift towards conventional lifestyles and behaviour as their permanent pattern of experience. However, Matza found that, if during the teenage years of drift there is official intervention and social reaction to specific kinds of unconventional behaviour, it may precipitate the movement of the juvenile into a permanent state of delinquency. The central policy concern of the labelling approach, therefore, is to find ways in which to prevent a young person from becoming a career criminal or long-term deviant. If we accept the proposition that contact with the criminal justice system—whether police, courts, or detention centres—serves to sustain deviant careers, then the solution is posed in terms of *diversion*. From a labelling perspective, individuals should be diverted away from the formal processes of the justice system in order to escape any possible negative consequences arising from the formal public labelling process. In this way, future commitment to a deviant career can be averted. For those young people within the system, deinstitutionalisation (that is, the removal of youth from institutions) and their placement in the community are advocated in order to minimise negative labelling.

In summary, labelling theory concentrates its attention on the social reaction to crime. The approach sees crime as maintained, perpetuated, or amplified by the labelling process. Criminality is thus something that is conferred upon some individuals, and on some types of behaviour, by those people who have the power to do it, and who have the power to make a label stick. The labelling perspective's implications for juvenile justice are that we should do what we can to minimise the harmful effects of labelling and stigmatisation. This can be achieved through a wide variety of diversionary practices that attempt to keep the young person from entering too far into the official criminal justice system.

SOCIAL INEQUALITY AND STRUCTURAL POWER

Marxist and feminist conceptions of society are based upon an analysis of structural power. In this view, individuals are defined not so much by personal attributes or by reference to universalising statements regarding 'choice' and 'determinism', but by their position and opportunities as dictated by class forces and unequal gender relations. To understand crime, therefore, we need to examine the actions of the powerful in defining and enforcing a particular kind of social order, and the activities of the less powerful in the context of a social structure within which they have fewer resources and less decision-making power than others.

A key characteristic of *Marxist* conceptions of crime and criminality is their focus on the way in which institutionalised power is organised and exercised in society. Specifically, where 'liberal' analysis views the state as acting in the capacity of a neutral umpire or arbiter of conflict, and as being independent of and not aligned to any particular class, Marxism sees the state as variously linked to the specific interests of the capitalist ruling class. In a capitalist society, power is concentrated, and the activities of the state reflect the interests of capital in general. These activities foster the accumulation of capital, maintain the legitimacy of unequal social relations, and control the actions of those who threaten private property relations and the public order. In other words, the state in a capitalist society is a capitalist state. As such, the general tendency of state institutions (such as the police, the judiciary, prisons, and community programs) is to concentrate on specific kinds of behaviour (usually associated with working-class crime) as being 'deviant' and 'harmful'. Other kinds of destructive or exploitative behaviour (usually associated with crimes of the powerful) are deemed to be less worthy of state intervention.

From a Marxist viewpoint, how issues are constructed, how crime is defined, and how crime is responded to relate directly to the individual's position in the class structure (see White & van der Velden 1996). If social power is concentrated in the hands of those who own the means of production, they will influence and generally dictate which behaviour is and is not defined as criminal. The Marxist concern with class and class analysis of society has led some theorists to draw attention to the specific ways in which the activities of working-class juveniles are subject to particular processes of criminalisation. The Birmingham Centre for Contemporary Cultural Studies (BCCCS) in England, for instance,re-examined the issue of youth subcultures from the point of view of the unequal material circumstances of working-class boys and girls (Hall & Jefferson 1976). It was argued by members of the BCCCS that class is central to any explanation of the experience of growing up, and that the relationship between young people and social institutions—such as school, employment, and the legal system—is characterised by different forms of class-based resistances to the dominant relations of power. Certain youth subcultural forms were seen in this work to 'solve', in an imaginary way, problems experienced by working-class young people (for example, unemployment, educational disadvantage), which at the material level remained unresolved (Clarke, Hall, Jefferson, & Roberts 1976; Brake 1985).

From the point of view of social control and policing, various studies have pointed to the ways in which the media portray certain types of youth subcultures, which in turn lead to a form of 'deviancy amplification' (Cohen 1973; Young 1971; Collins, Noble, Poynting, & Tabar 2000), that is, the sort of public labelling pertaining to some groups of young people actually generates further 'deviant' behaviour in the labelled group. More generally, the link is made between the actual cultural, social, and economic experiences of working-class young people, and the manner in which the state—particularly the police—intervenes in their lives, both coercively (shown by arrest rates) and ideologically (such as through the promulgation of 'moral panics' over young people's behaviour and attitudes).

The concern of the Marxist criminological approach is to highlight the inequalities of a class society (for example wealth versus poverty, business profits versus low wages), and the impact these have on the criminalisation process (Spitzer 1975). The powerful are seen as designing the laws in their own collective interest, while having greater capacity to defend themselves individually if they do break and bend existing rules and regulations. The less powerful in society are seen as propelled to commit crime through economic need and social alienation. They are also the main targets of law enforcement and wider criminal-justice agencies, something reflected in statistics that show an over-representation of the unemployed and poor in prisons, police lockups, and criminal courts (White & Perrone, 2005). By providing a structural perspective on social institutions, social processes, and social outcomes, Marxist approaches argue that revolutionary or profound social transformation is needed if 'crime' is to be addressed in a socially just manner. This implies that working with young offenders is inherently political and needs to be based on strategies that empower young people and their communities.

Feminism proceeds from the point of view that a fundamental division in society is that between men and women. The *feminist* approach, which came to prominence in the 1970s, sees differences between men and women as biological, and socially and historically constructed. A major emphasis in contemporary social analysis is to explain the different experiences and social realities of men and women in society, and to understand why women and men have different positions, roles, and status.

Feminism challenged criminology in at least two ways. First, there was the relative neglect within criminology itself of issues relating to female crime and women as victims of crime. Second, the theories and studies that did exist tended to reinforce certain stereotypes and conservative portrayals of the 'proper' place of women in society. Feminist writers sought to rectify these matters through critiques not only of the criminal justice system, but also of the dominant sexist assumptions underpinning mainstream criminological theories of crime (Smart 1976; Naffine 1987). Feminist theorists pointed out, for example, that the neglect of women in criminological enquiry was due in part to the overwhelming dominance of males in the criminology discipline and the criminal justice system. In terms of research and theory, and at the level of the practitioner, the system has traditionally been composed mainly of men. Judges, barristers, solicitors, prison officers, and police were predominantly male. Even when some men challenged the overt sexist practices of the law and law enforcement, this did not change the overall orientation of the system towards women. Similarly, it was recognised that women were well represented in social-control agencies such as welfare, social work, and the nursing professions. Nevertheless, the criminal justice and welfare systems together tended to police the behaviour of women in ways that reinforced the notion of women as only wives, mothers, sexual partners, nurturers, and domestic workers, rather than as complete individuals in their own right.

The neglect of women generally within criminology until the second wave of feminism in the 1970s is attributable to the subordinate position and limited participation of women within the criminal justice system. It is also related to the fact that women appear to be a less statistically significant problem than men, in that women generally commit fewer crimes. Furthermore, while women are over-represented in some categories of victimisation (for example rape, domestic violence), in general they did not appear to be victims of crime to the same extent as men. As a consequence, investigators within criminology did not regard the female offender or the female victim as worthy of much research attention.

One of the problems with the overall attitude and perspective on women and crime was that, when mainstream criminologists occasionally looked at female crime, they did so from within a male framework. Since mainstream criminological theories (such as strain theory and male subcultures) had hitherto tended to concentrate on male experience, there was a problem in trying to extrapolate such experiences into the analysis of women's place in crime (Naffine 1987). What, for example, does strain theory tell us about the opportunity structures and cultural goals of women? Similarly, labelling theory argues that it is *particularly* the less powerful in society who suffer most from the detrimental effects of labelling. How, then, do we account for the fact that powerless women are not involved in crime to the same extent as powerless men? What is it about the sex variable that influences the specific conditions under which male and female offending (and victimisation) occurs? The vast majority of criminological theories have ignored these questions altogether. When such theories have attempted to explain female crime as a distinct and specific social phenomenon, they have accepted a narrow, conservative view regarding the place and position of women in society, and more often than not have done so on the basis of a form of biological reductionism. *Biological reductionism* refers to instances where female experiences and behaviour are explained solely in terms of presumed biological imperatives, in that the biological sex of a person is seen to dictate or determine appropriate social roles and practices.

The response of feminist writers to biological explanations is that these represent a double standard in terms of morality and power. They argue that underpinning the double standard is a blurring of the distinction between 'sex' and 'gender'. Many criminological theories have presumed females have a fixed biological nature that is indistinguishable from their traditional social role as mother, housekeeper, sexual partner, and childcarer. Any 'maladjustment' to this stereotypical femininity is said to be closely linked to the activities of women as offenders (for example prostitution) and their experiences as victims (for example being subjected to male violence).

In the feminist perspective, the crucial issue is that of relative social power and access to community resources. The criminalisation process itself is seen to be heavily laden with sexist assumptions that reinforce and reproduce structural inequalities of gender in society (Gelsthorpe & Morris 1990). This is thought to occur with respect to the construction of offending behaviour, and with respect to the portrayal of victims. The central proposition of much feminist analysis is that women are treated differently in and by the criminal justice system because of the persistence of traditional gender-role expectations regarding 'appropriate' and 'feminine' behaviour for women (and men).

Underpinning this gendered division of the sexes is the question of power. Society is seen as male-dominated, and this is reflected in myriad social institutions, including the law and the juvenile justice system. Feminist theory places the nature of female offending into a wider social, economic, and political context, rather than one that reduces female experience to biological or psychological determinants. For example, as discussed in chapter 8, many young women committed to institutions have been victims of violence themselves. Similarly, women who commit social-security fraud or other minor forms of fraud and theft, usually do so not for themselves but to support children and other dependants. Hence, the generalised violence against women as a social category, and the relative disadvantages they suffer economically, are explored as vital preconditions to any individual offending behaviour. In the case of victimisation, feminist analysis pays much attention to the ways in which crimes against women have historically not been considered as such (for example domestic violence) or are subject to trivialisation and sexual bias (for example rape trials involving sex workers). Questions of what is an 'offence' and who is a 'victim' are thus often intertwined with gender stereotypes and biases that reflect a general inequality between the sexes in society.

In summary, the feminist perspectives within criminology challenge the male biases and areas of neglect of mainstream criminology (see Naffine 1997). Feminist criticism is levelled at historical and contemporary examples of the double standards applied to women and men in the criminal justice system. As well, active intervention has been called for by feminist activists, including lawyers and criminologists, in areas such as inappropriate responses to female offenders (for example imprisonment), law reform that prevents discrimination against women (for example equal employment opportunity), the legal recognition of certain crimes against women (for example sexual harassment), and active enforcement of laws to protect women from male violence (for example domestic violence, incest, rape).

MULTIFACTORIAL EXPLANATIONS

Most theories of crime causation at some stage refer to issues of 'free will' and 'determination'. That is, most writers on youth offending tend to speak about crime as entirely or mainly a matter of personal choice (thereby stressing the responsibility of the young person for their actions), or as something largely determined or shaped by forces outside of the young person's conscious control (thereby stressing the need for treatment or social reform of some kind).

At a very general level, writers tend to focus on and emphasise particular factors that may be related to young offending. If we are to construct general types or approaches to criminological theory, then it is useful to identify the central focus of any theory, and the level of analysis and explanation at which the theory is pitched. As box 2.1 indicates, there are three broad levels of criminological explanation: the individual, the situational, and the structural. Criminological theories tend to locate their main explanation for criminal behaviour or criminality at one of these levels. Occasionally, a theory attempts to combine all three levels in order to provide a more sophisticated and comprehensive picture of crime and criminality.

BOX 2.1   MAIN FOCUS OF THEORIES OF YOUTH OFFENDING

FOCUS ON INDIVIDUAL FACTORS

The focus is on the personal or individual characteristics of the offender or victim. Study considers, for example, the influence of intelligence, mental illness, substance abuse, or motivation on the nature of crime causation or victimisation. This level of analysis tends to look to psychological or biological factors that are said to have an important determining role in why certain individuals engage in criminal activity. The key concern is with explaining crime or deviant behaviour in terms of the choices or characteristics of the individual. Typical explanations for youth offending include:

- young people choose to commit crime
- biological reasons, such as lead poisoning, abnormal chromosomes
- psychological reasons, such as aggression, lack of self-control
- social-psychological reasons, such as abusive childhood, lack of love
- pathological conditions, such as mental illness.

FOCUS ON SITUATIONAL FACTORS

The site of analysis is the immediate situation or circumstances within which criminal activity or deviant behaviour occurs. Attention is directed to the specific factors that may contribute to an event occurring, such as how the participants define the situation, how different people are labelled by others in the criminal justice system, the opportunities available for the commission of certain types of offences, and so on. A key concern is the nature of the interaction between different players within the system, the effect of local environmental factors on the nature of this interaction, and the influence of group behaviour on social activity. Typical explanations for youth offending include:

- result of negative labelling, such as the stigma of being called a 'delinquent'
- poor school performance, including level of attainment, alienation
- poor parenting, including lack of supervision, neglect
- homelessness, for example lack of stable and safe shelter
- peer group and youth-subculture influences including youth gangs, media images, violent video games.

FOCUS ON SOCIAL STRUCTURAL FACTORS

This approach tends to look at crime in terms of broader social relationships—and the major social institutions—of the society as a whole. The analysis makes reference to the relationship between classes, sexes, different ethnic and 'racial' groups, the employed and unemployed, and various other social divisions in society. It also investigates the operation of specific social institutions, such as education, the family, work, and the legal system, in constructing and responding to crime and deviant behaviour. Typical explanations for youth offending include:

- inadequate socialisation, for example little education in 'right' and 'wrong'
- colonialism and social disempowerment, for example denial of culture
- racism and discrimination, for example negative biases in the system
- poverty, inequality, and social marginalisation, for example no means to attain desired ends, social exclusion
- unemployment, for example few opportunities for paid work.

The level of analysis chosen (see box 2.1) determines how crime and the offender are viewed, and how the criminal justice system should be organised. A biological positivist approach, for example, which looks at characteristics (such as genetic makeup) of the individual offender, sees crime as stemming from the individual offender's specific personal attributes. A situational perspective, on the other hand, might consider the interaction between police and young people on the street, and argue that 'crime' is defined in the process of specific interactions, behaviours, and attitudes. From a structural perspective, the issue might be seen in terms of the relationship between poverty and crime: that is, the elements of social life that underpin particular courses of action. The biological, the situational, and the structural approaches would each advocate quite different policies because of their particular perspectives. The vantage point from which one examines crime—from a focus on personal characteristics through to societal institutions—thus shapes the ways in which one thinks about and acts in regard to criminal justice matters.

The different levels of analysis apparent in criminology also reflect the diverse disciplines that have contributed to the study of crime over many years. Researchers, scholars, and writers in areas such as biological science, psychology, philosophy, law, sociology, forensic medicine, political economy, education, history, and cultural studies have all contributed to the multidisciplinary nature of criminology. Each discipline uses its own concepts, debates, and methods when examining a criminological issue or problem. This means that within criminology there is a natural diversity of viewpoints, as different writers and researchers see the world through very different analytical spectacles. Such differences are reflected in the adoption of a wide range of techniques and methodologies in the study of crime. These include the use of historical records, surveys, participant observation, interviews, evaluation of official statistics, clinical examination, study of policy documents, and discourse analysis.

Some researchers find the causes of crime in looking at the personal characteristics and background of individual offenders. Others examine aspects of situations within which the young person has been placed, and the types of interactions that person has with other people, and how these influence that person's behaviour. Finally, there are those who look to the nature of society as a whole for their explanation. A conservative perspective, for example, may see crime as ultimately stemming from the lack of moral values and inadequate discipline in a society. Liberal and more radical analyses point to issues relating to inequality and social divisions.

There are, then, myriad reasons for any particular young person to engage in crime, although broad social patterns in offending behaviour are apparent. As demonstrated in this chapter, theories and studies of juvenile offending point to a wide range of causal factors. These include individual factors (ranging from personal choice, to psychological damage arising from an abusive childhood, to mental illness), situational factors (including such things as poor school performance, homelessness, and deviant peer cultures), and social structural factors (relating for instance to inadequate moral education and socialisation, racism, and social inequality). There is, then, a multiplicity of specific factors that help to explain crime.

In a review of empirical research on the predictors and correlates of offending, Farrington (1996) provides a systematic outline of the key 'risk factors' associated with youthful offending. Among the many factors cited are:

- prenatal and perinatal factors (for example early childbearing, substance use during pregnancy, low birth weight)
- hyperactivity and impulsivity (for example hyperactivity–impulsivity–attention-deficit, lack of inhibition)
- intelligence and attainment (for example low non-verbal intelligence, abstract reasoning, cognitive and neuropsychological deficit)
- parental supervision, discipline, and attitude (for example erratic or harsh parental discipline, rejecting parental attitudes, violent behaviour)

- broken homes (for example maternal and paternal deprivation, parental conflict)
- parental criminality (for example convicted parents, poor supervision)
- large family size (related to parental attention, overcrowding)
- socioeconomic deprivation (for example low family income, poor housing)
- peer influences (for example male group behaviour, delinquent friends)
- school influences (for example use of praise and punishment, classroom management)
- community influences (for example high residential mobility, neighbourhood disorganisation, physical deterioration, overcrowding, type of housing)
- situational influences (for example specific opportunities, benefits outweighing expected costs, seeking excitement).

It is the combination of these factors, and their association with certain categories of young people, that explains variations in the propensity for criminal behaviour and/or criminalisation among young people. As Farrington (1996:105) observes:

> In explaining the development of offending, a major problem is that most risk factors tend to coincide and be interrelated. For example, adolescents living in physically deteriorated and socially disorganized neighbourhoods disproportionately tend also to come from families with poor parental supervision and erratic parental discipline and tend also to have high impulsivity and low intelligence. The concentration and co-occurrence of these kinds of adversities make it difficult to establish their independent, interactive, and sequential influences on offending and antisocial behavior.

In a similar vein, Canadian research (Canada, National Crime Prevention Council, 1996:11) identified the following factors as being associated with persistent crime:

- family violence and neglect
- lack of supervision from parents or other caring adults, parental rejection, and lack of parent–child involvement
- difficulties in school
- neighbourhoods characterised by poor housing, lack of recreational, health, and educational facilities
- the disintegration of social supports
- peer pressure
- youth unemployment and blocked opportunities
- poverty.

Recent Australian reviews and commentaries likewise identify a wide range of interacting and interrelated factors—pertaining to the individual, peer groups, family, school, and community—as integral to any explanation of youth offending (see Developmental Crime Prevention Consortium 1999;

Toumbourou 1999). However, and as indicated in the next chapter, the profiles of young offenders tend to look basically the same: young men with low income, low educational achievement, no employment, a weak attachment to parents, and who move frequently are the most likely to wind up in juvenile detention centres (see Braithwaite 1989). While researchers continue to identify a range of 'risk factors' (such as drug abuse) and 'protective factors' (such as family cohesion) that influence whether an individual engages in criminal or antisocial behaviour (Catalano & Hawkins 1996), it is the wider structural context of youth experience that shapes the overall life chances and life experiences of young people (White & Wyn 2004).

To say that the wider structural context is such a strong determinant of youth behaviour and opportunity is to assert that youth offending occurs within certain specific political, economic, and social contexts. Rather than treating such phenomena as 'socioeconomic disadvantage' and 'unemployment' as specific causal factors, among many others, it is necessary to view such phenomena as consequences of wider structural transformations in society. This is precisely the central concern of critical criminology (see Scraton & Chadwick 1991; Collins et al. 2000; Cunneen 2001a; Muncie 2004). Within this theoretical approach, some groups are particularly vulnerable to processes of criminalisation, marginalisation and social exclusion. Members of the working class (especially its more powerless sections, including the 'underclass'), women (especially those who are poor, who are sole parents, and who are socially isolated), ethnic minority groups (especially those from non-English-speaking backgrounds and refugees), and Indigenous people (especially those worst-affected by long-term colonisation processes and institutional disadvantage) are those most likely to suffer from the weight of oppressive social relations based upon class division, sexism, and racism. Yet, as analysis of neoliberal policy and practice indicates, a systemic process of 'responsibilisation' and 'individuation' shifts the public gaze and social policy away from structural disadvantage and toward the notion that each person is responsible for their own life chances (Muncie 2002; White & Cunneen 2006). It is up to individuals, families, and communities to cope with their situation as best as they can, and to be fully responsible for their actions. In contrast, critical criminology focuses on how crime is socially constructed through the interventions of the state and within the context of the political economy of advanced capitalism. To address youth crime therefore requires that analysis move from simple multifactorial analyses to consideration of broader social processes that give rise to and exacerbate particular 'risk factors'. It also requires critical scrutiny of responsibilisation processes that make the individual appear to be at the centre of explanations for criminality, with no or little consideration of structural disadvantage.

In practice, of course, why certain young people commit certain crimes is only answerable by consideration of their personal life history, their immediate life circumstances, and their position in the wider social structure. For example, the decision to commit vandalism may incorporate elements of an abusive childhood, difficulties at school, unemployment, and bad experiences with authority figures, or it could be as simple as 'having a good time'.

While it is important to think about general theories and causes of crime, it is also insightful to consider the specific reasons for young people to commit particular crimes, and how these might relate to the general theories. Take property offences, for example: a 1996 New South Wales study involving interviews with juvenile-theft offenders in detention centres found that the main reasons given for shoplifting were to obtain clothes or money for clothes, and to obtain food or money for food (Freeman 1996). The majority of young offenders also said they committed break-and-enter offences in order to obtain money, with about half of these young people wanting to use the money to buy drugs and/or alcohol. Almost half of the offenders convicted for stealing a motor vehicle said that they had committed the offence because of the want or need of transport. Similarly, a study in Victoria of teenagers in low-income neighbourhoods found that 80 per cent of young people in the study viewed illegal activity as an important means whereby people their age could supplement an inadequate income (White, Aumair, Harris & McDonnell 1997). Drug dealing and shoplifting were considered the main ways to get money, and in both cases the reason for the activity was primarily financial.

These examples illustrate that certain types of crimes (property crime, drug dealing) are very much related to particular groups of offenders (low income, unemployed) for very specific ends (obtaining money, having transport). This is important insofar as it indicates that it is crucial to consider the social context of crime in any genuine attempt to bring together crime's individual, situational, and structural elements. Taking into account social context, we can also better understand the place and role of alcohol and other drugs in the lives of some young people. Studies have shown, for example, that substance use—particularly the use of marijuana and alcohol—is strongly associated with young-offender status (Howard & Zibert 1990; Putnins 2001). Higher rates of tobacco, alcohol, and cannabis use have also been observed in those young people who, for whatever reason, are out of school but not in full-time employment (Tressider, Macaskill, Bennett, & Nutbeam 1997). Drug use (and abuse) have been associated with a lack of positive things to do, boredom, lack of employment and educational opportunities, and a general sense of pessimism that things are not going to get any better. Furthermore, many offenders report using substances at the time of their offence, with alcohol the substance most often associated with the actual act of offending (Putnins, 2001:14).

What young people think about their circumstances, how they think about themselves, and how others view them, all have major repercussions for the ways in which they relate to issues of crime and society. Invariably, as well, the social position of young people also brings them into regular contact with agents of the criminal justice system. Certainly, more theoretical and empirical work is needed to explore the lived experiences of youth crime—motivations, emotions, sensate experiences, and meanings associated with human behaviour. How young people perceive and emotionally respond to the world around them is central to this task. In this regard, recent developments in 'cultural criminology' emphasise both that the criminalisation of many aspects of everyday life is occurring and that 'transgressing and doing wrong are for many an exciting and pleasurable experience' (Presdee 2001:30). As Hayward (2002) observes, the vilification and pleasures of youthful transgression are important to study since they relate to broader changes in society (for example, commodification of social life, generalised feelings of insecurity) that, in turn, generate varying responses on the part of young people as they negotiate their everyday lives (for example, searching for excitement, going beyond the mundane and the boring). The phenomenon of juvenile crime has to be investigated from the point of view of how young people construct meaning, as well as in relation to the material and cultural resources that they draw upon in specific social circumstances. Understanding and explaining youth offending therefore demands that we be sensitive to the interconnections between individual biography, social history, and local context, and well as taking into account the interventions of powerful agencies and adults in the lives of young people.

CONCLUSION

The development of official responses to juvenile offending has been heavily influenced by the theories and perspectives outlined in this chapter. The 'special conditions' that have characterised the ways in which young people have been processed within the criminal justice system are in no small part due to the influence of ideas relating to the social structure and social processes and their impact on youth behaviour. The responses of the system to young people are by no means uniform or consistent, and the multiplicity of programs and institutions in part reflects the many different ideas about the causes of juvenile offending. The emphasis on group work and outreach work in some programs, for example, is related to the notion of peer-group influence and subcultural values, and how these shape a young person's attitude towards criminal or deviant behaviour. Provision of training and educational programs is clearly linked with concerns to enhance 'blocked opportunities' and encourage positive developmental outlets for young people. The decriminalisation of some juvenile offences, ongoing concerns to divert young people from the formal court system, and the development of alternatives to detention represent systemic responses to issues raised by the labelling theory (Coventry & Polk 1985).

The application by criminologists of the ideas summarised in this chapter tends to manifest in the form of multifactorial explanations for youth crime.

However, in doing this, criminologists generally refrain from presenting a hierarchy of causes. The result is that immediate causes are cited (such as unemployment, racism, labelling, poor schooling), and reformist measures are advocated (such as training schemes, alternative schools), but rarely are substantial changes to the social structure as a whole demanded. For those who wish to see major social change occurring, the questions of power and of social interests are of paramount importance. Where multiple factors are at the foreground of analysis, the tendency is to respond to the phenomenon of youth crime through emphasis on developing specific projects and programs. More radical perspectives view such proposals as very limiting, unless they are linked directly to a wider politics of social change.

The theoretical perspectives outlined in this chapter provide competing and at times complementary explanations regarding the causes of crime and the appropriate responses to it. While some theories concentrate on determining individual differences in the commission of offences and some focus on situational factors such as alcohol use and antisocial behaviour, others explore the way in which changing socioeconomic circumstances and the nature of society itself impinge upon particular groups and classes in society. The specific level of analysis and the particular political orientation of the writer in essence dictate the definitions, explanations, and control strategies that ought to be adopted. In a similar vein, the notion of 'scientific truth' in terms of theoretical understanding, and 'effectiveness' with regard to actual criminal justice practices, will vary according to the paradigm within which one is working. Perceptions and theories of juvenile offending are frequently reliant upon data regarding specific offences and offenders gathered by the formal agencies of criminal justice (as well as data generated through research study). Which young people and which offences come to the attention of criminal justice officials is the subject of the next chapter.

3 | The nature of contemporary juvenile crime

INTRODUCTION

This chapter discusses the nature and dynamics of juvenile crime. It is important to recognise at the outset that a complete picture of juvenile crime cannot be obtained. Our sources of information limit the picture of juvenile offending for a variety of reasons. Each source of information at the most provides only a selective glimpse—and, like any partial view, may actually disguise as much as illuminate. Sources of information about juvenile offending include official statistics, self-report studies, and other surveys and research. However, we should not underestimate the role of popular culture through film, video, music and literature—as well as the ubiquitous role of the media as definers of law-and-order news—in structuring our knowledge and understanding of juvenile offending and the range of possible responses to it.

THE EXTENT OF JUVENILE OFFENDING

Official sources of information deal with the end process of intervention by police, courts, and juvenile justice authorities. These sources may be useful in terms of understanding some juvenile offending patterns, and also for telling us about the priorities, practices, and nature of intervention by state agencies (for example, how many young people receive a police caution instead of being arrested and charged, or how many matters are processed by way of youth conferencing or other alternatives, rather than through the children's courts).

However, we need to be aware of the limitations of the official statistics that are, in the end, a product or outcome of a social and political process. Cicourel (1976), in an important study that examined juvenile justice in the 1960s, analysed the social processes that create knowledge about an 'offender'. In particular, he was concerned with the way police and probation officers construct documents and textual accounts that develop 'evidence' about an individual. In this sense, the routine bureaucratic processes incorporate and transform the young person into a 'juvenile delinquent', and official statistics concerning young offenders derive from these processes. Equally important is that our knowledge of the occurrence of 'crime' is also dependent on a range of factors.

For an event to be classified as a crime, a number of conditions must be satisfied. Some act or situation must be perceived by someone and then defined as being illegal. The observer must then decide to report the incident to police. The police must decide that what is being reported to them constitutes an offence, and record it as such.

We know that a great deal of crime is not reported to the police in the first instance. Crime victim surveys in Australia and overseas show that many offences of violence are never reported to authorities. Recent surveys in Australia show that only 20 per cent of sexual assaults, 31 per cent of assaults, and 50 per cent of robberies are reported to police (Australian Bureau of Statistics 2003). Reports of theft vary, with 95 per cent of motor vehicle theft and 75 per cent of burglaries being reported to the police. Furthermore, British studies have shown that between one in four and one in five crimes reported by the public to the police are subsequently not accepted by police as being crimes and are therefore not recorded (Bottomley & Coleman 1981; Sparkes, Genn & Dodd 1977). What emerges in the official crime statistics as the level of crime is clearly a partial picture.

There are also factors specific to juvenile crime that further limit the utility of official figures. These are:

- the level of unreported juvenile crime, particularly where young people are also the victims
- changes in enforcement practices with a specific focus on young people
- distortions caused by the nature of juvenile offending itself.

Young people may be reluctant to report crime to police for a variety of reasons. It has been noted that young women who are the victims of violence either at home or in public report few of these incidents to the police (Alder 1994:170–1). Homeless young people are also vulnerable to violence, and their already strained relationship with authorities makes reporting of incidents unlikely. Specific groups of young people from non-English-speaking backgrounds, and Indigenous young people, are unlikely to report offences when they have been victims, perhaps because they are suspicious of police or because they have a history of poor relations with police. People working in youth services have noted that a sense of resignation and powerlessness often prevents young people from reporting offences (Underwood, White & Omelczuk 1993:14). Routine crime-victim surveys such as those conducted by the Australian Bureau of Statistics or the British Home Office are unlikely to overcome the problems associated with the low levels of reporting by specific groups: homeless people are excluded from household surveys, as are those who are not on the electoral register. People with English as a second language may find the surveys difficult to complete. Perhaps most importantly for our discussion of young people is that a large section of young people are excluded from the survey process. In the United Kingdom, household crime surveys are completed by those 16 years and above, and in Australia the respondent must be 15 years of age or older.

Changes in juvenile justice enforcement practices and law can have dramatic effects on official figures, particularly in amplifying the incidence or participation of specific groups of offences or offenders. For instance, a police crackdown on graffiti groups can immediately boost arrests and court appearances for offences related to property damage. Yet this does not mean there has necessarily been any increase in the level of offending. Similarly, changes in legislation can 'cause' an apparent increase in court appearances, such as occurred with the introduction of the *Summary Offences Act 1988* (NSW), which redefined the elements of offensive behaviour and increased the penalties for that offence. The number of children's court appearances for offensive behaviour rose by 255 per cent between 1985–86 (before the legislative change) and 1989–90. The increase was primarily the result of changes in legislation and increased arrests by police (Cunneen 1993:186).

Changes in police powers can lead to increased levels of formal contact with juvenile justice agencies. The *Police and Public Safety Act 1998* (NSW) gave police specific 'move on' powers. According to the New South Wales Bureau of Crime Statistics and Research, some 10,000 orders were issued in the first 12 months. Refusal to obey such an order resulted in more than a thousand fines being issued (see *Sydney Morning Herald*, 21 December 1999, p. 11). The same legislation gave police the power to search young people they suspected of being in possession of knives and other prohibited implements (such as scissors, nail files, and so on). Possession of a prohibited implement is an offence, as is refusal to allow a search. Parents can also be found guilty of an offence if they knowingly allow their child to carry a prohibited weapon (NSW Office of the Ombudsman 2000). In the first 21 months after the legislation was introduced, more than 27,000 people were searched. Around one in five people were found to be carrying a prohibited implement (Fitzgerald 2000:2). Changes in existing child welfare laws or the introduction of new welfare-styled laws (which bridge 'protection' and issues relating to potential criminality) may also increase contact between young people and the police; for example, the *Children (Protection and Parental Responsibility) Act 1997*

(NSW) provides police with the power to remove children from public places under particular circumstances.

Changes in law enforcement approaches to illicit drugs can also influence young people's contact with juvenile justice. In recent years, many states have introduced police diversion for minor cannabis offences, under which eligible offenders can be diverted to a drug diversion program for assessment and education. If the offender attends the program, he or she is not charged with a criminal offence, does not attend court, and does not receive a criminal record.

There are a number of specific features of juvenile offending that likewise can increase young people's representation in crime statistics. Young people are more likely to get caught by police than adult offenders, for the following reasons:

- young people are less likely to be experienced and accomplished criminals
- young people tend to commit offences in groups, which leads to greater visibility and risk of detection
- the social dynamics of the offence may lead to easier detection if it is public, gregarious, and attention-seeking
- juvenile crime is often episodic, unplanned, opportunistic, and related to the use of public space in areas such as public transport and shopping centres, where there is a high level of visibility and surveillance
- young people tend to commit offences close to where they live. As a result, they are more likely to be identified by the victim and reported.

These issues have been discussed more fully in a number of reports (Mukherjee 1983, 1985; Freiberg, Fox & Hogan 1988). There are also a number of other factors that lead to distortions in the figures on juvenile offending. These include the following:

- because young people commit offences in groups, several young people are often arrested for a single offence, which distorts the statistics on the relationship between offenders and offences
- the offences for which juveniles are most overrepresented when compared to adults are also offences that have high reporting rates because of insurance requirements (motor vehicle theft, burglary)
- motor vehicle theft and burglary are also offences for which police clear-up rates (that is, rates of crimes solved) are very low. The apparent high level of young people's participation in these offences may in part reflect their inexperience and the greater likelihood of their being apprehended.

Some examples will clarify the points just noted. For instance, young people are likely to steal cars for reasons different from those of professional thieves, and are more likely to be caught joy-riding because of the nature of their public behaviour and their youth. Yet the vast majority of car thefts are not solved. In fact, almost 95 per cent of reported motor vehicle thefts are not cleared by police (New South Wales Bureau of Crime Statistics and Research 2005b:38). If the theft of a single car has been committed by a group, this produces multiple offenders in police and court statistics. Thus, while we know juvenile offenders comprise some 42 per cent of those who are caught by police for motor vehicle theft in Australia (see table 3.1, below), this figure is itself based on a very low percentage (5.5 per cent) of cleared crimes (New South Wales Bureau of Crime Statistics and Research 2005b:38). In addition, the 42 per cent proportion of juvenile offenders is not equivalent to saying that juveniles account for 47 per cent of car thefts where offenders are known, because of the likelihood that there were several young people involved in each incident.

A similar scenario is applicable to burglary ('break and enter' or 'breaking and entering'), where young people's inexperience and their propensity to commit offences in groups lead to a greater chance of apprehension and a distorted presence in the offender statistics. For example, Mukherjee (1985:36) found that nearly 80 per cent of adults arrested for breaking and entering were apprehended acting alone. Conversely, the majority of young people arrested for breaking and entering were apprehended in groups of two or more. In addition, the clear-up rates for burglary are extremely low, with only 5.2 per cent of offences cleared (New South Wales Bureau of Crime Statistics and Research 2005b:38). We cannot assume that the characteristics of the few offenders who are caught are representative of the 95 per cent of offenders who are not.

TABLE 3.1   ALLEGED OFFENDERS AND RECORDED CRIME, NSW 2004

OFFENCE	NO OF JUVENILES	% OF ALL OFFENDERS
Murder	1	1.2
Assault	9855	15.8
Sexual assault	422	15.4
Other sex offences	493	15.8
Robbery w/o weapon	854	46.8
Robbery with a firearm	39	19.5
Robbery with other weapon	337	30.7
Burglary dwelling	2797	34.4
Burglary non-dwelling	2475	49.2
Motor vehicle theft	2282	42.0
Steal from motor vehicle	1505	40.9
Steal from retail store	5595	37.4
Steal from dwelling	1468	32.0
Steal from person	471	38.7
Fraud	980	7.4
Property damage	8381	32.9

Source: Unpublished data, NSW Bureau of Crime Statistics and Research, 6 March 2006.

Even when young people commit the most serious offences (such as homicide), the pattern of their offending is different from that of adults. Homicides committed by young people are more likely to occur between unrelated people, and are more likely to occur in public environments than homicides perpetrated by adults.

The proportion of offences committed by young people

Official police figures can be used to give some indication of young people's participation in reported crime. One set of data that is available relates to offences cleared by police through the arrest of an offender or where there is a suspect identified by police.

These data show that the offences for which the highest proportion of young people are thought to be involved are related to various forms of property theft or robbery without a weapon. There are difficulties in drawing too many conclusions from police arrest figures because of the assumptions underlying such figures and because of their mode of collection (Tait 1994), but they do tell us something about who gets arrested for particular offences. More than 40 per cent of motor vehicle theft cleared by police involved young people. One-third or more of those arrested for shoplifting, theft, and property damage were also young people.

The Youth Justice Coalition (1990:21) has concluded that juvenile offenders tend to be underrepresented in the more serious offence categories (offence categories being groupings of distinct criminal offences). Such an argument is consistent with earlier findings by Mukherjee (1983) and Freiberg et al. (1988:40–1). Arrest rates for juveniles showed that juveniles were underrepresented for homicide and serious assault. Juvenile arrest rates were the same as adult arrest rates for robbery, and higher than adult arrest rates for burglary and motor vehicle theft. More recent analysis of Australian data by Mukherjee, Carcach, and Higgins (1997) confirms that juveniles are more likely to be arrested than adults for less-serious assaults. The higher juvenile arrest rates for burglary and motor vehicle theft are open to influence by the factors discussed earlier, such as the commission of the offence in company, a lack of criminal experience, and the greater likelihood of detection (Freiberg et al. 1988:41).

Not only are young people not overrepresented in the most serious offence categories, but the offences they commit are also less serious than adult crimes because:

- there is a greater likelihood that the attempted property crime or robbery will be unsuccessful
- there is less frequent use of weapons when committing an offence
- when injuries to victims occur, they are less serious than those caused by an adult offender
- the financial loss suffered in theft offences is less than that caused by adult offenders.

While the overall picture shows that about one in four offenders in offences cleared by police is a juvenile, young people are overwhelmingly concentrated in less-serious property offences. For example, in Victoria only 4 per cent of the juveniles proceeded against by police were in the major violent crime categories of homicide, rape, serious assault, and robbery (Mukherjee 1997a:7).

Another way of considering the information available on young people who come into conflict with juvenile justice agencies is to look at the apprehension of young people by police. A young person who is apprehended is not necessarily arrested and charged, and does not necessarily appear before the children's court. In most states, a range of options is available to police, which might divert the young person from the court system. In short, the information on apprehensions shows the nature of the offences for which young people are likely to come into contact with police.

Table 3.2 is based on South Australian police data, and shows the offences (in order of frequency) for which young people were apprehended by police during 2004. It shows that offences relating to theft (larceny) are the major reason for young people's contact with police. Shoplifting, in particular, far outnumbers any other reason for apprehension within the broader category of larceny (comprising nearly 40 per cent of larceny apprehensions). The second major reason for apprehension by police relates to public disorder, and includes such offences as offensive behaviour, offensive language, loitering,

TABLE 3.2   ALLEGED OFFENCES BY JUVENILES APPREHENDED BY POLICE, SOUTH AUSTRALIA, 2004

OFFENCE	N	%
Larceny and receiving	1764	27.2
Offences against good order	1392	21.5
Offences against the person	835	12.9
Property damage	727	11.2
Criminal trespass	708	10.9
Driving offences	574	8.9
Drug offences	141	2.2
Sexual offences	103	1.6
Other offences	104	1.6
Fraud and misappropriation	69	1.1
Robbery and extortion	65	1.0
Total	6482	100.0

Source: Office of Crime Statistics and Research (2005:55).

and resisting arrest. In the category of offences against the person, some seven out of ten apprehensions by police were for common assault, which is the least serious among these offences. The major offences for which young people were apprehended were similar to those of previous years, with the exception of a decline in apprehensions for drug offences over recent years arising from a Police Drug Diversion Initiative.

Court appearances by young people

Another source of information on young people's contact with juvenile justice agencies is available through the children's courts. As we noted above, not all young people who come into contact with police end up before the children's court. However, the court data do provide important information on who is selected for prosecution. Young people appear in the children's courts for a variety of offences, from the very serious (such as homicide) to minor forms of youthful misbehaviour. Table 3.3 relates to 8125 criminal matters determined in the New South Wales Children's Court in the 12 months to the end of 2004, and shows the different offences for which young people came before the courts. The major offence categories relate to property theft and offences against the person. Theft is the largest category of offences (21.6 per cent) dealt with by the children's court, and ranges from motor vehicle theft to shoplifting. Burglary offences make up 12 per cent of matters dealt with by the court, followed by public order offences (10.4 per cent). Justice offences, such as breaching bail or other existing court orders, comprise 8.5 per cent of matters.

Offences against the person (homicide, sexual assault, acts intended to cause injury, and dangerous negligent acts) account for 18.5 per cent of offences dealt with in the children's court. Robbery offences account for a further 7 per cent, and these can be classified as both property and violent offences.

Broadly speaking, the data from the New South Wales Children's Court are comparable with that from other jurisdictions in Australia. Wundersitz (1993:30) has analysed various jurisdictions and concluded that 'property theft dominates the charge profile of young offenders processed by the system'. Her study, which covered various jurisdictions between 1988 and 1991, found that:

- in South Australia, Victoria, and New South Wales, around 50 per cent of charges dealt with were property offences
- in Tasmania and Western Australia, around 45 per cent of charges concerned property offences
- the less serious categories of 'other theft' and 'shoplifting' predominated
- offences against the person were relatively infrequent in most states.

TABLE 3.3 CRIMINAL MATTERS IN THE NEW SOUTH WALES CHILDREN'S COURT, 2004

	MALE		FEMALE		TOTAL	
OFFENCE	**N**	**%**	**N**	**%**	**N**	**%**
Homicide	19	0.3	2	0.2	21	0.3
Acts intended to cause injury	903	13.3	266	20.2	1169	14.4
Sexual assault and related offences	102	1.5	5	0.4	107	1.3
Dangerous/negligent acts endangering persons	176	2.6	13	1.0	189	2.3
Abduction	15	0.2	3	0.2	18	0.2
Robbery	508	7.5	58	4.4	566	7.0
Burglary and related offences	908	13.3	65	4.9	973	12.0
Theft (including motor vehicles)	1430	21.0	324	24.6	1754	21.6
Deception	112	1.6	39	3.0	151	1.8
Drug offences	170	2.5	41	3.1	211	2.6
Weapons	42	0.6	6	0.5	48	0.6
Property damage	481	7.1	87	6.6	568	7.2
Public order offences	718	10.5	125	9.5	843	10.4
Motor traffic offences	534	7.8	88	6.7	622	7.6
Justice offences	539	7.9	156	11.8	695	8.5
Miscellaneous	151	2.2	39	3.0	190	2.3
Total	6808	100.0	1317	100.0	8125	100.0

Source: Adapted from New South Wales Bureau of Crime Statistics and Research (2005a:58–73).

Recent data on juvenile court appearances in South Australia paint a similar picture to those from New South Wales. In 2004, 23 per cent of cases involved theft and receiving, 19.2 per cent involved driving offences, 12.9 per cent concerned offences against the person, and 14.8 per cent were burglary-type offences (Office of Crime Statistics and Research 2005:123). American juvenile arrest data suggest almost identical patterns, particularly when compared to the New South Wales data. In the USA during 1990, crimes against the person accounted for 14 per cent of arrests, compared to 57 per cent of arrests for larceny-theft (Lundman 1994:7).

Returning to the New South Wales data in table 3.3, some further comments can be made on a number of offence categories that give a greater indication of the actual nature of the alleged offending behaviour. In the homicide category, half of the offences were 'driving causing death'. In the public order offences category, 35 per cent related to offensive behaviour, 13 per cent of the offences related to offensive language, and a further 31 per cent were for trespass.

The costs of juvenile offending

Various attempts have been made to estimate the costs of juvenile crime (Potas et al. 1990; Walker 1992; Chan 1994; Mayhew 2003). Any attempt will involve some degree of estimation, given the limitations of official crime statistics. Costs can be measured both in relation to the direct costs of crime (for example, car theft), as well as 'intangible' costs involving an assessment of the monetary value of pain, suffering and lost quality of life.

There is no doubt that the total cost of crime is very significant, with recent estimates placing it at $19 billion per annum, plus a further $13 billion for police, prisons, private security, etc. (Mayhew 2003:1). These figures represent the cost of crime irrespective of whether it is committed by adults or juveniles.

The most expensive crimes are those that are overwhelmingly offences committed by adults. Fraud accounts for 31 per cent of the cost of crime, followed by crimes of violence, which account for 14 per cent. By way of contrast, motor vehicle theft accounts for 5 per cent and robbery 3 per cent (Mayhew 2003:5).

The New South Wales Crime Prevention Division (1999:4) noted that:

> In publicity and visibility terms juvenile crime is far more prominent than white collar crime although the latter is more costly financially and is largely committed by adults. Assuming that juveniles committed all shop-lifting, all auto-theft, all robbery, all break and enter, and all theft offences ... the direct economic cost to the community would still be almost four times smaller than the financial losses which result from fraud.

The economic costs of juvenile crime are significant. However, in the broader comparison of other—predominantly adult—economic and property crime, the costs of juvenile crime are relatively modest.

Changes in the rate of juvenile offending

There has been a great deal of public discussion about whether crime rates are rising and whether young people are committing a greater number of offences now than in the past. We know that many types of crime declined during the early 2000s, with lower incidents of car theft, homicide, robbery and burglary. Some offences have also increased, most notably assaults (Australian Institute of Criminology 2004:8).

One way of finding out whether there has been an increase in juvenile offending is to look at trend data in terms of the number of interventions by the juvenile justice system. The term 'interventions' refers to all court appearances and other formal diversionary processes, such as cautioning and/or appearances before youth conferences. Over recent decades, a relatively stable proportion of young people have faced some form of intervention by juvenile justice authorities in Australia. Wundersitz has analysed the rate per thousand of youth population for matters processed by juvenile justice systems in each state for the period 1979–80 to 1990–91. She found that, with the exception of Western Australia, the rates remained stable across jurisdictions, with only small variations (Wundersitz 1993:22–3). In other words, at the beginning of the 1990s, the rate of intervention in Australia was much the same as it had been more than a decade previously. Even in Western Australia, where the data showed a major increase in the rate of intervention during the 1980s, this trend was reversed at the end of the decade. By 1991, Western Australia was processing juvenile offenders at about the same rate as it had been in 1981.

Despite perceptions at the time of rising juvenile crime rates, figures throughout the 1980s were remarkably stable. Arrest rates of juveniles during an earlier period—from the 1960s to the end of the 1970s—show a slightly different pattern, however. The data for this period are available only for a limited number of offences, including homicide, serious assault, robbery, burglary, fraud, and motor vehicle theft, and show increases in all these categories for both boys and girls (Mukherjee 1985:30–1). Although the arrest rate for girls remained much smaller than that for boys, there were some important changes during this period, with the arrest rate increasing more rapidly for girls when compared to that for boys, and when compared to that for women. For instance, in 1964 the ratio of arrest rates for serious assaults for women and girls was 3:1 (three women arrested for assault for every one girl per 100,000 of population), and for boys and girls 25:1 (twenty-five boys arrested for every one girl per 100,000 of population). By 1981, this pattern was reversed between women and girls, with girls having a higher arrest rate than women, while the ratio for boys to girls had dropped to 6:1 (Mukherjee 1985:28). More recent data by Mukherjee (1997a), covering the period to the mid-1990s, show that arrest rates for robbery, serious assault, motor vehicle theft, and break, enter, and steal showed some stability during the first half of the 1990s. One exception to this stability was an increase in arrest rates for girls for the offence of robbery. The most recent data show recorded offending rates by girls declining by 28 per cent in the early 2000s (Australian Institute of Criminology 2004:61).

Some comparative US data from the Office of Juvenile Justice and Delinquency Prevention are useful. Between 1987 and 1994, the violent crime arrest rate more than doubled for females, while increasing by 64 per cent for males. However, declines since the mid-1990s brought the rate in 1999 to below the 1980 rate for males, but not for females. The 1999 arrest rate for females remained 74 per cent above the 1980 rate. Between 1980 and 1999, male juvenile property crime arrest rates declined by 41 per cent, while the female rate increased by 8 per cent (Office of Juvenile Justice and

Delinquency Prevention 2000). However, it appears that the female rate is also now declining.

Australian figures for the period 1964–95 that Mukherjee (1985, 1997a) has compiled are not completely compatible with those that Wundersitz (1993) has collected for 1979–91, because the former are based on arrest data for a limited number offences, while the latter look at total interventions for all offences. However, they imply that the apparent increase in juvenile arrests experienced during the period of the 1960s to the 1980s may have levelled off during the 1990s. Such a finding is compatible with US data, which show an increase in juvenile arrest rates from 1960 to 1980 (Lundman 1994:8). Between 1980 and 1999, the juvenile arrest rate for all offences in the USA reached its highest level (in 1996), and then declined 16 per cent by 1999. The overall juvenile arrest rate had risen only 7 per cent from 1980 to 1999 (Office of Juvenile Justice and Delinquency Prevention 2000).

There is some evidence to suggest an increase in the seriousness of offences for which juveniles have been apprehended. In New South Wales, both the number and proportion of charges for offences against the person determined by the children's court doubled between 1985–86 and 1989–90. There was an increase again in offences against the person in the later half of the 1990s (NSW Department of Juvenile Justice 1999:6–7). There appears to be a similar pattern regarding proportions of offences against the person in other states and territories. However, overall, offences against the person still constitute a relatively small proportion of offences, even in New South Wales (see table 3.3).

Finally, there is evidence to suggest that the 'levelling off' in juvenile offending in the mid- to late 1990s had now moved to an actual decline in recorded juvenile offending levels. Research by the Australian Institute of Criminology (2004:55) shows that from 1995–96 to 2002–03, the rates of offenders by age have declined for the 10–14 age group by 26 per cent and for the 15–19 year old age group by 21 per cent. A similar picture emerges from the South Australian data, where police apprehensions of juveniles have declined by 36 per cent from their peak in 1995 (Office of Crime Statistics and Research 2005:15–16). Data from NSW also show a decline between 1999 and 2004 in the number of juveniles proceeded against by police for a range of offences including property offences and assaults (unpublished data, NSW Bureau of Crime Statistics and Research, 6 March 2006).

The possible reasons for the decline in the frequency of particular crimes are complex. Some possible causes of the downward trend in property crime include a fall in heroin consumption and greater use of methadone maintenance treatment programs, a rise in average weekly earnings, and a fall in long-term unemployment among young men (Moffatt, Weatherburn & Donnelly 2005). Motor vehicle theft has consistently declined since 2001. The rate of motor vehicle theft in 2005 was half of the 2001 rate, decline that has been largely attributable to the introduction of engine immobilisers as standard equipment on new vehicles (National Motor Vehicle Theft Reduction Council 2006).

Self-report studies and juvenile crime

Self-report studies provide an alternative method to official statistics for gaining a picture of the extent and nature of offending by young people. Such studies rely on young people to provide information on their involvement in behaviour that could constitute a criminal offence. Self-report studies can be useful in gaining knowledge about the subterranean nature of juvenile crime where, for example, it is connected to the underground economy and particularly difficult to quantify (White et al. 1997).

Studies in the 1950s compared self-reports on delinquency between male high-school students and males in a juvenile detention centre. While both groups admitted to committing offences, those who were incarcerated admitted to more frequent and serious offences (Lundman 1994:12). However, self-report studies do suggest that juvenile offending occurs more uniformly among young people than is suggested by arrest data. Two points are of particular relevance to issues discussed further on. First, self-report studies indicate that both boys and girls engage in a range of activities definable as delinquent (Alder 1985:54–5). Second, in the USA, groups of black youth and groups of white youth have both reported similar levels of offending or delinquent behaviour (Gale et al. 1990:17).

Generally, more attention has been paid to self-report studies in the United Kingdom, and particularly in the USA, than in Australia. In the early 1980s, there were some local studies (Kraus & Bowmaker 1982; Warner 1982). More recently, the New South Wales Bureau of Crime Statistics and Research conducted a self-report study of offending behaviour with 5178 secondary school students (Baker 1998). The results indicated that in the twelve-month period prior to the interview, 29 per cent of students had assaulted someone, 27 per cent had damaged property, 15 per cent had received or sold stolen goods, and 5 per cent had been involved in burglary and car theft (Baker 1998:vii). Self-report studies also cast light on how young people who commit offences may explain their own behaviour. For example, Salmelainen (1995) interviewed young people convicted of property offences who had been subsequently committed to detention. Some 50 per cent of those convicted of car theft stated that the main reason they stole the vehicle was because of transport needs. A further 24 per cent stated that they stole the vehicle for excitement or thrills (Salmelainen 1995). Self-report studies have also been used in New South Wales to understand the social environment surrounding violence among school students and the factors that might inhibit such violence (Grunseit, Weatherburn & Donnelly 2005).

Self-report studies are also useful for making comparisons across different countries. A review of self-report studies in thirteen Western countries (Junger-Tas 1994:371, 379) found similarities in the rates of delinquent behaviour and in the nature of offending behaviour generally. There were also similarities with respect to higher rates of reported offending among males than females. There were differences, however, in reported drug use, with lower levels in southern Europe than in western Europe or the USA. International comparisons of self-report studies also reveal a disparity between the self-reported level of offending by ethnic minorities and their over-representation in official juvenile justice statistics when compared with their non-minority counterparts. This highlights the difference between actual offending behaviour and the processes of criminalisation that appears to be a common phenomenon in many countries (Junger-Tas 1994:179).

Contact with the juvenile justice system

There are a number of ways we can consider the question of how many young people come into contact with the juvenile justice system in Australia. First, there are figures on arrest rates of juveniles from various states, which indicate formal police contact. These figures are available only for the more serious offences of homicide, serious assault, robbery, break and enter, motor vehicle theft, and fraud. They indicate quite substantial differences between jurisdictions, with the highest arrest rate in the Northern Territory at 72.1 per 1000 of the juvenile population, compared to 15.8 per 1000 in New South Wales (Freiberg et al. 1988:39).

Second, there are the formal intervention rates, which combine court appearances with data from formal diversionary appearances (police cautions and youth conferences in jurisdictions where these diversionary alternatives exist). Wundersitz (1993) compiled data from these sources and estimated that the intervention rate is 40.8 per 1000 young people. She concluded from her analysis that about 4.1 per cent of juveniles come into formal contact with juvenile justice agencies in any one year. These figures ranged in the data from around 3 per cent in Victoria and New South Wales to 6.4 per cent in Western Australia. The Northern Territory and the Australian Capital Territory were omitted from the analysis because of the problem of obtaining accurate data (Wundersitz 1993).

Another way of considering how many young people come into contact with the system is through the use of cohort studies. In South Australia, Morgan (1993) conducted research on two groups of young people (or cohorts) who were born in 1962 and 1972. The research indicated that about one in five young people appeared before either the South Australian Children's Court or the Aid Panel (which were used before the introduction of youth conferences) during their adolescence. The analysis has shown that approximately one in four boys, compared to one in ten girls, had contact with either the court or the panel. More than half of the Aboriginal youth in the 1972 cohort had contact with these agencies. Skrzypiec and Wundersitz (2005) used a more recent cohort of young people born in 1984, and analysed their formal contact with the South Australian juvenile justice system through police apprehensions. They found one in six (16.7 per cent) young people were formally apprehended by police during their adolescent years of 10 to 17. This represented about one in twelve girls and one in four boys.

Thus, intervention rates indicate that in any one year only a very small proportion of young people come into formalised contact with the juvenile justice system (aside from casual contact with police). A different picture emerges from studies that consider the likelihood of contact over the entire period of adolescence. In general terms, the majority of young people have no formalised contact with juvenile justice agencies; however, some 25 per cent of young males (based on the South Australian study) do find themselves at some time before the authorities within a formal setting.

SOCIAL FACTORS

Data consistently show that young people who enter the juvenile justice system tend to exhibit certain social characteristics, and these characteristics become more pronounced with greater involvement in the system. Many come from a non-nuclear family, have left school early—possibly after expulsion or suspension—are unemployed, have other family members who have had contact with either the juvenile justice or adult criminal justice systems, are more likely to be homeless, are more likely to have drug and alcohol problems, and are more likely to come from minority backgrounds (see, for example, Salmelainen 1995).

These are the key social characteristics that must be considered when looking at offences by young people. Many of these factors will be considered in more detail throughout the book; for the present it is important to put juvenile offending within the context of social relations. The key social characteristics are:

- age
- gender
- ethnicity
- Indigenous status
- social class
- family
- drug and alcohol use
- mental illness and intellectual disability.

An understanding of these social factors allows us to contextualise and understand both the nature of offending by young people and the response to offending by state agencies. We do not suggest that these social characteristics cause juvenile offending as such, but they have an enormous impact on the young people concerned.

Age

Age is an important characteristic in understanding juvenile offending and its classifications. Until recently not all jurisdictions legally defined 'child', 'juvenile', or 'young person' in the same way. Australian jurisdictions have now legislated for criminal responsibility to begin from 10 years old. The age at which a young person is treated as an adult by the criminal justice system is 18 years. However, this commonality in definition across Australian jurisdictions was not reached until 2006–a century after the introduction of children's courts. It is worth noting that the United Nations Convention on the Rights of the Child (CROC) requires that 18 years should be the age of adult criminal responsibility. The Australian Law Reform Commission (ALRC) and Human Rights and Equal Opportunity Commission (HREOC) had recommended that all Australian jurisdictions set the minimum age of criminal responsibility at 10 years and the age of adult responsibility at 18 years (ALRC & HREOC 1997:469–72).

We often see references to 'juvenile crime' as if all young people were equally likely to be offenders irrespective of age. However, the level of offending is related to a young person's age. This is demonstrated in a number of ways:

- Offending rates for particular offences peak during the teenage and early adult years—depending on the type of offence—and then decline dramatically. According to Mukherjee (1983:36), the peak age for theft is 16, for robbery 17, for homicide 19, and for aggravated assault 21 years of age.
- In general terms, offending rates are much lower the younger the age of the person. For example, court appearance rates for 18–19 year olds are nearly six times higher than for 14–15 year olds, and the rates of 14–15 year olds are nearly five times higher than 12–13 year olds (NSW Bureau of Crime Statistics and Research (2004:1).
- A large proportion of juvenile offenders stop offending as they get older— that is, they 'grow out of crime'.
- A small proportion of juvenile offenders go on to commit a large number of offences, and these tend to be young people who started offending at an early age.

Several studies in New South Wales (Coumarelos 1994; Cain 1996), Queensland (Juvenile Justice Branch 1998) and South Australia (Morgan 1993) have confirmed the phenomenon that many juveniles brought before the courts do not reappear on further offences (see also Carcach & Leverett 1999). The Coumarelos study involved a sample of 33,900 young offenders brought before the children's court between 1982 and 1986. It was found that 70 per cent of the young people did not reappear in the children's court. A further 15 per cent had two appearances. The average age at the first appearance was 16 years old.

The study also confirmed that a relatively small group of reoffenders accounted for a large number of court appearances. The 15 per cent of young people who had more than two court appearances accounted for 45 per cent of all children's court appearances, and the 3.4 per cent of young people who had more than six court appearances accounted for 20 per cent of all children's court appearances during the period under examination (Coumarelos 1994:7). In line with these results, it was found that the probability of returning to the children's court increased as the number of appearances increased. There was a low probability that a young person appearing for the first time would return to the children's court. About half the young people who had two appearances returned for a third appearance. However, about three-quarters of those who had six appearances returned for further appearances (Coumarelos 1994:19–20).

More recent research in New South Wales showed significantly different results than the Coumarelos study, partly because the research was able to track whether young people later appeared in adult courts. Chen et al. (2005) analysed the reappearances of 5476 juveniles who had appeared for the first time in a New South Wales children's court in 1995. The researchers found that 68 per cent reappeared at least once in an adult or juvenile court over the next eight years.

The research by Cain (1996) analysed the records of 52,935 young people who were first convicted of an offence before the New South Wales Children's Court from 1 January 1984 and who had reached the age of 18 years by the end of 1994: in other words, those who had commenced and ended their juvenile criminal careers within that period. The study found that juveniles who reoffended tended to be younger at first court appearance and were more likely to be given a more severe sentence for their first offence. They were also more likely to have been dealt with by a non-specialist magistrate. Persistent offenders did not demonstrate any escalation to more serious or violent offences (Cain 1996:1–2).

Morgan's (1993) South Australian study had similar findings to the study by Coumarelos. The majority of children had only one appearance before either the South Australian Children's Court or the Aid Panel (69.3 per cent of the 1962 cohort and 64.6 per cent of the 1972 cohort) (Morgan 1993:176). However, a small number of young people accounted for a large number of offences dealt with by either the court or panel: 5 per cent of young people accounted for a third of offences (Morgan 1993:180). The Queensland study looked at 22,462 finalised appearances between 1987 and 1995, and found that just under 60 per cent of young people did not reappear in the Children's Court (Juvenile Justice Branch 1998:18).

Such research, identifying peak ages for various offences and showing that many young people appear before the children's court only once, has given weight to the notion that young people grow out of crime. The maturation process is as important as any rehabilitative or reformative measure (Mukherjee 1985:33). Conversely, we know the younger the child is when first having contact with juvenile justice, then the more likely it is the child will become entrenched in the justice system (Chen et al. 2005).

There is considerable research from various countries that lends weight to these ideas. A famous study of juvenile males in Philadelphia by Wolfgang, Figlio, and Sellin (1972) confirmed that about half of those with a police record were only apprehended once, while a small group committed a large number of offences. Hirschi and Gottfredson (1983) also found consistency in the age distribution of crime across countries and various time periods. The British study by West (1982) found that with increasing age there was increasing conformity among those previously designated as delinquent. In terms of policy, such findings have led to an emphasis on developmental strategies that reinforce the role of the home and the school, and that argue against the use of incarceration (Rutherford 1986).

Gender

There are enormous differences in the number of young men and young women arrested and brought before the children's courts. While levels of unreported crime and differential treatment by state agencies may obscure some criminal behaviour by young women, the overwhelming feature of the data is that boys are about five to six times more likely than girls to be charged with a criminal offence and appear in court. Table 3.3 shows the magnitude of difference in court appearances in New South Wales, where young women account for one in six (or 16.2 per cent) of finalised criminal matters. Such a difference is typical of all Australian jurisdictions.

Another feature of intervention specific to girls is that, proportionately, they are more likely to receive a diversionary outcome (such as a caution) than boys. Such a finding is typical across Australian jurisdictions where information is available (Western Australia, Victoria, New South Wales, and South Australia) (Wundersitz 1993:28).

The data from New South Wales show that, once before the court, the two major offence categories for males and females ('acts intended to cause injury' and 'theft') are similar, although there are greater proportions of girls concentrated in those categories (see table 3.3). A notable difference relates to burglary offences. For boys, these comprised 13.3 per cent, and for girls 4.9 per cent.

However, there are no offence categories where the actual number of offences by girls is the same as that of boys. Table 3.3 shows that, among the more significant offence categories, the closest parity is for fraud (deception), where 26 per cent of court appearances were by girls. The next closest is for 'acts intended to cause injury' (23 per cent of appearances by girls). Self-report studies confirm this general picture, with some exceptions. In a study by Baker (1998), young men reported significantly higher participation rates in offences, particularly car theft and break and enter. Shoplifting was the one offence more equally reported across the sexes; for final-year senior school students, young women reported a slightly higher participation rate in shoplifting than males (Baker 1998:20–21).

As noted earlier, offence categories are groupings of distinct criminal offences. One specific offence where the number of court appearances by young women exceeds that of young men is for convictions relating to prostitution, which is usually categorised within 'offences against good order'. The extent to which prostitution is criminalised varies between jurisdictions, and is also dependent on police discretionary practices. However, it can be an important mechanism through which young women enter the juvenile justice system.

A further feature of the difference between males and females brought into the juvenile justice system is their relative likelihood of reoffending. The South Australian cohort study showed that females were significantly less likely to appear more than once before the South Australian Children's Court or Aid Panel than were boys. Some 37 per cent of boys of the 1962 cohort went on to reappear, compared to 13 per cent of girls (Morgan 1993:176). In the Queensland study, 39 per cent of boys compared to 29 per cent of girls went on to reoffend (Juvenile Justice Branch 1998:19). New South Wales studies of recidivism found that males were one-third more likely to reoffend while juveniles than females (Cain 1996:38), and were more likely to go on appear in an adult court than females (Chen et al. 2005:4).

Ethnicity

Since the Second World War, Australia's population has become increasingly culturally diverse as a result of immigration. By the mid-1980s, it had been estimated that between one in five and one in six young people between 15 and 24 years old were either born in non-English-speaking countries, or had one or both parents born in non-English-speaking countries (Federation of Ethnic Communities' Council of Australia 1991:3). The cultural diversity of Australia's population increased further during the next decade. By the mid-1990s, 23 per cent of people in Australia were born overseas and, of these, more than half were born in non-English-speaking countries (Race Discrimination Commissioner 1995:31). The cultural diversity of young people has given rise to a number of issues relating to juvenile crime and the administration of juvenile justice. Some of those issues have concerned the over-representation of specific groups of young people (Indo-Chinese, Lebanese, and Pacific Islanders) in court appearances, and whether discrimination is a matter worthy of attention (HREOC 1993b:251). In New South Wales, there was an increase of more than 200 per cent in the number of Indo-Chinese juvenile detainees between 1991 and 1993. The custody time for Indo-Chinese detainees in juvenile justice centres was also three times longer (16.3 months) than the average custody (Cain 1994a:5).

In addition, some sociodemographic indicators, such as unemployment, poverty, refugee status, and lack of family support in Australia, place at least some young people from non-English-speaking backgrounds (NESB) in high-risk categories for contact with juvenile justice agencies.

There has also been concern over insensitivity and police harassment of NESB young people (NSW Office of the Ombudsman 1994; Youth Justice Coalition 1994; Collins et al. 2000). A report from the Youth Justice Coalition found that the rates at which young people from Asian, Aboriginal, and Pacific Islander backgrounds were contacted, searched, questioned, fingerprinted, and detained by police indicated unacceptably high levels of racism: 'Our survey shows that young people from Asian backgrounds are nearly twice as likely to be searched, four times more likely to be arrested, and three times more likely to be injured during their contact with police than young people describing themselves as from an Australian background' (Youth Justice Coalition 1994:1).

Ethnicity has in the main been ignored as a factor in juvenile justice policy. Yet clearly, specific groups of young people come into contact with agencies in a way that calls into question whether their ethnicity is a factor in intervention. The only Australian self-report study on juvenile offending that has considered the issue of ethnicity found that ethnic-minority young people were not associated with any particular type of reported offending. 'In fact where we found any relationship between ethnicity and participation in crime it indicated that students from an ethnic background had lower rates of participation in crime' (Baker 1998:55). The issue of ethnicity is discussed more fully in chapter 7.

Indigenous status

A key social factor of young people who are processed by the juvenile justice system is the over-representation of Indigenous youth. We discuss the evidence of over-representation at greater length in chapter 6. For now, it is important to note that a key characteristic of the juvenile justice system is the extent to which Aboriginal and Torres Strait Islander young people, more than other identifiable groups, dominate arrest, court, and detention figures.

The over-representation has been persistent and severe, and needs to be understood within the context of colonial and neocolonial politics. In other words, there has been a distinct and special relationship between Indigenous young people and non-Indigenous authorities since the time of colonisation. Aboriginal and Torres Strait Islander young people have historically been discriminated against. As a result, it is by no means self-evident that the current over-representation of Aboriginal young people is simply the result of greater levels of offending in that group than in any other.

Many of the factors that are commonly associated with young people who are arrested and brought before the courts simply do not hold true for Indigenous young people. For example, the South Australian cohort study showed that, while the majority of young people only appear once before courts or panels, this was reversed for Aboriginal young people. Some 60 per cent of Aboriginal young people were brought into the juvenile justice system on two or more occasions (Morgan 1993:177). A New South Wales study found that an Aboriginal young person brought before the children's court was nine times more likely to later appear before an adult court than a non-Aboriginal young person (Chen et al 2005:4). Aboriginal young people who come into contact with juvenile justice authorities are also more likely to come from rural backgrounds, to be female, to be younger, and to be incarcerated (see chapter 6).

Social class

A determinant in relation to social class and the likelihood of contact with the juvenile justice system is unemployment.

Unemployment is characteristic of young people brought before the children's courts. One study indicated that 67 per cent of young people over the age of 15 years who appeared in the children's court were unemployed (cited in Freiberg et al. 1988:50). Similar findings were made in a South Australian study where more than 60 per cent of school-leavers who appeared were unemployed (Gale et al. 1990:56).

We deal more fully with the issue of unemployment and economic adversity in chapter 5, but for now it is important to note a number of essential features. Unemployment and poverty are not equally distributed across the population in terms of age, gender, ethnicity, or geographic location. Unemployment rates among 15–19 year olds are regularly two to three times higher than those for the general population.

Unemployment is also differentiated by area. Many of the working-class suburbs of Australian cities have significantly higher rates of unemployment than affluent areas. It has been noted that the suburbs with the highest number of young people appearing in court are also the ones with high levels of unemployment and disadvantage on other social indicators, including welfare dependency (Freiberg et al. 1988:49–50; Gale et al. 1990:59; Devery 1991; Carrington 1993:15). Unemployment is also concentrated in particular groups, and this factor tends to be registered in children's court appearances. The unemployment rate for some ethnic minority young people (15–19 years old) is higher by more than three percentage points than the general rate of youth unemployment. Among specific groups—such as Vietnamese male youth—the unemployment rate is double the general youth rate (HREOC 1993b:223; Blacktown Youth Services 1992:16). Similarly, among Indigenous young people the unemployment level is considerably higher than the general youth rate. Research in the 1980s found that in some communities the level of unemployment among Indigenous young people was almost 100 per cent (Cunneen & Robb 1987:27). In South Australia, it was found that the unemployment rate among Aboriginal school-leavers who appeared in court or before an Aid Panel was 91 per cent (Gale et al. 1990:56).

Unemployment is not equally distributed across the general population or across the youth population. Particular groups of young people are susceptible to a greater likelihood of being without work and/or without money. Economic adversity is a factor strongly associated with those young people who appear in the juvenile justice system.

Family

It is apparent that many young people who appear before the children's courts do not live in nuclear families. These include young people who live with one parent, with relatives, with other young people, or in a de facto relationship, and those who are homeless.

There are a number of complex issues here relating to culture, economics, and politics. Some young people live in extended families because it is part of their culture of child-rearing and familial relations—for instance, research done in South Australia in the 1980s found that three-quarters of Aboriginal young people brought before the courts did not live in a nuclear family (Gale et al. 1990:57). Young women who are homeless and brought before the courts may well be there as a result of escaping from an abusive home situation.

Another way of considering the issue of family is that juvenile justice agencies may seek to supervise through the children's court what are defined as abnormal families. There are two aspects to be considered here. First, there is the question of the perceived abnormality of the sole-parent family. In a South Australian study, about one in four appearances were of young people from sole-parent families (Gale et al. 1990:57) and in a New South Wales study, specifically of girls, about one-third were from sole-parent families (Carrington 1993:73). The prevalence of sole-parent families among these young people was about three to four times the national average. Second, there is the issue of the extent to which all family members, including all the siblings, come under surveillance. In one study of fifty-nine girls who were institutionalised, more than half of the siblings appeared in the children's court at some time (Carrington 1993:73).

Family background is an important social characteristic of those young people brought into the juvenile justice system. It is those young people without family, those living in what is defined as an 'abnormal' family relationship, and those in the most economically marginalised families who are the most susceptible to intervention. Young people who live outside 'normal' family arrangements are subject to different responses once inside the system. Issues of parental neglect have been directly associated with lack of economic and social resources, and with family poverty. All of these in turn have been linked with greater likelihood of contact with the juvenile justice system (Weatherburn & Lind 2001).

Drug and alcohol abuse

National surveys indicate that illegal drug use among young people in the 14–19 year age group is widespread. In 1995, 32 per cent of young people in this group had used an illegal drug. In 1998, the percentage had increased to 38 per cent (New South Wales Law Reform Commission 2001:29). The relationship between drug abuse, young people, and the juvenile justice system is multifaceted. Drug dependency, particularly heroin dependency, has been linked with the incidence of property crime. At the beginning of 2000, there were an estimated 74,000 dependent heroin users in Australia. About half lived in New South Wales. Other studies have indicated links between substance abuse and juvenile offending (see Copeland & Howard 1997, Putnins 2001).

Monitoring of drug use by young people detained by police also shows widespread use of illicit drugs. In 2004, 93 juvenile detainees were interviewed at Bankstown and Parramatta police stations. Some 72 per cent of these agreed to provide a urine sample. Forty-three per cent in Bankstown and 40 per cent in Parramatta tested positive to at least one drug. Juveniles were most likely to test positive to cannabis, although 19 per cent in Bankstown tested positive to methylamphetamine, and 7 per cent in Parramatta tested positive to heroin (Schulte et al. 2005:26).

A survey of 302 youth in New South Wales detention centres found that more than 90 per cent reported having used cannabis, 56 per cent amphetamines, 50 per cent heroin, 46 per cent hallucinogens, 34 per cent cocaine, and 27 per cent ecstasy or similar drugs. The average age of the sample was 16.5 years (NSW Juvenile Justice Advisory Council 2001a:Appendix D; see also Copeland & Howard 2001). A South Australian survey of drug use among 900 young people in detention centres also showed widespread use. The survey measured reported use in the month prior to interview, and revealed that 73 per cent had used alcohol, 81 per cent marijuana, 25 per cent hallucinogens, 23 per cent sedatives (without prescription), 10 per cent narcotics, 22 per cent stimulants, and 11 per cent inhalants. The data were compared with drug use by male 16 year old secondary school students, and showed that young offenders have significantly greater use in all drug categories except alcohol, which was only slightly higher (Putnins 2001:7).

Official responses to illicit drug use and dependency also have an impact on the types of laws, programs, policies, and sentencing options that are put in place. Whether criminalisation or harm minimisation policies are followed can have a significant impact on the way in which the juvenile justice system might respond to young people who are drug-dependent. The level and nature of services available for treatment will also impact on the response of juvenile justice agencies. As we discuss more fully in chapter 10, drug courts are being introduced in many jurisdictions in Australia, and a new development has been the introduction of youth drug courts in a number of states.

Mental illness and intellectual disability

There has been little research done on the incidence of intellectual disability or mental illness among young people who become involved in the juvenile justice system. However, research on adults shows there is a significant problem in relation to intellectual disability and the criminal justice system. The New South Wales Law Reform Commission (1996:25) conducted an inquiry in the area, and the research results show that some 12–13 per cent of the prison population have an intellectual disability, which is around six times higher than the general population. People with intellectual disabilities were over-represented before the magistrate's courts, comprising possibly a third of those who appear as defendants. Possible reasons for this over-representation include police reaction to and criminalisation of perceived abnormal behaviour, and the possibility that people with intellectual disabilities were more likely to commit certain types of offences.

The Commission found that young people in the juvenile justice system who suffered from an intellectual disability were likely to be doubly disadvantaged. The Commission noted that:

> 'Specific concerns for juveniles are their enhanced vulnerability in custody and the desirability of maintaining community links, as well as the danger that they will fall between the gaps of youth services and disability services despite being at risk of becoming victims and/or offenders' (New South Wales Law Reform Commission 1996:39).

Mental illness is also a significant problem, particularly among those young people who are incarcerated. A survey of 302 youth in New South Wales detention centres found that 23.7 per cent had attempted suicide, with females more likely to attempt suicide than males (cited in Juvenile Justice Advisory Council 2001a:Appendix D). An earlier survey of 100 detainees had found that 26 per cent had thought of suicide, 9 per cent had attempted suicide, and 46 per cent had previous contact with mental health professionals (Fasher et al. 1997). A more recent survey of young people in custody in New South Wales provides some insight into the mental health issues facing young people in custody. Some 88 per cent of young people reported mild, moderate, or severe symptoms consistent with a clinical disorder (New South Wales Department of Juvenile Justice 2003:9). We discuss this research further in chapter 11.

The HREOC conducted a National Inquiry into the Human Rights of People with Mental Illness in 1993. Of relevance to the relationship between mental illness and juvenile justice, the inquiry found that:

- of people with mental illnesses, young people are among those who are hardest to place in accommodation
- there is an extreme shortage of child and adolescent psychiatrists, as well as other child and adolescent mental health professionals
- there are serious deficiencies in the provision of staff, services, facilities, and programs for children and adolescents with mental illness

- there is an alarming lack of knowledge among many health, education, welfare, and juvenile justice professionals about various psychiatric, behavioural, and emotional problems that can affect children and young people (HREOC 1993a:919, 932).

The Mental Illness Inquiry made a number of specific recommendations relating to juvenile justice agencies, which focused on appropriate psychiatric assessment and treatment for young people in detention centres (HREOC 1993a:934). The ALRC and HREOC (1997) Inquiry into Children in the Legal Process also made specific recommendations in relation to the sentencing of young people with mental illness or severe emotional or behavioural disturbances, including the need to obtain psychiatric reports prior to sentencing, the need for sentences to provide for ongoing assessment and treatment, and for relevant juvenile justice staff to be appropriately trained (recommendation 249).

EXPLANATIONS

Many of the attempts to identify the predictors for juvenile offending have been tautological, highly generalised, and often profoundly ideological in nature. For instance, it has been argued that the background characteristics of delinquents are below-average intelligence, parental criminality, sibling criminality, low income, and discordant family environment. Other factors cited are poor academic performance, antisocial behaviour, and inadequate parental supervision and discipline (see Potas et al. 1990:52–4; Weatherburn & Lind 2001).

Braithwaite (1989:44–9) has outlined the strongest known variables that relate to crime. With the exception of white-collar crime, crime is disproportionately committed by males aged 15–25 years, by unmarried people, by people in cities, and by people who have experienced high residential mobility. People who are disadvantaged by socioeconomic status, who are unemployed, and who belong to an oppressed racial minority group have higher offending rates.

In addition, young people strongly attached to school are less likely to commit offences, while young people who do poorly at school are more likely to engage in crime. Young people with high educational and occupational aspirations are less likely to commit offences. Young people who are strongly attached to their parents are less likely to engage in crime. Young people who have friendships with criminals are more likely to engage in crime themselves.

The list that Braithwaite has developed shows the potential danger of making sweeping generalisations concerning young people and juvenile justice. In the end, all that can be said is that these factors are associated with young people brought into the juvenile justice system. This is a very different proposition from stating that these factors are the cause of juvenile crime.

More recent work looking at developmental factors associated with juvenile offending has concentrated on enumerating and analysing what are considered to be 'risk factors' associated with 'antisocial and criminal behaviour', and 'protective factors' that are likely to prevent such behaviour (Developmental Crime Prevention Consortium 1999). Both risk factors and protective factors are considered within categories of child factors, family factors, school context, life events, and community and cultural factors (see chapters 2 and 12). The researchers are at pains to point out that their lists are not static or constant, and should be seen as 'process linked rather than having some purely statistical connection to an outcome' (Developmental Crime Prevention Consortium 1999:141). Yet there appears to be little analysis of the political and economic context within which such factors occur. For example, how can we consider such 'risk factors' as absent father, large family, long-term parental unemployment, and so on (Developmental Crime Prevention Consortium 1999:136) outside of specific state policies that are class- and gender-based? These include federal family policies that provide tax incentives and financial support for two-parent, mother-staying-at-home 'families', and the dearth of labour-market policies that offer full employment opportunities. Surely a 'small family size' and 'more than two years between siblings' are protective factors (Developmental Crime Prevention Consortium 1999:138) only under particular economic and cultural conditions. In fact, many cultures would see an extended family as highly protective and economically sound.

The danger of multifactorial approaches is that too often we are left with an apparently scientific picture that children from a middle-class, home-owning nuclear family of the dominant culture are quintessentially law-abiding, and that all those who do not fit this stereotype are potentially delinquent. Such images of normality and delinquency are profoundly ideological. Regardless of developmental intentions, such analyses lend themselves to greater punitive interventions rather than strategies for social support. This is particularly so under conservative and law-and-order governments that are hostile to providing the resources identified as necessary for community development.

The most fundamental difficulty with explanatory predictors or factors associated with juvenile offending is whether they can be divorced from the operation and processes of criminalisation. Are young people who have trouble at school more likely to commit offences, or are they more likely to be reported to authorities and become the subject of surveillance and intervention? Similarly, are children from single-parent families more likely to be subject to welfare and police surveillance because they are already connected to regulatory bodies as a result of welfare dependence? Are the young of minority groups more likely to appear in arrest rates because they commit more offences, or because they are members of minority groups and therefore subject to differential treatment and sometimes racism by authorities? In other words, the factors that are often presented as predictors of delinquency may in fact be the predictors of intervention.

MEDIA REPRESENTATIONS

For many years, there has been concern about the way the media present images of youth, particularly in relation to crime and social disorder. For most people, their knowledge concerning crime does not come from the direct experience of victimisation, offending, or detection by authorities; nor does it come from academic studies or policy documents. Rather, knowledge about juvenile offending and juvenile offenders is partly mediated and partly constructed through the stories circulated in the news broadcasts and cop shows, the daily tabloids, and talkback commentaries. What we have are constructed simulations dealing in images of youth and crime.

Hogg and Brown (1998:21) have identified the key assumptions in what they refer to as 'law and order commonsense'. These include assumptions that:

- crime rates are soaring
- crime is worse than ever
- the criminal justice system is soft on crime
- the criminal justice system is loaded in favour of criminals
- there should be more police
- police should have more powers
- courts should deliver tougher penalties
- greater retribution against offenders will satisfy victims' demands.

These elements of law-and-order commonsense form part of the routine reporting by the media on issues of crime and criminal justice.

Four broad categories in the contemporary representations of young people have been identified: the 'ideal' young person, the young person as 'threat', the young person as 'victim', and the young person as 'parasite' (White 1990:107). Evidence discussed further on indicates that the dominant representation of young people is as a threat. The media are big business, and their representations need to be understood within the context of profitability (what sells) and of discourses about social normality.

There is a tradition in criminological writings of looking at the relationship between young people and the media. Stan Cohen's classic work on the clashes between the mods and the rockers in England during the 1960s showed the power of negative representation in amplifying disorder and bringing about a political crackdown on youth (Cohen 1973). Similarly, Hall et al. (Hall, Jefferson, Critcher, & Roberts 1978) analysed the creation of a phenomenon of 'mugging' and its association with young people, in particular black British youth. In Australia, researchers have looked at the role of the media in riots at the Bathurst motorcycle races through their amplification of anti-police sentiment and limited portrayal of events (Cunneen, Findlay, Lynch, & Tupper 1989). Others have noted earlier media representations of bodgies and widgies (Stratton 1992) and contemporary youth subcultures (Walton 1993). An underlying theme in such work is the way in which young people and their subcultures are portrayed as deviant and criminal. Much of this literature utilises the concept of 'moral panic'. By 'moral panic', we refer to the situation in which (see Goode & Ben-Yehuda 1994):

- the behaviour of a social group is defined as deviant
- there is serious concern over the behaviour of, and hostility towards, the particular group
- there is a level of consensus over the negative definitions of the group and its behaviour
- there is a disproportionate and punitive response, usually by the criminal justice system, towards the group.

Moral panics also tend to be volatile, in that they erupt suddenly and disappear around particular issues or subcultural groups.

Many empirical studies have confirmed the media's preoccupation with crime (see Cunneen et al. 1989). By and large, crime is sensationalised by the media. This means that atypical—usually violent—crimes are given more prominence than common crimes. Crime is presented as basically random in nature and thus a threat to everyone in the same way (Grabosky & Wilson 1989; Ericson, Baranek & Chan 1991).

In the specific case of youth crime, the images are equally powerful, and equally distorted (see, for example, Bessant & Hil 1997). The media are saturated with stories about 'young thugs', 'hooligans', 'ethnic youth gangs', 'school vandals', and 'lazy teenagers'. In an examination of newspaper reporting about youth in Western Australia between 1990 and 1992, Sercombe (1993) found that the major issue reported in relation to young people was crime. Crime stories easily dominated the reporting agenda, comprising 63 per cent of newspaper reporting on youth (Sercombe 1993:16). Later research also revealed that the 'face' of youth crime was also heavily racialised. Some 85 per cent of stories that referred to Aboriginal youth were principally about crime (Sercombe 1995:78).

The high profile given to illegal drugs in the mass media has been accompanied by moral panics over drug use among teenagers. Headlines about deaths linked to the taking of ecstasy, and lurid details about deaths due to heroin overdoses, have reinforced public concern over how to tackle the presumed 'war on drugs'. Much of the media coverage of youth crime hinges on the idea that there is some kind of youth crime wave.

Sercombe (1993) found that two sources of information (police and court) dominated the news in relation to youth. He suggests that the reason for this lies in the economics of news production and in the news values of the media. In terms of production, statements from the courts and police are routine, cheap, and easy to collect. The close connection between the police and journalists has been commented on in a number of Australian studies (Grabosky & Wilson 1989; Cunneen et al. 1989). The propriety or otherwise of these connections has been questioned in judicial inquiries such as the Fitzgerald inquiry into police corruption in Queensland (Fitzgerald 1989).

Official views, whether through press releases, spokespersons, or government statistics, dominate what is said about young people. Young people themselves are in a particularly disadvantaged position in terms of having their own opinions or views on matters heard in the media. They have neither official legitimacy, nor the institutional means of making their views known.

There has been concern about the reporting of young NESB people. The New South Wales Ethnic Affairs Commission, in a 1985 report on fights between young people in Marrickville and Bankstown, was highly critical of what it saw as superficial and selective reporting by the media, which presented the conflict in racial terms. The Commission described some of the headlines as sensational, misleading, and hysterical (Ethnic Affairs Commission of New South Wales 1986:3). More recently, research by Collins and others (2000) has been critical of media reports linking Arabic-speaking youth with crime in Sydney. There have been similar concerns regarding the reporting of Indo-Chinese and other ethnic minority young people and crime in Melbourne and other cities (White, Perrone, Guerra, & Lampugnani 1999; Pe-Pua 1999). One article described Vietnamese young people who had arrived in Australia as unattached minors as follows: 'They live in transient, shared households, stay up late, smoke, drink and watch hours of cheap "chop socky" videos. They roam in packs, drifting from pool halls to petty crime to drug-taking' ('Suburbanasia!', *Time Magazine*, 8 April 1991, p. 23).

The images of young people in the media are not always left uncontested. An interesting and successful defamation proceeding was undertaken by the National Children's and Youth Law Centre on behalf of twenty-eight former high school students against News Limited, the publisher of the *Daily Telegraph*. In January 1997, the newspaper had published a front-page photograph of Year 12 students from Mt Druitt High School in Sydney's western suburbs and a story about how badly the class had done in the Higher School Certificate (HSC). The students took action for defamation against the newspaper on the basis that the article implied that they were so stupid they failed the HSC, that their lack of application and discipline contributed to their failure, and that the students had no commitment to their studies. A jury found the article was defamatory. The settlement included a public apology to the young people from the *Daily Telegraph* and undisclosed financial settlements with the students (Floro 2001:6–7).

We need to consider how the representations of young people coincide with their positioning as a law-and-order problem within electoral politics. Virtually all state and territory elections in Australia now have law-and-order issues as a central component of the campaign. In most elections, the extent of juvenile offending and the appropriate responses to it have been used as an electoral issue. Often, Labor and the conservative parties have attempted to outdo each other to be seen as the more punitive.

In the post-election period, punitive policies are often put in place as a result of earlier promises. Recent Australian history is replete with examples, such as the introduction in the early 1990s of 'boot camps' in Western Australia; and, in New South Wales, changes to juvenile cautioning procedures and the introduction of the *Summary Offences Act 1988* (NSW). Electoral politics and the role of media reporting on young people and crime go hand in hand. Neither is fettered by appeals to rational discourse about the nature of juvenile offending. Empirical evidence and calls for reasoned debate on juvenile justice policy are lost when populist politics are in command.

The potential appeal of the politics of law and order, 'getting tough' on juveniles, and the collapsing of media into government is shown by the Western Australian 'Rally for Justice'. The rally was organised by Perth Radio station 6PR and a local talkback radio commentator. One result was the introduction of the first recent wave of mandatory sentencing legislation, the *Crime (Serious and Repeat Offenders) Act 1992* (WA) (see White 1992).

Indeed, substantial changes to police powers found in the New South Wales legislation (the Police and Public Safety Act and the Children's (Protection and Parental Responsibility) Act), as well as the introduction of mandatory sentences of imprisonment for juveniles in the Northern Territory and Western Australia, have been generated more by political perceptions of what constitutes successful electioneering than by concern for the actual effects of such legislation on young people or their human rights.

The role of the media in representing young people as delinquents can have tangible results, from changes in legislation to variations in policing practices. The interconnection between popular fears, media reporting, and political responses was captured by the former Director-General of the New South Wales Department of Juvenile Justice (Buttrum 1998:63) as follows:

> Current policy is flawed by political expediency and 'knee-jerk' responses to perceived problems ... talk back radio is a principal medium for propagating the urban myths about juvenile crime. Members of parliament are regularly invited to discuss law and order issues on these shows and are commonly badgered by the hosts and radio audiences to give a commitment to toughening the government's stance toward youth lawlessness.

More broadly, the intersection between media reporting and the political use of community fears over law-and-order constructs a certain reality that inhibits our understanding of the nature of juvenile offending and constrains our conceptions of the possible responses. Within this climate, mandatory sentencing, increased police powers, and restrictions on community-based sentences appear popular, while community development and social justice strategies are portrayed as ineffectual and 'soft'.

YOUNG PEOPLE AS VICTIMS OF CRIME

Ironically, an important and neglected aspect of the relationship between young people and the law is that they are often the victims of offences. Usually, the images and public knowledge about young people and crime paint a picture of youth as perpetrators of offences. However, significant research has identified the extent to which young people are also the victims of crime. This recognition is in line with the current focus on victims' rights and the move towards 'restorative justice', which emphasises the participation of victims in dealing with young offenders. Unfortunately, despite all the emphasis on the role of the victim in the new methods of dealing with young people, there is often no recognition that young people are as likely to be victims as perpetrators (or in some cases more likely). For all that has been written about victims' rights, one is hard-pressed to find literature that deals with the simple empirical observation that young people are, indeed, victims themselves. Recent crime victimisation surveys show that the group with the highest level of victimisation for personal crimes is young males between 15 and 24 years of age, with nearly one in ten reporting being a victim in the previous twelve months (Australian Bureau of Statistics 2004).

Using South Australian police data, Tait (1994:70) found that young people between 15 and 20 years old were the most likely group to be the victims of robbery, and that more young people reported being victims of robbery than were apprehended by authorities as perpetrators of the offence. Alder (1991) has identified high levels of victimisation of young people who are homeless. Underwood, White, and Omelczuk (1993) surveyed youth workers in a number of different youth services, such as refuges and drop-in centres, throughout Western Australia. The survey ascertained that young people were exposed to incidences of violence in the private sphere of the home and in the public sphere (Underwood et al. 1993:15–17).

Similarly, Mukherjee (1983:71) has noted that children under 16 years old are about four times more likely to be victims than suspects in homicide cases. Alder and Polk (2001) have extensively analysed the nature of homicides against children and young people, particularly within a family setting. This type of research is rare. As noted earlier in this chapter, surveys of crime victims do not adequately deal with juvenile victimisation. However, Australian surveys do show that those in the 15–19-years age group are more likely to be victims of personal crime such as assault, sexual assault, and robbery than are older age groups. Unemployed young people are more likely to be victimised than those in employment (Mukherjee, Carcach, & Higgins 1997:51). Data from the National Crime Statistics collection show that 12 per cent of homicide victims are under the age of 20, 61 per cent of sexual assault victims are under the age of 20, and 45 per cent of victims of kidnapping and abduction are under the age of 15 (Mukherjee et al. 1997:51).

There is also a large body of research that identifies young people as being susceptible to violence on the part of the authorities, particularly police (see chapter 9).

CONCLUSION

The nature of juvenile offending is not as straightforward as it might seem at first glance. The official figures are limited for a range of reasons: some limitations relate to all recorded crime statistics; others are specific to measuring juvenile offending. Arrest rates and court appearances show that property crimes predominate among young people. The available data also show that juvenile offending is less serious than adult offending because of a number of factors.

We know that many young people who are apprehended for an offence come into contact with the juvenile justice system only once during their adolescent years. We also know that in any one year a very small proportion of young people will be apprehended by police and brought before courts or diversionary schemes. Over the length of a person's adolescence, the likelihood of contact is much greater, but still the majority of young people have no formal contact with the juvenile justice system. We also know that there is a range of social factors that increases the likelihood of a young person's contact with the juvenile justice system.

Rather than present arguments about the causality of juvenile crime, we have preferred to provide an analysis of the key social characteristics of young people who end up in the juvenile justice system. We have sketched such a profile in terms of age, sex, ethnicity, Indigenous status, social class, family, drug and alcohol abuse, and intellectual illness and mental disability.

In summary, the general pattern of offending can be broken down in terms of extent and seriousness of offending. Typically, it is the case that a large proportion of juvenile offenders stop offending as they get older, and that a relatively small group of reoffenders account for a large number of court appearances (Coumarelos 1994; Cain 1996). Children and young people who offend can be categorised into three main groupings (McLaren 2000; New Zealand Ministry of Justice & Ministry of Social Development 2002; see also Leober & Farrington 1998):

- low-risk or minor offenders, who do not commit many offences and who generally 'grow out' of offending behaviour as part of the normal maturation process
- medium-risk offenders, who commit a number of offences, some serious, mainly due to factors such as substance abuse and antisocial peers

- high-risk offenders, who begin offending early (between 10 and 14 years of age), offend at high rates and often very seriously, and are likely to keep offending into adulthood.

The age at which offending first occurs, or at which criminalisation of the young person happens, has a major bearing on subsequent contact with the criminal justice system (Harding & Maller 1997). The younger the person, the more likely that person will engage in future reoffending. It is necessary to recognise that different ages and different types of offending demand different kinds of responses.

It is important to acknowledge that the dominant images of young people and crime that circulate in the social world are not real reflections of youthful offending. These images magnify the social threat of young people, and particularly isolate groups of young people such as Indigenous youth and NESB youth. Politicians grab eagerly at these simulated images of youth, and develop public policy that has more to do with the image of threat than the reality of the world in which young people live.

We need to recognise that viewing young people as a law-and-order threat has serious consequences for our ability to develop socially just responses for young people and for our ability to respect young people's human rights. International human rights instruments require that we develop juvenile justice responses on the basis of a recognition that much juvenile crime is not serious and is transitory. Yet law-and-order politics has been translated into zero tolerance policing strategies and mandatory prison sentencing for minor offences—strategies that run contrary to what we know about the nature of juvenile crime.

4 | The institutions of juvenile justice

CHAPTER HIGHLIGHTS

Introduction
The legislative framework
The key players
Accountability and regulation
The principles of juvenile justice
The effects of the system
Conclusion

INTRODUCTION

The purpose of this chapter is to describe and analyse the institutions of juvenile justice and to ask what these institutions are.

It is accepted in everyday language to talk about juvenile justice or the juvenile justice system. The implication is that there is a system that is, to a greater or lesser extent, coherent in terms of policy and practices. In a formal sense, there certainly is a system created by the body of legislation and regulations that govern interactions between institutions and young people of a certain age. However, it would be simplistic to imagine that there are no competing interests, indeed, no different interests in the way various juvenile justice agencies deal with young people. If the so-called system of juvenile justice has any competing interests within, there are important implications in terms of political change and policy development. What is seen as a progressive policy change at one level may be thwarted and undermined at another.

Another characteristic of the juvenile justice system is that it is not closed. While the age of a young person defines the jurisdiction of parts of the juvenile justice system, these boundaries are somewhat fluid. Young people accused of serious offences may be transferred to the adult courts.

Under particular circumstances, young people may be transferred to the adult prison system. Conversely, young adults may be kept in the juvenile detention system although they are no longer juveniles. There are close links with the welfare system in terms of historical development, personnel, clientele, and operational practices. Young people may be 'dual clients' of both welfare services and juvenile justice. Furthermore, there is an increasingly important international context in which juvenile justice operates: various United Nations conventions set standards for juvenile justice law, policy, and practice.

We can discuss the institutions of juvenile justice by asking some central questions:

- What is the legislative framework?
- Which international human rights standards are applicable?
- Who are the key players?
- What are the mechanisms of accountability and regulation?
- What are the principles of the system?
- What are the effects of the system?

In the following sections, we will look at these questions to understand how juvenile justice in Australia operates at an institutional level.

THE LEGISLATIVE FRAMEWORK

Young people are subject to criminal law and to a range of other laws. When we talk about juvenile justice legislation, we primarily mean the legislation that establishes a separate system for dealing with young people suspected or convicted of committing a criminal offence. Juvenile justice legislation in Australia is a matter primarily for the states and territories, and varies between jurisdictions. Although each jurisdiction is different, generally speaking juvenile justice legislation covers:

- the principles applicable to dealing with young people
- the definition of a young person or child
- the way police may proceed against a young person through the use of arrest, court attendance notices, and summons, including any preference for attendance notices or summons over arrest
- what diversionary schemes are available (such as cautioning or family group conferences) and how they should be utilised
- any special considerations for young people in regard to being released or detained through bail or custody
- how the children's court is established as having special (or exclusive) jurisdiction over children

- which criminal matters the children's court can determine, and which matters must go before a higher court
- the mechanisms for appealing against a decision by the children's court
- the sentencing options available to the court
- any special requirements relating to restitution and compensation
- the establishment of juvenile detention centres and their operations.

Juvenile justice legislation may be split between a number of legislative acts, and not all legislation necessarily covers each of the points just listed. The key juvenile justice legislation current in Australia in 2006 is shown in box 4.1. As is evident from box 4.1, in most states and territories the legislation governing juvenile justice is embodied in several different pieces of law. These Acts may be substantially amended from time to time to reflect legal change. For example, the introduction and later repeal of mandatory sentencing in the Northern Territory was brought about through amendments to the 1983 Juvenile Justice Act.

As well as being subject to specific juvenile justice legislation, young people are also subject to general criminal laws and to laws relating to criminal justice procedure, such as the Crimes Act or Criminal Code in force in various states. Indeed, most of the offences for which a young person is likely to come before the children's court are violations of the law under the Crimes Act or Criminal Code. Young people are also subject to the law governing public order under the various Summary Offences Acts and Police Offences Acts in different states, and a sizable proportion of young people brought before the courts is there for violations of public order governed by this type of legislation.

Legislation covering criminal justice procedure also has an impact on young people. Legislation of this nature covers, for example, the issuing of search warrants, commitment warrants, and summonses, the collection of DNA and other bodily samples, and finger-printing. Young people are also subject to the legislation covering bail in each state, which sets out the criteria for bail and any presumptions for or against bail. Juvenile justice legislation in some states modifies the requirements of the general Bail Act in its application to young people, for instance specifying special conditions relating to the release of young people.

Finally, young people are also subject to general sentencing laws. Sentencing legislation sets out requirements in relation to fixed terms, minimum terms, and additional terms of imprisonment, as well as the relationship between parole periods and imprisonment. In New South Wales, for example, sentencing legislation establishes that all sentences of detention or imprisonment for the period of six months or less must be fixed terms without any possibility of parole. This requirement affects both adults and juveniles.

We mentioned above that not all juvenile justice legislation covers each of the areas specific to the administration of juvenile justice. In other words,

BOX 4.1 JUVENILE JUSTICE LEGISLATION IN AUSTRALIA, 2006

AUSTRALIAN CAPITAL TERRITORY
Children and Young People Act 1999

NEW SOUTH WALES
Children (Criminal Proceedings) Act 1987
Children (Detention Centres) Act 1987
Children's Court Act 1987
Children (Community Service Orders) Act 1987
Sentencing Act 1989
Children (Protection and Parental Responsibility) Act 1997
Young Offenders Act 1997

NORTHERN TERRITORY
Juvenile Justice Act 1983

QUEENSLAND
Young Offenders (Interstate Transfer) Act 1987
Juvenile Justice Act 1992
Children's Court Act 1992

SOUTH AUSTRALIA
Young Offenders Act 1993
Youth Court Act 1993

TASMANIA
Youth Justice Act 1997

VICTORIA
Children and Young Persons Act 1989
Sentencing Act 1991
Children and Young Persons (Miscellaneous Amendments) Act 1996

WESTERN AUSTRALIA
Children's Court of Western Australia Act 1988
Young Offenders Act 1994
Sentencing Act 1995

in some states there may be serious gaps in the legislation. There is often inadequate recognition in legislation of the following points:

- a child's family should participate in decision-making, and their views should be taken into account
- consideration should always be given to the wishes of the child

- decisions should be made that correspond to a child's sense of time
- the special vulnerability of children entitles them to special protection during investigation
- special consideration should be given to the cultural background of the young person.

There are also considerable variations in the legislation concerning the extent to which police procedures in dealing with young people are set out in law. In some states, the process by which police should give cautions, or the criteria that should be used in deciding which children should be cautioned for particular types of behaviour, are not clearly articulated in the legislation. As a result, the administration of such schemes is left to Police Instructions or Standing Orders, which do not have the force of law. Similarly, the entitlement of a young person to consult a solicitor before questioning, the notification of parents that a young person has been arrested, and the entitlement of parents to consult with their child, often have no basis in legislation. While some of these matters are dealt with in some states through Police Instructions or Standing Orders, they are not obligatory by law (Warner 1994).

Over a decade ago, the Youth Justice Coalition (1990:70–1) identified three characteristics of juvenile justice legislation in Australia, these being few rights, wide discretion, and few criteria. As shown in box 4.1, new legislation was introduced in Australia during the 1990s; however, the criticisms of the Youth Justice Coalition still provide a benchmark against which we can measure more recent change. In general, juvenile justice legislation does not identify the rights of young people within the system. At best, implicit rights are created through legislation that imposes conditions and requirements on certain behaviour of officials—for instance, the requirement of a magistrate to give reasons for the imposition of a detention order. However, the recognition of some implicit rights is far weaker than legislatively enacted national standards and a charter of rights that lists the entitlements of a young person. As we note later, international human rights standards can provide the framework for national standards and a charter of rights. A further development has been the introduction in 2004 in the Australian Capital Territory of the Human Rights Act–the first 'bill of rights' in Australia.

The second characteristic identified by the Youth Justice Coalition was wide discretion. For example, legislative requirements relating to the administration of juvenile detention centres allow wide discretion in relation to visits, phone calls, mail, and so on. Such wide discretion undermines the notion that young people have any rights to certain conditions, and makes it difficult to challenge official decisions. Some recent legislation provides for the review of police decisions regarding the use of diversionary alternatives. In New South Wales, for example, referral to a community conference can be made not only by police, but also (should they decline) by the Director of Public Prosecutions or children's court magistrates. Given the wide discretionary powers available in juvenile justice, review of discretionary decisions still requires greater attention.

The third characteristic is few criteria. In general, legislation does not stipulate the criteria that should be used when important decisions about young people are being made. The lack of criteria is evident from the beginning of a young person's involvement in the system, when police are required to decide the important issue of who will benefit from a diversionary option rather than criminal proceedings, through to the end of the system, where segregation and transfers in detention centres can be used capriciously. Again, there have been some developments in a few states in the use of legislatively defined criteria for the use of diversion and the development of sentencing principles applicable to young people. Legislation in Tasmania (the *Youth Justice Act 1997* (Tas.)) now establishes criteria for the use of isolation and other matters affecting young people in detention centres, but such developments are exceptions to the rule in most of Australia.

International human rights standards

Gaps in the legislative framework also raise the issue of the extent to which juvenile justice legislation is consistent with Australia's international obligations in relation to the treatment of young people. The two major United Nations instruments relating to juvenile justice are the Standard Minimum Rules for the Administration of Juvenile Justice (the Beijing Rules), and the CROC. Australia helped to develop the Beijing Rules, and is a signatory to the CROC. There are also other conventions, rules, and guidelines relevant to juvenile justice. The international human rights framework affecting juvenile justice is shown in box 4.2.

BOX 4.2 INTERNATIONAL HUMAN RIGHTS: JUVENILE JUSTICE

PRINCIPAL CONVENTIONS, RULES, AND GUIDELINES
Convention on the Rights of the Child (CROC)
Standard Minimum Rules for the Administration of Juvenile Justice 1985 (Beijing Rules)
Standard Minimum Rules for Non-custodial Measures 1990 (Tokyo Rules)
Guidelines for the Prevention of Juvenile Delinquency 1990 (Riyadh Guidelines)
Rules for the Protection of Juveniles Deprived of their Liberty 1990

OTHER CONVENTIONS OF RELEVANCE
International Covenant on Civil and Political Rights (ICCPR)
Convention for the Elimination of All Forms of Racial Discrimination (CERD)
Convention Against Torture and Other Forms of Cruel, Inhuman or Degrading Treatment or Punishment (CAT)
Convention for the Elimination of All Forms of Discrimination Against Women (CEDAW)

International human rights affecting children and young people provide a broad and internationally agreed upon set of rules, principles, and standards with which states need to comply. The CROC is the key international instrument in relation to children and young people, and specifies a wide range of rights. Australia adopted the convention in 1989 and ratified it in 1990. In particular, the CROC establishes the principle of the 'best interests of the child' as one of the fundamental principles underpinning all the rights and freedoms of children. Article 3.1 states that: 'in all actions concerning children, whether undertaken by public or private social welfare institutions, courts of law, administrative authorities or legislative bodies, the best interests of the child shall be a primary consideration'.

The CROC deals more specifically with juvenile justice issues in Articles 37 and 40, which cover a range of matters relating to the rights of young people accused of an offence, and their trial, sentencing, and punishment. For example, Article 37 states that:

(a) No child shall be subjected to torture or other cruel, inhuman or degrading treatment or punishment. Neither capital punishment nor life imprisonment without possibility of release shall be imposed for offences committed by persons below eighteen years of age;

(b) No child shall be deprived of his or her liberty unlawfully or arbitrarily. The arrest, detention or imprisonment of a child shall be in conformity with the law and shall be used only as a measure of last resort and for the shortest appropriate period of time;

(c) Every child deprived of liberty shall be treated with humanity and respect for the inherent dignity of the human person, and in a manner which takes into account the needs of persons of his or her age. In particular, every child deprived of liberty shall be separated from adults unless it is considered in the child's best interest not to do so and shall have the right to maintain contact with his or her family through correspondence and visits, save in exceptional circumstances;

(d) Every child deprived of his or her liberty shall have the right to prompt access to legal and other appropriate assistance, as well as the right to challenge the legality of the deprivation of his or her liberty before a court or other competent, independent and impartial authority, and to a prompt decision on any such action.

Article 40(2)(b) stipulates that every child accused of having infringed the criminal law has at least the following guarantees:

(i) to be presumed innocent until proven guilty according to law;

(ii) to be informed promptly and directly of the charges against him or her, and if appropriate, through his or her parents or legal guardian, and to have legal or other appropriate assistance in the preparation and presentation of his or her defence;

(iii) to have the matter determined without delay by a competent, independent and impartial authority or judicial body in a fair hearing according to law, in the presence of legal or other appropriate assistance and, unless it is considered not to be in the best interest of the child, in particular taking into account his or her age or situation, his or her parents or legal guardians;

(iv) not to be compelled to give testimony or to confess guilt, to examine or have examined adverse witnesses and to obtain the participation and examination of witnesses on his or her behalf under conditions of equality;

(v) if considered to have infringed the penal law, to have this decision and any measures imposed in consequence thereof reviewed by a higher competent, independent and impartial authority or judicial body according to law;

(vi) to have the free assistance of an interpreter if the child cannot understand or speak the language used;

(vii) to have his or her privacy fully respected at all stages of the proceedings.

It is important to note that juvenile justice legislation in general does not provide any legislative base to enforce the rights that are spelt out in these human rights instruments. The CROC is not directly part of Australian law; however, under particular and limited circumstances the Human Rights and Equal Opportunity Commission may investigate whether it has been violated. The Australian High Court found that ratification of the CROC gave rise to a legitimate expectation that decision-makers will take its provisions into account. The High Court also established that international law is relevant to the interpretation of domestic law and to the development of common law (*Minister for Immigration and Ethnic Affairs v. Ah Hin Teoh* (1995) 183 CLR 273). Both Labor and conservative governments have sought to limit the effect of this High Court decision by introducing legislation that would enable officials to disregard human rights treaties like the CROC without fear of legal consequence. Amnesty International has noted that such legislation robs Australians of the right to use international human rights standards in complaints to domestic courts, even though Australian governments have ratified such conventions (Amnesty International press release, 28 March 2001).

As noted previously, an important development in Australia has been the introduction of the *Human Rights Act 2004* (ACT). The Act sets out a number of rights relating to the operation of the criminal justice system which affect both adults and juveniles, including rights to humane treatment and a fair trial, and prohibitions against torture and cruel, inhuman or degrading treatment. Section 20 of the Human Rights Act refers to children in the criminal process, and provides that:

- an accused child must be segregated from accused adults
- an accused child must be treated in a way that is appropriate for a person of the child's age who has not been convicted

- a child must be brought to trial as quickly as possible
- a convicted child must be treated in a way that is appropriate for a person of the child's age who has been convicted.

Human rights standards also provide important benchmarks by which we can evaluate the legislative and administrative operation of juvenile justice systems (see Crane 1993; Alston, Parker & Seymour 1992). Some examples of where international human rights standards have been used as such are in studies dealing with police powers (Blagg & Wilkie 1995) and the operation of detention centres (NSW Office of the Ombudsman 1996). Recently, the National Children's and Youth Law Centre and Defence for Children International combined to produce an important report on Australian governments' compliance with the Convention on the Rights of the Child (National Children's and Youth Law Centre 2005). The report was critical of governments' compliance on a range of issues, including access to public space and the use of move-on powers, the over-representation of Indigenous young people in juvenile justice, and the need for increased use of diversion (National Children's and Youth Law Centre 2005:16, 60–2).

THE KEY PLAYERS

We began this chapter by discussing whether there is a 'system' of juvenile justice. To a certain extent, each state's legislation imposes a regulatory framework within which the major agencies operate. The major agencies involved in juvenile justice are clearly the police, the courts, and the family or community services department with responsibility for offender supervision. Yet there are also many other players in the field. These range from small, community-based organisations (such as an Aboriginal-run bail hostel dependent on government funding), through to the state cabinet, which must pass any proposals for legislative change.

There are not only many players in the field, but also many interests at work in the way juvenile justice operates. The Youth Justice Coalition (1990:74) has identified some of these as:

- the party political interests of government and opposition
- the personal political interests of responsible ministers
- the personal and professional interests of senior bureaucrats
- the organisational needs of the agencies and departments directly involved in juvenile justice administration
- the interests of associations representing the industrial and professional interests of people working in the field (for example, police associations, law societies)
- the interests of other connected agencies and departments (for example, ombudsman's office, attorneys-general, education and training, corrections, children's commissioners, crime prevention offices, law reform commissions, local government associations)

- government advisory bodies (for example, juvenile justice advisory councils)
- the interests of lobby groups (for example, church groups, youth justice coalitions)
- the interests of major media and local media organisations.

The list illuminates some of the powerful vested interests that can be involved in juvenile justice. The political interests of government and opposition may coincide to bring about progressive change, or—more likely in the current climate—their interests may coincide to push for more punitive intervention, with both groups attempting to be seen as being tough on juvenile crime. As we identified in chapter 3 pp. 58–61, the media also play a powerful role in identifying presumed problems of juvenile offending. The personal and political interests of ministers with responsibility for various aspects of juvenile justice are also important. Progressive reforms to procedures introduced by departments have been abolished almost immediately by ministers when such reforms have perceived backlash from the public or the media. Similarly, senior bureaucrats may see their own personal prospects fulfilled more quickly if they control the department in a manner that does not court public controversy. Overall, the articulation of these different interests helps us to understand that the interests of the young person, their family, and the victim may indeed be a minor consideration when placed in the broader picture.

The police

The state police services play a major role in juvenile justice through the apprehension of young people who have allegedly committed offences. Apprehending young people is a significant component of police work. Around one-quarter of offences cleared by police involve juveniles (Cunneen & White 1995:98). Besides the obvious aspect of police work in apprehending offenders, police are involved in many other aspects of juvenile justice. Police play a role in diversion schemes, such as youth conferencing, by selecting the young people to be involved; and in the case of police cautions, they directly control and administer the first level of diversion. Police are involved in determining bail and in prosecuting cases before the children's court. They are involved in detaining young people in custody if such people have been refused bail, and in escorting young people to detention centres.

Police also collect information on juvenile offending, and provide information to the community and the media about juvenile crime. They formulate policy regarding their own role with young people, as well as responding to policy initiatives from other services or departments. Police services also play a part in police training and in determining the nature of information that new recruits receive about juvenile offending and young people. Police services also allocate resources and services, prioritising attention to particular forms of juvenile crime or prioritising resources to specialist youth officers.

Juvenile justice departments and/or divisions

Traditionally, departments of community services in various states have the key function of administering juvenile justice services (support services, non-custodial programs, detention centres, and so on). There is usually a division within the relevant community services department that administers juvenile justice, separate from child protection and child welfare. In many ways, this organisational arrangement has reflected the view that young people need special treatment separate from adults, and there is a perception that the focus should be on the social and rehabilitative needs of young people.

The functions of such divisions include the preparation of court reports, the supervision of young people placed on a probation order or some other supervisory order by the court, and the provision of specialist counselling services to young offenders. The departments of community services also have responsibility for establishing and administering detention centres for young people who have been committed to an institution.

The divisions of juvenile justice collect and disseminate information relating to the number of young people appearing in court and relating to young people who end up in detention. The divisions have a key role in developing policy on responses to juvenile offending. Finally, although welfare and juvenile justice matters are separated in all states of Australia, the links between welfare and justice are strongest in these departments. Welfare functions such as child protection and family support operate from the same offices that administer community-based programs for young offenders.

There was a trend during the 1990s to move the administration of juvenile justice into its own portfolio area under the general administration of justice, or to subsume it within departments of adult corrections. At various times over the last decade, juvenile justice was under the Department of Correctional Services or the Department of Justice in Queensland, New South Wales, the Northern Territory, and Western Australia. The physical relocation of juvenile justice administration also represented a symbolic change in the view of young people as more akin to adult offenders, and a shift from seeing the special needs of young people to emphasising their responsibility for offending behaviour.

Statutory bodies

There are a number of bodies with a role as advocacy and/or investigatory bodies for matters that may involve juvenile justice.

Commissioners for children

Internationally, many jurisdictions have children's commissioners or children's ombudsmen (for example New Zealand, Denmark, Sweden, and Norway). Australia has fairly recently seen the establishment of commissioners for children in Queensland (Children's Commissioner and Children's Services Appeals Tribunal Act, 1996), New South Wales (the Commission for Children and Young People Act, 1998), and Tasmania (Children, Young People and Their Families Act, 1997). The responsibilities and functions of the commissioners emphasise child protection, however, commissioners can also deal with a range of human rights matters relating to young people up to the age of 18 years.

Ombudsmen's offices

Offices of the Ombudsman exist at Commonwealth, state and territory level throughout Australia. The function of the Ombudsman has traditionally been to deal with individual complaints against government authorities. However, some offices have instigated inquiries to consider systemic issues. For example, the New South Wales Office of the Ombudsman (1996) has conducted perhaps the most exhaustive inquiry ever held into detention centres in that state as a result of a series of complaints and disturbances in various centres.

The Human Rights and Equal Opportunity Commission

The federal HREOC has responsibility for promoting the CROC in Australia through education and the promotion of guidelines. It can investigate complaints against the Commonwealth where there is an alleged inconsistency with children's rights. The HREOC has recently published three Human Rights Briefs on matters relating to juvenile justice. Brief No. 1, 'The Best Interests of the Child' (March 1999), details the meaning of the principle in the CROC that the best interests of the child shall be a primary consideration—and sometimes paramount—in all actions concerning children. Brief No. 2, 'Sentencing Juvenile Offenders' (June 1999), sets out the eleven principles governing the sentencing of juvenile offenders, which are found in the CROC. Brief No. 5, 'Diversionary Principles for Juveniles', sets the requirements for diversionary schemes.

Other state bodies

The departments of attorneys-general also play a key role in juvenile justice administration. These departments are responsible for the administration of the children's courts as well as the higher courts, and allocate staff and resources to the courts. The departments are also active in other areas of relevance to juvenile justice through preparing legislation and developing policy on criminal proceedings. Finally, the departments may be involved in prosecutions of children in the higher courts, through directors of public prosecution.

Other state bodies include legal aid commissions, which provide legal representation for some young people; law reform commissions, which provide reform proposals that may impact on young people; judicial commissions, which monitor sentencing and provide education and training for magistrates and judges; crime prevention units, which coordinate government crime prevention policies and information; bureaus of crime statistics, which publish crime data; and victims' compensation tribunals, which provide compensation to victims of crime, including juvenile crime.

In addition, there may be specifically constituted advisory bodies on issues relating to children and young people (such as the Children's Interest Bureau, which reports to the Minister for Family and Community Services in South Australia), or with specific focus (such as the Youth Justice Advisory Committee, established under the *Young Offenders Act 1997* (NSW).

Many other state departments have either a direct or an indirect role in relation to juvenile justice in terms of prosecutions, policies, and programs. They include school education, technical education, health, industrial relations and employment, state railways, youth affairs, housing, public works, sport and recreation, treasury, and cabinet. Often these departments are not recognised for the role they play. For instance, treasury departments advise on departmental budget allocations, including the money that is allocated for juvenile justice. Another example is the state rail authorities, which are involved in prosecutions of young people for offences committed against railway regulations.

The Commonwealth government

The Commonwealth government plays an important but often unrecognised role in juvenile justice. The Commonwealth provides money for jointly funded services, and money in the form of general and tied grants to state governments. The level of provision of this funding can directly affect a range of services, from legal aid to emergency accommodation.

Commonwealth policy on youth employment, training, higher education, income support (including allowances for the unemployed and young homeless people), and so on directly affects the wellbeing of young people and their opportunities for growth and development. The nature and level of income support and social services can determine the lifestyle and immediate conditions of existence for many young people, which in turn have major consequences with regard to the factors underlying juvenile offending.

In addition to playing a crucial role in social provision, the federal government has a major contribution to make in the ratification, promotion, and monitoring of international treaties and conventions. In the specific area of juvenile justice, it has been suggested that the Commonwealth government can play a much stronger role in defending and enhancing the rights of young people. For example, since the mid-1990s the National Children's and Youth Law Centre has advocated that a Charter of Rights for Children and Young People should be enacted in Commonwealth legislation, and that the federal government should actively intervene in instances where state governments have passed laws that ignore or run contrary to the provisions contained in international instruments such as the CROC.

The Commonwealth has also taken on a relatively new role in relation to crime prevention. National Crime Prevention, part of the federal attorney-general's department, has undertaken major research reports on developmental issues and juvenile delinquency, domestic violence and young people, and young people's use of public space (see, for example, *National Crime Prevention* 1999).

Local government

Local governments play an important but often neglected role in juvenile justice. There are various facets to the relationship. On the negative side, local governments are victims of juvenile crime, particularly in regard to the vandalism of public property. We have also seen local governments demand more punitive approaches to young people, which have included attempts to impose youth curfews (Simpson & Simpson 1993). In addition, local governments have played a role in the direct regulation of public space through the use of by-laws. In several states of Australia, local government has the power to introduce alcohol-free zones and to regulate the use of public places and shopping centres in relation to activities like skateboarding. Such regulations may bring local government officers or private security guards into a direct policing role in relation to young people.

On the positive side of the relationship, local government is also a provider of services and facilities. The provision of services for young people can be used by progressive local government bodies as an important crime prevention tool. Rather than seeing young people as a problem, progressive local governments use part of their resources to provide facilities for young people, and treat them as part of the local community that this tier of government represents.

Non-government organisations

There are many community-based organisations that play a role in juvenile justice. Some provide general services to young people, but because of their nature a large proportion of such organisations' clientele has usually had contact with juvenile justice agencies (youth refuges that provide emergency accommodation are one example). Some service clubs are also involved in the supervision of young offenders who undertake community service work.

Some community legal centres, such as Marrickville Legal Centre in Sydney, have lawyers who specialise in juvenile justice. There are also a few community legal centres that work solely with young people, such as the Youth Legal Service in Perth and the Youth Advocacy Centre in Brisbane.

The National Children's and Youth Law Centre is an important advocate for justice for young people and children. The centre is active in a wide range of research projects, legal test cases involving children's rights (such as the defamation case mentioned in chapter 3), and coordination of a network of youth legal and advocacy services. A central aspect of the centre's work has been to lobby for the establishment of a National Commissioner for Children to act as a watchdog for children, and to monitor and report on the implementation of children's rights in Australia. As mentioned earlier, the centre has also advocated national legislative protection of the rights of children and young people, and in relation to this has developed a draft Charter of Rights for Children and Young People (National Children's and Youth Law Centre, 1995).

There are Youth Affairs Councils (or their equivalent) in each state. Their purposes are to lobby governments and to express the interests and opinions of young people to elected representatives and state officials on a wide range of issues. Often these non-government youth organisations provide support to, or work in tandem with, specific juvenile justice lobby groups such as the Youth Justice Coalitions in various states. These organisations are dependent on external funding, which is often precarious, depending on the political priorities of the government.

There are also many religious groups that provide a range of services, from specific programs for young offenders (such as post-release and wilderness camps) through to accommodation services and assisting police by attending interviews with young people. Other religious-based groups act as advocates for young people in the area of government policy. The Catholic Commission for Justice, Development and Peace (Melbourne), for example, has been active in publishing discussion papers on reforming the juvenile justice system in Victoria.

Many of the community organisations that provide services for young people receive their funding through the state and/or federal governments. Finally, there are also internationally based non-government organisations that play an important role in monitoring compliance with the human rights of young people. These include Amnesty International and Defence for Children International. Amnesty International has had an important role in drawing attention to issues affecting Indigenous young people, and Defence for Children International has been important in considering potential human rights abuses that arise as a result of mandatory sentencing. As noted previously, both the National Children's Youth and Law Centre and

Defence for Children International have had an important role in evaluating government compliance with human rights for children and young people.

ACCOUNTABILITY AND REGULATION

The agencies that play a role in juvenile justice can exert enormous power over young people. If young people are convicted of an offence, they receive some form of sanction that at worst can deprive them of their liberty. Even without such an extreme outcome, police, courts, and community services personnel can exert significant control over the lives of young people once such young people have entered the system. It is important to ask, therefore, whether there is adequate review of and accountability for the decisions made by juvenile justice agencies. Are decisions made fairly? And, if not, how are these decisions reviewed?

The accountability and regulation of juvenile justice agencies operate through a range of different mechanisms. There are legal forms of regulation through legislation, the courts, and disciplinary and complaint bodies; and the setting of standards with which agencies must comply. There are non-legal forms of accountability through management structures, public participation in advisory and consultative bodies, and the provision of research and evaluation. We explore these different methods of achieving accountability in the sections that follow.

Review and complaints mechanisms

How accountable are juvenile justice agencies for the decisions they make in regard to young people? Both young people and the community in general have the right to expect that juvenile justice is administered fairly, responsibly, and appropriately. One way of achieving such administration is through adequate mechanisms for review and complaints.

In practice, a number of review mechanisms specific to juvenile justice have been identified (Youth Justice Coalition 1990:110–19). These are discussed in the following pages.

Management review

Managerial techniques, such as program budgeting, corporate planning, performance contracts, and program evaluation, have been adopted by agencies working in juvenile justice. However, the major impact has been from economic rationalism, with its particular focus on budgeting, accounts, and economic responsibility. For accountability to operate through managerial techniques, far greater attention needs to be paid to issues of access, equity, and citizenship. Conversely, government services should not treat users solely and simply as customers when in reality there are substantial inequalities in power, in the ability to participate in decision-making, and in community resources.

Inspections

One way of achieving accountability is through inspections of the closed institutions of juvenile justice: detention centres and police stations. Some states have moved to establish lay visitors' schemes in police stations, and some have official visitor schemes in institutions. In addition, in some states the Ombudsman's office makes regular visits to detention centres (for further details, see the ALRC & HREOC 1997:605–7), and in Western Australia, the Inspector of Prisons also has jurisdiction over juvenile detention.

Case planning

Jurisdictions vary in the extent to which they use case planning with individual young people who are either in detention or under the supervision of the community services department. However, generally speaking, there has been a significant increase in case planning as a preferred model of supervision and service delivery. Case planning can allow some participation by young people and parents, as well as making it more likely that there will be ongoing reviews of what is happening to an individual young person (for further details and discussion of the limitations of case planning, see the ALRC & HREOC 1997:588–91).

Complaints

In theory at least, young people can complain about matters relating to their treatment. Such complaints can be directed to a number of people: the responsible government minister, the officer in charge of the institution or police station, official visitors' schemes (where these exist), the Ombudsman's office, or the police complaints tribunal. The mechanisms available for complaint vary from state to state, but a central problem is providing young people with the confidence, necessary information, and opportunity to make complaints where appropriate. It is a recognised failing that organisations established to handle complaints do not deal adequately with issues affecting young people. For example, a survey of official police complaints in New South Wales showed that only 3 per cent of the complaints received were from or on behalf of young people (New South Wales Standing Committee on Social Issues 1996:162–3).

Quasi-judicial review

Some states at various times have established review boards for the purpose of reviewing and making decisions about the release on parole of young people in detention (for instance, the Training Centre Review Board in South Australia) or the classification of young people in detention (for instance, the Serious Young Offenders Review Panel in New South Wales). In general, though, young people have not had the type of review boards that operate in relation to adult offenders.

Judicial review

Young people generally have not had access to courts to review matters in relation to the way juvenile detention centres operate. Decisions made in detention centres in relation to transfer, segregation, and punishment have not been open to the scrutiny of the courts to the same extent as equivalent matters in the adult sphere.

Professional regulation

The extent to which personnel working in the juvenile justice system are regulated by legislation or professional bodies varies. Lawyers, magistrates, and police face some regulation through professional bodies, tribunals, and commissions, although there are frequent and consistent criticisms concerning their usefulness. Personnel working in detention centres and non-custodial environments usually have no professional regulatory body, with the exception of social workers, psychologists, and the like.

It is clear that there are specific problems relating to the mechanisms for achieving regulation and accountability in the sphere of juvenile justice. Even where there are specific measures for complaints, there are substantial problems in enabling young people to utilise what is available.

Establishing standards

It has been acknowledged that standards have not been used widely as a way of ensuring consistency in the operation of juvenile justice agencies in Australia (Youth Justice Coalition 1990:106–10). However, developments in the USA show that national standards can be of use in promoting common approaches to operational matters. The development of national standards seems particularly applicable to Australia, given the eight different state and territory juvenile justice systems.

Much of the United Nations' involvement in juvenile justice has been about setting standards (see Crane 1993). The Standard Minimum Rules for the Administration of Juvenile Justice (the Beijing Rules) provide that:

- a comprehensive social policy be in place to ensure the wellbeing of juveniles
- reaction to juvenile offenders always be in proportion to the circumstances of both the offenders and the offence
- police officers who deal extensively with juveniles be specially instructed and trained
- detention pending trial be used only as a measure of last resort and for the shortest possible period of time
- placement of a juvenile in an institution always be a disposition of last resort and for the minimum necessary period

- necessary assistance such as housing, vocational training, and employment be provided to facilitate the rehabilitative process.

The United Nations has also published *Rules for the Protection of Juveniles Deprived of Their Liberty*. Minimum standards have been increasingly used in other areas of social policy in Australia, including hospitals, aged care, and residential care in child welfare.

In the area of juvenile justice, standards could have a range of functions, including establishing criteria for evaluating, reviewing, and funding programs and services. They might help to establish consistency in approach within and among different jurisdictions. One area where standards have been developed in Australia is in relation to juvenile detention. The National Quality of Care Standards (QOC Standards) and Design Guidelines for Juvenile Justice Facilities in Australia and New Zealand (Design Guidelines) were endorsed by all states and territories in 1996. The standards draw on international treaties as well as the *Royal Commission into Aboriginal Deaths in Custody* reports (ALRC & HREOC 1997:582–3).

Community input

Community input into juvenile justice policies and operations can possibly be achieved through formal advisory bodies. Some states have established such bodies (for example, the New South Wales Juvenile Justice Advisory Council and the South Australian Juvenile Justice Advisory Committee). These groups tend to be heavily dominated by institutional interests, including representatives from the police, children's courts, and the Department of Juvenile Justice. Members are typically nominated by the Minister, and young people are not well represented.

Another potential area for community consultation, including the views of young people, is the development of crime-prevention plans at the local government level. For example, in New South Wales a local government authority has a legislative obligation to develop a crime prevention plan, if it wishes to have sections of the *Children (Protection and Parental Responsibility) Act 1997* (NSW) declared operational for its particular area.

However, the existing advisory mechanisms offer little scope for community input into juvenile justice administration. There is little opportunity for young people's involvement.

Research and evaluation

Research and evaluation can be important tools for ensuring accountability in juvenile justice. Unless we know how the system is operating and to what effect, it is extremely difficult to hold agencies accountable for what they are doing. At the beginning of the 1990s, the Youth Justice Coalition sounded a despairing note: 'The situation in relation to planning, research and evaluation in the juvenile justice area is so underdeveloped that it must be questioned whether those responsible for the system really want to know what is going on' (Youth Justice Coalition 1990:95).

Generally, research in and evaluation of juvenile justice had been poor. There were some exceptions, such as South Australia's relatively sophisticated information base, and some of the research that has used the information from this base shows the need for reliable monitoring (see Gale et al. 1990). However, since the beginning of the 1990s, research and evaluation has improved significantly in a number of jurisdictions. New South Wales, Victoria, Queensland, and Western Australia all have the capacity through various organisations to provide research and evaluation reports.

Sound research and evaluation are important for a number of reasons. Policy must be based on an understanding of whether programs are effective or not, and on an understanding of existing problems within the system. Without adequate information, policy development is susceptible to misjudgment, and can take the form of crisis management. Research and evaluation inform the public, parliament, and media how particular programs are working or can be expected to work. Finally, research and evaluation enable departmental resources to be allocated effectively.

THE PRINCIPLES OF JUVENILE JUSTICE

We have outlined the legislative framework of juvenile justice, the key players, and the issues of accountability and regulation. It is also necessary to consider the philosophy and principles underlying juvenile justice systems. Juvenile justice has often been seen as alternating between models of 'justice' and 'welfare'. Although juvenile justice as it has developed historically has never actually conformed to either the justice or the welfare models, these ideal types have been invoked in order to conceptualise changes within the system and to measure the system against the principles elaborated in either model.

The welfare and justice models are usually considered as being at opposite ends of the spectrum, and as representing quite different approaches to dealing with young people. But in practice, particularly in Australia, the juvenile justice system represents aspects of both models. In addition, it is also important to remember that there is a significant movement of children and young people from the formal welfare system into the juvenile justice system, and vice versa. What, then, are the features of these different models of juvenile justice?

The welfare model

The welfare model of juvenile justice has the following characteristics:

- behaviour is regarded as arising from a range of factors outside the control of the individual

- the emphasis is on 'needs' over 'deeds', that is, the offender is more important than the offence
- rehabilitation is the primary goal in sentencing
- the needs of the young person must be treated through appropriate intervention
- treatment can occur outside the formal justice process through diversion, but still involves professionals and experts
- the protections of criminal justice procedures are not required because the focus is on rehabilitation rather than punishment.

It is clear that the focus on a welfare approach has close connections with the theories of positivism outlined in chapter 2, as well as incorporating aspects of contemporary rehabilitative views about corrections.

The justice model

The justice model of juvenile justice is as follows:

- emphasis is on the offence rather than the offender
- the model promotes due process, that is, the rules applicable to the adult courts concerning prosecution and criminal procedure are applied to young people
- young people are seen as responsible for their actions, and offending is seen as the result of a choice
- the model promotes 'just deserts' in sentencing, that is, it focuses on the responsibility of the young person for the offence and on a punishment that 'fits the crime'
- rehabilitation is seen as a secondary goal in sentencing.

We can see the similarities between the justice model and the classical theory of criminology previously outlined in chapter 2, with its stress on individual responsibility for offending behaviour. Indeed, the emphasis on justice in the approach to juvenile justice can be seen as part of the resurgence of neoclassicist approaches to law and order. To some extent, this move has been at the expense of those promoting rehabilitation. However, as we discuss later, the actual effect on sentencing practices is not so clear.

Much of the impetus towards a justice approach arose in the USA during the 1960s, where there was disillusionment with the failures of rehabilitation (Freiberg et al. 1988:4). There were calls for a greater concentration on retribution and deterrence, as well as concerns about the degree of discretionary power and the failure to consider the rights of due process for young people. Labelling theorists (see chapter 2) also had an impact with their argument that the agents of juvenile justice could themselves expand and confirm the likelihood of criminal careers (Freiberg et al. 1988:4).

The Australian experience

As we noted in chapter 1, children's courts in Australia never moved as far towards the welfare model as they did in the USA. However, there were substantial differences between the adult and juvenile courts in Australia, not the least being the court's power to deal with both criminal matters and welfare matters, and to use welfare-style interventions in relation to a criminal offence. From the late 1970s through to the end of the 1990s, there was a move to separate welfare from justice matters in most jurisdictions. South Australia was the first state to achieve the separation, in 1979. This separation has been accomplished in some jurisdictions by separate legislation governing criminal matters and welfare matters, such as the *Children (Criminal Proceedings) Act 1987* (NSW) and *Children (Care and Protection) Act 1987* (NSW). Other jurisdictions have made use of a single piece of legislation, such as the *Children and Young Person's Act 1989* (Vic.), which establishes separate divisions of the children's court in the Family Division and the Criminal Division—effectively separating welfare from crime. Tasmania was the last Australian state to continue to operate a system that mixed welfare and criminal matters. It introduced new juvenile justice legislation (the Youth Justice Act) in 1997. The existing legislation, which was finally repealed at the end of the twentieth century, provides an example of the old-style welfare legislation. When contrasted with new justice legislation, it provides a window on the broader changes that have been occurring in juvenile justice. The philosophy was clearly stated in s. 4 of the *Child Welfare Act 1960* (Tas.):

> As far as practicable and expedient, each child suspected of having committed, [being] charged with, or found guilty of an offence shall be treated, not as a criminal, but as a child who is, or may have been, misdirected or misguided, and that the care, custody and discipline of each ward of state shall approximate as nearly as [possible] to that which should be given to it by its parents.

The old Tasmanian Child Welfare Act of 1960 highlights many of the general criticisms that have been levelled against welfare-model legislation. The court's assessment of the welfare needs of a young person could result in a far longer sentence than an adult would have received for the same offence. The court could determine that the young person appearing for a criminal matter was in need of wardship, and thus declare them a ward of state until their eighteenth birthday. The legislation allowed for indeterminate sentencing by magistrates, and the release of the young person was dependent upon the discretion of the department (Stokes 1992:11).

The problems with the welfare approach can be summarised as follows:

- there is a failure to protect the rights of the young person
- the issues of neglect and offending are intertwined
- there is no proportionality between the offence and the sentence

- indeterminate sentencing is permitted
- there is excessive administrative discretion.

Much of the recent juvenile justice legislation in Australia sets out to a greater or lesser extent the principles under which juvenile justice and the children's court operate. It is possible to see the shift that occurred over the last two decades of the twentieth century towards a justice-oriented approach. For example, the South Australia Young Offenders Act of 1993 notes in s. 3 the following statutory policies of juvenile justice:

- young people should be made aware of their obligations under the law and of the consequences of breaching the law
- the sanctions imposed against illegal conduct must be sufficiently severe to provide an appropriate level of deterrence
- the community, and individual members of it, must be adequately protected against violent or wrongful acts.

The legislation refers to responsibility, deterrence, and community protection, which are seen as components of a justice approach. Similarly, the *Juvenile Justice Act 1992* (Qld) sets out the principles of juvenile justice in s. 4. Subsection (e) states that 'a child who commits an offence should be … held accountable and encouraged to accept responsibility for the offending behaviour'. Again, accountability and responsibility are hallmarks of a justice approach.

However, legislation provides some special considerations for young people. For instance, subsection (e) of the Queensland legislation goes on to state that the child should be punished in a way that provides opportunities for development in responsible, beneficial, and socially acceptable ways. Similarly, the South Australian legislation in s. 3(1) states that the object of the Act is to secure for youths who offend against the criminal law the care, correction, and guidance necessary for their development into responsible and useful members of the community, and the proper realisation of their potential (for a similar discussion of the Victorian and New South Wales legislation, see Naffine 1993).

Thus, there is clearly still a preference for rehabilitation and special considerations of care and guidance. Currently, juvenile justice legislation is moving towards a more justice-oriented model, but it has retained a commitment to welfare-related principles as well. How these essentially contradictory moves relate to practice is, of course, a separate issue. O'Connor (1998:4–5) has noted what he sees as the 'growing tension' in Australian juvenile justice legislation as a result of these changes:

> In all states there has been a shift to the justice model with a renewed focus
> on the offence, proportionality of punishment, the payment of lip service
> to due process rights and a superficial commitment to non-intervention
> for non-criminal behaviour. … The justice model has eschewed the welfare

model's focus on the needs of the child and the harsh coercive responses to these needs. However, many of the needs were real, even while the responses were inappropriate. Lack of income, homelessness, abuse and exploitation, all have detrimental effects on children [and] the social circumstances of youth in the last two decades in Australia have worsened substantially.

THE EFFECTS OF THE SYSTEM

The justice-versus-welfare debate has come to be regarded by many as a limited way of conceptualising events in the juvenile justice arena. Many commentators in Australia and elsewhere have argued that the debate about welfare or justice is essentially sterile because it fails to explain either how the system operates or what effects it has. Pitts (1988) has noted that both the justice and the welfare models are ultimately attempts to ensure the social conformity of young people, and that they disagree only on how to achieve this objective. One method advocates conformity through the punishment of the rational actor, thus deterring future aberrations, while the other promotes conformity through various approaches that rest on social engineering and rehabilitation to the existing social conditions and norms.

It is difficult to match the claims of either a justice or a welfare model with the real operation of juvenile justice. The large institutions that have dominated most of the twentieth century have been sites of petty oppression rather than rehabilitation. Specifically in relation to Indigenous young people, the welfare approach saw large-scale social disorganisation imposed on young people and families. Far from any notion of rehabilitation, the system was deliberately and actively destructive.

Similarly, the justice-based model, which emphasises responsibility, accountability, and due process, has offered punishment as a panacea. The emphasis has been on greater punishment of young offenders, rather than on ensuring the other supposed benefits of a justice model, which include proportionality in sentencing and the protection of legal rights. As we note in chapter 10, most young people plead guilty in court, and generally they are not in a position to assert their various rights. The 'back to justice' movement in the United Kingdom, in which the justice model was emphasised, was by and large an anti-welfare movement that saw an attack on social workers by police, magistrates, and lawyers. In this sense at least, the shift occurring in juvenile justice from the 1970s onwards fitted closely with attacks on the welfare state in general (Clarke 1985). More recently, theorists have considered changes during the last decade of the twentieth century in the context of neoliberalism (O'Malley 1999).

During the 1980s and 1990s in Australia, there were considerable changes: the separation of juvenile justice and child welfare jurisdictions, and the introduction of new policies. However, these changes were not a simple shift between two dichotomous models. Some were aimed at progressive reforms—such as reducing the number of children in institutions, those going to court for first and minor offences, and those committed to institutions without having received community-based sanctions—and to reducing sentencing disparities (Youth Justice Coalition 1990:43). Yet there was also a noticeable swing to the political right by the late 1980s, which intensified during the 1990s, particularly in the area of sentencing young people. The emphasis was on punishment.

A further area that is often neglected is the 'drift' of children and young people from the welfare system into the juvenile justice system. A New South Wales study in the mid-1990s revealed that a young person who was a ward of the state was fifteen times more likely to end up in a juvenile detention centre than a non-ward. For girls, wards were thirty-five times more likely to enter a juvenile detention centre than non-wards (Community Services Commission 1996:8). The group of state wards who were Aboriginal who appeared before the children's court for juvenile offences was also dramatically overrepresented, comprising 37 per cent of all wards who appeared on criminal matters (Community Services Commission 1996:24). Thus, the institutional links between welfare and juvenile justice practices mean that the same families and young people are targeted for intervention.

Finally, we would like to consider differing but complementary ways of conceptualising the operation of the juvenile justice system through notions of 'corporatism', 'social class', and 'governmentality'. In the late 1980s, Pratt (1989) argued that the justice–welfare dichotomy did not account for the changes that were occurring in juvenile justice. Pratt argued that significant changes included:

- an increase in cautioning and disposal of matters prior to court
- the growth of cooperation between a range of agencies, with a focus on greater efficiency and crime prevention
- the development of alternatives to custody (non-custodial programs are intermediate between detention and an unsupervised order)
- a decline in the autonomy of professionals and the judiciary through attempts to control discretionary power
- an increase in the role of the voluntary sector, particularly in providing intermediate treatment and programs
- the development of juvenile justice technology, which has increased the level of planning
- bifurcation in policy for 'hard-core' and 'minor' offenders (that is, young people who are defined as recidivist and dangerous are dealt with punitively, mainly through adult sentencing structures and regimes, while those defined as minor offenders are dealt with through pre-court diversionary options).

The importance of Pratt's approach was that it attempted to move beyond the justice–welfare conceptualisation. He found that the changes could be considered within the context of *corporatism*. Pratt argued that corporatism is a characteristic of advanced welfare states, whereby the 'capacity for conflict and disruption is reduced by means of the centralisation of policy, increased government intervention, and the cooperation of various professional and interest groups into a collective whole with homogeneous aims and objectives' (Pratt 1989:245). These were precisely the types of changes that were occurring in juvenile justice, through increased administrative decision-making; centralisation of authority, decision-making and planning; greater involvement of non-government agencies; greater sentencing diversity; and high levels of control in some sentencing programs.

We can also consider the theoretical analysis of the juvenile justice system in terms of social class. For example, Clarke (1985) argues that the 'presentation of juvenile justice as a site of an opposition between principles of justice and welfare is ill-conceived, and leads to potentially dangerous political consequences' (1985:407). It is not helpful to consider two abstract principles: what needs to be analysed is the way in which juvenile justice essentially criminalises working-class young people, and manages those young people defined as being delinquent through a patchwork of processes and programs that draw on a range of philosophies and principles. In particular, Clarke argues that concentration on the 'rule of law' masks class inequalities. Equality before the law as due process rests on assumptions of the formal equality of citizens. However, the class inequality of young people who are criminalised undermines that formal equality. Furthermore, there is a class bias in the selection of activities that are prohibited by the law and policed— in particular, those activities that are regulated in public places. Finally, the process of the law acts against working-class young people, since, despite notions of formal equality, the use of discretion in the juvenile justice system acts against the interests of young people from working-class backgrounds.

A further conceptualisation of the juvenile justice system that we wish to consider is the application of Michel Foucault's ideas of governmentality and power. *Governmentality* refers to the collection of institutions, knowledge, procedures, and practices that allow the exercise of power over and through the population. According to Rose (1989), childhood is the most intensely governed part of personal existence; in other words, the process of governmentality has a particular application to children and young people. There have developed around children a complex of laws, agencies, and practices that determine delinquency and pathology. According to Rose, the most powerful outcome of the study of 'delinquency' is that it has been used to define 'normality'. 'Knowledge of normality has not in the main resulted from studying normal children … It is around pathological children—the troublesome, the recalcitrant, the delinquent—that conceptions of normality have taken place' (Rose 1989:131).

Government of the child through education, child welfare, and juvenile justice is important because it is concerned ultimately with the management and regulation of the self in contemporary society. The issue is not whether regulation is good or bad in its own right, but rather to unravel the process through which it occurs. According to Rose (1989:1), our 'personalities, subjectivities and relationships are not private matters ... on the contrary they are intensely governed'. The process of governmentality begins in childhood: through various institutions public power targets and regulates the personal and subjective characteristics of the population. Children and young people are intensely governed through a range of agencies, among which juvenile justice is important because of its role in detecting pathology and abnormality. It is clear that this view of the function and effects of juvenile justice is far removed from any debate about justice or welfare. As with Pratt's argument, discussed earlier, Rose is considering juvenile justice within the context of a regulatory practice. What is important is the way in which juvenile justice regulates young people and children, not which guiding principles might be invoked to explain its existence.

This discussion shows the need to move beyond a conception of the juvenile justice system as a body of agencies working within a framework of ideas constrained by notions of welfare or justice. In other words, juvenile justice must be *theorised* in terms of practices as well as ideas. The various approaches just outlined have a concept of political power and a particular view of the function of institutions and the state. For Pratt, the role of the state is to regulate and manage conflict and dissent. For Rose, power and regulation operate through discourses and institutions. For Clarke, the state—through juvenile justice—is essentially concerned with class control.

More recently, O'Malley (1999) has specifically considered the developments in various approaches to punishment within the context of New Right politics. He argues that there has been a 'bewildering array' of developments in punishment that are often apparently contradictory and incoherent. Such punishments range from disciplinary obedience (boot camps) to entrepreneurial autonomy (training for future opportunities), and from punishment and incapacitation (mandatory sentencing) to reintegration and restitution (youth conferencing). O'Malley's (1999:185–6) argument is that these different approaches are united under the competing strands of neoconservatism and neoliberalism of the New Right. *Neoconservatism* is socially authoritarian, and rests on punitive disciplinary approaches. In contrast, *neoliberalism* privileges the market and individualism for achieving social order, and emphasises managerialism in its approach to criminal justice policy. The outcome is a range of inconsistencies in punishment, with some programs harking back to a nostalgic past (emphasising either discipline or 'shaming'), and others emphasising individual responsibility (just deserts).

CONCLUSION

We began this chapter by asking whether there is a juvenile justice system, and discussing whether those whose function is to administer juvenile justice differ in their interests. We considered the role of legislation in providing a legal framework for the operation of juvenile justice. We identified the key players in juvenile justice at the level of each state, and in the Commonwealth and the non-government sectors, and we looked at the various systems of accountability and regulation of those who administer juvenile justice. Finally, we considered the formal principles and philosophies underlying juvenile justice, and the debates that have occurred about justice and welfare approaches.

For many, the debate between justice and welfare has been sterile and does not really come to grips with the broader functions of juvenile justice within the social fabric. One way of moving beyond such debates is to consider the role of the state and institutional power in a wider social context. Clearly, at this level we are talking about a 'system' of juvenile justice that regulates, controls, and manages particular groups of young people for particular, although varied, reasons. To adequately understand the operation and effects of the 'system', we need to know precisely how, under particular historical conditions and economic and social circumstances, the institutions of juvenile justice actually operate. It is to this we turn in part II of this book.

PART II
THE SOCIAL DYNAMICS
OF JUVENILE JUSTICE

5 | Class and community

INTRODUCTION

The processing of young offenders is heavily oriented towards dealing with working-class young people, in particular the most marginalised sectors of the youth population. In chapter 3, we analysed in general terms the extent and nature of juvenile crime; the aim of this chapter is to explore the economic and social reasons for certain categories of young people to engage in specific types of crimes, and how the state attempts to enforce a particular kind of order with regard to the public presence of working-class and minority young people on the streets. We argue that the impetus or motivation for offending by young working-class people lies in the limited availability of adequate means of subsistence, and in the denial of the opportunity to participate in a meaningful way in consumption and social activities. In particular, we explain the high incidence of property crime among juveniles through the application of the concepts of class and marginalisation.

Australian society is a capitalist society that is divided into a number of identifiable classes (such as capitalist class, small-business class, working class). As a structural relation, class reflects people's different positions and their differing capacity to marshal economic and political resources as dictated by their relationship to the means of production. The ownership of the means of production (for example factories, banks, telecommunications, mining companies, farms) is central to the distribution of wealth and power

117

in society, and to the overall allocation of community resources. The working class comprises those people who live by the sale of their labour power on the labour market in return for a wage or salary. Indeed, the wage is a crucial determinant in the wellbeing and social status of working-class people. Unemployment, and the threat of unemployment, is therefore one of the conditions of the working class, given the importance of the wage for economic survival and the general dependency on business to provide work in return for a wage or salary.

Youth unemployment and youth poverty, in particular, are and will continue to be among the most disturbing and profound social issues of the twenty-first century. Specific studies and overviews of the youth studies literature indicate that young people are seriously 'at risk' across a range of broad social indicators—whether these be suicide, health, employment patterns, or other facets of youth lifestyle—all of which have been affected by wider economic conditions (Furlong & Cartmel 1997; White & Wyn, 2004). One consequence of the vulnerability of many young people to economic and social hardship is the creation of a marginalised 'underclass' stratum of the working class. Members of this social stratum are part of a wider 'surplus population' that has been progressively swelled by the advent of structural, long-term unemployment.

From the point of view of juvenile justice, it is essential to understand the broad processes of marginalisation that separate certain young people from mainstream institutions economically, socially, and culturally, and that provide fertile ground for various kinds of low-level property and interpersonal crime. Such processes are also associated with varying degrees of alienation, antisocial behaviour, riots, and violence, which in turn are symptomatic of a system that privileges the economic over the social, and that relegates the needs of the majority behind the dictates of the market.

In a similar vein, it is likewise important to consider the manner in which marginalisation is related to particular processes of criminalisation, whereby certain groups of young people are targeted above others for state intervention. In essence, the criminalisation process is, by and large, directed at the comparatively powerless and most marginalised sectors of society. Thus, the young people who are most vulnerable to being discarded by the formal labour market and to experiencing difficulties within institutions such as schools and the welfare system are also the most vulnerable when it comes to the activities of coercive state institutions such as the police, courts, and jails.

This chapter provides an examination of the relationship between young people, crime, and community resources. In so doing, it poses the question of how we address issues relating to the definitions and causes of particular types of youth crime, and official state responses to youth offending, in a period of gross economic and social inequality. Our approach to youth crime is in terms of political economy: this approach offers the prospect of an integrated analysis that incorporates structural, situational, and personal factors in explaining youth behaviour. It also exposes some of the limitations of existing state responses to this behaviour.

A POLITICAL ECONOMY OF CRIME

The basis for a political economy of crime is an appreciation of the changes that have occurred in the spheres of production and consumption as they have affected young people over the last 25 years. The marginalisation of young people in the sphere of production, specifically in relation to paid work, has had a profound impact upon their wellbeing and life opportunities. Indeed, there can be little doubt that many young people are experiencing life in this sphere as victims (and survivors), and are bearing the brunt of economic restructuring.

The current social context for youth is one characterised by high levels of youth unemployment and poverty, reductions in state welfare and educational services and benefits, and a public culture of competitive individualism (White & Wyn, 2004; Senate Community Affairs References Committee, 2004). It has been argued that, in historical terms, the present era is significantly different from previous time periods: whereas for most of the twentieth century the state played a major supporting and interventionist role in assisting young people in the areas of education, welfare, and rehabilitative juvenile justice—particularly when youth employment was stagnant—the same is not the case today. Rather, we are seeing a simultaneous reduction in youth employment prospects *and* in state support programs for young people, leading to what has been described as the phenomenon of 'abandoned youth' (Polk 1997a).

Major shifts have occurred in the youth labour market. For example, the proportion of teenagers in full-time work plummeted from 58.3 per cent in 1966 to 16.9 per cent in 1993. In 1997, estimates of youth unemployment for 15–19 year olds was in the order of 30 per cent nationally, and much higher in some regional areas. Meanwhile, insecure part-time and casual positions have proliferated dramatically, with the number of 14–24 year old part-time workers more than doubling between 1980 and 1996 (Spoehr 1997:2). While the number of full-time jobs available for those 25 years and over increased by 12.1 per cent between 1995 and 2003, the number for teenagers declined by 6.9 per cent, and for young adults by 15.1 per cent (Senate Community Affairs References Committee, 2004:278). Systematic study of labour market trends indicates the dramatic nature of the shifts in youth participation from full-time to part-time work, from paid work to educational participation, and from educational and work participation to unemployment (see Dusseldorp Skills Forum 1998; Senate Community Affairs References Committee, 2004).

Paid work available for teenagers tends to be reserved for students, and is located primarily in the retail and services sectors (White et al. 1997).

It consists of low-skilled work in both the formal and informal (cash-in-hand) waged economic spheres, and youth wages continue to be pegged at a level below that of other workers, regardless of the productivity of young workers (White 1997). Figures show that real earnings from full-time work among 15–19-year-olds fell by 6 per cent between the early 1980s and the mid-1990s, and that earnings from part-time work fell by 29 per cent in that period (Sweet 1998:9). It is notable that minimum full-time wages have fallen well behind average wages over the last two decades to just 50 per cent of average earnings, a reduction of 15 per cent since 1983 (Senate Community Affairs References Committee, 2004:80).

The income of young people has been severely affected by broader economic restructuring, both directly in terms of potential paid work performed by the young person, and indirectly through the financial pressures placed on families to support their children. Many young people have no income at all and are dependent upon their parents. For those receiving income, the average income of 15–19-year-olds has fallen significantly in real terms since 1982. This includes incomes for full-time workers, part-time workers, and those receiving government benefits (Landt & Scott 1998). The struggle to make ends meet is a major problem for young people and their parents, particularly in low-income areas.

Australian research has indicated a process of 'ghettoisation' in a number of localities around the country (Gregory & Hunter 1995; Vinson 2004). That is, particular neighbourhoods are filled with poor, unemployed people who, because of low skill levels, few educational opportunities, and longer physical distances from potential job sites, are mired in ghetto-like conditions. The spatial entrenchment of poverty is manifest in analysis of the impact of economic upturn as well. As Gregory and Hunter (1995:33) comment, it is 'people who live in poor neighbourhoods who are increasingly not at work … part-time jobs are going to young people and women who live in high SES [socioeconomic status] neighbourhoods and … income is rising in the best SES neighbourhoods but falling in poor neighbourhoods.' In other words, when job growth does occur, it tends to benefit people living in the better-off socioeconomic areas rather than incorporating the poorer neighbourhoods.

The changed economic opportunities and prospects for young people generally have not affected all young people in the same way. There are clear class and social differences in the allocation of valued social resources, including that of paid jobs and educational opportunities (White & Wyn 2004). Some young people continue to be privileged by existing institutional arrangements, while a growing proportion are experiencing profound economic hardships. The difficulties facing the latter group are manifest in social indicators that show unemployed and poor young people to be overrepresented among those who commit suicide, who die prematurely due to a range of causes, and/or who end up in youth detention centres (Australian Institute of Health and Welfare 1996; Hassan 1996; Vinson 2004; White and Perrone 2005).

The social worth of many of these young people has been further undermined by constant negative media images and stories regarding youth. The problems experienced by a growing proportion of young people in making ends meet, in finding secure full-time employment, in coping with stress and educational competition, and in forging a meaningful social identity are often transposed in such a way as to make young people themselves the 'problem'. The very lack of social and economic power exercised by these young people means they are easy targets for media campaigns that pathologise their behaviour and that present them as agents of their own lack of opportunity (see Bessant & Hil 1997, and Poynting et al. 2004, for examples).

The level of resources and facilities available at a local level, the income sources that are available to young people and their families, and the public perceptions of young people all influence what young people do to get money, and what they do with their time. For example, the income-generating activity of young people on low incomes is diverse, and involves a range of legal, illegal, and criminal activities (White et al. 1997). We shall return to some facets of these activities shortly. Why young people commit crime, and certain types of crimes, is a complex issue and one that can be answered only by taking into account a range of individual, situational, and social structural factors. For present purposes, our concern is with the idea that crime and antisocial behaviour tend to be exacerbated in circumstances of economic adversity and social dislocation—times when young people are feeling most vulnerable, most alienated, and most disfranchised.

The status and position of young people generally, and of specific groups of young people in particular, therefore has important implications for their economic, social, and emotional wellbeing. It is notable, for example, that violence is perceived by young people as a major issue in their lives. It is seen as being pervasive, as something that affects them at home, in the schools, through the media, and on the streets (White et al. 1999; White & Mason 2006). For young people, according to Daniel and Cornwall (1993:16), community violence has a number of dimensions: 'Violence is a problem in public places, like train stations, between racial groups, with the police. Violence was linked to the media, to adult behaviour and to young people's own levels of anger and frustration.'

Furthermore, it is crucial to consider that, while many young people may come to see violence as an unavoidable part of their lives (due to particular family circumstances, neighbourhood conditions, and community relationships), and that they themselves may partake occasionally in violent acts, the broad desire of most young people is to have safe spaces of their own. Indeed, it has been argued that the 'lack of safe havens makes children more vulnerable to youth crime, both as perpetrators and victims' (Meucci & Redmon 1997:140). The low social status of young people, as manifest in the lack of positive programs and the lack of adequate community resource allocation, is thus intertwined with the escalation of fear and vulnerability among young people themselves.

The sphere of production

Under capitalism, the key mechanism for the distribution of economic resources is the market. The sale of one's labour in return for wages is the basis for economic wellbeing. For those who, for whatever reason, are excluded from participation in the labour market or who simply cannot earn enough to make ends meet, there is the welfare state. In essence, the welfare state plays a residual role in Australian society, compensating for the shortfalls in resource distribution in the market sphere (see Watts 1987). A third area in which economic and other resources are transferred is that of informal community structures and networks (Jamrozik 1984). This area includes informal economic activities of an illegal nature, and the sharing of resources within a particular family, household, or community.

Changes in resource allocation in the dominant sphere of the market affect each of the other spheres as well. Certainly, the phenomenon of widespread unemployment constitutes the biggest single factor—but by no means the only factor—in the transformation of the relationship between the market, the state, and informal community sectors. For example, in 1992 there were more than 300,000 children living in families dependent on unemployment benefits, and an even greater number living below the after-housing poverty line (Australian Council of Social Services 1992; see also Carter 1991). Since then, there has been a further age-related shift in poverty levels, with greater numbers of younger people compared with the aged experiencing poverty (Gregory & Sheehan 1998; Senate Community Affairs References Committee 2004). While structurally playing a residual role in relation to overall resource distribution, the state has come to be a primary or major source of economic resources in the lives of a large proportion of Australian residents. This, in turn, has placed considerable pressures on the state to balance the demands of the economy through fiscal, monetary, and labour market polices with the demands of social policy. The latter stem from the general decline in living standards accompanying the movement of people out of paid work and into the welfare queue.

The result of the state's balancing act has been manifest: the tightening of regulations covering benefit provision, moves towards privatising public services (through the sale of assets, the introduction of user-pays principles into areas such as education, and the farming out of government functions to private contractors), more selective allocation of state resources through tests on means and assets, and redefinition of areas of state responsibility and private responsibility. Simultaneously, the ways in which the Australian state has intervened in the market sector, particularly in the areas of taxation and wage policies, have affected the living standards of the majority of those in the paid workforce. All of this adds up to enormous hardships for people as a result of the substantial increase in unemployment, underemployment, and precarious employment since the 1970s. For young people in particular, the impact of the changing nature of work has been especially profound and in some instances devastating.

Many young people today are struggling to come to grips with two essential facets of their lives: what to do with their time, and where to get enough money to do what they wish to do. The issue of income looms large for many young people, for in a capitalist consumer society, one in which most services, amenities, and activities require cash payment in return for participation, the importance of a regular, adequate income becomes highly significant. How young people interact with and choose their peers, and how they deal with the mainstream institutions of family, leisure, sport, education, and criminal justice, are very much influenced by their access to financial as well as social resources.

Analysis of the employment and work-related activity of young people has indicated that for most young people there are five broad spheres of economic activity within which they may be active (see White et al. 1997). These are:

- the *formal waged* sphere, which includes paid employment that is taxed and state regulated
- the *informal waged* sphere, which includes paid employment on a 'cash-in-hand' basis, and which is 'off the books' in terms of formal state regulation of work
- the *informal non-waged* sphere, which includes goods and services being exchanged without monetary payment, as in the case of domestic labour within the parental home
- the *welfare* sphere, which includes income benefits received from the state to assist young people in education, training, and while unemployed
- the *criminal economic* sphere, which includes activities that cannot be undertaken legally in the economic sectors, either on or off the books.

The most prevalent ways of gaining money are through paid work in the formal and informal waged spheres. However, even here the issues of low wages, part-time work opportunities, and poor working conditions affect the amount of income available to teenagers.

Most under-18 year olds rely primarily on their parents as their main source of income (see White et al. 1997), so that the level of resources available to any particular young person depends upon household circumstances, family relationships, and expenditure patterns. For many young people, the opportunity to engage fully in recreation and leisure activities—let alone attain basic everyday necessities—requires that they seek an income beyond that available from their parents and relations. Employment and finding paid work that yields a sufficient level of remuneration are crucial factors in immediate lifestyle and longer-term life prospects.

One of the important general conditions that shapes the current situation of economic adversity for young people is the collapse in the availability of full-time work for the young. In Australia, youth unemployment figures have had various peaks and troughs across the years since the worldwide jump in unemployment in the mid-1970s, with the low point being in the 12 per cent range in 1982, and the highest peak at more than 25 per cent in 1991 (with regional variations showing much greater levels of unemployment in some localities). But the long-term underlying trend has been such that unemployment is distinctly 'ratchetting upwards' during each recession peak, 'and never quite returning to pre-recession levels' (Wooden 1996:151). As Jamrozik (1998:76) further points out: 'In 1966, young people accounted for 13.6 per cent of all employed persons, but by 1995 they accounted for only 6.9 per cent. They lost their share of employment in all sectors of industry, including those industries which over this period achieved a very high rate of employment growth.' In a similar vein, it is notable that between 1986 and 1991 the proportion of young people (15–25 years) in full-time employment decreased by 11 per cent (ABS and NYARS 1993). This decrease was most significant for those aged 15–17 years, of whom 57 per cent were full-time employed in 1986 but only 30 per cent full-time employed in 1991.

The instability and dilemmas associated with new patterns of work organisation are also apparent in discussions of 'precarious employment' (see Campbell 1997). This refers to a combination of low levels of pay and high levels of labour insecurity. In substantive terms, there is evidence that a large and growing proportion of workers, including those working in casual and full-time positions, are now working under conditions in which insecurity, irregularity, and unpredictability have become hallmarks of their employment. The result is the production of an increasing proportion of low-wage, low-quality jobs within the workforce. Furthermore, such jobs do not translate into enhanced career prospects. As noted by Campbell (1997:9), we are increasingly seeing in many countries the consolidation of patterns of 'intermittent employment' in which 'persons fluctuate between periods of unemployment, short-term and low-paid employment, participation in government-sponsored training or employment schemes and periods of withdrawal from the labour force'. It is significant that industries that lend themselves to such precarious employment patterns include those that young people might be expected to be most involved in, namely wholesale and retail trade, and recreation and personal industries. However, as Jamrozik (1998:76) points out, although youth employment between 1966 and 1995 increased only in these two sectors (while decreasing in all others), the increase was nevertheless still lower than the increase of total employment in these sectors.

Hence, what work there is tends to be insecure part-time and casual, and tends to go to students rather than unemployed young people. A substantial proportion of Australian young people are today locked into marginal activities, precarious forms of work, and withdrawal from the labour market (see Dusseldorp Skills Forum 1998; Senate Community Affairs References Committee 2004). This part-time work tends to be casual, with minimum pay and conditions, and limited prospects for either training or further advancement. While technically keeping some young people off the unemployment roll, such work will not generally provide avenues into full-time, long-term, and career-oriented jobs. The work tends to be a temporary measure associated with the educational and recreational financial needs of students, or simply a stepping stone into yet more work of the same nature.

Not surprisingly, much has been written in recent years about the relationship between unemployment and youthful offending (see, for example, Weatherburn 1992; Watts 1996; Moynihan & Coleman 1996; Polk & White 1999). While the debates and literature on this relationship have not been able to provide a consistent or accurate statistical correlation between unemployment rates and levels of criminal offending, at the level of personal experience, unemployment does appear to be of great significance when it comes to who is actually criminalised for their offending or antisocial behaviour.

Any analysis of unemployment and crime must take into account a range of variables that influence individual and group behaviour. In concrete terms, questions can be asked regarding how particular groups of young people are affected by factors such as lack of paid work, inadequate levels of income, poor neighbourhood amenities, unequal distribution of community resources, and uneven employment prospects. Through addressing such questions, crime and unemployment trends can be put into a more meaningful social context. For example, while youth unemployment may cut across many types of household and income groups, its impact will be felt more acutely in some cases than others. Young people from affluent families have long experienced 'poverty' and 'unemployment' as part of the normal process of gaining a higher-education degree or as part of the travel and settling-down process (Graycar & Jamrozik 1989). The situation is usually transitory and experienced by the young person as part of a personal growth life experience. Middle-class parents tend to have the resources, the capacity and the desire to support their offspring through the hard times of education or labour market transitions (see Pusey 2003, 2004). The options and experiences of working-class young people generally differ markedly, however. Unemployment is experienced as neither transient nor as simply a passing phase in the life cycle: it is often a condition to be endured, with many ups and downs in terms of hands-on work opportunities and income-generating activities.

Further to this, employment is often distributed unevenly in geographical terms, with clear regional biases in youth unemployment rates (Centre for Labour Studies 1997). It is particularly devastating for specific groups of young people, such as Indigenous Australians or young migrant refugees (Johnston 1991; Moss 1993). The concentration of large numbers of unemployed young people in particular geographical locations or among certain population groups increases the difficulties of specific individuals gaining paid work. It simultaneously fosters the shared identification and physical segregation of unemployed young people with each other. Thus, it can act to preclude such young people from attaining jobs, and also make them more visible in the public domain as an identifiable 'outsider' group.

For such young people, there are fewer financial and parental resources to cushion the experience or to act as a safety net if things go wrong. In these kinds of circumstances, it is more likely that young people will view crime as a significant option if things go from bad to worse in their economic life (see, for example, Daniel & Cornwall 1993). This was affirmed in a 1997 Sydney study of forty unemployed young people who were living in a socially disadvantaged inner-city suburb. The study showed that the young people had a high degree of motivation to work, but were handicapped in pursuing work by having relatively few employed relatives and friends who could introduce them to job opportunities and prospective employers. The young people in the study acknowledged reliance on crime as a way to make ends meet (Vinson, Abela & Hutka 1997).

Other research has confirmed the importance of the 'neighbourhood effect' when it comes to youth offending (see Reiss 1986). In other words, the social status and crime rate of a neighbourhood have an effect on a young person's chances of becoming involved in offending behaviour independent of their socioeconomic status. For example, a young person from a low-income background who lives in a high crime-rate area is far more likely to engage in offending behaviour than the same person living in a low crime-rate neighbourhood. Community context is therefore an integral part of why some unemployed and marginalised young people may have a greater propensity to commit crime than other young people in a similar social position. This is discussed in greater depth later in this chapter.

The sphere of consumption

The flip side of income-generating activity—whether this be paid work or criminal activity—is consumption. The post-Second World War period saw dramatic changes in the nature and place of consumption in Western society. During the long boom of economic development—up to the late 1960s and early 1970s—paid work for young people was readily available and a disposable income there to be spent. One consequence of shifts in spending ability and the market weight given to young people was a significant change in leisure activity and the use of time and space. Stratton (1992:163) comments: 'With the advent of an increasingly consumption-oriented society independence came to be measured more and more as a function of possible expenditure. This relates directly to the rise of institutionalised and commercialised leisure activities.' In other words, leisure pursuits were increasingly reliant upon money.

The shift towards more commercialised forms of youth leisure and recreation also helped to consolidate the city as a prime site of consumption. Shopping became a type of leisure activity in its own right, and shopping centres and malls began to feature more prominently in civic life. The distinction between 'commercial' and 'community' spaces became conflated as shopping districts became the central focal point for much community interaction and socialising (see White 1999a). Shopping centres have now become major sites at which many young people 'hang out', for a wide variety of social purposes.

Meanwhile, the cultural importance of consumption changed in the postwar period as well. Fads and fashions—youth-oriented and otherwise— have increasingly dominated public life. It seems that who you are is, in essence, a reflection of what you wear and where you shop. Alternative and mainstream fashion dictates that the right clothing be worn, at whatever cost. The rise of the 'spectacular' youth subcultures in the 1950s onwards (Hall & Jefferson 1976; Hebdige 1979; Brake 1985; White 1993a) provides an indication of the importance of style and presentation in youth cultural life. Youth group cultures have continued, although the shift from 'sub' to 'club' cultures (among other changes) has seen youth cultural forms moving through new stages and transitions (see Redhead 1997; White 1999b).

Social identity for young people is an active process involving several different dimensions. The processes of cultural formation are such that youth identity is forged through how young people consume what is provided in the mass commercial market and how they consciously produce their own self-generated cultural forms (see Wyn & White 1997). A 1998 British study on youth consumption points out that 'it was the symbolic qualities of consumer goods, as opposed to their intrinsic qualities, that appeared to provide the cultural capital with which social peer groups could interact' (Miles, Cliff & Burr 1998:89). The study concluded that young people consume material items as a means of facilitating social participation and thereby constructing a recognisable identity. A crucial issue raised by these findings is the experience of those young people who do not have the basic resources they need to become participants in this sort of consumer culture. To some extent, insight into this issue can be found in consideration of the sites of consumption.

The focus of much of the cultural life of cities and towns today is the central business district (CBD) or similar major regional centre. Not only a major site of commercial consumption, but the CBD is also equated with large flows of people, exciting places to hang out, entertainment centres, fast-food outlets, proximity to public transport services, and a wide range of people from many different types of social backgrounds. For many young people, the construction of social identity is intertwined with being in a public place and exhibiting a noticeable presence among their peers. To be seen, and to watch others, is part of a ritual process of identity formation and affirmation.

The growing importance of the city as a site of social identity is due to a range of factors, including the need for community connection in an increasingly globalised social environment. In his study of youth patterns of 'going out' in Newcastle, England, Hollands (1995:1) observed that economic restructuring has had major effects on work, education, and domestic identities, and that the city has an increasing role in shaping young people's experiences. He argued that: 'The shift from these more traditional sites of identities to increased identification with the city through consumption, and their participation in extended socialising rituals, represents a broader response and re-adjustment by young people to "modernity" and post-industrialism.' Hollands (1995:18–19) points to several factors that affect the relationship of Newcastle young people with city life:

> First, it is a 'public space' in the sense that going out is a visible display of identity. Second, urban regeneration, in terms of leisure, public entertainment and the redevelopment of clubs and pubs, occurred in the same time frame as the region experienced its most rapid economic decline. And finally, this new consumption space did not readily discriminate against either students or the local population on the basis of age, class or gender criteria, and many young adults responded by appropriating sections of the city by claiming them as their own.

While city space has its attractions and compelling qualities for many young people, economic status has an impact on how they experience the city, and on how others view them in general (see also Chatterton & Hollands 2003; White & Wyn 2004).

For instance, from the point of view of commercial consumption, many young people today are 'worthless'. They are unable or unwilling to purchase the goods and services on offer in the commercial spaces, yet they utilise the 'consumer' spaces as public spaces for their own uses. Often this involves the production of 'noise', literally and figuratively. It means being who they are through adopting particular kinds of dress and language, through demonstrating certain kinds of 'style' by acting in particular ways, and through establishing themselves as beings with social worth in a wider societal context that emphasises financial value.

The mass privatisation of public space, and the transformation of community space into commercial space (Sandercock 1997), has meant a considerable narrowing of places where young people can comfortably hang out for 'free'. Simultaneously, the public visibility of young people has been heightened by the concentration of people into more selected gathering places (such as malls, train stations, shopping centres) by the fact that young people tend to hang around in groups, and by the diversity of social and economic circumstances within which young people find themselves. Public concern has also been expressed over 'unpoliced' or 'unwatched' places—such as beaches or parks after dark—that are associated with the activities of young people.

Accompanying the visibility of young people have been rising public perceptions that young people, especially those in disadvantaged social positions, are engaging in more antisocial behaviour and criminal activity (White 1996ab, 1997/98; Schissel 2002). The fear of crime in recent years has largely stemmed from a fear of young people (see Males 1996; Bessant & Hil 1997). The exclusion of young people from the traditional means of income and social status in the sphere of production has certainly altered their position in the sphere of consumption. It is in this sphere of activity that young people are most prevalent as offenders, and are most likely to be identified as threats to existing consumer practices and institutions.

Media-generated moral panics regarding youth 'crime waves' and the stereotyping of certain young people as being particularly 'troublesome' or 'dangerous' can stimulate general fear and anxiety at a popular level (see chapter 3). This is especially so as regards 'street kids' and 'youth gangs' (White 1999b). Coupled with the concerns of businesspeople and market traders regarding actual losses suffered due to offending behaviour, such images affect large numbers of young people, offenders and non-offenders alike. The suspicion that (some) shopkeepers and traders have of (some) young people is grounded to a certain extent in experience. It is significant, for instance, that shoplifting constitutes one of the largest categories of offences for which juveniles are actually apprehended by police. A major victim of youth offending, therefore, is not the individual citizen *per se* but business enterprises of various kinds.

Given the prevalence of shoplifting as an offence, it is useful to explore more fully the meaning of such offences in the lives of different groups of young people. More research is needed, for example, to examine the dynamics of shoplifting as an activity that plays different possible roles in relation to personal situation and household economic relations. Do young people steal items for their immediate-use value, or for their exchange value—that is, as something to be exchanged in the criminal economy for cash? In which ways can shoplifted items, or cash from their sale, be linked to immediate physical needs (for example, fast food, drugs), youth culture (for example, items related to dress and appearance), psychological needs (for example, self-esteem, status, peer-group pressure), or to purchases of other goods and services on the market (for example, commercial entertainment)? As well, it would be of interest to investigate class, gender, and ethnic differences in the patterns and content of shoplifting. Clearly, there are bound to be differences in the perceived causes of such behaviour, which will range from issues of powerlessness stemming from general social restrictions placed upon all young people, through to immediate economic needs relating to physical survival. In other words, if we are to understand the nature of juvenile offending of this kind, we need to have insight into the significance and meaning of such activities in the lives of the young people involved.

Nevertheless, it is logical to suggest that, given the poverty, unemployment, and homelessness affecting large numbers of young people, shoplifting represents one means to 'consume' when one does not have the resources to pay. And in a consumption-oriented society, there are considerable pressures on young people to participate in consumption activities regardless of their financial ability to do so.

One of the consequences of both the prominence of shoplifting as a youth crime and the visibility of the social impact of economic restructuring, is what can be called the 'criminalisation of the non-consumer'. For many young people, the central logic of the shopping centre or mall—to consume—is either not realisable or is not the primary reason for their use of this space. Other motivations for young people to congregate in such centres include social activity and escape from close parental or adult control. But the social response to young people will be shaped by their position as consumers (and producers) in the context of general street life. For example, young people who do purchase goods and services, or who exhibit a level of affluence that makes them appear as potential consumers, are rarely seen as problematic by businesspeople or the police.

On the other hand, the social position of the dispossessed, the obviously poor, and the visible minority-group member is usually mirrored in the suspicion and confrontational attitudes of those around them. Shopkeepers may see the presence of these young people as unacceptable on at least two grounds. First, such young people are often implicated in or suspected of shoplifting, which directly affects shopkeepers' profit levels. Second, even if no offence has been committed, the very presence of these young people may put off other consumers and thus be bad for business (see White 1999a for shopkeeper perceptions and opinions).

From the point of view of young people, public spaces mean many different things, reflecting different social circumstances (youth homelessness), patterns of use (street frequenting versus living on the street), social relationships (activities of young men and young women), and affiliations (shared musical interests, ethnic group identification). Generalised images of 'youth' often provide misleading and inaccurate portrayals of group activities and actual uses and experiences of public spaces. Why and how different individuals and groups of young people use public space the way they do is of crucial importance in understanding the ways in which the lives of young people in general are shaped by broader economic, social, and political forces (White 1999ab).

There is also a need to consider space itself as a community resource. Increasingly, it seems to be the case that public space is being redefined as, and constricted to, 'consumption' space. As such, it is also subject to intensive and extensive forms of social control, involving both state and private police (see chapter 9). The private ownership and/or state regulation of public space, which is based primarily on the construction of this space in commercial terms, thus forms part of the context within which particular activities and particular young people are more prone to be criminalised than others.

CRIME AND COMMUNITY

Transformations in the material resources available to young people have had a profound impact on their lifestyle and life opportunities. The issue of economic provision is not, however, simply one of quantity, but quality as well. For example, an important distinction can be made between physical survival and social functioning. The first refers to basic human needs (such as nutrition) that are necessary for the sustenance of life itself. The second is more closely related to the question of life chances. Social functioning, as Jamrozik (1987:48) explains, 'depends on the provision of, and access to, an adequate quantity and quality of material resources sufficient for the achievement of a certain minimum standard of living and a certain quality of life'. The cash resources available to young people, whether through the labour market or as a result of state transfers, therefore mean different things in real terms, depending on the overall economic situation of particular young people, their position in the class structure, the family and community resources that can be drawn upon, and their immediate work, study, or lifestyle requirements.

Social problems such as unemployment, poverty, and declining opportunities directly affect the physical and psychological wellbeing of young people (White 1994). The marginalisation of young people economically, socially, and politically undermines their own self-conceptions of 'worth'. It is also linked to feelings of resentment at promises unfulfilled, with boredom over and frustration at their present social state, and with a search for meaning and satisfaction in an era of no jobs. As Pixley (1993) demonstrates, people who are excluded from mainstream work become powerless and experience significant problems in coping with their lack of status in society.

Any discussion of crime and community must also take into account the role played by schools in shaping the social resources and social identities of young people. In financial terms, the weight of government policy change has been in the direction of bolstering youth participation in school and tertiary education by providing enhanced government benefits for those in full-time study (see Szukalska & Robinson 2000). This has taken the form of changes in eligibility requirements and in disposable income, with full-time students being better off than their unemployed counterparts. The general trend has been twofold: on the one hand, a large and growing proportion of the 15–24-year-old age group attend an educational institution (85 percent in 1998); on the other hand, a growing number of such young people are combining full-time study with part-time work (Szukalska & Robinson 2000). This is creating enormous stress for many young people as they attempt to negotiate their multiple responsibilities and to forge an existence on a relatively low income.

For other young people, existing financial incentives to remain in some form of education are simply not sufficient to ensure continuing participation. This may be due to a range of reasons. For example, student alienation within the school context can lead to detachment from the institution, feelings of resentment or failure on the part of the young person, the turning towards alternative peer groups (such as gangs) for support and identity networks, and active resistance to what the school has on offer (White 1996c). Intergenerational experiences and attitudes to education also have a major bearing on how each young person perceives and acts within the schooling context (see Hunter 1998). In other words, how one's family sees education influences how children are socialised with regard to the learning process and educational institutions. Meanwhile, schools are confronted with higher retention rates and, simultaneously, 'discipline' problems on the part of students who may not really desire to be there but who, financially, have few alternatives. This may result in high levels of school absenteeism and/or the use of school exclusions as a disciplinary measure.

Whatever the specific case or circumstance, the end result is that many young people find themselves outside school during class hours. For these young people, the 'street' is both somewhere to escape to and a place where conflict is inevitable (with each other, and with authority figures). The specific kind of schooling available, the nature of youth relationships at the local neighbourhood level, and the specific community context will all shape how young people deal with their own personal circumstances. This is demonstrated in recent Australian studies of how local conditions shape youth behaviour and opportunities, and how these in turn influence engagement in criminal and antisocial activity.

Local neighbourhoods and social disadvantage

Research on youth unemployment shows a clear regional and neighbourhood-level bias in youth unemployment rates (Centre for Labour Studies 1997; Hunter 1998). The work of Hunter (1998) in particular has been very informative regarding the impact of unequal distributions of unemployment, employment, and educational opportunities at the local level. By comparing low and high socioeconomic-status areas, Hunter (1998) showed, among other things, that:

- teenagers in low-status areas are more than 10 percentage points more likely to be unemployed than those in other areas
- the residents of low-status areas are more than 50 per cent less likely than those in other areas to be attending either secondary school or a tertiary institution
- not only is the proportion of unemployed students higher in low-status areas, but such people are also more likely to be searching for full-time employment (which raises questions concerning the commitment of students in low-status areas to the educational process)

- there is a 10 percentage-point difference between the proportion of youth working part time in high- rather than low-status areas (and even greater differences in the case of full-time students being employed part time)
- greater numbers of youth in low-status areas were relatively inactive compared to those in high-status areas, as measured by patterns of involvement as either full-time students or full-time workers
- the peer group provides less job-finding information in low-status areas, due to the lesser likelihood that friends, contacts, and relatives are employed
- based upon experience, individuals, families, and peers of low-status-area youth tend to place a lower valuation on education, an issue influenced partly by government financial incentives, and partly by quality and availability of local educational infrastructure.

Similarly, research into youth unemployment and social disadvantage in New South Wales demonstrated that 'a lack of jobs for the young can be embedded in a lack of other community resources, including education, income, work qualifications, work experience, and links via members of one's family and social networks with the world of work' (Higgins & Vinson 1998; see also Devery 1991). In other words, the social and economic character of a region has an influence on the activities and opportunities of unemployed individuals who live there.

Local neighbourhood conditions therefore have a major effect on schooling and employment prospects. This is significant insofar as poverty and unemployment are becoming entrenched at a spatial level, and are increasingly concentrated in specific locations around Australia, including some rural areas (Gregory & Hunter 1995; Vinson 2004). It has been observed that income inequality across households 'exert[s] a strong and systematic neighbourhood effect' that in turn results in fewer opportunities for young people and a greater likelihood of negative 'neighbourhood pathologies' (Gregory & Hunter 1995). At a very general level, then, it would appear that local community context is an integral part of why some young people have a greater propensity than others to commit crime.

But the circumstance of economic adversity in and of itself is insufficient to explain fully the relationship between disadvantaged youth and crime. For instance, Weatherburn and Lind (1998, 2001) examined the role of parenting and delinquent peers as mediating factors in the relationship between economic stress and youthful criminality. They found that parental neglect (more so than abuse) was a major factor in juvenile participation in crime, and that 'economic and social stress exert most of their effects on crime, at least in urban areas, by increasing the risk of child neglect' (Weatherburn & Lind 1998:4). They further argue, in a similar vein to Reiss (1986), that living in a high crime-rate area influences the likelihood of a person from a low-income background engaging in criminal behaviour. In this case, the argument is that parenting and peer-group activity interact in shaping the rate of entry into crime. Specifically, in addition to a positive correlation between reported parental neglect and poverty, there are higher rates of crime in those neighbourhoods where the level of economic stress is sufficient to push the number of crime-susceptible juveniles above a certain limit. Thus, according to Weatherburn and Lind (1998:4): 'Low socioeconomic status neighbourhoods will generally have larger populations of delinquents and will therefore produce higher rates of interaction between juveniles susceptible to involvement in crime and juveniles already involved in crime.'

The precise nature of peer group interaction is, however, also influenced by other local neighbourhood factors. It is not simply a case of there being a critical mass of young people who together contribute to the creation of a crime-prone neighbourhood: the social dynamics of specific areas also shape the nature and extent of juvenile offending. American (Sampson 1991, 1993) and British (Hirschfield & Bowers 1997) research has pointed to the importance of 'social cohesion' in understanding the relationship between crime and disadvantage. Here it is argued that areas of disadvantage with high levels of social cohesion will tend to have lower levels of crime than similarly disadvantaged areas with low levels of social cohesion. Social cohesion, albeit a difficult concept to define and measure, generally refers to ties at the local level that bind people together in a positive way, such as familiarity with one's neighbours, shared interests, a sense of community, engagement in formal and voluntary organisations, the presence of local friendship and acquaintance networks, and so on.

Residents in neighbourhoods with strong social cohesion—which tend to be fairly stable in terms of residential tenure and home ownership—are able to exert greater informal social control. This control can include monitoring the play of local children, intervening to prevent acts of truancy or vandalism by local youth, ostracising 'troublemakers', and confronting people who are exploiting or disturbing public spaces (Foster 1995; Sampson, Raudenbush & Earls 1997). These types of analysis suggest on the one hand that 'The more that an area that is at a disadvantage economically pulls together as a community, the greater its capacity to combat crime' (Hirschfield & Bowers 1997:1296). On the other hand, it is argued that concentrated disadvantage will decrease collective efficacy, and thus informal controls will be undermined (Sampson et al. 1997). Interestingly, better-off middle-class neighbourhoods that generally have low crime rates do not usually display the characteristics associated with social cohesion, nor do they draw upon informal social-control mechanisms. Rather, such neighbourhoods tend to have weak ties among residents, and to rely upon police to enforce privacy and safety. Thus, specific types of social and economic circumstances give rise to different forms of offending behaviour, and to reliance upon different forms of social control (see Crawford 1998).

The idea of an underclass

In theoretical terms, the linking of disadvantaged areas with youth offending has been interpreted in several different ways. Because of the sheer extent and scope of such marginalisation, much concern has been directed in recent years to the concept of an 'underclass'. Such a notion carries with it various connotations, including the distance of certain groups from the mainstream institutions and processes of society. For example, the term has been used to distinguish different categories of unemployed people on the basis of their relationship to the labour market (Morris & Irwin 1992). Thus, the unemployed can be divided into two main groups:

1   *Outside the labour market*: These people by virtue of their age or disability are ineffective in competing for jobs; they are outside the labour market because they lack 'marketability'. They suffer systematic disadvantage in the market. At an experiential level, they still maintain an interest in entering the labour market, and state policies relating to education and training—that is, labour market re-entry—are central to their lifestyle and efforts to become employed.
2   *Excluded from the labour market*: These people are non-participants in the labour market, and have no stable relationship to employment. They are, in essence, excluded from the job market through a combination of long-term unemployment, inadequate work histories, and declining motivation to compete in apparently hopeless circumstances.

Each category of the unemployed constitutes a sizable proportion of those people living in poverty (which also includes aged pensioners, sole-parent families, and so on), and as such includes people who would under normal circumstances rely upon state welfare provisions of some kind. The important distinguishing factor is whether individuals are defined as 'deserving' or 'undeserving' with regard to the claiming of state benefits or services. It is crucial to acknowledge here the ways in which social policy encapsulates and structures the social division of welfare (Rodger 1992; White 1996b). In the Australian context, it is clear that more stringent conditions for the claiming of state support simultaneously constitute rules of inclusion and exclusion in relation to state welfare provision. It is notable in this regard that young people under the age of 25 are disproportionately likely to be penalised by governments for breaching social security rules. For instance, in February 2001, while jobseekers under 25 years of age represented only 30.6 per cent of those people receiving Newstart Allowance and Youth Allowance, they made up 50.6 per cent of all Activity Test breaches (for example, not accepting a 'suitable' job) and 57.6 per cent of all administrative breaches (for example, failure to attend an interview). The consequences for the young person are particularly severe, given the already low level of payment: a breach leaves a person on a Youth Allowance with only $110 to $119 to live on each week (Australian Council of Social Services 2001:26).

For those who play by the established rules of the game, the reward is a meagre sum with which to achieve a modicum of physical survival. However, there are many who persistently find it difficult to succeed within the terms of the policy agenda (because more training does not necessarily guarantee greater employability), who refuse to accept the notion that welfare resources exist principally as a privilege (rather than a right), or who exhibit high degrees of alienation, resentment, and loss of faith in themselves or the system (through accumulated 'failures'). Such people may find themselves subject to the label 'underclass'. The 'underclass' is not simply marginal to the labour market; it is excluded from the labour market by virtue of family history, structural restrictions on education and job choices, geographical location, racial and ethnic segregation, and stigmatised individual and community reputation.

The principal defining features of the 'underclass' include:

- it is non-working in the conventional sense (although it might be noted that the expansion of part-time work could be explored as a boundary issue between the underclass and the marginal sectors of the working class)
- the primary source of income lies permanently (or effectively permanently) outside the capital–wage labour relationship
- the economic conditions of life for this group lie at or below relative subsistence
- there is a strong intergenerational component, with 'underclass' conditions persisting from one generation to another, and
- there are significant cultural, ideological, and political factors that reinforce a subworking-class position, associated with such things as ethnicity, race, and so on.

Entry into the 'underclass' is generally through movements and transitions in the class structure that propel some people into the lower echelons of the social hierarchy. These transitions include shifts in the number of long-term unemployed, the never-likely-to-be employed, and the part-time working poor.

The marginal sectors of the working class are the transitory repository for movement into the 'underclass', but are not members of the 'underclass' *per se*. Marginality is constituted through permanent part-time work, through seasonal or irregular employment combined with unemployment, through minimum or substandard conditions at, near, or even below the poverty line, through short-term contract employment, and through accelerated reductions in the social wage (for example, education, health) through the privatisation of services and introduction of user-pays services. This describes a condition of existence for an expanding proportion of the working class. It also provides the structural floor upon which rests the 'underclass' proper. The movement between these categories is ultimately shaped by the contours of unemployment and the general status of wage-labour. It is also influenced by distinct neighbourhood and social factors (Lee 2005).

The concept of underclass can refer to an objective position of exclusion (from the labour market and/or state welfare provision), and a subjective dimension of experience (general social attitudes, values, and behaviour). From a right-wing perspective, it is the 'habitual' and long-term unemployed who are seen as a threat to the economic fibre of the nation; it is the 'culturally impoverished' and 'socially deviant' unemployed who are seen to threaten the standards of decency and respectability in society. As a substratum of the working class, the so-called underclass can thus appear as a highly visible blight on the social landscape and an 'unnecessary' drain on public and private resources.

Discussion of the underclass could be used to heighten awareness of social polarisation and human deprivation, and as a means to focus attention on the structural conditions that exclude some categories of people from community resources. However, in popular discourse, the concept has largely been appropriated by those who use it as a stigmatising label, referring in the main to forms of undesirable behaviour. It is this perceived behaviour that has informed various law-and-order policies and that partly shapes the way in which law-enforcement agencies operate in relation to marginalised young people. As has been pointed out, this approach to dealing with members of the underclass focuses on kinds of people rather than on social conditions (Rodger 1992). From this conservative perspective, the problem lies with the personal pathologies of many of the underclass, and with self-perpetuating 'pathological communities' that are characterised by a 'hand-out' mentality, immorality, and criminality (see Jones & Smyth 1999 for a review of the different explanations for social exclusion).

Where large numbers of young working-class people congregate in particular areas, they constitute the visible evidence of the failures of capitalism and the threats to social order posed by these failures. The echoes of class situation are seen in vandalism, 'making trouble', gathering on the streets together, theft, and generally asserting public spaces as youth spaces. The dominant ideological and repressive responses to social change are manifest in the notion of the 'underclass' as a moral category. Thus, members of the 'underclass' are perceived and portrayed as morally corrupt and as a group needing to be disciplined and reformed. One way in which to neutralise the social expense of inequality and disadvantage is to construct official state ideology that reinforces the individual nature of the problem (for example, you are unemployed because you don't have the right skills, training, attitude, or work ethic) and the responsibility of individuals to the state (for example, in varying forms of 'mutual obligation' welfare requirements). Another response is through state coercive action, generally involving some form of criminalisation of the poor, and containment of social differences via geographical segregation of rich and poor.

One consequence of the perceived threat posed by the 'underclass' is increased state intervention in the affairs of some young people as a matter of course. This intervention takes many different forms, and involves various state agencies, including welfare authorities, the police, educational staff, and others. The impact of pervasive and strong official intervention into such young people's lives in this manner combines with prior difficulties of economic hardship, low self-esteem, few social resources, and general boredom associated with exclusion from the spheres of production and consumption, to make an explosive mix of desperation and anger. Young people caught in the web of no money, no job, and no future nevertheless often have very creative survival skills and a rebelliousness sparked by knowledge that they are the most disfavoured and disowned by society.

The marginalisation of young people economically, socially, and politically is uneven, and is based on wider social divisions in Australian society, being linked to class position, ethnicity, Indigenous background, and gender relationships. The social costs of marginality are inevitably translated into the economic costs of crime. But the social costs of marginality are also transformed into behaviour that is officially defined as 'antisocial' and 'dangerous'. As much as anything, this reflects the ways in which the state attempts to manage disadvantaged youth at the ground level. In other words, official social reaction to the marginalised in turn makes worse the already tense relationship between these young people and other members of the public who perceive the young marginalised through the lens of law and order.

All of this is bound to have an impact on the self-image of marginalised young people, and to influence their efforts at self-defence in a hostile environment. The pooling of social resources and the construction of identities that are valued by others (if only one's peers) find expression in a range of cultural forms, including various youth subcultures and gang formations (see, for example, chapter 7). The actual behaviour and activity of young people is thus shaped by their position as producers and consumers in society, their relationship to the major social institutions, and by the ways in which they are subject to various social-control measures by the state and private policing agencies. Structural dislocations are affecting a large and growing number of young people, giving rise to a range of experiences. These experiences are shaped by situational factors, such as the nature of a local community and the type of policing in particular social locations. Analysis of the conditions underlying the advent of the Macquarie Fields riots in 2005, for example, demonstrate how and why poorly resourced and poorly policed neighbourhoods become socially primed as sites for explosive events (Lee 2005). More generally, young people respond to adverse circumstances with diverse personal coping strategies, with negative strategies ranging from substance abuse and suicide through to petty crime. Positive coping strategies are also apparent in the form of creative street art and music, renewed commitment to formal education, and innovative business enterprise. Any strategy designed to address youth crime must therefore seek to transform young people's reality at the structural, situational, and personal levels.

CONCLUSION

Criminality associated with economic marginalisation and social alienation stems from the subordinate position of the working class in society. Unemployment and the threat of unemployment constitute central factors of the capitalist organisation of paid work. This means that social vulnerability by way of the growth in surplus populations, and social polarisation by way of unequal distributions of community wealth, will be ongoing in Australian society. In such circumstances, working-class crime will flourish even as the state redoubles its efforts to contain it.

Portrayals of the 'underclass' as increasingly threatening, dangerous, irresponsible, and immoral serve to justify the introduction of more hurdles for claimants of state benefits, and the enactment of law-and-order policies that target particular groups of young people and penalise certain types of behaviour. Such portrayals represent a movement from concern about welfare to the criminalisation of the poor. If there is to be an adequate response to the issue of youth crime, then it is essential to come to grips with changes occurring in the spheres of production and consumption, and understand how these are radically transforming the life experiences of young people in Australia today.

A realistic, meaningful, and humane response to the issues surrounding young people, crime, and community would have to be built upon interrelated policies that acknowledge and attempt to transcend the unequal distribution of power and resources in current sociostructural arrangements. Briefly, these might include the following:

- *More action to redistribute community resources*: The right to the means of life should not be contingent upon activity, but should be based on need. For both the working poor and the unemployed, there is a great need to increase social resources such that physical survival and enhanced social functioning are guaranteed institutionally.
- *Concerted action on employment and job creation*: The right to work could be grounded concretely in policies that recognise the transformation of paid work, the essential creativity, and necessity of labour in the self-worth of human beings, as well as the necessity to involve all members of society in carrying out tasks essential to preserving and improving the social and natural environment.
- *Acknowledgment of the importance of community space in the construction of social life*: The right to space of one's own means there needs to be greater community control over privately owned areas that have a high public usage, such as shopping centres. The managers of such space should be compelled to provide greater control and usage of such space by young people.
- *Greater community involvement in local decision-making, particularly public service provision*: The right to accountability is crucial in the case of institutions and agencies such as the police and social services. As

the wielders of legitimised violence in society and/or as the holders of considerable social power, public service providers must be fully accountable for their actions.

Such measures are central to a reform program that sees young people first and foremost as active, valued members of their communities. When society disfranchises the young and the communities of which they are a part, youth crime and greater state intervention in the lives of the young necessarily follow. This is a recipe for social conflict, not social empowerment.

6 | Indigenous young people

INTRODUCTION

In this chapter, we consider why Aboriginal and Torres Strait Islander young people have high levels of contact with juvenile justice agencies. To answer this question involves analysing many interlocking issues, including the history of colonisation, the links between welfare intervention and criminalisation, the effects of social and economic marginalisation, and the extent to which racism and discrimination are part of the regulatory practices of juvenile justice agencies.

We also consider some Indigenous responses to the current situation, including demands that Australia respect its international obligations in relation to its treatment of Indigenous young people, particularly in regard to the right of self-determination for Indigenous communities. Finally, there is discussion of the way Aboriginal and Torres Strait Islander people are dealing with youth who engage in offences within their communities.

To gain an appreciation of the extent to which Aboriginal people are caught up in the juvenile justice system, it is worth noting the level of over-representation in juvenile institutions.

Table 6.1 shows that the majority (54 per cent) of young people incarcerated in Australia are Indigenous. This is truly an extraordinary situation given that Indigenous people are 2.4 per cent of the nation's population. On the basis of specific youth populations, Indigenous young people are 26 times more likely to find themselves in detention than non-Indigenous youth.

New South Wales has the greatest number of Indigenous young people in a detention centre (110), although not the highest rate, which is in Western Australia (654 per 100,000). In every jurisdiction in Australia, the rate of incarceration for Indigenous youth is much higher than the non-Indigenous rate. The level of over-representation, as measured by the difference between the Indigenous and non-Indigenous rates, is greatest in Western Australia, where an Indigenous young person is fifty times more likely to be in a detention centre than a non-Indigenous youth.

In a submission to the National Inquiry into the Separation of Aboriginal and Torres Strait Islander Children from Their Families (referred to as NISATSIC throughout this text), the Australian Institute of Criminology (quoted in NISATSIC 1997:498) noted the following on the long-term trends of Indigenous juvenile incarceration.

TABLE 6.1   INDIGENOUS YOUNG PEOPLE 10–17 YEARS OLD IN DETENTION CENTRES IN AUSTRALIA, AS AT 30 JUNE 2004

STATE	INDIGENOUS NO.	NON-INDIGENOUS NO.	INDIGENOUS RATE*	NON-INDIGENOUS RATE	O/R**
New South Wales	110	88	372	13	28.6
Victoria	12	50	193	10	19.3
Queensland	55	36	201	9	22.3
Western Australia	91	27	654	13	50.3
South Australia	21	30	390	19	20.5
Tasmania	4	14	105	27	3.9
Northern Territory	8	2	74	14	5.3
Australian Capital Territory	5	11	620	32	19.4
Australia	306	258	313	12	26.0

*Rate per 100,000 of the respective juvenile populations
** Over-representation measured by comparing rates per 100,000

Source: Adapted from Veld and Taylor (2005:24–7).

There appears to be little cause for optimism in relation to the overrepresentation of Indigenous juveniles in detention. Of particular concern are the consistently high numbers of Indigenous youth in detention in NSW, Queensland and WA; the likelihood that very young detainees will be Aboriginal, the steady increase in the rate of detention of Indigenous juveniles in Australia; and, an apparent upward trend in the proportion of Indigenous remandees to sentenced Indigenous detainees. The level of overrepresentation of Indigenous juveniles in detention in Australia appears to be rising.

Data on the extent to which Indigenous young people are held in police custody also demonstrate the extent of intervention by juvenile justice agencies into the lives of Indigenous youth. The first National Police Custody Survey, conducted in 1995, showed that 40 per cent of all young people held in police custody during the survey period were Indigenous. The most recent National Police Custody Survey was conducted in 2002. It also showed that 40 per cent of young people in police custody were Indigenous. The rate of custody per 100,000 Indigenous young people was 1129 compared to a rate of 73.6 for non-Indigenous youth. The over-representation factor was 15.3 (Taylor and Bareja 2005:27).

Another way of understanding the extent of intervention into the lives of Aboriginal young people is to look at the number of juveniles who, at some time in their life, come into contact with juvenile justice agencies. South Australian research that has been able to consider this question includes Morgan's 1993 study, and Skryzpiec and Wundersitz's 2005 study of cohorts in South Australia, to which we referred in chapter 3. Morgan found that 55 per cent of Aboriginal youth born in 1972 had either appeared in a children's court or before a panel during their juvenile years, while Skryzpiec and Wundersitz found for the 1984 cohort that this had decreased somewhat to 44 per cent. When broken down by sex, Skryzpiec and Wundersitz found that 63.1 per cent of Aboriginal boys and 26.7 per cent of Aboriginal girls had formal contact with the juvenile justice system. These figures can be compared to 24.2 per cent of non-Indigenous boys and 7.3 per cent of non-Indigenous girls (Skryzpiec and Wundersitz 2005:5–6). The figures give some idea of the extensive formal contact of Aboriginal young people with children's courts.

The data presented above show the formidable nature of the dilemma. It is impossible to consider the operation of juvenile justice agencies without looking at the impact on Aboriginal and Torres Strait Islander young people. And it is impossible to understand the position of Indigenous young people in Australia without considering the extraordinary level of criminalisation directed at them.

HISTORY AND CULTURE

Indigenous societies in Australia had and continue to have very different cultural notions in relation to childhood and young people. Generally, there is not the same separation or exclusion of children from the adult world. Responsibility for children and young people tends to be allocated through the kinship system and the wider community (Sansom & Baines 1988; Watson 1989). Colonisation has wrought changes in these social patterns to varying degrees, either by disruption to whole communities and nations through expropriation of the land or through specific policies aimed at the removal of Aboriginal children and young people. However, it is also important to recognise that distinct cultural patterns relating to child rearing have remained intact.

There have been at least three modes of colonial and neocolonial intervention into the lives of Aboriginal and Torres Strait Islander young people during the last two centuries. These forms of intervention have included the period of open warfare and resistance, the period of 'protective' legislation, and the contemporary period of criminalisation. The different phases of colonial expansion over the last two centuries have meant that these modes of intervention have often overlapped. For instance, at the same time as the Native Mounted Police were engaged in open violence on the frontier in Queensland during the mid-nineteenth century, the Victorian government was introducing protective legislation.

During the period of open colonial warfare, Aboriginal young people were treated the same as Aboriginal adults. The massacres of Aboriginal tribal and kinship groups meant that Aboriginal young people were killed alongside other members of the group. Age was irrelevant at this level of state intervention: an overriding concern was Aboriginality. Aboriginal people were murdered because they were Aboriginal, that is, because they were the Indigenous people in possession of the land, and because they resisted colonial expansion. Thus, the accounts of various massacres by mounted and other police suggest that the killing was indiscriminate, and occurred throughout Australia at various times. It is also important to remember that conflict involving the killing of Aboriginal adults and children by punitive parties of Europeans went on at least until the late 1920s in the Northern Territory and Western Australia (Cunneen 2001a).

Missionaries and colonial administrators looked to children and young people as explicit targets for interventionist policies. Their policies were aimed at removing Aboriginal children from their families and kinship groups (Attwood 1989; Markus 1990). From the beginning of colonisation, 'those seeking to absorb Aborigines into European culture have looked to children as their best hope' (Markus 1990:22). Some of the earliest institutions established by Europeans to deal with the 'natives'—such as the Parramatta Native Institution, established in 1814—were designed to remove Aboriginal children from their families and communities (Brook & Kohen 1991). Indigenous young people had to be captured and sent to the institution, and those who were caught often absconded. The plan by Governor Macquarie to use the Institution to 'rescue' these children needs to be seen alongside the simultaneous use of punitive expeditions against the Indigenous peoples around the Sydney settlement (Brook & Kohen 1991).

By the mid-1800s, Victorian missionaries were concentrating on removing Aboriginal children from their families and placing them in dormitories. The policy was designed to prevent the continuation of Aboriginal culture (Attwood 1989:18). By 1850, all the religious missions that had come and gone in eastern Australia had tried to raise Aboriginal children separated from their parents (Edwards & Read 1988:xi).

PROTECTION LEGISLATION

The removal of Aboriginal children from their families and communities had started at the beginning of the colonial period. However, the scale of removal by the missionaries was relatively modest compared to what was achieved under the 'protection' legislation introduced in the late nineteenth and early twentieth centuries. The legislation legitimated police and Aborigines Protection Board intervention into Aboriginal life in an unprecedented manner. The removal policy was large-scale and designed to prevent Aboriginal children growing up to identify as Aboriginal adults (NISATSIC 1997). Read (1982) has estimated that more than 5600 Aboriginal children were removed in New South Wales alone between 1909 and 1969, when the legislation was repealed. More recently, the Stolen Generations Inquiry estimated that between one in ten and one in three Aboriginal children were removed between 1910 and 1970, depending on the period and location. Most Aboriginal families 'have been affected, in one or more generations, by the forcible removal of one or more children' (NISATSIC 1997:37).

A feature of protection legislation was the absence of procedural justice (Chisholm 1988:321). The New South Wales protection legislation of 1909 was found inhibiting by the Board because it had to be demonstrated before a magistrate that the child or young person was neglected before that child or young person could be removed. The children the Board wanted to remove were not neglected, and the Board failed in a series of court cases because it was unable to demonstrate neglect (Goodall 1990). The legislation was amended in 1915 to allow for the removal of Aboriginal children without a court hearing if the Aborigines Protection Board considered it to be in the interest of the child.

The change in the New South Wales legislation was achieved through a campaign aimed at convincing parliament and the public that generally Aboriginal parenting was negligent. The Board gained greater powers and, in the process, reinforced racist assumptions about Aboriginal parenting. These assumptions about the incompetence of Aboriginal parenting and child nurturing have permeated the views of police and others when carrying out Protection Board policies (Goodall 1990). It is also important to understand how this process of intervention and removal was gendered. Between 1900 and 1940, Aboriginal girls bore the heaviest impact of removal policies. The policy was targeted at pubertal girls, and in its early years some 80 per cent of the children removed were female, the majority of whom were 12 years and older (Goodall 1990).

The human devastation wrought by the regime has been told in Aboriginal autobiographies (Tucker 1977), by historians (Read 1982; Haebich 2001), in the reports of the Royal Commission into Aboriginal Deaths in Custody (Wootten 1989), and most recently in the *Bringing Them Home* report of the Stolen Generations Inquiry (NISATSIC 1997). The links between early removal on welfare grounds and later juvenile and adult criminalisation were clearly articulated in the reports of the Royal Commission into Aboriginal Deaths in Custody (see, for example, Wootten 1989).

When the Aborigines Welfare Board replaced the Protection Board in New South Wales in 1940, and procedures relating to Aboriginal children were brought under the Child Welfare Act, there was the introduction of the new complaint of being 'uncontrollable'. Aboriginal children were particularly susceptible to being found uncontrollable, and as a result being placed in corrective institutions. It would seem likely that the over-representation of Aboriginal young people in the general juvenile detention centres dates from this period. Welfare complaints such as those of uncontrollability were a significant factor in this process.

It is important to recognise the contemporary effects of the earlier policies of forced removals. These effects are manifold. Twice as many Indigenous people who were removed as children reported being arrested; those who were removed reported significantly poorer health (NISATSIC 1997:15). Almost one in ten boys and just over one in ten girls reported that they were sexually abused in children's institutions; one in ten boys and three in ten girls reported they were sexually abused in a foster placement (NISATSIC 1997:163). There has also been a range of complex trauma-related psychological and psychiatric effects that have been intergenerational. These relate to issues such as parenting skills, unresolved grief and trauma, violence, depression, mental illness, and other behavioural problems. A survey conducted by the Aboriginal Legal Service in Western Australia of 483 Aboriginal people who had been forcibly removed found that one-third had also had their children removed (NISATSIC 1997:226). Indigenous children are still significantly over-represented in contact with welfare agencies. Nationally, around 20 per cent of children in care are Indigenous. A significant proportion of such children are placed with non-Indigenous families, which is particularly the case for those in long-term foster care (Cunneen & Libesman 2001).

A further long-term consequence of the protection period has been the way it influenced the relationship between Aboriginal people and the police, welfare, and juvenile justice authorities. The police played an important role in the administration of the protection legislation (Cunneen 2001a:62–79).

Aboriginal people were not passive victims to the policies of child removal. In New South Wales, for instance, there were individual and community struggles against the Aborigines Protection Board. The removal of Aboriginal children was resisted by parents at every step (Goodall 1982:73).

Indeed, early Aboriginal political organisations in south-eastern Australia, such as the Australian Aborigines Progressive Organisation, drew attention to the forcible removal of Aboriginal children and the role of police as 'guardians' during the 1920s (Markus 1990:176–7). The struggle concerning the removal of Aboriginal children has now reached the stage where people are demanding compensation and reparations for the effects of removal. Individuals have sought compensation through the courts for the psychological, material, and cultural damage caused by removal and institutionalisation. There is also a widespread movement for reparations and a public apology (Cunneen 2001b).

When considering the protection legislation, both the Royal Commission into Aboriginal Deaths in Custody in 1991 and the Stolen Generations Inquiry in 1997 found that the policy adopted by governments that led to the forcible separation of Indigenous children from their families and communities constituted genocide within the international law meaning of the term (Wootten 1989:19; NISATSIC 1997:249–75). 'Genocide' is defined as those acts committed with the intent to destroy, in whole or in part, a national, ethnic, racial, or religious group, and includes forcibly transferring the children of one group to another group. The Inquiry also found that the policy breached prohibitions against racial discrimination. There were also a number of civil and criminal harms caused by the policy, including deprivation of liberty, deprivation of parental rights, abuses of power, breach of guardianship duties, assault, and sexual assault. It is significant that past policies by Australian governments towards Indigenous children and young people have been characterised in this manner. This is an issue that must be considered when attempting to understand the operation of contemporary juvenile justice policy.

WELFARE TO CRIMINALISATION

One might have expected a decrease in the incarceration rates of Aboriginal young people with the demise of protection legislation and assimilation policies, and with the more stringent separation of welfare matters. However, Indigenous young people continue to be incarcerated in juvenile institutions at extraordinary rates as a result of the processes of criminalisation.

There is evidence to suggest that Indigenous young people are more over-represented in the juvenile justice system than Indigenous adults are in the adult criminal justice system. For example, in Western Australia in 2004, 27 per cent of all adults arrested were Aboriginal, but 50 per cent of all juveniles arrested were Aboriginal (Ferrante et al. 2005:54). In addition, the level of over-representation actually increases as Aboriginal young people move through the system. Aboriginal youth are least over-represented in the least punitive stages of intervention, and most over-represented at the point of police custody or committal to an institution.

These processes are evident in the data from South Australia, as table 6.2 demonstrates.

TABLE 6.2   ABORIGINAL PARTICIPATION AT VARIOUS POINTS OF THE JUVENILE JUSTICE SYSTEM, SOUTH AUSTRALIA, 2004

	ABORIGINAL YOUNG PEOPLE AS A PERCENTAGE OF ALL YOUNG PEOPLE
Total interventions	20.5
Police cautions	13.8
Referred to Conference	17.8
Referred to court	26.1
Detention orders	30.9

Source: Office of Crime Statistics and Research (2005:20, 43).

As the Office of Crime Statistics notes, 'these figures indicate that they [Aboriginal young people] are under-represented in terms of the numbers receiving a formal caution and ... over-represented among those referred to the Youth Court' (Office of Crime Statistics and Research 2005:20).

Another way of considering this issue is to compare police interventions between Indigenous and non-Indigenous youth, as shown in figure 6.1 for New South Wales. The issue that stands out clearly is that Indigenous young

FIGURE 6.1   INTERVENTION TYPE BY INDIGENOUS STATUS, NSW, 2004

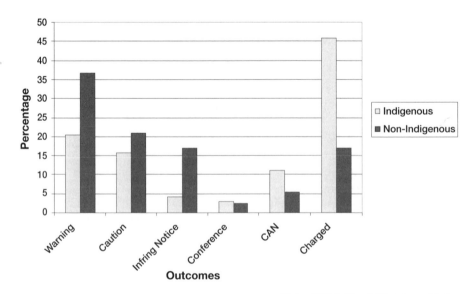

Note: CAN is Court Attendance Notice
Source: Cunneen & Luke (2006:64)

people are most frequently dealt with by way of arrest and charge, while non-Indigenous youth are more likely to receive a formal warning as an intervention.

Information from the New South Wales Department of Juvenile Justice (2005:11) also shows the greater penetration of Indigenous young people after police intervention. Indigenous young people comprised 29 per cent of youth conferencing referrals, 33 per cent of young people placed on community service orders, 37 per cent of those held in remand, and 45 per cent of those sentenced to detention.

The evidence above shows that Aboriginal young people are treated differently than non-Aboriginal in the juvenile justice system, tending to receive more punitive outcomes when discretionary decisions are being made—an issue we explore more fully later in this chapter.

CHARACTERISTICS OF OFFENCES COMMITTED BY INDIGENOUS YOUNG PEOPLE

One explanation for the over-representation of Indigenous young people in juvenile justice statistics is that they commit a greater number of offences, including more serious offences. We have already discussed in chapter 3 some of the difficulties in overly simplistic interpretations of the relationship between crime statistics and actual offending levels. We now turn to consider some of the specific aspects of Aboriginal offending patterns.

Studies in South Australia (Gale, Bailey-Harris, & Wundersitz 1990) and in New South Wales (Luke & Cunneen 1995) have compared offences between Aboriginal and non-Aboriginal young people. Statistics are now also more routinely available on differences in police apprehensions and court appearances between Aboriginal and non-Aboriginal youth in South Australia, Western Australia, and New South Wales. Studies from the late 1980s and early 1990s, and the more recent data, tend to show broadly similar patterns of offending for both Aboriginal and non-Aboriginal young people.

Table 6.3 shows police apprehensions of Aboriginal and non-Aboriginal young people by major-offence category for South Australia in 2004. For Aboriginal and non-Aboriginal young people, the greatest proportion of offences relate to property crime, including burglary, break and enter, stealing motor vehicles, shoplifting, and other forms of theft (59.8 per cent of Aboriginal offences and 47.6 per cent of non-Aboriginal offences in table 6.3). However, there are significant differences between the two groups in terms of the nature of the property offences. Aboriginal young people have a significantly greater proportion of more serious break-and-enter offences and motor vehicle theft than do non-Aboriginal young people.

There are a number of possible explanations for the difference. In commenting on the South Australian experience, Gale and her colleagues noted: 'it is not clear to what extent Aborigines actually commit more serious property offences or whether other factors and, in particular, police discretion in charging are at work' (1990:46). The authors cite examples of police discretion in charging where less serious offences, such as being unlawfully on premises and larceny, could be substituted for the more serious charge of break, enter, and steal. Similar results were found by Cunneen and Robb (1987:96).

TABLE 6.3   ABORIGINAL AND NON-ABORIGINAL JUVENILES:* POLICE APPREHENSION BY MAJOR-OFFENCE CATEGORY, SOUTH AUSTRALIA, 2004

OFFENCES	ABORIGINAL (%)	NON-ABORIGINAL (%)
Offences against the person		
Homicide/manslaughter	0.2	0.1
Serious assault	2.2	2.3
Other assault	9.8	9.5
Other offence against the person	0.9	1.4
Sexual offences	1.0	1.5
Subtotal	**14.1**	**14.8**
Robbery and extortion		
Armed robbery	0.3	0.5
Unarmed robbery and extortion	0.6	0.6
Subtotal	**0.9**	**1.1**
Fraud	0.2	1.3
Property offences		
Burglary and break and enter	19.8	9.5
Receiving/unlawful possession	4.5	2.6
Steal/illegal use of motor vehicle	10.2	5.8
Interfere with motor vehicle	1.6	1.1
Larceny from a motor vehicle	2.2	2.4
Shoplifting	10.2	10.4
Other theft	2.8	4.1
Property damage/environmental offences	8.5	11.7
Subtotal	**59.8**	**47.6**
Drug offences	1.0	2.4
Offences against good order		
Resist/hinder police	4.9	4.1

(table continued)

Table 6.3 continued

OFFENCES	ABORIGINAL	NON-ABORIGINAL
	(%)	(%)
Unlawful possession of weapon	1.5	1.8
Offensive behaviour/language	6.6	4.7
Graffiti	0.7	3.5
Other public order offences	5.6	7.2
Subtotal	**19.3**	**21.3**
Driving offences		
Drink driving	0.6	2.2
Dangerous driving	0.6	6.0
Driving unlicensed	1.0	2.2
Subtotal	**2.2**	**10.4**
Other offences	2.5	1.0
Total	**100.0**	**100.0**

* Excludes 469 apprehensions where Indigenous status was unknown.
Source: Adapted from Office of Crime Statistics and Research (2005:59).

As noted in chapter 3, offences such as break, enter, and steal, also have very low clear-up rates, these being sometimes as low as 5 per cent of reported crimes. The information available on the few offenders who get caught is particularly susceptible to policing practices, reporting levels in particular areas, and the relative sophistication or otherwise of the offenders. The greater proportion of Aboriginal young people in this category of offences may tell us more about detection by police than levels of criminality.

The issue of reporting and police detection is also connected to the issue of environmental opportunities. Gale and her colleagues argue that even if it could be shown that Aboriginal young people do commit more serious property offences, it would not demonstrate any greater 'criminality' because environmental opportunities and pressures influence the nature of property crime. In particular, urban–rural differences structure opportunities and pressures differently. Simple theft and shoplifting are primarily urban offences that are particularly associated with large shopping complexes. Similarly, there is increased likelihood of being caught either breaking into or attempting to break into a dwelling in a small country town or remote community.

The second most frequent group of offences are those related to public order. Table 6.3 shows that one in five police apprehensions are as a result of such offences. Within this category of good-order offences, it is public apprehensions for offensive language and offensive behaviour that cause the most pronounced differences between Aboriginal and non-Aboriginal young people. Such findings have been repeated in other studies

(Cunneen & Robb 1987; Gale et al. 1990:48; White 2002). These charges are also the ones most dependent on direct police intervention, with the potential for selective enforcement and the adverse use of police discretion. The use of offensive language and offensive behaviour charges against Aboriginal people have been consistently criticised for decades by researchers, academics, and members of the judiciary. It is widely acknowledged that these charges contribute significantly to the criminalisation of Aboriginal people and to poor Aboriginal—police relations.

The third significant group of offences are those that involve violence. Aboriginal and non-Aboriginal young people have similar proportions of offences in this category (14.1 per cent compared to 14.8 per cent). Earlier research has tended to show a greater proportion of Aboriginal matters involve violence. Gale and others (1990) argue that the differences might support the argument that poor living conditions lead to a greater degree of violence in Aboriginal communities. Or 'it may reflect nothing more than the well-documented fact that violence in an Aboriginal community is often an open and public event to which police are readily called' (Gale et al. 1990:48). Another factor to take into account is the large number of charges against Aboriginal people for assault of police (Cunneen 2001a:27).

Finally, it is worth noting that Aboriginal young people are proportionately less represented in the driving offence category.

Another way of explaining some aspects of the offending patterns of Aboriginal young people is to consider the extent to which the offences are specifically aimed at non-Indigenous targets or are responses and a form of resistance to non-Indigenous institutions and authorities. A number of researchers in the area have commented that some property offences, vandalism, assaults, or behaviour classified as offensive can be understood as a form of resistance (Brady 1985; Cunneen & Robb 1987; Cowlishaw 1988; Hutchings 1995). For instance, Brady notes that in the community where she did her research, the break-ins by Aboriginal young people were directed at school buildings, European staff houses, and the store (Brady 1985:116). Aboriginal organisations have also noted that resistance has become part of Aboriginal culture: 'What has been described as delinquency could also be regarded as acts of individual defiance. The scale and nature of Aboriginal children's conflict with 'authority' is reflective of a historical defiance' (D'Souza 1990:5).

A further way of explaining offending patterns and the over-representation of Indigenous young people in the juvenile justice system is to look at their socioeconomic or class position. In general, Aboriginal young people show very poorly on all social indicator scales in terms of health, housing, education, unemployment, welfare dependency, and so on (NISATSIC 1997:543–58). In this sense, they are substantially disadvantaged in comparison with non-Indigenous youth. Studies that have analysed juvenile offending have also discussed the socioeconomic disadvantage of Aboriginal young offenders (Cunneen & Robb 1987; Gale et al. 1990:56).

However, it is important not to paint an overly simplistic picture in relation to poverty and social disadvantage among Aboriginal young people. First, there is the need to understand 'social disadvantage' within the context of colonialism, dispossession, the destruction of an Aboriginal economic base, and specific colonial policies such as child removal (NISATSIC 1997). As many Indigenous people have stated, Aboriginal and Torres Strait Islander people are not simply a disadvantaged minority group in Australia. They are the Indigenous people of Australia whose current socioeconomic status derives from a specific history of colonisation, and whose political status as Indigenous people gives them a number of rights and entitlements. We will return to this issue later in this chapter.

Second, while in general terms there is a positive correlation between socioeconomic disadvantage, poverty, and juvenile offending rates, it is far too simplistic to say that Aboriginal young people actually offend more often and more seriously than their non-Aboriginal counterparts because they are more disadvantaged. The extent to which the offences of Aboriginal young people are greater in number than the offences of non-Aboriginal young people is difficult to assess because levels of surveillance (primarily policing) play such a fundamental role in producing the nature and number of offences brought into the juvenile justice system, as well as in selecting young people to be considered as offenders.

POLICE DECISION-MAKING

To a large extent, police determine which young people will enter the juvenile justice system, as well as the terms on which they enter. Police must continually decide whether to intervene and how to intervene. All the available evidence demonstrates that the discretionary decisions that are made work against the interests of Indigenous young people.

Deciding to intervene

There is considerable evidence that police intervene in situations (particularly 'street offences') involving Indigenous people, in often unnecessary and provocative ways. Two examples, both from Queensland, show the way in which initial police decisions to intervene can initiate a chain of events that have significant consequences for Aboriginal young people.

Daniel Yock died in police custody in Brisbane in November 1993. Nine Aboriginal young people (including Yock) aged between 15 and 18 years old were in Musgrave Park in Brisbane. The older youths had bought some alcohol and were drinking. A police van began circling the park, driving slowly around observing the youths. When the group left the park, the police van followed them slowly along the road. Although there was contradictory evidence, it appears that some verbal abuse and various gestures were directed at the police in the van, who called for assistance. Two other police cars responded. Police made a number of arrests for disorderly conduct. Yock was tackled to the ground by police during his arrest. He later died in the police van from a heart attack (Cunneen 2001a:134–5). The case provides an example of situations that the Royal Commission into Aboriginal Deaths in Custody sought to avoid in the future. Indeed, a number of the Commission's recommendations were designed to encourage police to think about whether intervention was necessary in such situations and which alternative types of intervention—rather than arrest and custody—might be appropriate.

In the incident involving Daniel Yock, police had considerable discretion as to how they might have proceeded. Perhaps a warning to the young people concerning their behaviour would have been sufficient. Perhaps no intervention was necessary, and police contact with the Aboriginal–police liaison officer would have been a better option. Irrespective of available alternatives, police decided to embark on the most confrontational approach possible in the circumstances.

The second case involves the so-called 'Pinkenba' incident, again in Brisbane. Three Aboriginal boys, aged 12, 13, and 14 years old, were detained by six police officers in a shopping mall in Fortitude Valley, Brisbane, some time after midnight on 10 May 1994. There was no evidence that the young people had committed any offence at the time they were detained. The boys were never charged with any criminal matter and were never taken to a police station. They were taken about 14 kilometres to an industrial wasteland and swamp in Pinkenba in three police cars.

The three youths later claimed they were terrorised by six police officers on the banks of a creek. The boys claimed that they were told to take off their clothes and shoes, and told they were going to be thrown in the creek. The children claimed that police threatened to cut off their fingers. Finally, the six police drove off and left the children to find their way back to Fortitude Valley at around 4 o'clock in the morning. The police officers were charged with unlawfully depriving the three Aboriginal young people of their liberty. The magistrate found that the police officers had no case to answer because there was no evidence that the children were held against their will. There was no dispute that they had been placed in the police cars, driven to Pinkenba, and 'dumped' there. The Pinkenba incident shows the way certain police are prepared to intervene and use a form of terror as a control tactic over what are perceived to be dissident and troublesome groups of Indigenous young people (Cunneen 2001a:114–16).

The problem of differential policing can also be seen in the way 'move on' and search powers have been used. The Crimes Legislation Amendment (Police and Public Safety) Act 1998 (NSW) provides police with the power to search for prohibited implements (knives, scissors, and so on) and to request young people in public places to 'move on' under certain conditions. An evaluation of the use of the legislation in areas with large Aboriginal populations shows wide disparity in its application. For example, police use of the 'move on' powers in Bourke and Brewarrina was at a rate thirty times higher than the state average (492.3 compared to 16.5 per 10,000 of population) (Chan & Cunneen 2000:32). Search powers of juveniles are also used more frequently in Aboriginal areas of the state. In Bourke and Brewarrina, nearly 90 per cent, and in Moree 95 per cent, of searches were 'unsuccessful', in the sense that the young person was not carrying a prohibited implement at the time (Chan & Cunneen 2000:39).

Cautioning

Throughout Australia, police have the power to issue a formal caution against a young person as an alternative to charging them with a criminal offence. If a caution is issued, the young person is not prosecuted and the matter does not proceed to court. Various studies over the last decade or so have found that Aboriginal young people do not receive the benefit of a police caution to the same extent as non-Aboriginal young people (Luke 1988; Luke & Cunneen 1995).

Luke and Cunneen found that in 1990 some 5.7 per cent of Aboriginal young people were cautioned compared to 12.9 per cent of non-Aboriginal young people. Even when young people had no prior record of either court appearance or caution, it was still found that Aboriginal first offenders throughout New South Wales had a greater chance of being prosecuted by police, and thus less chance of receiving a police caution. This pattern was particularly evident in country areas, where two-thirds of Aboriginal interventions occur (Luke & Cunneen 1995:19–21). This pattern of differential treatment was maintained when the offence type was held constant. For example, 91.2 per cent of Aboriginal first offenders apprehended for break-and-enter offences were charged rather than cautioned, while only 83 per cent of non-Aboriginal first offenders apprehended for the same offence were charged (Luke & Cunneen 1995:21). More recent data from New South Wales suggests this disparity remains, with 16 per cent of Indigenous interventions resulting in a caution compared to 21 per cent for non-Indigenous young people (see figure 6.1).

In Western Australia, Aboriginal youth comprised 50 per cent of young people arrested in 2004, but only 21 per cent of those who received a caution (Ferrante et al. 2005:50, 54). According to the Stolen Generations Inquiry, the cautioning system in Western Australia disadvantages Indigenous young people and 'further increases the disproportionately negative treatment they receive under the juvenile justice system'. The Inquiry was told that police were attaching conditions to cautions, although there was no provision to do so in the legislation, and, contrary to recommendation 240 of the Royal Commission into Aboriginal Deaths in Custody, police cautions were issued without the involvement of parents (NISATSIC 1997:514).

In Victoria, Indigenous young people are significantly less likely than non-Indigenous young people to receive an official police caution (11.3 per cent compared to 35.6 per cent of interventions in 1995–96). Thus, slightly more than a third of non-Indigenous youth apprehended by police avoid appearing in court (and thus avoid the likelihood of a conviction and criminal record). Such diversion benefits little more than one in ten Indigenous young people (Mackay 1996:9–10). In South Australia in 2004, 16.2 per cent of Indigenous youth apprehended by police received a police caution compared to 26.1 per cent of non-Indigenous youth. Thus, Indigenous young people were half as likely to receive a police caution as non-Indigenous young people (Office of Crime Statistics and Research 2005:82–3). Research in Queensland also found that Indigenous young people were about half as likely to receive a police caution compared with non-Indigenous young people (Cunneen 2005:46).

The failure to caution Aboriginal young people is particularly important, given that the majority of young people cautioned at the beginning of their contact with juvenile justice agencies do not go on to have further contact the juvenile justice system (Dennison et al. 2006:6).

Arrest, summons, or diversion

If police decide not to caution but to proceed against a young person, there is a range of options available. The specific options vary from state to state. However, the evidence shows consistently that Indigenous young people will invariably receive the most punitive option available. The use of a court-attendance notice (also referred to as a summons or notice to appear) is a less punitive way of bringing a young person before the courts on a criminal charge. Unlike proceeding by way of arrest, court-attendance notices do not involve being detained or having bail determined. Research also indicates that children's courts are more likely to impose custodial sentences on young people brought before them by way of arrest than on the basis of an attendance notice, because the process itself influences the court's view of the seriousness of the matter and the nature of the offender (Gale et al. 1990).

In many states, the evidence shows Aboriginal young people are more likely to be proceeded against by way of arrest and bail, and to be held in police custody, and less likely to be summonsed than non-Aboriginal youth. For example, in Victoria, Aboriginal young people apprehended by police were twice as likely to be proceeded against by way of arrest (46.6 per cent) compared to non-Indigenous youth (23.5 per cent) (NISATSIC 1997:514). In South Australia in 2004, 63 per cent of Aboriginal youth were brought into the juvenile justice system by way of arrest, compared to 42 per cent of non-Aboriginal youth (Office of Crime Statistics and Research 2005:19). In Western Australia in 2004, a higher proportion of non-Aboriginal youth

(31.5 per cent) were proceeded against by way of summons compared to Aboriginal young people (20.5 per cent). Conversely, a greater proportion of Aboriginal youth were arrested (Ferrante et al. 2005:46).

In New South Wales in 2004, 45.7 per cent of Aboriginal young people were proceeded against by way of arrest compared to 17.1 per cent of non-Aboriginal youth (see also figure 6.1) (Cunneen & Luke 2006:63). In Queensland, 36.9 per cent of Indigenous young people were proceeded against by way of arrest compared to 18.6 per cent of non-Indigenous youth (Cunneen 2005:46).

The evidence is very clear: throughout Australia, Aboriginal young people do not have the same benefits of less intrusive criminal justice processes. The one positive point to note is that in some jurisdictions, such as New South Wales and Queensland, there has been a general move over recent years to use attendance notices instead of arrest. However, the trend has not been universal. In South Australia, the practice of arresting juveniles instead of using other methods has been on the increase (Office of Crime Statistics and Research 2005:18).

Bail

Because Aboriginal young people are more likely to be proceeded with by way of arrest, they are more likely to face a bail determination. Two issues are important: first, whether bail will be refused and the young person held in custody, and second, if bail is granted, which conditions will be attached. In the first instance, Aboriginal young people are more likely than non-Aboriginal young people to be refused bail by police.

The Stolen Generations Inquiry found that, in Queensland each year between 1992 and 1995, more than half, and sometimes more than two-thirds, of overnight detentions of young people in police watch-houses involved Indigenous youth. The major reason for such detention was the refusal of bail (NISATSIC 1997:520).

In New South Wales, Aboriginal young people are nearly 40 per cent more likely to be refused bail. However, the difference is not as great when prior criminal records are controlled for, except in rural areas, where Aboriginal first offenders are still twice as likely to be refused bail as non-Aboriginal first offenders (Luke & Cunneen 1995:23–4).

The second issue of importance concerning bail is the nature of the conditions that are imposed when bail is granted. The Royal Commission into Aboriginal Deaths in Custody was particularly concerned with 'unreal conditions' that are imposed and then regularly broken. The result is that young people are recycled through the courts (Wootten 1991:353). Onerous and oppressive bail conditions may include curfews and residential requirements amounting to banishment (Cunneen 1994:139–41). Such conditions place enormous pressures on the young person and their family, and in the end may simply set up the young person for failure and further intervention.

It is clear that there has been a much more punitive attitude towards refusing young people bail and detaining them in custody. This change has had a very significant impact on Aboriginal young people in terms of detention. For example, in New South Wales between 2000 and mid-2005, the proportion of Indigenous young people on remand has risen from around 30 per cent to around 50 per cent of all remands over the period (Cunneen & Luke 2006:127). In Queensland in 2003–04, 84 per cent of all admissions to detention that involved Indigenous young people were as a result of being remanded in custody. For the period 2000–01 to 2003–04, only 16 per cent of Indigenous young people remanded in custody were subsequently sentenced to a custodial sentence (Cunneen 2005:79).

Conferencing

Youth conferencing has become a favoured option for diversion of young people from the courts in recent years, and various schemes exist in all Australian jurisdictions (see chapter 13). It is important to consider whether conferencing has provided Aboriginal young people with an effective diversionary option. The answer to this question is mixed.

Generally, the evidence shows that Indigenous young people are not being referred as frequently to conferences as non-Indigenous youth. A Perth survey in the first nine months of the scheme in Western Australia concluded that 'only a small percentage of Aboriginal young people are being referred to the Teams [for conferences]' (quoted in NISATSIC 1997:524). In 2004, Aboriginal young people were less likely to be referred to a juvenile justice team (for a conference) than non-Aboriginal youth. Aboriginal youth comprised 31.6 per cent of police referrals to a juvenile justice team. However, they comprised 42.1 per cent of young people appearing in court, and 50.5 per cent of young people who were arrested (Ferrante et al. 2005: 54; 107; 116).

In South Australia, some 14.7 per cent of interventions involving Aboriginal youth were referred to a conference, compared to 17.5 per cent of interventions involving non-Aboriginal youth (Office of Crime Statistics and Research 2005:82–3). As in previous years, the most recent data show that Aboriginal youth were also less likely to have a 'successful' conference than non-Aboriginal youth (23 per cent were unsuccessful compared to 11 per cent for non-Indigenous youth). The main reason was that Indigenous young offenders were less likely to attend the conference as required (Office of Crime Statistics and Research 2005:5).

In the first few years of the 1997 NSW Young Offenders Act, there were around 5000 referrals to conferences, about 20 per cent of which were Aboriginal young offenders. This was a slight improvement over the first year of operation of the Act, when Indigenous young people made up 14 per cent of referrals to conferences (Hennessy 1999). In more recent years, we have seen a further growth in the proportion of conferences involving Indigenous young people. In 2004–05, 29 per cent of referrals to conferences involved Indigenous young people (New South Wales Department of Juvenile Justice 2005:11). In fact, in 2004 an Indigenous young person was slightly more likely to be referred to a conference than a non-Indigenous young person. However, this also needs to be placed in the context of the relatively infrequent use of conferences compared to other interventions (see figure 6.1).

Significantly, in states where there is the possibility of the courts as well as police referring young people to a conference, there is less adverse discrimination. Courts appear more willing than police to refer Aboriginal youth to a conference, and this is reflected in the higher proportion of Aboriginal youth among court referrals to conferences in Western Australia (42.7 per cent of court referrals to conferences compared to 31.6 per cent of police referrals: Ferrante et al. 2005:116), in Queensland, 59 per cent of all Indigenous conference referrals were made by the courts compared to 45 per cent for non-Indigenous referrals (Cunneen 2005:62) and New South Wales (Hennessy 1999).

A further worrying trend in some jurisdictions is that police referrals to conferences are declining. Police referrals of young people generally fell by 21 per cent in Western Australia in 2004 (Ferrante et al. 2005:vii). In New South Wales, the proportion of police interventions resulting in a referral to a conference fell for both Indigenous and non-Indigenous young people between 2000 and 2004 (Cunneen & Luke 2006:63). In South Australia, referrals have declined slightly since 2002 (Office of Crime Statistics and Research 2005:26).

There are a number of issues that arise in considering the usefulness of conferencing programs for Indigenous young people. These can be summarised briefly as follows:

- There have been questions about the level of consultation with Indigenous people and Indigenous organisations in the establishment and operation of conferencing programs (Cunneen 1997; Blagg 1997; Kelly & Oxley 1999).
- There is the problem of referral: Who makes decisions about referring a young person to a conference? How important is a prior record in determining whether a young person is eligible for a conference? Which offences are included and excluded from the conferencing program?
- The general rule appears to be that the greater the police control of the referral process, the less likely Indigenous young people will benefit from the program, and the less likely will be the opportunity for Aboriginal communities to have a direct role in the decision-making processes around the conference.
- Issues may arise as to the cultural appropriateness of the conference format, the level of participation and satisfaction of Aboriginal people regarding the conference process, and the likelihood of successful completion of conference plans (Cunneen 1997; Urbis Keys Young 2001; Strang 2001).

While we have emphasised some of the problems with conferencing, we need to recognise some of the positive outcomes of conferences for Indigenous young people. Evidence on compliance is mixed. In Queensland, it suggests no difference in breach rates for Indigenous young offenders for failing to complete conferencing plans (Cunneen 2005:64), but in South Australia there is a 14 per cent lower compliance by Indigenous young people with undertakings from the conference (Office of Crime Statistics and Research 2005:35).

There appears to be no less satisfaction with the conferencing process by either Indigenous offenders or victims (Cunneen 2005:64, Trimboli 2000). Perhaps most importantly, research demonstrates that conferencing is more successful in reducing reoffending than the courts for both Indigenous and non-Indigenous participants (Luke and Lind 2002), although the impact is likely to be greatest among those with lower risks of reoffending (Hayes & Daly 2004).

COURT DECISION-MAKING

Aboriginal young people definitely have a greater chance of being sent to an institution than do non-Aboriginal offenders who appear in court. Similar evidence is available from most jurisdictions in Australia. For instance, in South Australia during 2004, 7.9 per cent of Aboriginal court outcomes resulted in a detention order compared to 4.6 per cent of non-Indigenous outcomes. While Indigenous youth comprised 23 per cent of finalised matters in the court, they received 31 per cent of detention orders (Office of Crime Statistics and Research 2005:38, 43, 141). In Western Australia in 2004, 20.7 per cent of Aboriginal court outcomes resulted in detention, compared to 8.9 per cent of non-Aboriginal court outcomes (Ferrante et al. 2005:109). In Queensland in 2004, Indigenous young people received five times the proportion of custodial sentences compared to non-Indigenous youth (Cunneen 2005:52). In New South Wales over the five-year period 2000–04, on average 16.7 per cent of Indigenous court outcomes resulted in a custodial order compared to 9.9 per cent of non-Indigenous court outcomes (Cunneen & Luke 2006:84).

The key question, then, is: Why does the children's court sentence proportionately more Aboriginal young people than non-Aboriginal young people to detention centres? The most simple explanation would be that Aboriginal young people commit more serious offences or offences that are more likely to attract a custodial penalty. There is some evidence to support this, in that Aboriginal young people have a greater proportion of matters relating to break-and-enter offences than non-Aboriginal youth, and these offences tend to be more likely to result in custodial sentences (Ferrante et al. 2005:113; Office of Crime Statistics and Research 2005:40).

However, South Australian research has shown that differences in penalties can remain even when specific charges are analysed. Thus, twice as many

Aboriginal young people compared to non-Aboriginal young people received a court outcome of detention for break, enter, and steal, and for assault and so on, meaning it was not the specific offence that determined the penalty (Gale et al. 1990:109). The major determinant influencing penalty was the young person's prior offending record. However, unemployment and family structure were also relevant, with those who were unemployed and living in a non-nuclear family situation being more likely to receive a custodial sentence. Research in New South Wales has reached similar conclusions in relation to the importance of prior criminal record. When differences in criminal record were controlled for, there were no significant differences in the percentage of Aboriginal and non-Aboriginal young people given a detention order (Luke & Cunneen 1995:27). A report by the New South Wales Judicial Commission confirmed that Indigenous and non-Indigenous youth received the same number and length of detention orders when factors including offence, prior record, bail, employment, and family structure were controlled for (Gallagher & Poletti 1998:17). However, Indigenous young people were also more likely to receive sentences at the harsher end of the sentencing scale, including community service orders.

At the other end of the sentencing scale, it has also been shown that Aboriginal young people are more likely to have their cases discharged. In South Australia during 2004, some 28 per cent of Aboriginal juvenile cases were found not guilty or otherwise discharged compared to 18 per cent of non-Aboriginal juvenile cases (Office of Crime Statistics and Research 2005:39). The large number of cases discharged by the court suggests that many of these young people should not have been sent to court in the first place, but rather should have been given some diversionary option. A further issue of importance is that, although a young person has an offence dismissed by the court, the matter is still regarded as proven, and the young person obtains a criminal record for the offence (Gale et al. 1990:107). Ironically, what may appear as a lenient court outcome still contributes to the overall process of criminalisation, particularly when we have identified prior record as such a key determinant in the decision of the court to incarcerate.

A further factor that may assist in explaining disparities in sentencing is different sentencing patterns between specialist children's courts (primarily in the large cities) and rural courts staffed by non-specialist magistrates. The majority of Indigenous young people appear in non-specialist country courts, so any sentencing disparity between courts disproportionately affects Indigenous children. For example, in Western Australia in 2004, 38 per cent of Indigenous court appearances were in the Perth Children's Court compared to 68 per cent of all non-Indigenous court appearances (Ferrante et al. 2005:107). The Stolen Generations Inquiry cited data from New South Wales that indicated that non-specialist country courts impose longer minimum terms and shorter additional terms of detention than specialist magistrates, and that in some country circuits, young people are about two-and-a-half times more likely to receive a custodial sentence than in specialist children's courts (NISATSIC 1997:532). More recent data would suggest that some rural courts are twice as likely to use detention orders for Aboriginal young people than specialist courts (Cunneen & Luke 2006:94).

Children's court magistrates are also guided when sentencing by the social background reports on young offenders, which are prepared by welfare and juvenile justice officers. Research indicates that social background reports are more likely to be ordered when the young person is Indigenous (Gale et al. 1990:101). From the late 1970s, there has been considerable criticism of the ethnocentric nature of the reports and of the psychological tests that were administered (Milne & Munro 1981). The reports gave free rein to express prejudices in relation to Aboriginal culture, family life, and child-rearing practices through descriptions of 'dysfunctional families' and 'bad home environment' (Gale et al. 1990:102; Carrington 1993:48).

The Stolen Generations Inquiry has summarised a number of points that are particularly relevant to understanding how the sentencing process might affect Indigenous young people differently from non-Indigenous young people.

- Indigenous young people brought before the courts are more likely to come from rural backgrounds, and are more likely to appear before non-specialist children's courts.
- Geographic isolation also raises issues of inadequate legal representation, the availability of non-custodial sentencing options, and harsher sentencing attitudes by non-specialist magistrates.
- In any one year, Indigenous young people appearing before the court are more likely to have been previously institutionalised, are less likely to have received a diversionary alternative to court, and are more likely to have a greater number of prior convictions. Each of these factors increases the likelihood of a custodial order.
- The existence of a prior record strongly influences the sentencing outcomes of the court. Indigenous young people tend to have a longer criminal history, and this results in a much higher use of custodial orders. Because intervention occurs at an earlier age with Indigenous children, they accumulate a criminal record at a much earlier age than non-Indigenous children.
- Earlier discrimination in the system results in Indigenous young people being less likely to receive diversionary options and being more likely to experience the most punitive processes and sanctions. These factors compound as the young person moves through the system. Apparently equitable treatment at the point of sentencing may simply mask earlier systemic biases.
- The current sentencing trend to treat 'repeat offenders' more harshly, either by way of mandatory sentences or through greater reliance on sentencing principles of retribution, general and specific deterrence, and community

protection, will have the greatest negative impact on Indigenous young people. They are precisely the group more likely to have longer criminal histories (NISATSIC 1997:528).

It should also be noted that the courts, at least in some jurisdictions, can take into account the cultural background of a young person as a relevant factor in sentencing. In South Australia, s. 3(3)(e) of the 1993 *Young Offenders Act* and in Western Australia, s. 46(2)(c) of the 1994 *Young Offenders Act* have these provisions. Amendments to the *Juvenile Justice Act 1992* (Qld) and the *Children's Court Act 1992* (Qld) enable elders and community justice groups to formally assist judges and magistrates when sentencing Indigenous young people. The extent to which such provisions are actually used is open to question.

ACCUMULATING A PRIOR RECORD

We have indicated the importance of a prior record in determining sentencing outcomes. A number of factors are important in understanding the accumulation of prior records among Aboriginal young people. Various studies have shown that intervention occurs earlier with Aboriginal young people and, as a result, Aboriginal young people receive a criminal record at an earlier age. For instance, in New South Wales, 26.4 per cent of Aboriginal young people who were cautioned or brought before the courts were aged 14 years or younger, compared to 18.6 per cent of non-Indigenous youth (Luke & Cunneen 1995:9). More recent data suggest little change in this profile. On average, between 2000–04, more than 9 per cent of Indigenous court appearances involved young people between the age of 10 and 13 years, compared to 4 per cent of non-Indigenous appearances (Cunneen and Luke 2006:89).

In South Australia during 2004:

- 10.8 per cent of Aboriginal young people apprehended by police were aged 12 years or younger, compared to only 6.6 per cent of such cases among the non-Aboriginal group (Office of Crime Statistics and Research 2005:16)
- 9 per cent of Aboriginal cases before the Youth Court involved children aged 12 years or younger, compared to 5.1 per cent of such cases among the non-Aboriginal group (Office of Crime Statistics and Research 2005:39).

Given what we have already established in relation to the adverse use of police discretion and the figures on early intervention, it is not surprising that Aboriginal young people develop extensive criminal records. Police decisions made at the time of apprehension have a compounding effect through the system. The most crucial decisions being made in relation to a young person are often being made by the least experienced police officers.

Police decisions about Aboriginal young people also need to be put in the much wider context of the relations between Aboriginal and Torres Strait Islander peoples and non-Indigenous Australian society. We have already indicated in this chapter the historical function of policing within a colonial context. It is also important to consider the function of policing within the contemporary context of neocolonial and post-colonial relations in Australia. This issue has been dealt with at length elsewhere (Cunneen 2001a).

The impact of a prior record can also be seen in the young age at which Indigenous youth find themselves in detention. For example, in New South Wales in 2004, 80 per cent of children aged between 10 and 14 years old in detention were Indigenous children (Cunneen and Luke 2006:123). We need to be particularly concerned with children under the age of 15 years in detention because of the long-term impact and increased likelihood that this group will become entrenched in the juvenile justice and then criminal justice system (Lynch et al. 2003).

RESPONSES TO THE OVER-REPRESENTATION OF INDIGENOUS YOUNG PEOPLE

The Royal Commission into Aboriginal Deaths in Custody dealt extensively with the issue of Aboriginal and Torres Strait Islander young people in the juvenile justice system. Many of the recommendations put forward were designed to deal with issues that are discussed in this chapter, and included an emphasis on the greater use of summons and diversionary mechanisms, realistic bail conditions, and the establishment of bail hostels. In addition, many of the general recommendations made in relation to police and custodial authorities, if implemented, would have a positive impact on Indigenous young people. A fundamental recommendation in relation to young people was that there be negotiation between authorities and Aboriginal communities on the causes of offending and the development of suitable responses.

Most states maintain that they are responding to Aboriginal over-representation in the system by implementing the Royal Commission recommendations, and by developing a range of programs, including the employment of Aboriginal community workers, the development of Aboriginal community responses, and specific alternatives to custody such as bail hostels, mentoring, and so forth. In Victoria, the government response has focused on providing local communities with resources to develop alternatives to incarceration under the Koori Justice Workers Program. Some local programs have included restoration of sacred sites, elders teaching culture and history, and Aboriginal artists providing tuition in music, dance, and painting (Ghys 1994).

Three responses in particular are worth discussing in further detail: mentoring, Aboriginal justice groups, and circle sentencing.

Mentoring

Juvenile justice authorities in New South Wales, South Australia, and Western Australia have developed mentoring programs for Aboriginal youth. Mentoring programs are premised on the belief that positive developmental relationships with adults will assist young people to stop offending. In New South Wales, the aims of the program are to:

- provide assistance and support to Aboriginal juvenile offenders
- assist young Aboriginal offenders to successfully reintegrate into their community by encouraging community members to participate in the provision of culturally appropriate services to young Aboriginal people
- encourage the active participation of local communities in the support of Aboriginal offenders through the community networking of mentors
- empower Aboriginal communities through their involvement in the rehabilitation process of young Aboriginal people
- improve the provision of departmental services to Aboriginal juvenile offenders.

Mentors act as role models where young people may lack a positive relationship with a significant adult. Aboriginal community members are recruited, trained, and matched with clients to provide mentor support.

Aboriginal justice groups

In many parts of Australia where communities have access to land, there has been the development of outstations. These outstations often provide the opportunity for Aboriginal elders to work away from settlements with young people convicted of offences. With support from local police and the visiting magistrate, Aboriginal elders have been able to devise and enforce sanctions for young offenders that are culturally appropriate. An offshoot of the outstation movement from the 1980s, as well as the ongoing demand for recognition of customary law, has been the development of Aboriginal community justice groups.

Aboriginal justice groups are known by various names, but basically comprise Indigenous people who meet around law and justice issues. These groups have been established in Queensland, the Northern Territory, and Western Australia. Often a major reason for the establishment of a group is perceived problems with juvenile offending. Perhaps the most extensively documented and evaluated program has been the Kowanyama Justice Group (KJG) in Queensland. In the early 1990s, pilot projects were commenced in Kowanyama, Pormpuraaw, and Palm Island. Each community planned a justice-group structure appropriate to the particular community, and each justice group identified issues of importance. The best-known and longest running of these community justice groups is the Kowanyama Justice Group (KJG).

The KJG was established in 1994 in response to increasing calls by Aboriginal communities for local autonomy and self-management in matters concerning law, order, and justice. It is run by a community-elected group of elders (usually including three men and three women elected by the three main groups in Kowanyama: the Kokobera, the Kokomenjena, and the Kunjen). Consultations between the KJG and the local Aboriginal community, local Aboriginal organisations, and key personnel from the non-Indigenous organisations ensure that the KJG deals with important social, cultural and legal concerns. The KJG became a registered corporation in June 2000, which has increased its autonomy at the local as well as regional level.

The aims of the KJG include, among other things, to:

- address the issues of law and order in a way that the community understands to be right and in accordance with its own customs, laws, and understandings about justice
- consult with magistrates about punishments and sanctions considered appropriate by Kowanyama people
- recommend and, if appropriate, carry out certain kinds of community punishments for offenders
- take action to prevent law-and-order problems in the community
- work closely with the Aboriginal Council to put appropriate by-laws in place and help the Council make Kowanyama a more peaceful place
- identify social and justice issues in the community
- provide recommendations and advice to government departments and the children's court and the Department of Family Services about juvenile justice matters
- provide advice and assistance in setting up programs and supervising offenders.

According to a Queensland Government Discussion Paper, since 1993 the situation in the pilot communities of Kowanyama and Palm Island has improved dramatically, with juvenile court appearances falling by two-thirds, and reductions in a number of offences (Premier's Department (Queensland) 1999:32).

In May 1999, the Department of Aboriginal and Torres Strait Islander Policy and Development (DATSIPD) released an Interim Assessment of the Community Justice Groups (DATSIPD 1999). The Interim Assessment found that community justice groups were 'developing innovative and successful strategies for tackling community justice issues by working within the formal justice system and within the community itself' (DATSIPD 1999:6). The Interim Assessment concluded that, 'despite their infancy, community justice groups are already achieving notable successes in various areas of community concern, according to their local priorities and their particular skills' (DATSIPD 1999:10).

Aboriginal courts and circle sentencing

Circle sentencing originated in Canada, based on Aboriginal dispute-resolution mechanisms. One of the key differences between sentencing circles and youth conferencing is that circles allow for input beyond the victim and offender to include community representatives more directly (see also chapter 13). Sentencing circles have been operating in parts of Canada since the early 1990s.

Although the procedures for circle courts may differ in limited ways from community to community, the usual process is that participants are welcomed to the circle by community Elders and the judicial officer, with each person then introducing themselves and explaining why they are there. The facts of the case are presented to the circle by the prosecutor, and the defence is then allowed to comment. The discussion that follows in the circle then usually focuses on:

- the extent of similar crimes in the community
- underlying causes of such crime
- an analysis of what life was like in the community before the increase in crime
- the impact of such crimes on community and family life
- the impact of such crimes on victims
- what can be done in the community to prevent this type of behaviour
- what must be done to heal the victim
- what must be done to heal the offender
- what will constitute the sentence plan
- who will be responsible for carrying out the sentence plan
- who will support the offender to ensure that the sentence plan is completed
- what support can be provided for the victim (New South Wales AJAC 2000).

Participants then develop a sentence plan, which the judge uses to sentence the offender. In New South Wales, a pilot project has commenced with Aboriginal adult offenders, and there has been some discussion on extending the model to children's courts.

Aboriginal courts (Koori Courts, Murri Courts, and Nunga Courts) have been established for both adult and juvenile offenders in Victoria, Queensland, and South Australia over the last few years. The courts typically involve an Aboriginal Elder or justice officer sitting on the bench with a magistrate. The Elder can provide advice to the magistrate on the offender to be sentenced and about cultural and community issues. Offenders might receive customary punishments or community service orders as an alternative to prison. Aboriginal courts may sit on a specific day designated to sentence Aboriginal offenders who have pleaded guilty to an offence. The court setting may be different to the traditional sittings. The offender may have a relative present at the sitting, with the offender, his or her relative, and the offender's lawyer sitting at the bar table. The magistrate may ask questions of the offender, the victim (if present), and members of the family and community in assisting with sentencing options (see Harris 2004; Marchetti & Daly 2004; Cunneen 2005).

As an example, the Brisbane Youth Murri Court sits once a month. Eligibility for the Youth Murri Court is that the offence is one within the jurisdiction of the children's court, and that the young person requests the matter to be determined by the Murri Court. There are usually two (and sometimes three) Elders who sit with the magistrate. The young person's family also have the opportunity to speak to the magistrate and the Elders. The Murri Court appears to have a positive impact on the young people who appear before it. Tony Pascoe, the magistrate at the Brisbane Children's Court, has stated:

> The [Youth] Murri Court sessions are intense, emotional occasions with a greater involvement of all parties. I can say that since the Youth Murri Court has been held that there has been a reduction in the number of serious offences committed by young Indigenous persons. There may be a number of reasons for this but I like to think that the Youth Murri Court, by involving the wider community in the concern for the futures of young Aboriginal and Torres Strait Islander people, has in some way contributed to this result (Pascoe 2005:7).

RECOMMENDATIONS FROM THE STOLEN GENERATIONS INQUIRY

The Stolen Generations Inquiry was completed seven years after the Royal Commission into Aboriginal Deaths in Custody, and its recommendations focus far more specifically on the importance of self-determination, as well as on greater controls over decision-making in the juvenile justice system. The Stolen Generations Inquiry noted that self-determination could take many forms, from self-government to the implementation of regional authorities, regional agreements, or community constitutions. Some communities or regions may see the transfer of jurisdiction over child welfare and juvenile justice matters as essential to the exercise of self-determination. Other communities may wish to work with an existing government department in ways that provide greater control in decision-making for Indigenous organisations. In any case, the level of responsibility to be exercised by Indigenous communities must be negotiated with the communities themselves (NISATSIC 1997:575–6).

Recommendation 43 is the key recommendation pertaining to self-determination. It requires that national legislation be negotiated and adopted between Australian governments and key Indigenous organisations to establish a framework of negotiations for the implementation of self-determination. The national framework legislation should adopt principles that bind Australian governments to the Act, that allow Indigenous communities to formulate and negotiate an agreement on measures best suited to their needs in respect of their children and young people, that ensure that adequate funding and resources are available to support the measures adopted by the community, and that ensure that the human rights of Indigenous children are respected. Part (c) of recommendation 43 authorises negotiations to include the complete transfer of juvenile justice´ and/or welfare jurisdictions, the transfer of policing, judicial and/or departmental functions, or the development of shared jurisdiction where this is the desire of the community (NISATSIC 1997:580). The Stolen Generations Inquiry's approach to self-determination provides a significant advance in serious discussion of the issue in Australia.

Recommendation 44 of the Stolen Generations Inquiry is concerned with the development of national legislation that establishes national minimum standards for the treatment of all Indigenous children and young people, irrespective of whether those children are dealt with by government or Indigenous communities and organisations.

The Inquiry set out a number of national minimum standards that provide the benchmark for future developments. Standards 1–3 consider principles relating to the best interests of the child. Standard 4 sets out the requirement for consultation with accredited Indigenous organisations thoroughly and in good faith when decisions are being made about an Indigenous young person. In juvenile justice matters, this includes decisions about pre-trial diversion, bail, and other matters. Thus, all discretionary decisions relating to Indigenous young people need to be made in consultation with Indigenous organisations.

Standard 8 sets out fifteen rules relating to juvenile justice decision-making. Rules 1 and 2 seek to minimise the use of arrest and maximise the use of summons. Rule 3 requires notification of an accredited Indigenous organisation whenever an Indigenous young person has been arrested or detained. Rule 4 requires consultation with the accredited organisation before any further decisions are made. Rules 5–8 provide protection during the interrogation process. Rules 9–12 ensure that Indigenous young people are not denied bail and that detention in police cells is eliminated except in truly exceptional circumstances. Rule 13 prioritises the use of Indigenous-run community-based sanctions. Rule 14 establishes the sentencing factors that need to be considered. Rule 15 requires that custodial sentences be for the shortest possible period, and that reasons for such sentences must be stated in writing.

The development of national minimum standards recognises the need for immediate change in the level of control by Indigenous communities and organisations in the decisions that affect the future of their children and young people. Unfortunately, there has been an inadequate response to the recommendations of the Stolen Generations Inquiry (Cunneen & Libesman 2001).

CONCLUSION

During the 1980s and early 1990s, many Indigenous communities grappled with developing alternative mechanisms for dealing with young people who offend. These alternative Indigenous mechanisms have tended to be localised, inadequately funded, and without any legislative base. However, a key principle in these developments has been implementing self-determination at the grassroots level. Communities have continually sought their own solutions to the problem of the over-representation of Indigenous young people in the juvenile justice system (Dodson 1995, 1996; NISATSIC 1997).

Aboriginal and Torres Strait Islander peoples have certain rights and entitlements as the Indigenous people of Australia. These rights are increasingly recognised in international law, and in particular and most importantly, the right to self-determination. Further rights specifically in relation to Indigenous children can be found in the United Nations Convention on the Rights of the Child. A fundamental area for the application of self-determination must be in that of juvenile justice policy. The development of self-determination in this area must include the right to determine basic questions in relation to law, enforcement strategies and the application of sanctions.

At the moment, there is little recognition of the principle of self-determination in the delivery of juvenile justice services for Aboriginal young people. To a large extent, the dominant rhetoric is one of 'disadvantage'—that is, Aboriginal and Torres Strait Islander young people are disadvantaged by the system. The former Aboriginal and Torres Strait Islander Social Justice Commissioner, Mick Dodson, has argued that policies and programs that derive from a perception of 'disadvantage' often have the result of reinforcing the recipients' powerlessness. They are perceived to have been given justice rather than to have received their rights and entitlements (Dodson 1993). Clearly, in the context of juvenile justice, the implied right of Indigenous people is to develop their own systems of social regulation. At present, the best we have are essentially 'hybrid' systems working at the interface of the traditional juvenile justice system, such as community justice groups and Aboriginal courts.

7 | Ethnic minority young people

CHAPTER HIGHLIGHTS

Introduction
Ethnic minority young people
Ethnicity and criminal justice
Ethnic minorities and the police
Public spaces and ethnic youth gangs
Sociolegal issues and institutional responses
Conclusion

INTRODUCTION

Popular images of youth criminality and deviance have increasingly taken on a racialised character beyond the long-standing references to Indigenous young people. That is, newspaper and television reports frequently stress the ethnic background of the alleged perpetrators of crime, and youth 'gangs' more often than not are identified as 'ethnic youth gangs'. Such images shape popular perceptions of which groups of young people are more likely than others to engage in offending behaviour. They also instil a sense that criminality has distinct 'ethnic' overtones, and as such is intrinsically related to particular social groups rather than being due to other factors such as economic adversity. It is the specific group that is seen to be the problem, while the problems experienced by any particular group or community are ignored or downplayed.

Although Australia is one of the most diverse and polyethnic societies in the world, it is only in recent years that greater academic, community, and government concern has been directed at issues relating to ethnic minorities in the criminal justice system. With many different nationalities, cultures, and ethnic groups represented in the Australian mosaic, the area of 'race and ethnicity' certainly warrants more attention within criminology than it has hitherto received. This is also true in the specific area of juvenile justice.

The aim of this chapter is to consider the position of ethnic minority young people in Australian society, and their broad relationship to the institutions of criminal justice. The chapter begins by providing a brief discussion of 'ethnic minority youth' as a social category, and the importance of understanding the specific social context and social conditions under which diverse groups of young people experience life in Australia. This is followed by an examination of how ethnic minority young people are perceived by, and interact with, officials and agencies of the criminal justice system. The chapter concludes by considering various measures that are needed if the specific interests of ethnic minority youth are to be addressed in the society at large, as well as within the criminal justice system.

ETHNIC MINORITY YOUNG PEOPLE

Australia comprises people from more than a hundred different countries, speaking more than 150 different languages. Attempts to quantify 'ethnicity' can be rather complicated, however. Do we assign ethnicity on the basis of language spoken, cultural heritage, physical appearance, religion, and/or migration status? Is ethnicity an objective social characteristic ('you are who you are') or does it involve subjective elements ('you are who you say you are')? These are important questions, and how we answer them, will greatly influence the type of information and statistical data that are gathered, and the analytical generalisations being made about certain groups.

One way in which to deal with ethnicity is to compile classification lists based upon country of origin. That is, we might examine immigration trends over time and document from which countries people originate. As a social identifier, however, such classification is imprecise, and does not show differences within either the country of origin or the country of destination. Ethnicity is not simply about country of origin, language, or skin colour. For example, in Vietnam there is a variety of ethnic groups, including ethnic Chinese, Vietnamese, Montagnards, and Khmer. In Israel, the Jewish community comprises Europeans, Africans, and people from the Middle East, all of whom vary greatly in terms of appearance, language, and spiritual expression.

For the present purposes, while acknowledging the heterogeneity of diverse national and 'ethnic' groups, the term 'ethnic minority' will be used to describe those people who are non-Anglo-Australians who are non-Indigenous (see Zelinka 1995). It includes non-English-speaking background (NESB) migrants, but is not exclusive to this group, especially since many 'visible minorities' may come from regions or families where English is spoken (such as India, Sri Lanka, or the Pacific Islands).

Although Australia is ethnically, religiously, and culturally diverse, it is nevertheless the case that it remains dominated by the majority Anglo-Australian population, and that particular non-Anglo groups thereby have 'minority' status (Guerra & White 1995). This is reflected in a number of different ways, in terms of culture, economic patterns, and institutional arrangements (see Jamrozik, Boland & Urquhart 1995). Visible difference (relative to the white Anglo-Australian 'norm') is a key factor in membership of an ethnic minority. Membership is a status conferred both by self-identification and by the dominant culture. For example, Chinese people have been settling in Australia since at least the mid-1800s. Their descendants may simply refer to themselves as Australian: their language is English, their home life may be 'typically Australian'. However, strangers may still confront them with questions such us, 'Where are you from?', and in casual encounters they may be treated as though they know Chinese culture but are unfamiliar with Australian mores.

To appreciate fully the situation of ethnic minority young people, analysis also has to be sensitive to the diversity of backgrounds and life circumstances of different young people. It is worth noting, for example, that the migrant experience varies considerably. It depends upon such factors as time period of migration (job opportunities in the 1950s versus high unemployment in the post-1974 period), place of origin and circumstances of migration (war refugees, flight from an authoritarian regime), relationship between first and subsequent generations (conflicting values), availability of appropriate services (English-language courses), and government policies and rhetoric towards specific classes of migrant (business migrants, asylum seekers). Particular groups of ethnic minority young people, such as unattached refugee children, are more likely to experience disadvantage, for instance, than young people with well-established family and community networks.

To elaborate, we might consider the migration background of groups that were examined as part of a major study of 'ethnic youth gangs' (White et al. 1999). The bulk of Vietnamese migration to Australia took place between 1975 and 1985, and consisted of four 'waves' of migration, beginning with those who were educationally, socially, and economically advantaged, and subsequently including those who were destitute and who had been subjected to years of living in refugee camps. Most of this migration consisted of refugees, although the resources and circumstances of specific groups of immigrants varied considerably. More recent migration has generally been under the family migration program. Vietnamese settlement has tended to be spatially concentrated in particular suburbs, predominantly in Melbourne and Sydney. The Vietnamese community is one of the youngest—in terms of age profile—in Australia. Problems faced by many recent Vietnamese immigrants have included language difficulties, social dislocation, reduced social and economic opportunities, poverty, and lack of adequate qualifications.

By way of contrast, the migration of Turkish people began en masse in 1967. Most Turkish migrants settled in Melbourne and Sydney, in particular residential areas. Turkish migration was generally for employment purposes, and was initially perceived by many immigrants as a 'guest worker' experience.

The Turkish community has placed great emphasis on maintaining the Turkish language, community values, and Islamic religion. By the mid-1980s, the children of Turkish immigrants were exhibiting much higher educational participation and school retention rates than had previously been the case. Problems faced by many Turkish immigrants have included language difficulties, maintenance of distinctive ethnic identity and religious affiliation, disadvantages in the labour market, and economic hardship.

We might also consider the specific circumstances of another group as well. The Pacific Islander community comprises mainly Polynesian people, including Maoris, Samoans, and people from Fiji. There are about 100,000 Pacific Islanders in Australia, from a diverse range of islands and cultural backgrounds. Immigration has generally been due to economic and social factors, such as the search for employment and overpopulation in the homeland. The social structure of Pacific Islander communities tends to emphasise kinship networks and reciprocal obligations within a highly stratified system that has clear hierarchies of status and control. Problems faced by many Pacific Islander immigrants relate to feelings of dislocation and isolation, unemployment, and the tensions between the norms and expectations of Pacific Islander ways of life and the wider Australian social and economic culture.

A more recent addition to the Australian social landscape are migrants from the Horn of Africa. For instance, there are now a few thousand Somali people who have immigrated to Australia. The majority are refugees who have fled drought and war. Most Somalis are Sunni Muslims, and most speak Somali complemented by Arabic and English. The Somali migrant population is relatively young, in terms of average age. Problems experienced by Somali refugees include difficulties with language, low occupational skill levels, inability to find employment, and economic disadvantage. A particularly important problem relates to the trauma associated with famine and war in their homeland, and with the migration process itself.

It is important to realise that the largest category of migrants is the Anglo-Australian, which consists of people from the British Isles and selected English-speaking countries with European ancestry. The Anglo-Australian community is diverse, and includes people from a range of ethnic and national backgrounds, such as Scotland, England, Ireland, the USA, Canada, New Zealand, and South Africa. It is the dominant group in Australia in terms of numbers, and in terms of socioeconomic and political status and power. Problems faced by Anglo-Australian immigrants, and their descendants, tend not to be linked to ethnicity *per se* but to processes of class division and gender inequality in general.

Except for the Anglo-Australian population, issues of racism and discrimination feature prominently when identifying problems associated with settlement processes of the ethnic minority groups, and with their longer-term position and status in Australian society. The dominant policy framework within which issues of immigration and resettlement have been constructed remains that of 'multiculturalism', although the precise meaning of the concept has changed over the years (Jakubowicz 1989; Castles, Kalantzis, Cope & Morrissey 1990; Jamrozik et al. 1995; Hage 1998). Ostensibly, Australia has adopted principles of participation and entry based upon non-discriminatory practices. This extends to the area of juvenile justice, as well as to other public service domains.

At present, there are great pressures on multiculturalism as both a concept and a form of practice. These stem partly from tensions associated with the 'race debate', which was heightened by the election of independent candidate Pauline Hanson to the federal Senate in 1996. They are also associated with significant changes over the last decade in immigrant settlement policy, welfare provisions, bureaucratic reorganisation, and government benefits in the broad migrant services area. Perhaps the most significant source of difficulty and consternation with regard to multiculturalism today, however, relates to the 'war on terrorism' and the symbolic division of the world into the so-called Western and Muslim civilisations. Tragic events and propaganda wars reflect and reinforce serious divisions within Australian, and indeed, global, society, and these divisions are likewise evident at the level of neighbourhood politics and social relationships. For particular groups of young people, especially those identified as 'Middle Eastern', questions of social identity and social belonging are paramount and more important than ever before. How that these widespread and more generalised social processes—of integration, incorporation, exclusion, and vilification—get translated into specifically criminal justice concerns is one of the subthemes of this chapter.

ETHNICITY AND CRIMINAL JUSTICE

Media images and treatments of particular ethnic minority young people are generally very negative. This is especially the case today with respect to groups such as Vietnamese, Lebanese, and Pacific Islander youth, although many other groups, such as Italian young people and Latin American young people, have also felt singled out for negative and stereotypical media treatment (Foote 1993; White et al. 1999; Collins et al. 2000; Poynting et al. 2004). Which group or who, specifically, is the object of 'moral panic' can, to some extent, be linked to particular moments in Australian immigration history— in the 1970s, it was the Greeks and Italians who dominated the headlines; the 1980s saw 'Asians' as the 'folk devils' of the mass media, and by the 1990s, the problem began to feature those with 'Middle Eastern appearance'. In the early 2000s, it is Arabic and especially Muslim young people who constitute the key targets of media preoccupation. More generally, researchers have commented on how certain ethnic minority youth are often presented as being homeless, on drugs, members of gangs, school dropouts, and basically 'bad' and 'dangerous' (Pe-Pua 1996, 1999). Indeed, young people themselves see the media as a constant source of biased, sensationalist, and inaccurate information about their lives and their communities (Maher, Nguyen & Le 1999; White et al. 1999). It is frequently the case as well that particular events are seized upon by the media to reinforce the 'ethnic' character of deviancy and criminality in ways that stigmatise whole communities (Noble, Poynting & Tabar 1999; Poynting 1999; Poynting, Noble & Tabar 2001). The title of a recent book—*Bin Laden in the Suburbs*—tells us much about how distortions in the media are often constructed around particular images of evil, which are then transposed onto and associated with specific population groups (see Poynting et al. 2004).

The presence of identifiable groups of young people in public places has been especially disturbing for some sections of the media. Frequently, gatherings of ethnically identifiable young people have been publicly associated with images that are negative, dangerous, and threatening. The media have tended to emphasise the 'racial' background of youth groups—and their presumed criminality—to the extent that, for example, 'young Vietnamese' or 'young Lebanese' becomes equated with 'gang member'. The extra visibility of young ethnic minority people feeds the media moral panics over gangs, as well as bolstering a racial stereotyping based upon physical appearance (White 1996d).

It is notable, however, that until recently ethnic minority youth did not feature prominently, if at all, in official crime statistics (see Cunneen 1995; Easteal 1997). The existing data on ethnicity and crime tended to show a low incidence of criminal involvement for ethnic minority youth, and low rates of involvement with the criminal justice system. For example, Easteal's (1989) study of young Vietnamese refugees in New South Wales in the 1980s demonstrated that these young people were likely to be underrepresented in criminal statistics and behaviour. This appears to be changing in some jurisdictions, for both adults and juveniles, if we take country of origin as one indicator of 'ethnicity' (see Mukherjee 1999).

For example, in New South Wales there has been an increase in detention figures for Indo-Chinese, Pacific Islander, and Lebanese young people (Cain 1994a; Standing Committee on Social Issues 1995). Questions have been raised as to whether the rise in numbers of Vietnamese young people in detention has been due to increased police targeting of these youth, is an actual reflection of a rise in criminality, or is an increase specifically in involvement with drugs (Easteal 1997; Bhathal 1998). Analysis of social indicators in relation to specific groups of ethnic minority young people (such as refugees) does, however, point to two major trends (White 1996d:309): 'The first is that increasing numbers of these young people are being marginalised economically and socially from the mainstream institutions of school and work. The second is that these same people are increasingly coming to the attention of the criminal justice system. That is, they are subject to a growing criminalisation of their activities, as partially reflected in the statistics regarding detention rates.'

The increased frequency of involvement with the criminal justice system, particularly in relation to drug offences and use of violence, means that heightened media attention on ethnic young people does bear some relation to what is occurring at a grassroots level.

It needs to be stressed that in many respects ethnic minority youth in general are doing better than their Anglo-Australian counterparts, as evidenced for example in the area of educational achievement (National Youth Affairs Research Scheme/Australian Bureau of Statistics 1993; Lamb 1994). Notwithstanding, it is also salient to note that many ethnic minority youth, particularly those living in working-class areas where the manufacturing industry has collapsed or declined (and hence affected the livelihoods of their parents and their own employment prospects), are faced with bleak job futures. This is exacerbated by factors such as inadequate schooling facilities and resources, and the commodification of leisure and recreation, which means young people need the means to pay if they want to play. The problem, therefore, is inextricably linked to class situation, although ethnicity adds a layer of complexity to the lived reality of these young people.

The extent of the shifts in criminal justice involvement by some ethnic minority young people do not warrant the intensity and universalising tendencies apparent in much media coverage, which tends to provide negative images of ethnic minority people as a whole. The problems associated with police–ethnic-minority youth relations have probably contributed to this as well.

ETHNIC MINORITIES AND THE POLICE

There is now extensive literature on the relationship between police and ethnic minority young people in Australia (see, for example, Mass 1993; Guerra & White 1995; Pe-Pua 1996; Maher, Dixon, Swift & Nguyen 1997). The tension between the two groups is fostered by a range of stereotypical images pertaining both to young people ('ethnic youth gangs') and to the police (repressive figures associated with authoritarian regimes). Several studies and reports have highlighted the lack of adequate police training, especially cross-cultural training, in dealing with people from NESBs, particularly refugees and recent migrants (Chan 1994, 1997; NSW Office of the Ombudsman 1994). At any rate, the relationship between the police and young people with South-East Asian, Lebanese, and Pacific Islander backgrounds has been particularly negative in recent years.

A New South Wales study, for example, found that ethnic minority young people were more likely than other groups of Australian young people (with the exception of Indigenous people) to be stopped by the police, to be questioned, and to be subject to varying forms of mistreatment (Youth Justice Coalition 1994). Young Vietnamese Australians in Melbourne and Sydney have complained about unfair treatment, and racism, in their dealings with the police (Doan 1995; Lyons 1995). This is confirmed in a recent study of encounters between police and young people of Asian background in Cabramatta, which found that the young people (who were heroin users) were subject to routine harassment, intimidation, 'ethnic' targeting, racism, and offensive treatment (Maher et al. 1997). Furthermore, there were a number of specific problems relating to cultural issues, in that 'Crucial norms of respect, shame and authority are routinely transgressed by police officers' (Maher et al. 1997:3). In the context of police rhetoric about adopting harm-minimisation policies in dealing with drug issues, these coercive strategies were viewed by the young people as counterproductive.

In a study of Vietnamese youth and police relations in Melbourne, Lyons (1995:170) identified a range of factors that influenced the relationship between the young people and authority figures. These included:

- unwarranted targeting and harassment of young people in public spaces
- high incidence of body search procedures used by police
- denial of young people's legal rights
- verbal, psychological, and physical mistreatment by police
- non-reporting of police mistreatment through formal channels
- general lack of respect towards each other, demonstrated by subtle and overt means.

Lyons (1995) points out, as well, that ethnicity raised additional issues that complicated police–youth encounters. These included:

- police tendency to stereotype Indo-Chinese youth
- a lack of command of the English language
- a lack of knowledge of Australian law and legal rights, which influenced the nature of contact
- police prejudice.

Not only did the young people feel they were being treated as 'gangsters' by the police, but they also objected to the ways in which certain other stereotypes intruded into their interactions. For example: 'Vietnamese youth are troublemakers unless they clearly conformed to the "brainy Asian" stereotype which demonstrated respect for authority' (Lyons 1995:171).

An important feature of police–youth contact was the way in which misinterpretation of certain cultural traits could unintentionally exacerbate the negative aspects of an encounter. For instance, Lyons (1995:167–8) describes how 'yes' has many different meanings for Vietnamese youth: it may be used when the young person does not actually understand what is being said, or may be used so as not to offend an authority figure, or to avoid confrontation. Culturally specific forms of facial expressions, eye contact, and arm gestures were also identified as sources of possible misinterpretation, and thus possible conflict.

Police–youth relations are circumscribed by the status and the position of ethnic minority youth as young people, and by their standing as members of particular ethnic minority groups. Police perceptions of young people in general will colour how and when police intervene in young people's lives. Their perceptions and attitudes towards particular ethnic minorities likewise have an influence on how they use their discretion, and the manner in which they will intervene in relation to particular individuals and groups.

In a Melbourne study involving interviews with a variety of ethnic minority youth, the police were often seen to play a pivotal role in the affairs of the young people (see White et al. 1999). In summary, the study found that:

- Vietnamese young people were very critical of the role of the police in their lives, saying that the police targeted them unfairly and that the nature of the contact was generally unpleasant
- Turkish young people criticised the police for two main reasons: first, the young people said they were hassled, searched on the street, or threatened by the police; second, when police intervened, including in those instances when a crime had been committed, they did not treat the young people with respect or dignity, but treated them badly
- most of the Pacific Islander young people complained of police harassment, and described their contact with the police as generally bad
- the Somalian young people were conscious of the issue of police harassment, and the negative reputation of the police had an impact on their movements outside the parental home; however, in practice few had had direct contact with police
- most of the Latin American young people had had some kind of contact with the police, and of this contact most said that it had been good and that they had been treated well. Some of them objected, however, to being questioned, searched, or threatened by the police on the street.

The police were also prominent in the lives of Lebanese young people in western Sydney, with bad and intrusive experiences tending to dominate local stories and perceptions (Collins et al. 2000).

A negative interaction between ethnic minority young people and the police breeds mistrust and disrespect. A minority of people in any community is engaged in particularly antisocial behaviour and criminal activity. For example, Cain (1994a) estimates that only 3 per cent of Vietnamese young people in New South Wales commit criminal offences. The problem is that prejudicial stereotyping often leads to the differential policing of a whole population group. This not only violates the ideals of treating all citizens and residents with the same respect and entitlement to rights, but also can inadvertently lead to further law-breaking behaviour.

For example, as victims of racist violence, ethnic minority young people may be reluctant to approach state authorities for help when these same figures have done little to engender confidence or respect. As with similar cases overseas, the lack of police protection can lead some young people to adopt the stance that 'self-defence is no offence' and thus to arm themselves against racist attacks (Edwards, Oakley & Carey 1987). Concern about the carrying of weapons not only justifies even more intense police intervention, but it also feeds media distortions about the problem of 'ethnic youth gangs'. Clearly, there is a need for concerted effort to modify existing police practices and to rethink community policing as it applies to ethnic minority young people (see Chan 1994, 1997).

PUBLIC SPACES AND ETHNIC YOUTH GANGS

The notion of 'ethnic youth gangs' has featured prominently in media reports of youth activities, especially since the early 1990s. Around the country, tales are told of ethnic-based or multiracial groups of young people being involved in a wide range of illegal, criminal, and antisocial activities (see, for example, Healey 1996). Allegations of a 'Lebanese youth gang' participating in a drive-by shooting of a police station in Sydney in 1998 is just one example of the kind of media coverage and public outcry relating to particular ethnic minority youth in Australia today. Police and others have also expressed concern that the relationship between ethnic minority young people and the police is deteriorating at the street level. This was reflected in the first National Summit on Police–Ethnic Youth Relations, held in Melbourne in 1995, and is a topic consistently raised in academic and community reports on police–youth interaction (Youth Justice Coalition 1994; White 1996b; Maher et al. 1997).

Although media and police reports seem to indicate that 'ethnic youth gang' activity appears to be on the rise, there has in fact been very little empirical information regarding the actual activities of ethnic minority young people (but see Guerra & White 1995; Pe-Pua 1996). Even less is known about those ethnic minority young people allegedly involved in drug-related activities and other kinds of offending behaviour. Concern has been raised regarding state responsibilities to collect relevant data on these issues (see Cunneen 1995; Collins et al. 2000), but to date there has been a dearth of systematic statistical material regarding welfare, criminal justice, and employment trends in relation to these young people. The limited work that has been undertaken in the area of ethnic minority group experiences has nevertheless indicated that there are strong social reasons and economic forces that are propelling increasing numbers of these young people into extremely vulnerable circumstances (Guerra & White 1995). A number of factors are seen to affect their social development and integration into mainstream Australian society, including, for example, conflicts between their parents' expectations and their own behaviour and lifestyle choices, lack of parents; homelessness, unemployment; illiteracy and semi-literacy, poor self-esteem, racism, stress and trauma associated with settling into a new country, trying to adjust to a different cultural environment, language difficulties, and so on (Moss 1993; Byrne 1995; Pe-Pua 1996).

Much of the public consternation regarding so-called ethnic youth gangs relates directly to the use of public space by ethnic minority young people. The presence of large groups of young people on the street, or young people dressed in particular ways, or with particular group affiliations, appears to have fostered the idea that Australia, too, has a gang problem similar to that found in countries such as the USA. One of the most sustained analyses of how young ethnic minority people actually use public space is a study undertaken in four local government areas in Sydney (Pe-Pua 1996). A wide range of issues relating to the lives of 100 street-frequenting NESB young people was investigated. The discussions and interviews covered topics such as family issues, housing and accommodation issues, social and recreational needs, financial needs, employment issues, educational and training issues, physical and mental health, legal issues, and youth services.

With respect to the specific issue of public-space use, the study found that (Pe-Pua 1996:115):

> The activities associated with street-frequenting ranged from illegal activities to fun activities, socialising, fighting or stirring up trouble, smoking and others. The reasons for street-frequenting were boredom, family-related, for economic or moral support, because of the freedom it provides, and others. The perceived benefits were: widening one's social network; having fun; learning experience; freedom and a sense of power; escape from problems; economic gains, and others. The perceived disadvantages were related to problems with the police; a negative image or bad treatment received from others, especially adults; getting into trouble or being involved in fights; health or drug and alcohol problems; lack of adequate shelter or food; financial worries; emotional burden; and general safety.

For most of the young people interviewed in this study, the street was a temporary site used for recreation or adventure-seeking, but not as the sole or permanent living space. These users of public space have been described by Pe-Pua (1996) as 'street-frequenting youth'. As users of public space, ethnic minority youth are particularly visible due to 'ethnic' markers such as physical appearance and language, and because they often congregate in numbers. Whether these groups of young people constitute 'gangs' as such is, however, highly doubtful.

For instance, a New South Wales inquiry received little or no evidence that the overseas style of gangs exist in that state, and commented that usage of the term 'gang', which implies violence and an organised structure, has little relevance to youth activities in Australian communities (Standing Committee on Social Issues 1995). Furthermore, while the police service reported the existence of fifty-four street gangs in 1993, there was no other evidence to support either this or related allegations of extensive memberships. Nevertheless, there is evidence that certain types of youth gangs do exist, albeit not to the extent suggested in media accounts (Standing Committee on Social Issues 1995). Even here, it is noted that most gangs limit their criminal behaviour to petty theft, graffiti, and vandalism. Few gangs are of a violent nature. Moreover, when violence such as homicide does involve a gang member, it is usually not gang-related.

By and large, it can be concluded that most bands of young people in Australia are not 'gangs', but groups (Standing Committee on Social Issues 1995; White 1996d). Social analysis of 'youth gangs' in Melbourne, for example, found that while some characteristics of the groups mirror the media images (such as the masculine nature of youth gangs, their preferred 'hangouts', and shared identity markers, such as shoes or clothes), the overall rationale for the group is simply one of social connection, not crime (Aumair & Warren 1994). There is a substantial difference between specific criminal organisations, which are usually not age-specific and which are expressly concerned with criminal activity (for example, criminal bikie gangs), and youth groups, which tend to be based upon age-based peer associations, and in which illegal activity is incidental to group membership and formation (see Perrone & White 2000).

In the specific case of 'ethnic youth gangs', the activities and perceptions by and of ethnic minority youth present a special case. The extra 'visibility' of young ethnic minority people (relative to the Anglo 'norm') feeds the moral panic over 'youth gangs'. Whole communities of young people can be affected, regardless of the fact that most young people are not systematic law-breakers or particularly violent individuals. The result is an inordinate level of public and police suspicion and hostility being directed towards people from certain ethnic minority backgrounds.

The Melbourne study

Research specifically on the question of ethnic youth gangs in Melbourne (White et al. 1999) challenges the notion that such gangs exist, at least in the form presented by the media. The study argues that key distinctions need to be made between 'youth group formations' (comprising friendship networks, subcultural affiliations, and family ties) and 'youth gangs' (highly structured and organised groups). Likewise, it is important to distinguish between social-centred activities (such as sharing similar language, religious beliefs, musical interests) and criminal-centred activities (commission of offences), and identify where these fit into general group dynamics and group formations. The study found that very often the notion of 'youth gang' itself was ill-defined or contentious for the young people who were interviewed. It could refer to many different things: types of activities, group associations, use of violence, engagement in illegal activities, and so on. Certainly, the idea of being a member of a 'criminal' gang had much less relevance to the analysis than concepts pertaining to group identification and social identity.

The study found that membership of a defined group tended to revolve around similar interests (such as choice of music, sport, style of dress), similar appearance or ethnic identity (such as language, religion, and culture), and the need for social belonging (such as friendship, support, and protection). Significantly, however, group affiliation was simultaneously perceived as the greatest reason for young people to be singled out as members of a 'gang'. This identification process was in turn associated with harassment from authority figures such as the police and private security guards, and with conflicts between different groups of young people on the street or at school.

To some extent, the media image of 'youth gangs' does have an empirical reference point. That is, many young people do 'hang out' together in groups and on the street. And, as is the case with most young people, periodic offending and illegal behaviour does occur. But this type of activity tends to be a by-product of group interaction rather than a rationale for group formation. It is not gang-related as such, in the sense that it is not the central reason for the young people to be together.

Nevertheless, the identification of certain young people as members of this group or that group was also tied to real tensions and problems at the level of intergroup relations among the young people. For instance, the Melbourne study (White et al. 1999) found that street fighting and school-based fights were a fairly common occurrence. The specific reasons for the fighting between different groups of young people (often involving fights between specific ethnic minority groups) were varied. Racism and treating people with disrespect were crucial elements in the explanation; likewise was the sense of ownership and belonging associated with particular local areas and membership of particular social groups. Social status for these young people is thus something that is both contested and defended, and this in turn is generally tied to one's identification with certain people and places.

Regardless of circumstance and motivation, the very fact that fights do occur can heighten police concerns about street-frequenting youth, and be drawn upon by the media in their portrayals of ethnic minority youth and violence. Rather than examining the problems faced by many of these young people, the tendency is to focus on specific events, specific group formations, and specific images of criminality: in other words, to view the young people themselves as the problem. This is reflected in sensationalised media treatment of ethnic minority youth. It is also reflected to some extent in the manner in which ethnic minority youth are differentially policed by state authorities and by private security officials.

An interesting finding of the Melbourne study was that when criminal organisations—and especially drug-related businesses—were discussed, they had little relevance to the street-level activities of the young people. In fact, any young person involved in 'adult' gangs or criminal organisations of this nature was more concerned to have a low public profile on the street, rather than associate with highly visible groups of peers.

The Sydney study

The other sustained study of ethnic minority youth particularly in relation to the issue of gang-related behaviour was undertaken in Sydney's western suburbs (Collins et al. 2000). The research involved Lebanese young people and other community members, as well as media and policy analysis. The authors were very critical of the media for attributing criminality to 'cultural' factors (in this case, related to being Lebanese). The clear implication is that everyone associated with this particular community shared similar negative attributes. Conversely, the authors argued that existing research demonstrates crime to be more of a socioeconomic issue than a cultural one. There is in fact very little reliable evidence to show that 'ethnic crime' as such is a problem.

What is a problem, however, is the 'racialised' reporting of crime when the media deal specifically with 'Lebanese' youth (see also Poynting et al. 2004). Ethnic identifiers are used in relation to some groups, but not others (such as Anglo-Celtic Australians). Moreover, the 'explanations' for such 'ethnic crime' tend to pathologise the group, as though there is something intrinsically bad about being Lebanese or, more generally, Middle Eastern. Such explanations also suggest that the origins of the criminality stem from outside Australia, and are related to immigration and 'foreign' ideas and cultures, rather than being linked to social and economic inequalities within this country. Such racialisation has a major impact upon public perceptions of the people and the issues, and on how state agencies such as the police respond to these perceptions.

The Sydney study pointed out that the groups exhibiting the highest rates of imprisonment—including, for example, the Lebanese, Vietnamese, and Turkish—also have the highest unemployment rates. Put simply, the issue of social exclusion appears to be central in any explanation of youth offending involving particularly disadvantaged groups. Marginalisation was also central to explaining the perception of widespread involvement in 'youth gangs' among Lebanese youth. Collins and others (2000) observed in the study that the main forms of association among Lebanese young people were first and foremost friendship groups. As in the Melbourne study (White et al. 1999), the groups also functioned as a defence against experiences of racism and exclusion from the cultural mainstream.

An especially strong aspect of the Sydney study was its discussion of marginality and masculinity. Some of the young men presented themselves in a 'gang' in order to gain a measure of 'respect'. The symbolic representation of themselves as members of a gang, however, was more at the level of overt performance than in relation to particular kinds of professional criminal activity. There was an intersection of masculinity, ethnicity, and class in such a way as to affirm social presence, to ensure mutual protection, and to compensate for a generally marginalised economic and social position (Collins et al. 2000:150):

> This performance of the 'gang' functions in several ways: it provides a venue for cultural maintenance, community and identity; and at the same time provides the protection of strength in numbers in the face of physical threats by other youth, and harassment by police and other adults ... Central to their partial negotiation of their experience of racialisation, they affirm a masculine and 'ethnic' identity of toughness, danger and respect.

Thus, assertion of gang membership is interpreted in the context of attempts by the young men to 'valorise' their lives and empower themselves in the face of hostility, disrespect, and social marginalisation. One of the ironies of media representations of gangs is that it makes membership of such a group appear even more attractive than otherwise might be the case.

The national study

In addition to city-specific studies, an attempt to pull together national data on youth gangs has also been carried out. This research has included a survey of school students in Perth as well as interviews with street-present young people in each capital city (White & Mason 2006). The sample for the national study varied depending upon local variations in 'hot spots' and which groups of young people were deemed to be problematic vis-à-vis gang membership and activities. Membership of group formations tended to be based on ethnicity (for example, based on cultural or family links) or territory (for example, based around a particular location or venue) or activity (for example, graffiti). In most capital cities, however, issues surrounding youth group formation were publicly constructed around the notion of 'ethnic' youth gangs.

For present purposes, it is interesting to note the preliminary findings of the national study in regard to whether or not gang-related behaviour and membership are related to ethnicity (see White 2006). The study found that much of the serious gang violence (especially that involving homicide) in Australia is in fact intra-communal violence, involving different groups of young people within the same ethnic community (e.g., Vietnamese gangs in Perth). On the other hand, in other places (such as western Sydney) the marginalisation of certain young people, and often their experiences of racism, meant that some (but definitely not all) were seeking to identify themselves and friends as members of a 'gang' in order to protect themselves and to project a strong image that affirmed their particular community identity. In this instance, the 'enemy' lay not within, but outside of the group.

Over time, the marginalisation and vilification of select groups of young people can lead to dire consequences. For example, in December 2005 two local Anglo youth were beaten up by a group of 'Middle Eastern' appearance young men. The following Sunday saw thousands of people gather at Cronulla beach—many wrapped in Australian flags, and a number clearly identified with white supremacist organisations. Fuelled by alcohol consumed on a very hot day, members of the crowd became more and more aggressive, until they began to attack anyone of 'Middle Eastern' appearance who happened to be in the vicinity, and to vandalise beachside properties. The violence continued for several days.

The media had a significant role in framing the violence, both in the lead-up to the Sunday violence and in the aftermath. For example, a series of gang rapes by young Muslim men in Sydney during the late 1990s and early 2000s had led to a media frenzy over the alleged 'unassimilable' attitudes of Muslim men towards women—a theme which was to re-emerge in the riots at Cronulla. Much of the vilification during this time was led by a few key media radio commentators and newspaper columnists. Indeed, a leading radio personality was advertising attendance at the Cronulla demonstration to 'reclaim the beach' during the week prior to the riot. This kind of media intervention frequently plays a major role in reflexively creating violent events by publicising them in advance, sensationalising them when they occur, and exaggerating the enormity of particular events relative to 'the Australian way of life'—hence the stimulation and provocation to violence is to some extent inspired by the mass media itself.

Evidence from both the national study and the specific Sydney research (Collins et al. 2000; Poynting et al. 2004) indicate that the common everyday racism experienced by Lebanese young people is hurtful, persistent, relentless, and widespread. This has been confirmed in a study undertaken by the Human Rights and Equal Opportunity Commission, which found high levels of vilification and abuse directed at Arab and Muslim Australians, to the extent that many young people were finding it very difficult to cope (HREOC 2004). It is not unlikely that some of these young people will lash out occasionally, given the weight of the burden on their shoulders. However, a vicious cycle of violence and retaliation is also linked with these overall patterns of social ostracism and group exclusion. In a period witnessing extremely hostile portrayals of Muslims, and of young men of 'Middle Eastern' appearance, it is hardly surprising that the actions of a few would be readily seized upon by those who showed up expecting trouble that day on the beach.

SOCIOLEGAL ISSUES AND INSTITUTIONAL RESPONSES

There are a number of issues pertaining to ethnic minority youth that are in many ways unique to this section of the youth population. In addition to difficulties related to policing practices and media portrayals, many ethnic young people have to struggle with matters pertaining to distinctive social differences, whether this relates to migration and resettlement processes or to specific cultural practices. To put it differently, very often ethnic minority youth have particular social needs that have to be taken into account if they are to be treated justly and fairly within the legal system generally, and within criminal justice institutions specifically.

Immigration and resettlement

There are several issues affecting ethnic minority youth that stem from or are related to immigration processes. What happens to the parents of young immigrants has a major impact on children and young people. Immigration selection processes, appeal mechanisms, and categorisation influence whether young people will be allowed into Australia, the conditions under which they will live, and how they and their families will adjust to the resettlement process. These issues are particularly pertinent in the case of refugees and those seeking asylum in this country. Hundreds of 'illegal' immigrants are held in detention each year. In some cases, children and young people—along with other family members—may have to spend years in secure holding camps awaiting immigration processing. For youth and children, enforced confinement may have particularly detrimental effects on their education, nutrition, employment opportunities, language training, and development of social bonds with established Australian young people (Everitt 2001). These problems are even worse for unaccompanied minors who do not have family support during their period of detention. There are major human rights issues here, to the extent that in 2001–02 the situation prompted an inquiry by the Human Rights and Equal Opportunity Commission (HREOC) into the confinement of children and young people in immigration detention centres.

If applicants are allowed to stay in Australia, they, along with other recently arrived migrants, have to cope with a two-year minimum period without state welfare assistance. This can mean major economic hardships for families, and these hardships are compounded by difficulties associated with making the transition to a new society in which language, laws, cultures, and traditions may well be foreign to the newcomers. In addition to the usual problems of transition, many refugee young people also require specialist assistance to deal with trauma associated with war, repressive regimes, torture, and life in transit camps. All of this is on top of the pains of separation from other family members and loved ones, and from the physical and cultural familiarities of the country of origin.

For many recent immigrants, there may also be emergent family tensions and conflicts linked to economic factors (such as members of the family finding paid work) and to changing social relationships. For example, if the dominant cultural 'way of life' in the country of origin is based upon norms and expectations different from the mainstream Australian norms and expectations, then this can lead to children in particular feeling that they are between two worlds. Occasionally, this can erupt into major conflicts between parents and children, if disagreement over values and daily practices emerges. Young people cope with this situation in various ways. However, for some at least it may lead to expulsion from the family home and/or being ostracised from one's community group. Under such circumstances, the young person may be placed in an extremely vulnerable social position, both in terms of potential victimisation and exploitation, and with respect to engagement in potential illegal and criminal activity.

Alternatively, a shared sense of culture and origin is important in order for groups of young people from similar backgrounds to bond together. Speaking the same language (such as Vietnamese or Arabic), holding similar religious beliefs (such as Muslim or Hindu), and being familiar with family and cultural norms can provide relief and comfort for those who are strangers in a strange land. Such bonding, however, may also be perceived in negative ways by established Australian youth, whether as standoffishness or as a sign of 'otherness'. This, too, can lead to conflict between such young people and their peers, at school and on the streets.

For some young people, the tensions created by trying to retain elements of the cultural identity derived from the country of origin and finding a place in the host country manifests itself in the construction of 'hybrid identities' (see Noble et al. 1999). This refers to young people placing a different stress on 'who they are' depending upon specific social situations, for example being 'Australian' at school, being 'Lebanese' at home, and being 'Lebanese-Australian' at the sportsground. The question of identity and cultural location is crucial to understanding the effects of resettlement beyond first-generation migration. The social and financial resources available at the point of transition from one country to another are important, but so too is the manner in which mainstream institutions in Australia cater to social difference. Schools and teachers who actively promote 'multicultural' forms of educational practice, and who are strongly anti-racist in orientation, are more likely to 'speak the language' of those youth who may otherwise feel left out. This extends from physical settings and material resources (such as bathing facilities for Muslim students), to curriculum development and people management.

Racial vilification and violence

The issue of resources is one facet in enabling ethnic minority youth to develop their capacities as human beings to the fullest extent. Another factor in this is being able to do so without suffering racial vilification and being subjected to racist violence. There is evidence, for example, that the level of violence and vilification against ethnic minority people has risen in recent years, partly due to the impact of the 'race debate' accompanying the emergence of the One Nation party (see Cunneen, Fraser & Tomsen 1997). Earlier investigations carried out by the HREOC had already pointed to the prevalence of such violence directed at minority groups in Australia (HREOC 1991).

In a period of heightened political agitation around 'race' themes, it is not surprising that certain groups (especially people from South-East Asia and the Middle East) have had to cope with greater levels of aggression levelled at them. As mentioned earlier, a recent HREOC report highlights the problems experienced by Arab and Muslim Australians in particular, especially since the horrendous events of September 11, 2001 (HREOC, 2004). Things appear to be getting worse, as world events such as the Gulf war and mass protests over cartoon images (which were published in some Western newspapers, and which are highly offensive to many Muslims) congeal into hatred, violence, and conflict at the grassroots level.

But the problem extends far wider than any one particular group. A recent report on the perspectives of crime and safety held by ethnic minority people in Melbourne (Victorian Multicultural Commission 2000:8) found, for example, that 'Nearly all groups indicated they feared some form of racial discrimination including vilification as a result of looking different from others in the local area. Some participants considered that as they were easily identified as belonging to a certain community they were treated in a negative way by members of the general community, figures of authority and service providers.'

What this indicates is that racial discrimination and vilification are not reducible to the actions of a few individuals who engage in hate crime as such. Rather, the issues tend to be ingrained in wider community relationships, and police, among others, are implicated in this process. It is ironic indeed that the only Australian state to introduce racist motivation as an aggravating factor in sentencing was New South Wales. The irony lies in the fact that this was not introduced as a result of a HREOC recommendation arising from its report on racist violence in Australia (see HREOC 1991), but as a result of the gang rapes committed by young Muslim men against non-Muslim women. One of the perpetrators was given a total sentence of 55 years imprisonment (later reduced on appeal). A further recommendation of the HREOC that has been ignored is that Australian police services monitor the frequency and nature of hate crime. Unlike many European and American jurisdictions, it is not possible in Australia to determine whether official reports of racially motivated offences have been increasing.

In strict legal terms, racist violence and vilification are outlawed through specific incitement-to-racial-hatred legislation, anti-discrimination legislation, and, more generally, criminal law (McNamara 2002). In practice, however, there are major tensions at the street level between groups of young people. This was acknowledged in the Melbourne study of 'ethnic youth gangs' (White et al. 1999), in which young people from all ethnic backgrounds commented on the negative media surrounding 'Asians', and spoke about the constant fights with and/or involving Asian young people. It is reflected in the Perth school survey that found high levels of violence among all boys and young men, but especially among those who identified themselves as belonging to a 'gang' (White & Mason 2006). The police and schools have to consider carefully how they intervene in such matters. At a minimum, it requires a commitment to upholding anti-discrimination principles, to protecting youth from racial taunts and violence, and to being sensitive to the issues surrounding the experience of racism when fights do occur.

Cross-cultural policies

From a crime-prevention and community-safety perspective, a number of strategies can be adopted to minimise group conflicts and specific types of group-based offending (see White et al. 1999). Some of these might include:

- providing quality educational services and facilities that are based on a multicultural curriculum and atmosphere, where students are provided with adequate individual and group support, and where anti-racist strategies and practices are applied across the whole school population
- developing appropriate conflict-resolution and anti-violence strategies in order to reduce the number of such incidents and to reassure students of their safety and security within the educational institution
- adopting appropriate community policing practices, and establishing protocols for positive and constructive interaction between ethnic minority youth and police or security guards
- providing specific education in cross-cultural issues and anti-racist education for young people and authority figures alike, so that issues of discrimination, prejudice, and unequal power relations can be analysed and discussed in an enlightened, informative, and empathetic manner
- developing youth reconciliation projects that will promote the diversity of cultures among young people, aim to reduce violence between them, and give young people from diverse cultural and ethnic backgrounds the practical opportunity to get to know each other at a personal and group level.

Where a particular individual from an ethnic minority community does offend and comes to the attention of criminal justice officials, once again specific problems and difficulties tend to present themselves. Various reports on access to justice have pointed to several different areas where young ethnic minority people require assistance (ALRC 1992; Burley 1995). For example, in common with most young people, ethnic minority youth may lack knowledge of the criminal justice system and how it works. This may be compounded by difficulties in communication with police and court officials. Thus, for example, a police caution on right to remain silent is useless to a person who does not comprehend the words in which the caution is given. Similarly, the right of criminal defendants to hear all the evidence brought against them in court is meaningless if the evidence is not translated into a language that the non-English-speaking defendant can understand (Access to Justice Advisory Committee 1994).

The use of interpreters has a number of dimensions (see, for example, Access to Justice Advisory Committee 1994). It includes their use at the stage of police investigation for suspects who do not have adequate English skills, through to the courtroom process. In between, there are considerations of language that must be recognised in regard to bail processes, diversionary programs (including juvenile conferencing), and community-based orders. For adequate service, there is need for a range of measures to ensure the availability and competence of interpreters, including the availability of bicultural as well as bilingual interpreters, so that the cultural background and understanding of the young person is fully incorporated into any proceedings.

It is important to acknowledge that, for some young people, there may be a profound distrust of police or lawyers due to experiences in the country of origin. The police are viewed with deep suspicion by people from societies in which police have been agents of oppression. A resulting attitude of apparent evasion and non-cooperation may lead police to wrongly suspect young people of concealing criminal activities. Alternatively, people from cultures that prescribe deference to authority figures may acquiesce in suggestions put to them by police or judges, even where the facts suggested are not known to them (Bird 1988). In this kind of situation, it is important to have specialist lawyers and advocacy services to provide legal advice, representation, and education. It is also essential to take into account the food and religious needs of diverse cultural groups, whether in police stations, lawyers' offices, or courtrooms.

In general, the institutions of criminal justice and juvenile justice need to be able to respond to the realities of a culturally diverse society. At a minimum, this demands systematic and ongoing cross-cultural awareness training for legal practitioners, judges, court staff, and police to enhance their awareness of cultural and linguistic diversity. As well, police and legal institutions need to adopt recruitment policies to make such institutions more reflective of the population composition in the long term.

In specific terms, each area of justice has to evaluate its particular role and obligations in relation to ethnic minority youth. For example, in the area of detention centres (NSW Office of the Ombudsman 1996; ALRC & HREOC 1997), juvenile justice workers and their agencies need to address concerns such as:

- ensuring that plans, policies, and programs are sensitive to the needs and requirements of ethnic minority youth from different social and cultural backgrounds, and that staff are trained and supported in this
- making sure that interpreter services are available, appropriate, and of good quality
- providing information booklets in a variety of different languages, and making books, newspapers, and videos available in different languages

- employing staff from various cultural backgrounds and with knowledge of other cultures, and encouraging visits from workers and support groups from each ethnic minority community
- providing culturally appropriate food, and spaces for diverse religious practices.

Certainly, there will be major challenges over the coming years to provide services, facilities, and programs that are appropriate to the needs of ethnic minority youth, and that will foster their movement out of the criminal justice system rather than entrench them in it. This will require concerted, innovative, and systematic efforts across areas such as crime prevention, policing, youth conferencing, and corrective services (see, for example, Chan 1997; Bhathal 1998; Victorian Multicultural Commission 2000).

Making sense of crime statistics

A key issue in discussions about ethnicity and crime is how authorities construct and interpret relevant crime statistics. There are compelling arguments for a more systematic compilation of crime and criminal justice statistics pertaining to juvenile offending that incorporate ethnic background. There is also a need to quantify the differential treatment of specific groups within the juvenile justice system, and statistics can be useful in uncovering discrimination and providing the impetus for reform. Fundamentally, the purpose of improving data collection in these areas ought to be to assess how well the criminal justice agencies are dealing with issues of access and equity, as well as to expose the socioeconomic reasons behind certain crime and criminal justice trends (Cunneen 1995; Collins et al. 2000; Wortley 1999).

Another issue to consider is how changes in police recording practices might influence the construction of official crime rates in relation to particular groups, or how these might influence police attitudes towards intervention with such groups (see National Police Ethnic Advisory Bureau 1997). The way in which ethnic identity is related to an offender is a matter that is linked directly to the definitions used in police records. For example, the police may refer to specific categories of ethnic classification (such as 'Caucasian', 'Asian', 'Indigenous', 'Middle Eastern' or whatever). The extent of ethnic-related crime will reflect both police perceptions of ethnic background (since it is the police who usually identify a person's ethnicity for record-keeping purposes) and the arbitrary nature of categorisation itself (referring here to the criteria used to define each category, and the overall number of categories). As noted earlier, defining ethnicity is not simply about determining the place of origin, or about 'ethnic' appearance. It also involves subjective assessments on the part of the young people themselves. However, from a criminal justice perspective, ethnicity is often used primarily as a marker of social distinction that provides a shorthand means of identifying potential offenders or troublemakers. This type of record-keeping can exacerbate, rather than alleviate, tensions between police and ethnic minority youth, and serve to entrench stereotypes about the relationship between ethnicity and offending.

Particular crime trends associated with specific ethnic groups, as with the links between Vietnamese young people and injecting drug use, creates something of a paradox for those wishing to adopt progressive measures in dealing with juvenile offending. On the one hand, acknowledgment of the problem among this community may well feed populist attacks on Vietnamese people in general, and unduly stigmatise individuals and community members. On the other hand, close analysis of why some Vietnamese young people use these drugs reveals the social inequalities and social injustices underpinning their lives, and the difficulties they face in fostering a sense of social belonging (see Beyer, Reid & Crofts 2001). As noted in a Victorian report dealing with drug use (Drugs and Crime Prevention Committee 1997:182):

> In the context of the general social disadvantages that many ethnic communities face, the consequences of drug problems tend to be magnified, and become less amenable to the sorts of solutions and strategies that suffice for mainstream cultural communities. Some ethnic communities will have the social and economic capacity to tackle their drug problems, but other communities will not be as well positioned to do this, and will stand in need of additional resources and extra efforts.

Again, crime statistics, accompanied by qualitative evaluation of actual circumstances (such as the dynamics of the immigration settlement process), are essential to understanding and acting in the best interests of these young people.

CONCLUSION

Within the criminal justice sphere, there has been limited movement towards analysis of the nature and extent of ethnic minority youth offending (Easteal 1997), to examine sentencing disparities in relation to the ethnicity of juvenile offenders (Gallagher & Poletti 1998), and to consider the special requirements of ethnic minority offenders held in detention (NSW Office of the Ombudsman 1996). However, much more study and conceptual work is needed if we are to appreciate fully the place of ethnic minority youth in the criminal justice system, and the reasons for their involvement with this system.

One of the biggest issues requiring concerted action is that of how to improve police–youth interaction and to diminish the impact of media hype and negativity on criminal justice processes. The media tend towards presenting certain ethnic minority youth as 'troublemakers', 'gangsters', and 'drug dealers'. Generalisations based on these stereotypes congeal into forms of public opinion and political-speak that do great damage and injustice to ethnic minority communities as a whole. In such contexts, it will take great resolve and commitment to anti-racist ideals to develop more positive and sensitive systems and methods of dealing with ethnic minority youth.

In the end, any analysis of ethnic minority youth, and any positive strategic action taken with respect to juvenile justice issues, must grapple with two essential questions: the dearth of social and economic resources available to sections of these communities, and the racism that permeates the lives of so many of these young people. These are not simply issues of policy and practice: they are matters of principle, and, ultimately, they connect to the nature of Australian society itself.

8 | Young women, young men, and gender

CHAPTER HIGHLIGHTS

Introduction
Early feminist research on young women
Challenging essentialism
Girls in the juvenile justice system
Developing programs for young women in custody
Gender relations and masculinity
Conclusion

INTRODUCTION

The purpose of this chapter is threefold. First, we want to analyse specific issues relating to girls and juvenile justice. We are aware of the risk of marginalising girls' issues through this approach: after all, the entire spectrum of discussion in a book on juvenile justice must acknowledge that clients and personnel consist of males and females. However, in terms of specific issues affecting girls, there is some merit in dealing with the discussion separately. Second, we want to pose the broader question of how gender is related to juvenile justice, and a discussion of gender inevitably involves a consideration of masculinity. Third, we want to consider the extent to which masculinity and femininity as social and psychological constructs determine the nature of interactions with juvenile justice agencies.

These questions have become increasingly important since the 1970s as feminist criminologists have challenged the male-centredness of the criminological enterprise. Feminists have made women visible as victims and offenders within criminology. Feminists have challenged criminology with the demand to consider gender relations as necessarily implying a focus on masculinity as well as femininity (Gelsthorpe & Morris 1990:3–4). Finally, feminists have also demanded that the policy and practice of juvenile justice reflect the special needs of young women.

From the point of view of criminological research generally, it is important to acknowledge that feminist criticism relates not only to the subject of analysis but also to the method of analysis (White 1990). For example, it has been pointed out that a specific focus on young men, or young women, is not necessarily the main issue. Gender bias resides at the level of explanation, as well as at the substantive empirical level. Furthermore, greater attention needs to be directed not only to the nature of 'femininity' or 'masculinity' in explaining system discrimination or the gendered patterns of crime, but also at the relationship of each social construct to the other, how 'masculine' practices shape existing male behaviour towards young women, and how 'femininity' is actively used and shaped by girls in negotiating their way in a male-dominated social world.

Although they are beyond the scope of the present work, we also view as very important further analyses of the material constraints and opportunities available to either sex as shaped by wider social processes. Issues of parental control, the use of public space, the means by which different groups of young people communicate with each other, income and employment opportunities, and availability of sex-specific services all have an impact on youth behaviour and attitudes (see, for example, White 1990, 1993a; Carrington 1993; Alder & Baines 1996). An understanding of gender demands both an analysis of the ideological construction of 'difference' between the sexes based upon biological features, and an examination of the real, material differences in power relationships, economic resources, and cultural forms.

One indication of the differences between sexes in contact with the juvenile justice system is provided in table 8.1, which shows the different participation of females and males at various levels of juvenile justice. The data are from Western Australia and represent relatively common findings in relation to differences between males and females. In relation to criminal matters, the participation of girls decreases further into the system. Thus, they represent 29.4 per cent of police cautions, 22.9 per cent of police referrals to conferences, 20 per cent of arrests, 19.8 per cent of proven criminal matters, and 9.1 per cent of custodial outcomes.

TABLE 8.1   POLICE CAUTIONS, ARRESTS, REFERRALS TO CONFERENCE, AND CHILDREN'S COURTS DETERMINATIONS, WESTERN AUSTRALIA, 2004*

DETERMINATION	MALE %	FEMALE %
Police cautions	70.4	29.4
Police referral to conference/juvenile justice team	76.7	22.9
Arrested	79.8	20.0
Finalised court appearance	81.2	19.8
Sentenced to detention	90.9	9.1

* Cases excluded where sex not recorded

Source: Ferrante et al. (2005: 43, 50, 116, 110, 121).

Similar results can be seen in Queensland. Ogilvie, Lynch and Bell (2000) found that 15 per cent of police interventions with young women resulted in arrest, compared with 26 per cent for young males, that 24 per cent of young women received an attendance notice or summons to appear in court compared with 35 per cent of males, and that 60 per cent of females were cautioned compared with 37 per cent of males (Ogilvie et al. 2000:2). The Queensland researchers caution against interpreting these divergent results between young women and men as necessarily indicating that the offences that females commit are either different or less serious. We return to this point further on.

EARLY FEMINIST RESEARCH ON YOUNG WOMEN

Understanding the different position of young women and young men in the juvenile justice system requires analysis that allows for the specificity of experience of each group. The fact that the system is by and large oriented towards young men has fundamentally shaped its institutions, programs, and objectives along masculine lines. This has a number of implications with regard to how we explain the presence of young female offenders in the first place (given the overall gender bias of the system), and how the state has constructed and responded to female youth crime. It also has implications for how we develop policies and practices that specifically meet the needs of young women.

Juvenile justice research and theory had traditionally been preoccupied with the concerns of young male offenders. When female offending was considered, there were assumptions that there must be some 'lack' of femininity that caused the offending (since it was considered not in the feminine nature to offend), or that femininity itself facilitated a level of deceitfulness that rendered female offending relatively invisible. Early feminist research challenged these assumptions and was concerned with a number of key issues in the analysis of young women and the juvenile justice system. A major issue was the apparent preoccupation of juvenile justice agencies with the sexuality of girls and young women, and with so-called 'inappropriate' female behaviour. Feminists referred to this process as the sexualisation of delinquency. Their analysis was based upon an examination and critique of traditional notions of 'a woman's place' in society. Femininity as a social construct defined women primarily in terms of their location in the private sphere of the home, their dependent relationship to men as daughter, wife, or mother, their social role as childcarer, housekeeper, and sexual object, and their emotional state as 'naturally' caring, passive, and excitable. Young women who did not conform to the ideals of chastity before marriage, subservience to the male figure, and convention (defined in terms of biological and social roles) were particular targets for state intervention.

Issues surrounding the regulation of 'femininity' were linked in feminist analysis to the question of whether girls and young women were subjected to more punitive intervention by juvenile justice agencies—including welfare personnel, police, and magistrates—than were boys. It was argued that girls were more likely than boys to come into the juvenile justice system as a result of welfare complaints or status offences, such as being exposed to moral danger, or underage drinking. A variety of studies during the 1970s and 1980s by Chesney-Lind (1974), Shacklady-Smith (1978), Casburn (1979), Sarri (1983) and others sought to demonstrate the apparent differences in treatment of boys and girls. There have been several parts to the argument of differential treatment. First, it is argued that girls' sexual behaviour is scrutinised by juvenile justice agencies in a way that boys' sexual behaviour is not. Second, it is argued that other non-sexual behaviours or offences by girls are either overlooked or redefined as status offences relating to moral danger. Third, there is a preoccupation with defining and maintaining the boundaries of what is 'appropriate' behaviour for girls. An example of US research is that of Chesney-Lind (1974), who found that 70–80 per cent of young women compared to 1–10 per cent of young men were given medical examinations prior to their appearance in the children's court. Doctors' reports commented upon the apparent sexual experience of the girls, even though it might have been unrelated to the offence. In summary, early feminist research in the area indicated that there was a preoccupation by authorities with the sexuality of girls: girls' behaviour was sometimes redefined as sexual, and girls were more likely than boys to come into the juvenile justice system for status offences such as 'exposed to moral danger'.

One initial point of intervention is the police. Generally, studies of police behaviour have not examined the role of gender in police decision-making. However, evidence from a 1987 study showed that girls in England and Wales were more likely than boys to receive a police caution and be diverted (Morris 1987:96). Alder (1994:160) cites US research suggesting that the sex of an individual affected police decision-making. It is important to recognise, however, that differential treatment can reflect the commission of less frequent and less serious offences by girls than by boys.

Gelsthorpe noted that police dealing with juveniles in an English police station viewed boys' and girls' offending patterns differently and along stereotypical lines, seeing girls as engaged in shoplifting and boys as engaged in car theft. An analysis of offences at the station revealed that boys and girls shoplifted equally, and that girls were involved in a wide range of offences (cited in Alder 1994:161). It has been suggested that girls who commit offences outside the boundaries of defined 'feminine behaviour' can expect to receive greater disapproval and harsher treatment (Youth Justice Coalition 1990:26). Alder cites other American research, which suggested that police officers respond to young women on the basis of their image, rather than the offence they have committed. The demeanour of a young person very much influences police use of discretion (see chapter 9). And it is apparent that assumptions concerning appropriate demeanour and image are mediated by gender-based expectations.

In Australia, Hancock (1980) noted that police reports on juveniles were more likely to refer explicitly to sexual history in the case of girls (29 per cent) than in the case of boys (1 per cent). Sexual and moral activities were cited in police reports in 40 per cent of female court appearances and in 5 per cent of male court appearances. Alleged promiscuity was seen as one reason for intervention (Hancock & Chesney-Lind 1982:112). Alder notes that overseas research indicates that overall assessment of 'immorality' is determined by a range of factors beyond alleged sexual experience (Alder 1994:165). The work by Hancock draws attention to social variables such as attitude and cooperation with authority, 'credibility', and home situation, as well as 'moral reputation' (1980:10). The activities that were commented on in police reports regarding complaints of 'exposed to moral danger' included underage drinking, hitchhiking, living away from home, or being in the company of 'undesirable' people. Hancock also noted the importance of the relationship between class and gender: 'Those females who are most likely to be affected by a moralistic/welfare definition of the charge and thus presented on a "protection application" are working class females whose behaviour is more likely to bring them to police notice ...' (Hancock 1980:11).

A further area of concern has been the nature of punishment used in the case of young women. Such punishment has included not only the use of diversion but also sentencing by the courts. Alder (1984) has noted that, while girls appear to be disproportionately involved in diversion programs, they tend to be diverted for minor forms of misconduct. An unanticipated consequence of the expansion of diversionary schemes has been to draw more girls into processing by the juvenile justice system for non-serious matters. Diversion has occurred for matters that would not normally have been dealt with formally by the juvenile justice system in any case.

Sentencing of young women has also raised a number of questions. First, the sentencing rationales used for young women have been questioned. Morris (1987) cited an English study of the use of secure detention for girls, which showed, during a twelve-month period, that of thirty-two girls placed in an institution, eight were there for 'delinquent' behaviour and the rest for truanting, neglect, moral danger, and other status offences. The major reason for the secure placement was absconding. The reason the social workers sought a secure environment was because they believed protection was needed for the girls (Morris 1987:95). The issue of 'protective custody' is discussed further on.

Second, it has been argued that girls receive harsher sentencing outcomes than boys for status offences, and less severe sentencing outcomes than boys for delinquent or criminal matters. However, it has also been noted that these findings have often been made without adequate controls (Morris 1987:97). Research in this area requires the use of control variables, such as offence type, prior record, bail, and mode of intervention (summons, arrest, and so on). Research in Australia using control variables has found that girls were less likely to be arrested, less likely to be sent to the children's court, and more likely to be discharged (Wundersitz, Naffine & Gale 1988). Parker, Casburn, and Turnbull (1981) argued that girls in the United Kingdom were treated differently from boys by magistrates when charged with the same offence. The difference in treatment usually resulted in greater intervention, such as the use of supervision orders rather than fines. Similar findings have been made in Australia (see Wundersitz et al. 1988). A more recent study by the New South Wales Judicial Commission (Gallagher, Polletti & MacKinnell 1997) challenges the view that courts treat male and female young offenders differently at the point of sentencing. The study controlled for type of offence, age, plea, number of charges, criminal history, bail status, and type of case. The results showed that there were no significant gender-based differences in the type of penalty imposed.

Datesman and Scarpitti (1980) in the USA found that girls were given more severe dispositions for status offences (especially when repeat offenders), and boys were given more severe dispositions for criminal matters. Hancock (1980) found similar results in Victoria when analysing welfare matters and specific criminal offences such as break, enter, and steal. In the research by Datesman and Scarpitti (1980), however, the discrepancies were less apparent for black girls, who received more severe sanctions than white girls for criminal matters and less severe sanctions than white girls for status offences. The research appears to indicate that issues of race and ethnicity have an impact on sentencing decisions as much as gender.

In Australia, Carrington (1993:25–7) argues that both girls and boys who appear before the children's courts on welfare matters are likely to receive harsher dispositions than those who appear on criminal matters. Two issues need to be explained: why is the means by which a young person is brought before the court so important, and why are welfare cases treated more harshly? Carrington suggests that, because welfare matters are more likely to be guided by social and psychological discourses that justify early and long periods of intervention, the outcomes are more likely to be punitive.

Much of the early feminist work rested on the observation that girls were more likely to appear in children's court on a welfare complaint or status offence rather than a criminal charge. While acknowledging variations between states, during the 1970s a large proportion of girls brought before the courts were there as a result of welfare complaints. In fact, in some states, such as New South Wales and Victoria—at least until the mid-1970s—the majority of girls in court were there for welfare-related matters (Hancock & Chesney-Lind 1985:238).

Welfare to criminalisation

From the 1980s through the 1990s, there was a clear decline in the use of welfare complaints against girls, and an increase in the number of criminal matters involving girls. The change was accelerated by legislative reforms that removed many welfare offences. The vast majority of girls who now appear in the children's court do so as a result of a criminal charge. For example, by the early 1990s in New South Wales, girls were about four times more likely to appear in the children's court on criminal matters than on welfare matters (Cunneen & White 1995:156). Increases in the number of cases going to children's court nevertheless warrant careful consideration. For example, due to a crackdown on fare evasion and misbehaviour on Public Transport Corporation property in Victoria in the early 1990s, there was a dramatic rise in the number of criminal cases brought before the Victorian Children's Court. Many of these cases resulted from the inability of young offenders to pay hefty on-the-spot fines for various offences. The main impact of this prosecutorial zeal was felt among young women, as evidenced in figures that showed PTC cases making up a higher proportion of children's court criminal cases against females than against males. The prosecution of young women rose sharply to more than half of all cases in 1991 (O'Grady 1992).

The nature of offending behaviour by girls and young women still requires further research and explanation. Ogilvie and others (2000) have argued that although young women commit significantly fewer crimes than young men, the evidence at least from official statistics indicates that the patterns of crime and types of crime are similar between both groups. This insight poses a theoretical challenge: as Carlen has noted, the explanations for female crime may be much the same as those for male crime, particularly in relation to poverty and powerlessness, and race and class issues (Carlen 1992:206–7).

Changes in offending behaviour also require more research. As we noted in chapter 3, it is apparent that there has been a long-term increase in the rate at which young women are coming before the courts for offences related to violence, although this is now showing some decline. Research on New South Wales court appearances during the first half of the 1990s indicates that rates for assaults, robbery, and drug offences all show greater increases for young women than for young men, although the absolute rates are much lower for females (Gliksman & Chen 2001). In Queensland, Ogilvie and others (2000:4) note that, although young males commit a far greater number of serious assaults, serious assaults comprise about three times the proportion of finalised court matters for girls compared to boys (6 per cent compared to 2 per cent). In relation to less serious assaults by young women, a Queensland survey found that these frequently involved fights between girls in public places such as shopping centres. In one-third of cases, the victim was another young woman, and in another one-third of cases, the victim was a police officer (Beikoff 1996:18). Changes in the offending behaviour of young women require sustained research that needs to go well beyond simplistic questions of whether girls are 'catching up' with boys (see Gliksman & Chen 2001). Research needs to consider the relationship between offending and drug and alcohol use, changes in welfare regulation and social security, education and labour market access, drug enforcement policies, and responses of criminal justice agencies to young women. Unfortunately, much of the public concern relating to young women's apparent increase in offending has been driven by moral panics fired by events such as the involvement to 14-year-old girls in the murder of a Sydney taxi driver in February 2006.

It is also worth considering the extent to which the decline in welfare complaints against girls had the unintended consequence of leading to greater levels of criminalisation. Carrington (2006) has argued that the rise in official rates of female delinquency between the 1960s and mid-1990s reflects this shifting 'regime of governance' from welfare to criminalisation. It can be seen as an unintended consequence to the extent that reform of the earlier welfare complaints process against girls was influenced by feminist intervention in juvenile justice and welfare policy. Certainly, by the early 1980s, lawyers, social workers, academics, and others working in the area were highly critical of the use of welfare complaints—such as those of 'uncontrollable' or 'exposed to moral danger'—against girls and young women. For example, Marrickville Legal Centre, which had a specialist children's legal section, opposed the use of 'uncontrollable' complaints against girls in a published policy paper (Miller 1983). The paper stated, in part (Miller 1983:1):

> Girls are subject to controls on their behaviour that are not applied to boys, especially in relation to their sexual development. Further, girls are more often the victims of sexual abuse within the family than boys. In our experience these two factors feature predominantly in the case histories of girls on 'uncontrollable complaints'.

The later part of the 1980s and the early 1990s saw administrative and legislative changes in many Australian states that had the effect of separating welfare from criminal matters, that withdrew complaints such as 'uncontrollable' and 'exposed to moral danger', and that saw a legislative and policy focus on care and protection matters. In New South Wales, the Community Diversion Program in 1985 aimed to provide alternatives to incarceration (such as community service orders), and to separate welfare matters from criminal matters. Specifically in relation to girls, the diversion program was to encourage greater use of police cautions, discourage juvenile justice officers from recommending incarceration for minor offences, and discourage the setting of unrealistic bail conditions that could not be met by girls (Saville 1993:293–4). Howe (1990) outlines similar changes in Victoria, and Beikoff (1996) discusses similar issues for Queensland. However, there are still important concerns relating to the incarceration of young women, and some of these are precisely the concerns that policy and legislative reform were supposed to have remedied. These are discussed later.

A further issue raised by feminists, but still not adequately addressed, is the relationship between unemployment and young women's involvement with juvenile justice agencies. The failure to address this issue itself reflects the assumption that employment and unemployment relate primarily to males. However, Alder (1986:211) cites Australian research indicating that young women were more concerned about unemployment than are young men. Certainly, the impact of changes in the labour market during the late 1970s and the 1980s, and limitations on job opportunities, have affected young women as well as young men. Alder's interviews with young women indicated that unemployment affected identity, the ability to live independently of parents, and the sense of hope and expectations for the future. While there was no simple relationship between unemployment and criminal activity, some of the young women interviewed by Alder had resorted to property offences such as shoplifting, while others saw drug and alcohol abuse as a means of coping (1986:219–21).

Research shows that the link between unemployment and crime needs to be considered as a gender-specific issue (Naffine & Gale 1989). Perhaps a more fruitful approach is to consider the survival strategies utilised by young women. The concept of survival strategies incorporates the interstices between the experiences of sexual and physical abuse, homelessness, inadequate welfare support, poverty, criminalisation, and unemployment and lack of job opportunities (Bargen 1994). Comments by young women in the juvenile justice system both in Australia (Alder 1993) and in the USA (Chesney-Lind & Shelden 1992) have stressed their need to establish independent lives with economic independence, adequate long-term housing, and less dependence on social services. These comments imply recognition of the potentially destructive outcomes of criminal or quasi-criminal survival strategies that force young women into the net of juvenile justice.

CHALLENGING ESSENTIALISM

One of the most important changes to earlier feminist interpretations of juvenile justice has been the demand that issues of race, ethnicity, and class be seen as intersecting with gender. Challenges to feminist essentialism developed during the 1980s, and can be seen, for example, in the work of Eisenstein. She criticised the 'false universalism' that 'in spite of its narrow base of white middle-class experience, purported to speak about and on behalf of all women, black or white, poor or rich' (1984:134). Connell (1987:59) also discussed the problems with a 'categorical' theory of gender. Gender essentialism gives primacy to the category of woman, and presumes a shared interest of all women. In simple terms, women are the oppressed group and men are the oppressors. The effects of class, race, or ethnicity are seen as subsidiary to the central category of sex. It should be noted that gender essentialism equally presumes the shared interest of all men as oppressors.

In the Australian context, it was the omission of Aboriginal young women that was the most obvious point of neglect in feminist analyses (Carrington 1993:15). In chapter 6, we discussed the gendered forms of intervention in relation to Aboriginal young people. It is also worth considering that there is still a paucity of empirical data that consider specifically the issues relating to Aboriginal young women, although we know such young women continue to constitute a large proportion of institutional populations (Cunneen & Kerley 1995). However, there is some discussion now on the particular policy requirements of Aboriginal young women in the juvenile justice system (for South Australia, see Bartemucci 1996; for Queensland, see Beikoff 1996).

Similarly, with some exceptions (Hancock 1980; Carrington 1993), social class has not received the level of consideration it deserves in the contact between young women and juvenile justice. Some research has shown a positive correlation between appearances by girls and indicators of social disadvantage. More girls from working-class communities appear before the children's courts than those from more affluent areas (Carrington 1993:15). And, as noted above, Hancock's study indicated that class was related to police decisions about girls. There is a high incidence in our prisons of unemployed women, those with few formal educational qualifications, and those institutionalised for low-level welfare fraud, all of which provides some indication of the class background of women who are likely to have ongoing contact with the criminal justice system.

One of the theoretical issues raised initially by Connell (1987) and taken up by Carrington (1993), specifically in relation to juvenile justice, is that essentialist notions of gender cannot be overcome simply by adding or incorporating class and race issues if these structures are also treated in a categorical or essentialist manner (Connell 1987:59; Carrington 1993:17). For instance, an understanding of the relationship between Aboriginal girls and juvenile justice and welfare agencies demands an analysis of the historically specific practices of those agencies. Whether the nature of the relationship overlaps with what happens to non-Aboriginal young women is an empirical question to be answered on the basis of research: it cannot be assumed by asserting the primacy of the social category of gender. As we have seen (in chapter 6), the fact that more than one in four Aboriginal girls compared to one in thirteen non-Aboriginal girls are likely to have formal contact with juvenile justice agencies during their adolescence suggests a qualitatively different level of intervention. The extent of this intervention and the importance of gender and race being considered together are also reflected in police apprehension and arrest figures. In South Australia during 2004, Aboriginal girls made up 25.1 per cent of all girls apprehended, compared to Aboriginal boys, comprising 19.5 per cent of all boys apprehended (Office of Crime Statistics and Research 2005:16). In Western Australia during 2004, Aboriginal girls comprised 65.5 per cent of all young women arrested, while Aboriginal boys comprised 46.7 per cent of all young men arrested (Ferrante et al. 2005:54).

Essentialist notions of gender also affect how we conceptualise men and masculinity. Judith Allen (1990), for example, argues against the sex/gender distinction—that is, the distinction between the sex 'male' and the gender 'masculinity'—because such a distinction removes analysis from men as a group. She asks: 'What is it about men, not as working-class, not as migrant, not as underprivileged, but as men that induces them to commit crime?' (1990:39). On the face of it, this is a powerful argument. However, other writers in the area, such as Connell (1987), argue that theories based on the sexual dichotomy of male/female cannot grasp the historicity of gender relations. In other words, gender is an historical formation open to change.

To put it simply, we can say that gender is, demonstrably, a learnt role: it is not fixed according to biology, insofar as its actual behavioural content varies from society to society. The evidence from both historical analysis and cross-cultural study is that 'gender' (however defined in any particular society) can likewise be altered. Some indication that gender is open to change is provided in the various political struggles between progressives and conservatives over the specific relations, behaviours, and attitudes that ideally should be associated with maleness and femaleness. Often the activist interventions from the Right and the Left include attempts to acquire social resources precisely in order to shape particular gender conceptions and behavioural patterns, either by maintaining or transforming mainstream social institutions. For example, one need only think of the debates over the definition of 'the family', and the social and economic policies that are put in place to shape such social institutions in particular ways.

History is also important if we are to understand class and other social relations, which may have an impact on a person as much as, or more than, their gender at a given moment. These arguments have particular application to juvenile justice. For example, as discussed in chapter 6, the intersections between race, gender, and juvenile justice changed in Australia during the twentieth century, and continue to change. The earlier focus of government was on the removal of (mainly) Aboriginal girls through a protection-and-welfare approach. There is a contemporary law-and-order focus primarily on Aboriginal boys through the process of criminalisation. Another area demanding concrete historical and social research is the way specific cultural groups of young women are over-represented in juvenile detention centre figures. For instance, there has been a relatively recent growth in numbers of Indo-Chinese and Pacific Islander girls who are incarcerated.

A move away from gender essentialism also opens up the terrain to a discussion of masculinities. We return to this point later in the chapter, but note now that it is probably fair to say that 'criminological theory has not yet begun to recognize the hegemonic masculinity of its central concepts nor, therefore, to revise its deep-seated androcentrism' (Sumner 1990:27). Certainly, in discussions of juvenile justice, masculinity by and large remains unproblematised. The issue of masculinity is invisible.

GIRLS IN THE JUVENILE JUSTICE SYSTEM

We have indicated some of the broad explanations as to how and why girls come into contact with juvenile justice agencies. A critical focus has been on the treatment by juvenile justice agencies of young women, particularly in arguments about the way the system apparently sexualises girls' behaviour to facilitate intervention. We have also indicated the importance of social class, race, and ethnicity in determining the likelihood of intervention. Some of these broad social relations, such as class and race, also apply to boys and their contact with juvenile justice agencies.

We also need to understand which other factors increase the likelihood that some girls within this broader framework will be drawn into the juvenile justice net. There is a range of social conditions that increases the likelihood of contact with juvenile justice agencies, such as inadequate accommodation, family breakdown and abuse, and unemployment. Indeed, it is even more difficult with girls than with boys to separate victimisation-related issues from offending. Social and economic conditions like unemployment may also have a different impact on girls and young women when compared to boys. For instance, homelessness and the strategies developed to deal with it may be different between girls and boys.

Certainly, Australian studies have outlined the connections between violence, family break-up, negative contact with welfare agencies and police, and the move from welfare needs to eventual criminalisation (Women's Coordination Unit 1986). The following is a summary of the key issues, adapted from the New South Wales Standing Committee on Social Issues (1992:53–4).

- In the past, girls have been more likely than boys to come before the court a first time for welfare reasons rather than for criminal charges. Although the use of welfare complaints has decreased, the link between welfare and criminalisation is still strong.
- Girls are sometimes charged with a minor criminal offence when police are called to respond to a domestic conflict.
- Girls in state care who rebel against the institutional regime may be reported to the police by staff responsible for their care, then charged with a criminal offence and transferred to a detention centre.
- Girls who are state wards are forty times more likely to be detained in custody than other girls. Boys who are state wards are seventeen times more likely to be detained in custody than other boys.
- Girls who are state wards are frequently unable to meet the bail conditions regarding an approved place of residence, and, by default, remain in detention.
- Studies have found that girls charged with criminal offences have a history of being abused at home.
- A large proportion of the girls before the courts for criminal matters are dependent on drugs.

YOUNG WOMEN, YOUNG MEN, AND GENDER

It has been noted that a lack of safe and supportive accommodation is an important factor in bringing girls before the courts on criminal matters (Women's Coordination Unit 1986). The New South Wales Standing Committee on Social Issues (1992) noted that life on the streets for homeless girls is more dangerous than for boys, and that there is greater vulnerability to drug abuse and self-destructive behaviour. A large proportion of girls came into the juvenile justice system because of welfare-related issues that themselves arose from abuse or neglect at home (New South Wales Standing Committee on Social Issues 1992:35). It was estimated that between 80 and 90 per cent of girls in detention centres had been abused. A similar proportion was dependent on drugs (New South Wales Standing Committee on Social Issues 1992:139). Drug dependence has also been related to recidivism and, for some girls released from detention, death from drug overdoses (Bargen 1994:122). The inability of detention centres to deal with drug dependency has been a focus of concern.

Much of the recent policy development in relation to girls has focused on the special needs of female offenders once they are in the system. It has been noted that young women in custody live in an environment heavily dominated by male culture: more than 90 per cent of detention centre inmates are male, the majority of the staff are male, and there are few women in senior management positions (NSW Juvenile Justice Advisory Council 1993:189).

Various committees and inquiries have considered issues relating to girls and young women in the juvenile justice system. Recommendations have centred on:

- specific counselling for sexual and other forms of abuse
- specific counselling for drug and alcohol dependencies
- assistance with accommodation
- assistance with finding employment
- pre-release and post-release schemes specifically for young women
- more women with specialist training to staff detention centres specifically catering for girls.

Given the above discussion, it is important to consider the profile of girls who are in detention centres. The following summary is based on a survey of twenty-five girls held in New South Wales detention centres on 13 April 1993 (Cain 1994a:28–38), as well as a preliminary survey of 469 young women admitted to custody in New South Wales over an eleven-month period between 1992 and 1993 (Cozens 1993:2). Although these data are now quite old, there is a paucity of good empirical research on young women in institutions, particularly focusing on their experiences of criminalisation.

Of the twenty-five girls in detention centres on 13 April 1993, nine were on remand and sixteen had been sentenced. The girls were held in custody for a range of offences, including assaults (6), malicious wounding (5), armed robbery (1), assault and rob (1), robbery (1), drug trafficking and possession (3), break and enter (1), motor vehicle theft (1), receiving stolen goods (1), escapes (2), and breach of previous court orders (3).

It appears that offences against the person (crimes of violence) are the major reason for incarceration. It is important to note that static census surveys taken on a single day overestimate the number of people serving longer sentences (presumably for more serious offences). These surveys give no indication of the volume of traffic through detention centres. In contrast, the Cozens (1993:15) survey, covering an eleven-month period, showed that 39 per cent of girls detained had been charged with break and enter or other theft offences. The second-largest category was offences against good order (23 per cent); and the third category was offences against the person (17 per cent). The relevance of these data is that they show that crimes of violence account for a relatively small proportion of the crimes of those incarcerated. The majority of girls are detained for property or good-order offences. However, it appears that a large proportion of young women now entering the juvenile justice system do so on drug-related charges (NSW Department of Juvenile Justice 2000:14).

Detention figures show that ethnicity is an important issue. Ten of the twenty-five girls were recorded as coming from an Anglo-Australian background, seven were Aboriginal, and eight were from NESBs. The Cozens survey also indicated a significant proportion of girls from 'Island' background (4.9 per cent) and 'Asian' background (4.3 per cent) (1993:2).

A more recent survey of young women in detention in New South Wales by the Juvenile Justice Advisory Council (2001b:ii) seems to confirm these earlier studies. Monthly figures for the period 1997–99 indicated that:

- between 56 per cent and 83 per cent of young women were detained for less serious offences
- between 28 per cent and 57 per cent were detained because they had been refused bail, with the proportion increasing in the later part of 1999, when it was consistently over 50 per cent
- 36 per cent of young women refused bail were Indigenous.

In the Cain (1994a) study, all of the sixteen girls sentenced to detention had prior criminal convictions, while seven of the nine on remand had previous criminal convictions. Eleven of the twenty-five girls in detention centres had been previously sentenced to detention. We can make some conclusions concerning process from this information: at any one time, there are few girls in detention who have not been previously convicted of an offence, and almost half have been previously institutionalised. As a group, these young women have experienced contact, and in some cases extensive contact, with juvenile justice agencies.

Previous contact with authorities in relation to welfare matters is also of some importance. Seven of the twenty-five girls had first appeared in court in relation to welfare matters. Three had been institutionalised as state wards. The Cozens survey (1993) indicated that, in detention centres, girls were twice as likely as boys to be state wards (9.3 per cent compared to 4.6 per cent).

Studies and surveys of girls in detention centres point to a number of broad issues. First, there were 'links between the welfare needs of young women, the progression into crime, and the difficulties of escaping the juvenile justice system' (Cozens 1993:9). Proportionately more females than males in custody are likely to be wards, and at least for some girls their first contact with the children's court is through a welfare complaint. However, these girls are not the majority. It needs to be recognised that in future fewer girls will have been first detained as a result of a welfare complaint. The separation of welfare and justice administration, the repeal of welfare complaints such as 'uncontrollable' and 'exposed to moral danger' from the statutes, and the closing down of state ward institutions have led to a decline in this form of intervention. Indeed, in some jurisdictions the whole concept of wardship has been abolished. For example, in New South Wales, under the 1998 Children and Young Persons (Care and Protection) Act, the children's court can make an order relating to the care of the child, including placing the child under the guardianship of the Minister as a last resort. However, the emphasis now is on the care and protection of children (particularly young children) rather than the notion of welfare. This change does not necessarily mean that girls will cease to be institutionalised; rather, we are witnessing a long-term transformation in the mode of intervention. The transformation is from welfarisation to criminalisation. Alder (1998:57) has noted that separating care cases from criminal matters does not mean that the difficult situations in which some girls find themselves have been removed:

> A consistent theme ... is the need to re-think the links, the nature of the responsibilities and the methods of referral between welfare and juvenile justice agencies. The consequences of the more limited use of care applications need to be monitored closely. Some initial statistical analysis in Victoria and Queensland suggests there is a relationship between the decline in care and control applications and the increase in young women appearing before the court on criminal matters.

Thus, it seems apparent that increasingly young women's contact with the justice system will be through the criminalisation process. It is possible to see how criminalisation replaces welfare intervention through the following processes: bail refusal, conditions relating to bail and probation, and the use of offences against good order. It should be noted that at least some of the issues—such as bail—were already the subject of concern during the 1980s. It has been suggested that detention centres may be used inappropriately for young women who are homeless. Certainly, Cozens estimated that 25 per cent of young women held in remand did not in fact receive a sentence of imprisonment (1993:9). Others have estimated that as many as 68 per cent of girls refused bail are not subsequently sentenced to detention (Youth Justice Coalition 1990:281).

It has been noted that young women are more likely to be refused bail than young men (Youth Justice Coalition 1990:281). Generally, a higher proportion of young women in detention centres have been remanded in custody than is the case for young men. The data from the New South Wales Juvenile Justice Advisory Council (2001b) indicate that more than 50 per cent of girls in custody are there on remand. The suggestion is that custodial remand is being used essentially as a substitute welfare measure, and is seen in terms of protecting the interests of the young women. In this sense, one can see the continuities with the previous use of welfare matters (and their overlap with criminal matters) to incarcerate girls for 'their own good'.

The conditions that apply to bail and to probation and parole orders also need to be considered within the context of the continuities with earlier welfare intervention. These conditions typically include being of good behaviour, accepting supervision from juvenile justice officers, attending school or counselling as directed, residing where approved, and not attending certain areas (such as Kings Cross, for example). Breaching such conditions is a further criminal offence and may lead to further incarceration.

It was noted in the Cozens study that 23 per cent of girls in custody during 1992–3 were held for offences against good order; comparatively, 12 per cent of boys were in custody for the same offence category. Court data from Queensland also show that a greater proportion of offences for girls than boys involve public order (11 per cent compared with 4 per cent) (Beikoff 1996:18), although New South Wales data show greater proportional similarity (see table 3.2). Offences against good order include public order offences (such as offensive behaviour, offensive language, and prostitution), and offences against justice procedures (such as breach of court orders and conditions). To the extent that these figures can be interpreted as showing process, there seem to be two related issues: the criminalisation of welfare needs, and the use of incarceration within the framework of protection. Certainly, feminists considering these issues have shown that authorities— welfare officers, police, and magistrates—continue to use custody as a means of 'protecting' girls from perceived risks associated with lifestyle (Moore 1994; Bargen 1994). Beikoff (1996:18) suggests that 'the "Care and Control" girls of the past were often highly visible on the streets and in their use of public space'. She questions whether charges for obscene language, resisting arrest, and assaulting police have replaced the welfare applications of the past.

In terms of policy, it has been noted for many years that, unless there are community-based preventive and supervisory services available for girls, the unnecessary use of custody will continue (Women's Co-ordination Unit 1986). For girls in need of assistance because of homelessness, abuse, or drug and alcohol problems, the choice facing agencies will be either neglect or enforced containment (Moore 1994:5). The ALRC and the HREOC (1997:563) noted the need for the full use of non-custodial programs designed specifically for young women and, where possible, the use of female caseworkers in these programs. The New South Wales Juvenile Justice Advisory Council has found that, because of the lack of data, it is nearly impossible to determine the extent to which young women utilise community-based options and accommodation programs. However, it is known that some alternatives to custody, such as Aboriginal bail hostels, are exclusively for young men (NSW Juvenile Justice Advisory Council 2001b:15–16).

DEVELOPING PROGRAMS FOR YOUNG WOMEN IN CUSTODY

We have discussed some of the issues arising from the use of detention for young women. Many inquiries have specifically identified the special needs of young women in detention centres. One research project (Youth Justice Coalition 1990:314) summed up the problems:

> Those girls interviewed by the Youth Justice Project were among the most distressed and resentful of all our respondents. A higher proportion of girls than boys in our sample had serious drug problems, for which there was little or no treatment available. Of the six girls from one detention centre interviewed for the Project, two girls had mutilated themselves ... There were a series of disturbances in this centre during our period of research ... Ambulances and the police Tactical Response Group had been called in on [one] occasion.

Seven years later, the ALRC and HREOC (1997:620) reiterated the importance of recognising the special needs of young women in custody:

> The number of girls in detention is very small ... girls in larger male-dominated institutions often find that the management, staff training and programs cater primarily for the majority male population. Consequently, girls often become marginalised in the system ... Girls admitted to detention can have serious social, emotional and health problems and their small numbers often mean that they are not given priority in allocation of resources.

In response to the criticisms concerning girls in detention centres, there has been greater consideration of the nature of custody by juvenile justice authorities. In New South Wales, a specific Young Women in Custody Program was developed in the early 1990s, which recognised that the majority of girls in custody 'have been abused, subjected to discrimination and that systemic issues have impacted upon their lives' (Yasmar Juvenile Justice Centre 1994:3). Ten years later, the same department introduced a *Girls' and*

Young Women's Action Plan 2002–2004 (NSW Department of Juvenile Justice 2000), and again recognised the particular needs of young women.

The New South Wales detention centre established for girls in the early 1990s (Yasmar) aimed to strengthen the girls' self-concepts and to empower them to manage their futures in a non-destructive manner. To achieve its objectives, the centre has concentrated on providing a stable and therapeutic environment. A psychotherapist position was also created (for a history of the development of the Young Women in Custody Program, see Clancey and Kirwin (1996)). The program has been criticised for overemphasis on individual change, despite the official recognition of structurally oppressive conditions. Indeed, the techniques being utilised—such as psychotherapy—are premised on the individual and her ability to effect change. There is also a perceptive analysis of problems that have arisen and need resolving from the perspective of two staff members. These include:

- staff attitudes and perceptions of young women
- dealing with self-harm, suicide, and staff assaults
- the potential for net-widening because of the Young Women in Custody Program
- confusion and inconsistencies that arise because young women in the program in some cases are both perpetrators of serious violence (20 per cent had been remanded or sentenced for homicide) and the victims of serious crimes, including incest, sexual assault, and child abuse (Clancey & Kirwin 1996:52–6).

The program at Yasmar was criticised for not satisfactorily separating young women convicted of serious violent offences from those on less serious offences. The centre was also incapable of accommodating young women with babies (NSW Juvenile Justice Advisory Council 2001b:iii). At any time, about one-quarter of young women at the centre are either pregnant or have children. In Parkville detention centre in Victoria, about 20 per cent of young women have children (NSW Juvenile Justice Advisory Council 2001b:8).

Moreover, the same level of resources has not been provided for non-custodial girl-specific support to achieve diversion from custody. Such programs might include day-attendance centres, short-term supportive accommodation, and open custody programs (Moore 1994:142). The resources are still focused on the custodial setting.

In Victoria in the early 1990s, the then Community Services Victoria (CSV) released a specific policy on young women, which—like the New South Wales policy—recognised structurally oppressive conditions. The policy was to 'help young women become independent in ways which recognise the inequalities which have shaped their development as children and young women and have impact on their ongoing opportunities for independent adulthood' (quoted in Alder 1993:305). According to Alder (1993:306–8), those who implement such a policy must understand and challenge several issues specific to young women, particularly the following:

- the workforce is still segregated along gender lines, so that it is difficult for young women to achieve economic independence
- there are fundamental social assumptions about femininity that undermine achieving independence
- young women who have been institutionalised face particular stigmatisation
- the previous sexual abuse of many girls who are institutionalised has to be sensitively understood and resolved in some form for the young women involved
- there needs to be a sufficient range of services for young women despite their relatively small numbers in the juvenile justice system.

State departments continue to build new institutions for girls, such as the Juniperina Centre in Sydney at a cost of $30.5 million, and they continue to develop specific policies for young women. However, these policies are often inadequately implemented and resourced. For example, the NSW *Girls' and Young Women's Action Plan* 2002–2004 required a policy officer specifically to oversee the implementation of the Plan. The position, once established, soon became overburdened with a range of other responsibilities, and before the Plan had reached its final phase, the position had disappeared completely.

Finally, we need to remember that there are specific international human rights standards applicable to young women in custody. Rule 26.4 of the Beijing Rules requires that young female offenders placed in an institution deserve special attention as to their personal needs and problems. They should not receive less care, protection, assistance, treatment, or training than young male offenders, and their fair treatment should be ensured.

GENDER RELATIONS AND MASCULINITY

We have already mentioned that discussions of juvenile justice fail to address gender issues in a way that considers masculinity. We want to show how notions of masculinity are useful in discussing offending behaviour as well as the response by juvenile justice agencies. Self-concepts of masculinity and femininity imply a complex relationship with the social world, and significant differences in how young women and men engage with each other as well as with mainstream social institutions.

The idealised male sex-role is to be tough, competitive, emotionally inexpressive, public, active, and autonomous. The specific content of these characterisations varies, however, depending upon the cultural, class, and ethnic background of the young men in question. Thus, in stereotypical terms, a 'working-class male' might construe masculinity in terms of brute strength, physical attributes, competency in using one's body and machines (such as cars), and peer-group solidarity. By way of contrast, a 'middle-class male' might exhibit masculinity through expressions of intellectual agility, a detached 'professional' attitude, performance of mental labour, and assertion of the importance of individual autonomy. The picture gets more complex once we start to explore the variety of masculinities that are shaped by cultural, national, and ethnic backgrounds and histories.

It has been shown already that boys make up the overwhelming majority of young people brought before the children's courts on criminal matters. We note, however, two caveats to this point. First, self-report studies imply that the level of over-representation of young males in crime is not as great as the official statistics suggest (Ogilvie 1996). Second, we need to acknowledge that criminalisation itself is a product of official processes of selection, apprehension, and prosecution (Tomsen 1996). A simplistic view of male power as all-encompassing would be hard-pressed to explain the fact that it is overwhelmingly young men who are criminalised.

During most of the twentieth century, those theories that attempted to explain male delinquency with respect to notions of masculinity tended to assume that gender relations were 'natural', and as a consequence often focused attention on the mother as a cause of male offending. This is because delinquency was seen to reside in the formation of masculinity itself: if young men were not socialised in the right way, then they would not express their manhood in the appropriate manner. Some theorists, such as John Bowlby, concentrated on explaining delinquency through maternal deprivation: delinquent behaviour could be understood as a form of compensation for inadequate mothering (Bowlby 1947, 1952). Others explained forms of masculinity and delinquency as a compensation for too much mothering (Miller 1958). Delinquency and toughness became an expression of protest against maternal domination. Delinquents were thought to come from families where there was a weak or absent father, and where the mother was effectively the household head. One can see that these theories, which, on the face of it, contradict one another, are based on tacit assumptions about the 'natural' family, with a mother at home and a father as head. Deviations from the norm are held to cause delinquency. Such theories, although they attempt to explain male delinquency, still accept dominant gender relations (Cunneen 1985).

One approach to understanding masculinity is the notion that there is a hegemonic masculinity that is constructed in relation to various subordinated masculinities, as well as in relation to women (Connell 1987:183). The concept of a hegemonic masculinity is useful: it recognises that there is no one masculinity, but that there is a dominant masculinity that prescribes particular behaviour as normal and that devalues other forms of behaviour. In reality, ethnic differences, generational differences, class patterns, and sexual preference come into play in the construction of masculinities; however,

These are subordinated to the dominant definition of what it is to be a 'man' (see Segal 1990; Connell 1987). Hegemonic masculinity emphasises male domination and women's subordination, the sexual division of labour in both the private and the public spheres, and heterosexuality as the dominant—and exclusive—categorisation of male sexuality.

The idealised male sex-role as defined in and by hegemonic masculinity is essentially built upon contempt for women—and for gays and lesbians—and emphasises success in terms of wealth, power, and status, rather than in terms of meaningful and open relationships. In practice, being a man may involve a range of strategies designed to shape the behaviour of oneself and those around one in accordance with the ideal. For example, the activities of young men often parallel those of the criminal justice system in that they constantly police the behaviour of young women, both in terms of sex and sexuality, and, more generally, with regard to what are deemed to be acceptable feminine behaviours (Nava 1984). Hegemonic masculinity is dependent upon, and implicated in, the enforcement of particular masculine and particular feminine modes of behaviour and social interaction.

The last decade has seen a great deal of theoretical debate on how masculinity should be conceptualised, and much of the debate has involved developing and critiquing Connell's groundbreaking work. Messerschmidt (1993) has been interested in considering how men 'accomplish' masculinity in different social settings and the cultural resources they draw upon to bring about this accomplishment. For Messerschmidt, gender, race, and class relations are all implicated in any given social practice, including crime. In addition, the field of gender relations is embedded within hegemonic power relations. Messerschmidt also draws upon phenomenology to consider the 'situational accomplishment' of gender: how gender is achieved in particular social settings. Crime becomes a way of accomplishing gender, particularly where other 'resources' are not available. Resources for accomplishing masculinity are affected by the hierarchies of class, gender, and race. Crime can become a replacement when other conventional resources are not available.

Jefferson (1996) has argued that we need to go beyond notions of hegemonic masculinity to consider how the subjective experience of masculinity is developed before we can understand the cultural forms masculinity takes. He criticises Connell and Messerschmidt for their failure to deal adequately with subjectivity. In relation to Messerschmidt, Jefferson notes that a critical question is not asked: Why is it only that some men from a given class/race background 'come to identify with the crime option, while others identify with other resources to accomplish their masculinity'? (1996:341). For Jefferson, the answer lies in post-structuralism and contemporary psychoanalysis, in particular, theories of the unconscious and the work of Jacques Lacan and Melanie Klein. It should be noted that Jefferson's theoretical demand is a movement away from a sociological explanation for offending behaviour to essentially a psychosocial and individualised explanatory framework. Collier (1998) also argues the

215

limitations of the work of Connell and Messerschmidt from a theoretical standpoint of feminist post-structuralism. Collier sets out what he sees as the limitations of 'social constructionist' and 'sociogenic' explanations (that is, sociological explanations), preferring instead to use theories of subjectivity that collapse the gender/sex dichotomy, rely on the notion of 'sexed bodies', and see identity as 'always contingent and precarious' (Collier 1998:31).

Until relatively recently, the application of these diverse theoretical insights on masculinity had been lacking in considerations of juvenile justice and juvenile offending. Yet they promise insight into the nature of some types of male offending. For example, we could explore the specific nature of young men's offending behaviour (defined narrowly in terms of official violations of the law, rather than with regard to issues of sexism *per se*). We might examine the gender differences in the use of public spaces such as the street (where traditionally males have had a dominant presence), or look at the gendered dynamics of the so-called private sphere of the home (where there is differential regulation of girls' and boys' behaviour by parents). In each case, there are clear implications regarding opportunities, material resources, choices, and group affinities, all of which can have an impact upon patterns of offending (White 1989, 1990).

Research into the nature of street violence, for instance, has demonstrated its prevalence in the lives of young people, and especially young men (White et al. 1999; Collins et al. 2000). This is particularly the case with working-class and marginalised young men, in that being tough and engaging in acts that put one's bodily integrity at risk are generally associated with working-class male culture (in its many varieties and permutations). That is, matters of physique and the physical have typically been central to working-class forms of aggressive masculinity that celebrate strength, speed, agility, and general physical prowess (White 1997/98). Street violence is often associated with pubs and drinking behaviour—a form of celebratory violence (Tomsen, 1997)—as well as fights between groups of young people. It has been noted that under conditions of economic disadvantage, social stress, and group marginalisation, there is even greater recourse to 'the body' as a key site for identity construction and affirmation (see Connell 1995, 2000). This manifests itself as self-destructive behaviour or as violence directed at other people. Behind the façade of toughness and aggression, and the realities of conflict and pain, lies a 'claim to power where there are no real resources for power' (Connell 1995:111). This type of analysis certainly demands greater theoretical sophistication than hitherto has been the case in many criminological accounts of juvenile offending. This is especially so when we examine how ethnicity, racism, and masculinity combine to reinforce particular kinds of behaviour and group formation (Collins et al. 2000). Issues of class, social status, and gender are essential not only to understanding the specific circumstances of young people, but in constructing positive and effective responses to offending and antisocial behaviour.

A theoretical understanding of the dynamics of gender opens up the world of crime and crime-control in new ways. As Tomsen (1996:191) has perceptively noted:

> The complexity of the cultural construction and reproduction of certain masculinities that are interwoven with much criminal activity is a likely reason why prevention, deterrence and rehabilitation have universally taken the form of such elusive and intractable problems, and why single-factor explanations of crime (poverty, unemployment, drinking, or even age and social class) so often fail to hold up to the further scrutiny of researchers seeking causal explanations.

For present purposes, we wish to illustrate the explanatory potential of such analysis by discussing several examples.

The first example is that of homophobia. A 1985 phone-in survey concerning violence against homosexuals revealed that the majority of attacks on gay men were carried out by teenage boys or young men. A more recent Victorian survey of more than 1000 lesbians and gay men revealed that 70 percent of lesbians and 69 per cent of gay men reported being verbally abused, threatened, or assaulted in a public place (GLAD 1994; see also Lesbian and Gay Anti-Violence Project 1992 for discussion of New South Wales). One in five gay men reported actual physical assault in public places; the typical perpetrators were gangs of young men (GLAD 1994:18–19). Overseas literature also stresses the participation of young males in assaults on gay people (Comstock 1991). In Sydney, a number of murders of gay men have involved male juveniles as perpetrators. For example, in 1990, eight young men aged between 16 and 18 years old were responsible for the bashing and death of Richard Johnson in a Sydney park (Tomsen 1997).

Interviews with attackers note their inability to accept and understand sexual attraction and affection between men (Herek & Berrill 1992). Connell has noted that this raises 'disturbing questions about the role of violence and homophobia in the construction of masculinity' (1987:12). Those responsible for the deaths of gay men have often claimed they were simply 'out for some fun', or defending their own heterosexual male 'honour'. In this sense, we can see that homophobic assaults receive some social approval through the dominant definition of masculinity, which devalues and disapproves of homosexuality. As Tomsen has noted, while concerns about male identity and honour may motivate such killings, 'it is the institutional heterosexism of the entire criminal justice system and criminological discourse, and the long history of the construction of gay men as targets of police violence and prosecution, which has made possible and condoned this form of violence' (1996:192–3). Research by Mason (1997) on violence against lesbians, and research by Tomsen (1997) on seventy-four gay-hate killings consider the role of masculinity in understanding violence by young men. Both authors argue that the violence commonly reflects the hatred and stigma felt towards men and women whose sexuality falls outside acceptable gendered identities. Violence and harassment becomes important for attaining and protecting the masculine identity of the perpetrators (Tomsen and Mason 2001:265).

A common way in which young men are brought before the courts is for offences related to motor vehicles, including theft. As we indicated earlier (in chapter 3), young males make up a large proportion of all people apprehended for motor vehicle theft. In previous work, we have drawn attention to the relationship between the expression of masculinity and the theft of vehicles (Cunneen 1985:84–6; White 1990:135). Cars and motorbikes need to be seen as symbolic objects of masculine power, linked to fantasies of material and sexual domination and success. They are powerful emotional and cultural symbols that define aspects of what it is to be a man (Walker 1999; Forrester 1999). Motor vehicles are also commodities that are produced and consumed in the marketplace. Time, space, and patterns of social life are also predicated to a large extent on the private ownership of motor vehicles. For those without a wage, access to the commodity may be available only through theft. In this brief summary, we can begin to see the links between the symbolic and social values of particular commodities and how they are intertwined with the subjective meanings attached to gender. We would argue that, without an understanding of masculinity, it is not possible to understand why young men are so often criminalised through offences related to motor vehicles. To argue this position is not to deny that young women are involved in motor vehicle theft. However, the concept of masculinity provides a basis for understanding why young men are so much more involved in this criminal activity than young women.

On the one hand, our subjective understandings of the world are structured through gender. On the other hand, it is necessary to consider how state agencies—and the forms of regulation in which they are engaged—are gendered. Such an analysis in the area of juvenile justice is an examination of gender-specific control of boys and girls within an institutional setting. Kersten (1989) has argued that there is a 'salvationist' attitude by institutional staff towards the boys in relation to homosexuality. While there is scope for employment and sport, caring and emotional needs remain unmet. Certain taboos are prevalent, including taboos on speaking about problems or on serious discussions about relationships unless such discussions are defined as being within a therapeutic environment. While there is a taboo on physical touching, a certain level of violence is permitted. Kersten also noted in the study that the use of space reflected the images of an aggressive masculinity, with posters of macho figures and pin-up girls. Without any challenge to this form of masculinity, it is likely that those young men who have been institutionalised will go on to further criminalisation.

It has been argued that the social practices that construct gender relations do not express natural patterns or reflect natural differences between boys and girls. What these practices do is establish the social marks of gender. They weave a structure of symbol and interpretation around what it is to be a boy or a girl (Connell 1987:79–80). We have only sketched the way in which a theory of the construction of masculinity can help our understanding, both of the nature of offending and of the ways in which the juvenile justice system itself operates within the parameters of the dominant gender relations. Of course, we add that it is not necessary that men and women working in the area of juvenile justice must reproduce the dominant conceptions of masculinity and femininity; they may be in a position to challenge those relations.

CONCLUSION

This chapter has shown some of the transformations that have occurred in feminist thinking about young women and juvenile justice over the last three decades. The concern has shifted from a focus on welfare complaints and juvenile justice agencies' preoccupation with girls' alleged sexual misconduct. There is still concern about the links between welfare and criminalisation; however, this is increasingly within the context of the failure to deal adequately with the oppressive conditions young women experience. Juvenile justice is still focused on detention. There has been a challenge to simplistic categorisations that ignore the importance of class, race, and cultural difference. Alder (1997:51–5) has argued that to understand the place of crime in young women's lives, it is necessary to:

- consider the inappropriateness of the victim—offender dichotomy
- understand the diversity of young women's experiences
- recognise the significance of economic factors in young women's lives.

To describe the operation of the juvenile justice system as 'sexist' or 'patriarchal' is to oversimplify the processes in operation. There is a range of social processes that mediate the treatment of male and female young people. These include race and ethnicity, class and economic background, family arrangements, and demeanour, style, and membership of subcultural groups. In the case of young women, we need to specify how these social attributes are simultaneously constituted with gender. Furthermore, we must think about what individual factors are important. After all, many girls from working-class backgrounds never come into contact with juvenile justice agencies. Individual considerations must include abuse, homelessness, and drug and alcohol problems.

There is also a range of organisational and administrative factors that influence the processing of offenders. Gender relations are mediated by the work practices of social workers, police, court staff, and so on, and also contribute to the construction of those work practices. For instance, to what extent does the police definition of 'proper' police work influence their treatment of young women?

Studies that simply compare the treatment of girls with that of boys have been criticised for their theoretical limitations. These approaches assume equal treatment: the treatment of males is the norm against which the treatment of young women is measured. As feminists have noted, even if it were found that there was no difference in treatment, such studies avoid the more difficult political question of how young people should be treated, as well as the theoretical problems of explaining why juvenile justice agencies operate in the way they do (Cain 1989).

It is apparent that there has also been a growing demand to deal adequately with masculinity in the context of juvenile justice. The vast majority of young people who appear before the children's courts are young men. Yet, by and large, masculinity remains the invisible social relation, uncommented on and unproblematised. The chapter has shown some specific instances where theories of masculinity can contribute significantly to our understandings of juvenile justice.

PART III
THE STATE,
PUNISHMENT,
AND COMMUNITY

9 | Policing the young

INTRODUCTION

The police are the gatekeepers of the criminal justice system. The formal contact young people have with the system—as victims or offenders—usually begins with some kind of contact with police officers. The nature of this contact can have far-reaching consequences. For example, a young person who does not cooperate with the police might find themself being brought further and further into the criminal justice system. On the other hand, simple compliance with everything the police demand of the young person may in fact constitute a violation of their legal and human rights.

The aim of this chapter is to survey the general relationship between young people and the police in Australian society, to explore the roles and activities of the police in relation to young people, and to assess the major issues surrounding police–youth contact. We begin by examining the different roles of public and private police in society. This is followed by a discussion of the range of powers the police have to deal with young people. How police interact with young people is partly determined by adoption of different styles and operational practices. The use of zero tolerance methods and youth curfews is relevant to this discussion. The next section considers issues pertaining to differential policing both of young people generally relative to adults, and of specific groups of minority youth. The chapter concludes with a summary critique of coercive forms of policing and crime prevention.

YOUTH, POLICING, AND PUBLIC ORDER

Most contact young people have with police today involves state or public police and, increasingly, private police such as security guards. State police have a wide range of tasks to perform (White & Perrone 2005). These include such things as law enforcement (detection, investigation, and prosecution of cases involving commission of an offence), order maintenance (policing of public order, domestic or family violence), crime prevention (working with community groups and individuals to prevent home burglary or to reduce the fear of crime), social services (finding lost children, dealing with potential suicides), and traffic management (drink-driving campaigns, attending traffic accidents). As public employees, state police are meant to be accountable to the public and to perform their work first and foremost in the public interest.

By way of contrast, private police are generally hired for specific purposes and are accountable directly to the private employer (which in some instances may include government departments). Private policing usually has a security focus. Such police include, for example, those personnel hired to protect commercial property, premises, employees, and customers (malls, banks, sports arenas), and residential communities (apartment complexes, gated communities). They may also be used by businesses and government agencies to provide security with regard to computer information systems (see Bayley 1999). In many cases, private policing is oriented towards the regulation and movement of people in public places such as malls and residential sites. In the case of both public and private policing, the location for most youth–police contact is 'the street', although the precise nature of the contact varies according to the police agency involved and the circumstances surrounding the contact.

State policing and social regulation

The systematic regulation of young people in public spaces has long been a key aspect of the maintenance of public order as conceived by authority figures (Cohen 1979; Hogg & Golder 1987; Finnane 1994). This is largely due to the fact that, historically, public space was generally publicly owned, and public order primarily a responsibility of the state. Hence the police have been central players in the leisure and spare-time activities of young people, especially working-class young people and Indigenous young people. Young people have used streets, beaches, malls, and shopping areas as prime sites for their unstructured activities, and it is these areas that have received the main attention of state police services.

The specific tasks of the police are generally framed in terms of particular social objectives. For example, police services in Australia today have mission statements that spell out the diverse roles of the service. Generally speaking, these aims include minimising the level of crime and maximising the extent to which people feel secure from the effects of crime, ensuring a level of public order that enables people to safely go about their lawful business, providing assistance to the public in circumstances of personal emergency, promoting road safety and effective traffic management, and engaging in crime prevention (White & Perrone 2005). The broad task areas of the police are thus varied and complex.

In order to carry out their tasks, the police have a variety of operational methods and powers of intervention (see further on). Legislatively, the police are guided by what constitutes public order and disorder by a range of laws, such as those referring to loitering, offensive behaviour, offensive language, obstructing traffic, and so on. So-called anti-gang laws, welfare legislation, and parental responsibility Acts, have also been put forward as providing further legal bases for police intervention in young people's activities.

How the police intervene in youth affairs is contingent upon a range of factors, that include, for example, the local political context, especially relating to 'law and order' debates. It also depends on how the media and the general public respond to incivilities in the public domain, whether in the form of direct experience of such things as noisy groups taking up the footpaths, or indirect experience of 'bad behaviour' in the form of graffitied walls and trains, and vandalised buildings and amenities. The general fear of crime in a community—whatever its origins or how accurate the perceptions—can have a major effect on policing practices.

Another factor in how the police go about their tasks relates to the culture and nature of policing itself. Blagg and Wilkie (1995:21) observe that:

> There is a considerable body of evidence suggesting that 'rank and file' police officers are extremely skilled at adapting the criminal law to meet the immediate requirements of 'the job', as they define it. The police task in relation to the policing of youth and social space (which is more or less the same thing) is a notorious 'grey area'; a shadowy domain defined precisely by its fluidity and the absence of clear, over-arching rules.

The use of discretion by individual officers tends to be socially patterned in the sense that individual decisions tend to manifest themselves as broad patterns of selective intervention. This is seen, for example, in the over-representation of some groups (Indigenous people), and some types of offences (offensive language), in police interventions; and in the underrepresentation of other groups (corporate businesspeople), and other types of offences (racist violence).

In the specific area of police–youth relations, the use of discretion is moulded by things such as the attitude and demeanour of young people in public spaces, their physical and social attributes, and how they interact with the police directly. A number of academic and community research projects in recent years have highlighted that many young people have a negative perception of the police and particular styles of intervention (see, for example, White & Alder 1994; Youth Justice Coalition 1994; Blagg & Wilkie 1995; NSW Standing Committee on Social Issues). The kinds of things young people are concerned about in their contact with the police are summarised in box 9.1. Obviously, how young people view the police will have some bearing on how the two groups get along.

BOX 9.1   YOUTH AND POLICE PERCEPTIONS OF EACH OTHER

YOUNG PEOPLE'S PERCEPTIONS OF POLICE

- perceptions of unnecessary police intervention and contact
- regular experience of verbal intimidation and the threat of violence
- experience of physical violence as a 'normal' part of contact with police
- experience of direct and indirect racism
- perceptions of underpolicing in cases of youth victimisation.

POLICE PERCEPTIONS OF YOUNG PEOPLE

- perception of lack of respect by young people for the law and law officials
- experience of constant hassles from young people on the street
- experience of lack of cooperation by some young people
- concern with the poor attitude and demeanour of some young people
- experience of verbal and physical violence directed at police by young people
- acknowledgment of youth dilemmas but having necessity for police action.

The use of police powers and discretionary decision-making at street level are affected not only by how young people respond to the police, but also by how the police feel about young people. A study undertaken in the early 1990s, for example, found that very often the police were less than impressed by the attitudes and behaviours of young people (Alder, O'Connor, Warner & White 1992). This, too, is shown in box 9.1.

Community pressure and political concern about the relationship between young people and the police helped to generate change within some police services in Australia in the 1990s. Increasingly, police around the country have begun to implement various schemes and policies that are intended to improve police–youth relations. This is reflected, for example, in official policy statements in New South Wales and Victoria, where the aims of new 'youth policy' require that children and young people be treated fairly and with respect, that police are to work to reduce youth crime, that courts are to be used as a last resort, that police are to support and involve victims, and that police are to work towards positive social change. In South Australia, the youth policy includes the following types of prescriptions:

- young people will be provided with the full range of services available to all citizens
- young people will be treated fairly and with respect
- young people will be informed of their legal position and rights

- police will show due care in the exercise of discretionary powers
- police will be aware of the difficulties young people can experience during questioning
- the lawful use of public places by young people will be respected
- police will act to minimise the negative stereotyping of young people
- police will work with other agencies to address issues involving young people
- the service is committed to identifying and implementing appropriate programs for young people.

In the Northern Territory, an extensive research project was undertaken to discuss ways of improving policing strategies in Aboriginal and non-English-speaking background (NESB) communities (O'Neill & Bathgate 1993). Among the recommendations were references to improving liaison between the police and the diverse communities, development and extension of cross-cultural training for police, and recruitment of people from diverse backgrounds. Similar types of recommendations were made by the New South Wales Office of the Ombudsman (1994) in relation to issues of race relations and policing in that state. Also of note is the work of Blagg and Wilkie (1995), who have developed a series of 'model clauses' that provide examples of how contact between young people and the police can be framed by specific legal procedures and guidelines, which are designed to respect rights and improve relationships.

Most jurisdictions now incorporate sessions relating to young people and youth issues into their pre-service and in-service police training programs. In a similar vein, specialist units (such as the Youth Advisory Unit in Victoria), designated positions (Youth Liaison Officers), and special programs (such as Police in Schools in a number of jurisdictions) have been set up in many states, and provide some indication of the organisational responses to police–youth issues.

Whether such strategies translate into large-scale change to current policing practices, especially given the countervailing pressures associated with adoption of tough 'law and order' laws and campaigns, is open to question. Furthermore, any substantial—rather than token—change demands a major shift in overall police departmental orientations and allocation of resources. As Chan (1996:171) comments: 'To be taken seriously, policy statements must be developed with the participation of operational police, backed up by relevant programs, adequate resources, appropriate administrative support, rigorous monitoring and an effective accountability structure.' For this to occur, there must be concerted political support for such changes, both outside and inside the police services.

Commercial enterprise and private interests

The relationship between state policing and private policing is reflective of broader changes occurring to the urban landscape. Whether a site is publicly accessible, while privately owned, or if it has explicit restrictive access, makes a difference in the kind of policing and legal regulation that will be in place. In some residential areas and sites, for example, residents are protected by private security firms. Access is controlled by the firms, as is routine patrolling of the site. The architecture and planning of such residences and residential areas tend to be designed with specific security and access objectives, which, by their very nature, exclude the general public. Interestingly, it has been suggested that, in such circumstances, off-site areas such as surrounding streets become the proper domain of state police, with the implication that 'good' citizens will remain in their enclaves, while 'bad' citizens are identified by dint of being on the streets (see Davies 1995).

For most young people, however, public-space issues revolve around publicly accessible, privately owned sites such as shopping centres. The regulation of public space in this instance is not driven by concerns with public order *per se*. Rather, most policing strategies are premised on the idea of promoting such spaces as 'consumer' spaces, and doing whatever is necessary to facilitate consumption.

The main concern of commercial enterprises is to prevent crime in the most effective way possible, and to ensure that behaviour in the site best matches the commercial objectives of the trader or corporation. This is reflected, for example, in a report that discussed the ways in which groups of young people gathering in Launceston's Mall caused concern to some citizens and business owners (Challenger 1997). The sorts of behaviours that were identified as being undesirable in the groups of young people included:

- occasionally intimidating or harassing mall users
- fighting with one another outside, sometimes spilling over into stores
- causing anxiety to staff and customers when roaming within stores
- causing damage to property
- being nuisances in stores and jeopardising the safety of customers and staff (for example, running through stores)
- stealing goods from the stores.

Similar findings were also apparent in a Melbourne study, which found that retail staff in a large shopping complex felt that 'loitering', 'rowdiness', 'offensive behaviour', and 'shoplifting' were significant issues (Bruce 1997).

In response to these kinds of activities, many site managers attempt to modify their sales environment or to beef up security in some way. Rules of access, public availability, and behaviour are set by site managers. These vary from site to site, and can include both dress and behaviour codes. The breach of such rules can lead to exclusion from the site (Youth Action and Policy Association NSW 1997:50). The usual message behind these sorts of rules is that the purpose of using the centre is one of specified types of consumption only (rather than socialising).

Leaving aside for the moment the social nature of shopping centres, and the multiple social uses of space within them, it is sufficient to note simply that much of the policing of commercial public spaces is undertaken by private police. In many cases, private security firms and guards work closely in tandem with state police in regulating privately owned spaces. The situation is rendered even more complex when the responsibility for security in publicly owned spaces is given over to private security firms (as with Southgate in Melbourne). A number of important questions can be asked, therefore, regarding the precise relationship between private and public policing, and issues of accountability, powers, and rights (see Blagg & Wilkie 1995).

Due to their physical layout and construction, city sites such as shopping complexes and recreational and entertainment centres are more amenable to the adoption of highly intensive systems of surveillance and control. The use of security guards and closed-circuit cameras, for example, is not uncommon.

Furthermore, there are instances where private companies and corporations are granted extraordinary powers to police users of their privately owned but publicly accessible urban spaces. In 1994, for example, the Queensland government introduced the South Bank Corporation Amendment By-Law (No. 1) 1994, which provides power for security officers to stop people, ask for their name and address, and direct them to leave the site (Murray 1995). The by-law was amended in December 1995 to enable security officers to unilaterally ban people with written notice from returning to the site for up to ten days if the person disobeys a direction, is drunk or disorderly, or even if a security officer simply considers the ban 'justified in the circumstances'. Security officers can also apply to the court to ban people for up to one year. It is important to note that not only does the law give the private police greater powers of exclusion than those available to state police, but these powers are also available to security officers regardless of training or attitudes towards young people.

The relationship between private security guards and young people has some parallels with that of the relationship between state police and young people. A study by White and others (1997) for example, found that many young people who had had bad experiences with security guards complained of constant harassment, being under surveillance, and being told to move on. What many young people felt was a sense of unfairness in terms of how the guards responded to them, particularly because of their age. More generally, it is often assumed that young people are simply hanging around and that they necessarily have a negative impact on retail investment and management. Yet, as Queensland research demonstrates (see Crane, Heywood, Earl, Egginton & Gleeson 1997:44), the spending impact of young people in shopping centres is not inconsiderable, and they have significant influence on parental spending choices.

On the other hand, young people do have positive experiences with security guards as well (and likewise with police). Young people in a Melbourne study

(White et al. 1997:122) described how they were friends with some security guards, and how they had been helped or protected by them. Having a 'positive experience' was also interpreted as simply being treated well when being hassled by the security guard to move on. As with recent state police initiatives (generally undertaken under a broad 'community policing' umbrella), there has been some movement around the country to develop more constructive relationships between young people and private security guards. In developing a more inclusive, less coercive approach to shopping centre security, public space consultants in Queensland have recommended detailed strategies designed to improve security services (see Heywood et al. 1998). These include the development of guidelines for shopping centre security provision in relation to young people, and security personnel training that is consistent with a 'customer service' approach and a 'crisis response' approach, depending on the circumstances. Issues of communication, accountability, problem-solving, appropriate types of security, and so on are central to reform (see also Crane 2000). Again, as with state police reforms, the impetus for significant alteration of existing security practices very much depends upon management support for such reform. In part, this depends upon whether or not shopping centre managers recognise the commercial benefits of having inclusive policies regarding those who visit the site (see White, Kosky & Kosky 2001).

POLICE POWERS AND OPERATIONAL STYLES

There are different models of policing, each stressing different approaches and strategies, but in the end what counts are the actions of the police on the beat and in direct contact with members of the public. In the course of their dealings with young people, the police have a range of choices in terms of how to proceed, which are outlined here. Importantly, what the police do in practice involves a high degree of discretion.

Police procedures and young people

Police procedures for dealing with young people include the following:

- *Assistance*—Advice to young people, general information, street directions, traffic regulations and responsibilities, anti-theft suggestions, and information about safety and personal security.
- *Informal caution*—Casual dealing with young people with no formal charges laid, may take young people home or phone parents or guardians, minor intervention, may be recorded administratively on caution sheet at the police station or in the police notebook, and includes warning or telling young people to move on.
- *Formal caution*—Formal record of a caution administered at a police station and authorised by senior police officer; a parent or guardian must attend or be notified to contact the police station within a set period. A formal caution

can be administered whether or not the young person is arrested for an offence. In some jurisdictions (such as South Australia) police can issue a formal caution accompanied by a range of specified requirements, such as undertaking community work; in other jurisdictions (such as Tasmania), the formal caution may take the form of a youth conference (see chapter 13).

- *Interrogation*—Common law rules of voluntariness and discretion apply. The presence of an adult witness is required when juveniles are interviewed; questioning may take place in the absence of an adult in some instances (safety of others, serious offence). Cautions and legal advice should be offered; generally, police have no power to involuntarily detain suspects or witnesses solely for the purpose of questioning or investigation, or to hold them pending enquiries.

- *Search*—There are common law and statutory powers to search for certain classes of suspected persons, to search persons who have been arrested, and to search for specific articles and material relevant to the investigation of crime. Search without a warrant applies only in cases where, on reasonable grounds, the arrested person is believed to have committed a serious indictable offence.

- *Summons*—The usual procedural option is a summons (citation notice or attendance notice) calling for the alleged offender to appear on a specified date before a magistrate's court. In less serious offences, the legislatively preferred option is by way of charge and summons.

- *Arrest*—The decision to arrest and place in custody is meant to be used in exceptional circumstances (such as with a serious or violent offence). Parents or guardians are informed of charges that are laid at the police station. Reasonable force may be used. The person arrested is entitled to know on what charge or on suspicion of what crime they are being arrested.

- *Fingerprinting and bodily samples*—Usually subject to statutory provisions and restrictions. A court order may be required, depending on the age of the young person. In some cases, the young person must be in custody or on a charge of an indictable (serious) offence before fingerprints or bodily samples (such as those for DNA testing) can be taken.

- *Custody*—Once arrested, a young person must be taken before a justice as soon as practicable unless bail is granted. Bail may be refused on the grounds of the seriousness of the offence, or for the welfare or protection of the child. Every person taken into custody must be released, granted bail, or taken before court; in some jurisdictions, time limits are set by legislation.

- *Complaints*—There are no special procedures where the complainant is a juvenile. Complaints may be made to another member of the police service or to the Office of the Ombudsman.

The exercise of police discretion is influenced by a range of institutional and occupational factors. In the specific case of young people, discretion is based partly on broad departmental policies and guidelines, and partly on the officer's perception of the event and individual in question. According to the police, the decision to deal with a young person one way or another is determined by the seriousness of the offence, and by the degree of cooperation displayed by the young person (Alder et al. 1992).

The general attitude and appearance of young people obviously play a part in shaping police perceptions and decisions (see especially chapters 6 and 7). The police develop expectations regarding the potential threat or trouble posed by certain groups of young people. This leads them to pre-empt possible trouble by harassing those young people whose demeanour, dress, and language identify them as being of potential concern. Indeed, distinctions are often made between the 'respectable' and the 'rough', the 'haves' and the 'have-nots', and police action is taken in accordance with these perceptions (Smith 1975; James & Polk 1989; Conway 1992; Omaji 2003).

In aggregate terms, then, we know that such 'personal' discretion is in fact social in nature. That is, the same people tend to receive the same kind of treatment—positive or negative—depending on overt social characteristics and social background. For example, a report prepared by the Federation of Community Legal Centres in Victoria (Biondo & Palmer 1993) pointed out that police mistreatment of the young was more prevalent among unemployed young people and students—that is, the more marginalised youth in terms of income. Charges of police mistreatment and harassment also predominate among groups such as Aborigines and Torres Strait Islanders, young homeless people, and young people who use the streets (White & Alder 1994).

The different task orientations of the police can subject them to contradictory demands. For example, calls to 'clean up the streets' and for law enforcement or public order may go against the more benign objective of providing for the general welfare of young people in city centres. Or, regardless of the motivation, the mix of different functions and the coercive powers available to the police may cause young people to perceive any kind of intervention in their lives as threatening or unwanted.

Within police departments, there is often an informal division of police tasks into 'real' police work and those of the 'plastic cops'. The first emphasises the use of force, intervention, and the muscled arm of the law; the second features dialogue with members of the community and the peaceful resolution of conflict. One's view of these methods rests on one's preference for traditional policing or problem-centred policing. The traditional style of policing emphasises the response to individual incidents, with a focus on the incident and the specific offender and victim. This approach is reactionary and police-centred. By way of contrast, problem-centred policing encourages identification of recurring problems and the causes of antisocial behaviour and crime. This approach analyses underlying problems (for example, ongoing conflict between police and young people in a particular locale) and devotes time and funds to determining causes and solutions. This perspective encourages coordination between police and other public-sector agencies. Hence, it is not simply police-centred as in the traditional style of policing, but seeks to broaden its activities to incorporate public participation.

Within the various police departments and service divisions, there are strong conflicts over the definition of what is real, positive, effective policing. Indeed, there are deep divisions within political parties and the public at large, and among police officers themselves, as to what constitutes a 'good cop'. Traditionally, this concept has been associated with the notion of exerting authority, a masculine street presence, and the fighting of crime. Problem-centred and community-based policing presents a different image, preferring to concentrate on deep structural issues of crime and the responses to it, and doing so in ways that do not intimidate or alienate community members. Attempts to change the face of policing have included, for example, employment of greater numbers of women, and people from other than English-speaking backgrounds.

Zero tolerance policing

How governments respond to youth behaviour, let alone youth criminal behaviour, is heavily influenced by the media and the political climate of 'moral panic' and anti-youth reporting. One consequence of this has been to evoke controlling and punitive measures on the part of some jurisdictions and policymakers, with major implications for policing and police strategies.

The populist crime-fighting terminology adopted in many jurisdictions is that of 'zero tolerance'. This refers to a broad philosophical stance with regard to how best to counter 'street crime', and to specific techniques and methods of state and private intervention that are deemed to be the most effective in combating crime. The zero tolerance approach is especially popular in the USA, has come to the fore in the United Kingdom under the Labour government, and has gained some currency among politicians and police in Australia.

Philosophically, the concept of 'zero tolerance' refers to the idea of 'taking crime seriously' by getting 'tough on crime' at its source. This is interpreted as taking pre-emptive police action in certain places (city 'hot spots') and against certain people (youth gangs). The approach is essentially coercive in nature, and involves stepped-up general surveillance, monitoring of specific areas and groups of people, and active use of force and arrest, even in the case of relatively minor offences (such as street littering or offensive language). Any behaviour, activity, or group deemed to be antisocial is not to be tolerated by authorities (see Dixon 1998; Cunneen 1999; Grabosky 1999; Marshall 1999). The response to the Cronulla riots in Sydney in the holiday period 2005–06—which saw the use of police road blocks across major arteries, the passing of legislation that greatly extended police powers, the deployment of huge numbers of police in the southern beaches area, and an emphasis on paramilitary style of intervention—provides a prime example of zero tolerance 'no nonsense' policing.

Such an approach relies heavily upon police intervention, and, increasingly, intervention by private police and security guards. It puts police at the centre of responding to 'disorderliness' (see Palmer 1997:234), and insofar as this is the case, represents a form of coercive crime control that has little direct or meaningful community involvement. It is a top-down approach to crime and social regulation.

Such an approach also goes well beyond a crime-control focus as such. For example, it has been noted that zero tolerance policies have as much to do with limiting the presence of selected groups in the public domain as they do with combating actual criminal behaviour. As Palmer (1997:236) points out:

> As places seek to compete as 'most livable cities' or countries or municipalities, those things that are deemed to have a negative impact on perceptions of 'quality of life' are likely to be subject to greater intervention. Crime is one of these. More generally though, it will be 'disorderliness' and 'anti-social behaviour'. These are being seen as the signs of either actual or future decline in quality of life and therefore a threat to the very viability—economic and social—of a particular place.

Zero tolerance is thus concerned with maintaining particular kinds of public order, in particular kinds of public spaces, using particular policing strategies that target particular groups of people. It is the most evident and pervasive form of crime 'prevention' pertaining to young people. Such policing effectively sees juvenile crime prevention as a matter of deterrence, usually through proactive interventions that attempt to stop young people from engaging in certain activities, or aim to exclude them from being in certain kinds of public spaces at particular times.

The coercive and authoritarian nature of such policing is reflected in the negative perceptions of some young people of police, and in the ambivalence among police regarding the best way to deal with young people. For example, a British study (Loader 1996) suggests that often the police do understand some of the problems experienced by young people in their use of time and space, but the police themselves are under organisational pressure to do something about the youth presence. As mentioned above, 'doing something' generally means engaging in some kind of coercive intervention—moving young people on, disbanding groups of young people, or bringing to a halt certain kinds of activities that are deemed undesirable (if not always criminal).

While the legislative basis for action varies from state to state, the general trend over the last decade or so around Australia has been for police services to be granted extensive new powers regarding young people (see, for example, Sandor & White 1993; Blagg & Wilkie 1995; Mukherjee, Carcach & Higgins 1997). These range from casual use of 'name-checks' (asking young people their names and addresses), to 'move-on' powers (the right to ask young people to move away from certain areas), to searching for prohibited implements, to the enhanced ability to take fingerprints and bodily samples of alleged young offenders.

Some legislation that increases police powers may be designed in a manner that is age-neutral, but that in practice frequently has a disproportionate impact upon young people. For instance, the *Crimes Legislation Amendment (Police and Public Safety) Act 1998* (NSW) commenced in July 1998. The Act made amendments to the *Summary Offences Act 1988* (NSW), so as to make the carrying of a knife in a public place an offence, to permit police to conduct searches for knives and other dangerous implements, and to enable police to give reasonable directions in public places to deal with people whose behaviour or presence constitutes an obstruction, harassment, intimidation, or causes fear.

The Act was monitored by the New South Wales Ombudsman over the first 12 months of its operation. The Ombudsman found that people from 15–19 years of age were much more likely to be stopped and searched for knives than those in any other age group. While there were more knives found on 17 year olds than on anyone else, the proportion of productive searches was relatively low for teenage suspects. In other words, there was a particularly high number of knife searches of young people in which no knife was found. In a similar vein, it was observed that a high number of teenagers were given directions by police under the terms of the Act. Significantly, it was also pointed out that 'the proportion of persons aged 17 years or younger affected by the directions power is higher than for the knife searches. The police data indicate that 48 per cent of persons "moved on" were aged 17 years or younger, while 42 per cent of persons searched were juveniles' (NSW Office of the Ombudsman 1999:37). The Ombudsman recommended that the New South Wales police service closely monitor the use of these powers, and be aware of the adverse impact this activity might have on police relations within the community in general or on those sections of the community subjected to such activity.

From an operational perspective, the use of specific campaigns, such as Operation Sweep in Western Australia from 1994, likewise denotes the concern of some police departments and political leaders that the activities of the police should be directed at, literally, cleaning the streets of young people. This campaign is particularly instructive to examine insofar as it demonstrates the ways in which law-and-order commonsense informs policy, and how media and police discourses shape the representation of key issues.

Operation Sweep was launched in January 1994 (see Blagg & Wilkie 1995; Sercombe in White 1999a). The impetus for the campaign stemmed from concerns expressed by the Northbridge Business Association about the threatening presence of young people, as well as the rumour that there was a gang problem in Northbridge (a major restaurant and café district of Perth). The intention of the campaign was to use provisions of s. 138B of the *Child Welfare Act (1947)* (WA) as a legal basis upon which to remove young people from the streets of Northbridge. This section allows the police to detain a child where, in their opinion, the child is on their own outside parental control and is, in the police's view, in physical or moral danger or truanting from school. Hence, while the campaign itself was clearly linked to a crime-control agenda, it nevertheless relied upon legislation intended for the care and protection of children.

The campaign involved picking up teenagers who were on the streets after a specified time (as early as 8 p.m.), taking them back to the police station, and then phoning their parents to collect them. In a fourteen-night period, more than 300 young people were detained. In Fremantle alone, in one weekend, 118 young people were reported as having been detained (Blagg & Wilkie 1995).

Within a short time, local opposition to the campaign was apparent, from civil libertarians, affected parents and children, and members of the wider community. This was particularly so in Fremantle. Community meetings were organised that condemned the initiative, affirmed young people's right to be in public spaces, and challenged the operation's legal basis.

Partly as a consequence of such opposition, the campaign was briefly stopped, to be replaced by a similar program titled Operation Family Values. The focus was now more on actual unlawful behaviour. This was followed in July 1994 by Operation Safe City. In 1997, Operation Zero Tolerance was launched in Perth, with the aim of cracking down on petty offences on the assumption that controlling such offences would have a positive flow-on effect in controlling more serious ones.

The removal of young people from public spaces has also been accomplished through specific youth-oriented legislative measures. For example, in 1994 in New South Wales the Children (Parental Responsibility) Act was passed, which increased parental responsibility for the behaviour of their children, and which increased police powers to remove young people from public places without charge. In 1997, Premier Carr announced the replacement of this legislation with the Children (Protection and Parental Responsibility) Act.

For present purposes, the sections of the Act dealing with police intervention are the most significant. The Act allows the police to remove young people under 16 years of age from public places without charge if the police believe that the young people are 'at risk' of committing an offence or of being affected by a crime, if they are not under the supervision or control of a responsible adult, or if it is believed the young person is in danger of being physically harmed, injured, or abused. The Act does not specify the sorts of offences that the young person must be suspected of being at risk of committing, but if an offence were actually committed, the police would not be picking up the young person under this Act.

The legislation does not automatically come into effect across the state: rather, local councils are required to apply to the attorney-general for their area to become a designated operational area (see Luker 1997). The legislation allows for 'officially approved' persons to have charge of young people for a period not exceeding 24 hours, without access to the courts, legal advice, or representation. The police priority is to get a young person to their home or to a family member. Local councils must consider a number of issues before their area is approved to become a designated operational area: these issues may include consulting with young people and examining the existence or possibility of alternative local crime prevention plans.

In the first six months of 1999, 145 young people were removed from public places in the four local government areas where the legislation was operational. Of these 145 young people, 90 per cent were Aboriginal children (Chan & Cunneen 2000:53). The apparent discriminatory use of the law by police led to a complaint under the Racial Discrimination Act. Evaluations of similar types of zero tolerance policing in the USA have likewise highlighted the discriminatory effects of such policing and the implication of such strategies in the violation of civil and political rights (see Dixon 1998; Cunneen 1999, 2001a).

Youth curfews

Zero tolerance policing has also been accompanied by other measures designed to contain and manage people, especially in regard to their access to and use of public places. Youth curfews, for example, represent yet another way in which to clear the streets of young people, regardless of whether they have done anything wrong, much less illegal. The use of youth curfews is extensive in the USA, and curfew ordinances are in effect in a majority of the largest cities in the USA (Bilchik 1996). Support for the imposition of curfews has also been highlighted in debates and political rhetoric on how best to deal with juvenile crime in the United Kingdom (Jeffs & Smith 1996).

The logic of the youth curfew centres on the problem of displacement. That is, at issue is how best to reduce the street presence of young people— particularly in circumstances where they are relatively free from adult supervision and control—by forcing them into situations of close monitoring where their activities and movements will be subject to stricter regulation, such as in the parental home or through structured youth pursuits such as recreation or social clubs.

Measuring the effectiveness of youth curfews is highly contentious. Proponents point to data on youth offending and victimisation rates that appear to demonstrate a decline in social harm associated with the imposition of curfews. Opponents, however, are likewise able to point to data that appear to show little is achieved by such measures (see Jeffs & Smith 1996). Part of the problem with any quantitative analysis is that the actual implementation of curfews varies so greatly in terms of local conditions, legal parameters, community resources, and style of criminal-justice intervention. The 'success' of youth curfews resides not in the coercive aspects of the curfew (that is, in aggressive street policing), but in the developmental accompaniments to the imposition of the curfew (that is, through recreation centres and counselling services). The presence or absence of additional community supports for young people in the context of curfew use is a central factor in how the curfew is put into operation and how it is perceived by residents and young people themselves (Bilchik 1996:9).

The use of formal curfews is not standard practice in the Australian setting. Arguably, some police operational campaigns (such as those in Western Australia, discussed earlier) and special legislation (such as that in New South Wales, also discussed earlier) constitute de facto youth curfews. However, the special legislation tends to have an element of selectivity built into it, in the sense of being based on defined criteria (according to which certain categories of young people are deemed to be 'at risk'), and thus intervention is not supposed to be universal in application. Nevertheless, the idea of curfews has continued to strike a popular chord among state politicians and local city councillors. In places such as Exmouth in Western Australia and Port Augusta in South Australia, periodical attempts have been made to impose curfews, either unilaterally through local council directives or through agreements between local council and police. However, in such cases questions have been raised regarding the lack of legislative authority for police to enforce curfews of a general nature (rather than those tied to bail or community service order conditions), and the ability of local councils to introduce curfews without prior legislation at the state government level that would extinguish common law rights relating to the right to move freely around the community (Simpson & Simpson 1993).

The presumed purposes of curfews vary from concern about the welfare of children to attempts to deal with young offending. While the curfew use is highly contentious in terms of its effectiveness in lessening criminal behaviour (Jeffs & Smith 1996), so too is the appropriateness of using coercive measures to tackle social ills. For instance, if the prime policy concern is with the welfare of the young (for example, the 12 year old who is roaming the streets after midnight), then the use of a curfew as such is inappropriate, since this is linked directly to the personnel, operation, and logic of the criminal justice system. Instead, a more suitable strategy might be to expand the range and availability of local social welfare services, including the number of community outreach workers, and to provide the police with information and training on where to take young people who need assistance.

In some localities, informal curfews may be in effect. This is where local police promulgate the idea that a youth curfew exists, and may take action against any young person caught outside their home beyond a certain time. However, there are relatively few formal curfews being introduced in local or regional jurisdictions around Australia at the present time. Curfews have been applied to selected sites, as with public parks in Logan, Queensland. They have also been imposed with regard to certain types of activity, as with anti-assembly by-laws pertaining to the mall area in Townsville. Historically, an important exception to group-specific curfews were the prohibitions placed upon the free movement of Indigenous people during the protection period (see chapter 6). Indigenous people in some cases were required to carry passes to move from one area to another, and were subject to set curfews (Sercombe 1997).

The main use of curfews in Australia is through the formal processing of young offenders who have been convicted or who are on bail. The imposition of curfews thus generally relates to bail conditions, and to court orders such as community service and other supervised orders (Mukherjee, Carcach & Higgins 1997). Curfews are generally imposed after a crime has been committed, and the young person has been apprehended and formally dealt with by the criminal justice system.

If the presence of young people is not necessarily subject to formal regulation through curfews, the same cannot be said about their activities. Few jurisdictions attempt to ban young people from certain sites at certain times of the day. However, particular activities and behaviours have been subjected to formal restrictions, as in the case of skateboarding. Efforts to regulate youth behaviour have included bans on certain types of activities, stepped-up surveillance, and intervention where groups of young people hang around together. There have been concerted attempts to curb obscene language, noise, and graffiti through intensive police campaigns. It needs to be emphasised that in most cases very little consultation has taken place between young people and other more powerful members of the community. Young people have generally been seen as the problem, not as part of the community; nor have they been seen as part of the solution to any perceived or real problems.

Community policing

Not all interaction between young people and the police is negative, nor does it occur exclusively on the street. 'Community policing', broadly defined, is now an important part of most police departments. Sometimes this term refers to a particular style of policing; more often, it refers to particular types of police practices or to specific policing projects. Many of these are linked to programs designed specifically for young people.

The precise nature of community policing is variable, ranging from crime prevention to legal information and safety measures. For example, Blue Light Discos provide young people under 17 years old with an opportunity for a night out in a secure environment under the supervision of off-duty police officers. The Police Schools Involvement Program in Victoria is another example of police commitment to developing a better relationship with young people. The long-term aim of such programs is to reduce the incidence of juvenile involvement in criminal behaviour (see James 1994). Information about criminal law, road safety, and the rules and regulations of bicycle riding are some of the topics covered in such schemes. Police youth clubs, which offer sporting activities, and which are intended, at least in part, to nurture citizenship in young people, are another example of community-based initiatives (James 1994).

The appeal of community policing principles was particularly popular in the 1980s. The idea was to generate a grassroots, participatory model of police–citizen interaction. To a large extent, this earlier emphasis on community participation (also involving young people) was submerged by the advent of new public sector managerialism. Progressively, over the last decades, the concern has shifted from community-initiated problem-solving approaches and the accountability of police to local communities, towards centralised corporate strategies. In such centralised strategies, the focus has tended to be on preparing strategic plans, mission statements, performance indicators, and measures of effectiveness. Some consequences of this change in management style and structure have been the continued marginalisation of specific police–youth units within police services, and little more than lip-service being paid by police and politicians to community policing ideals pertaining to young people.

The new corporate managerialism is driven by notions of evidence-based performance. The measurement of police effectiveness, however, is constructed around traditional, quantifiable concerns, such as number of arrests. The effect of this is to reinforce coercive styles of policing. Furthermore, it is to transform the idea of 'community policing' so that the emphasis is on the policing of communities, rather than policing by and for communities (see Cunneen & White 1995:212). The possibility that 'community policing models' may actually increase the degree of surveillance and control over young people is especially pertinent to the situation of young ethnic minority people (Chan 1994; Blagg & Wilkie 1995).

The pitfalls of dropping community policing down on the list of corporate priorities was highlighted by the recent, positive, policing experiences in the Sydney suburb of Woolloomooloo. Between 2001 and 2004, the local commander decided to rekindle community policing as a means to improve police relations and services in an area that includes many disadvantaged people and that poses its own unique challenges vis-à-vis public order and safety (Darcy, 2005). The commander encouraged police officers to build links with the local community, to get to know the physical layout and social dynamics and networks of the local area, and to foster positive interactions with local residents (for example, encouraging officers to 'play with the kids' at a local school as a means to genuinely engage with children and young people). The claimed benefits of 'reinvigorating a community policing model in a socially disadvantaged area' include:

- a stronger acceptance and participation by the community in policing services
- a community more willing to share information and experiences with local police

- a policing service more attuned to community expectations
- police less likely to indiscriminately focus on youth
- improved investigation efficiency
- a police community relationship that has the resilience to endure challenging or confronting events
- a genuine focus on interagency cooperation at practitioner level, and
- police confident in developing solutions to crime and disorder that are not necessarily legalistic in nature (Darcy, 2005:153).

In the specific case of New South Wales, it has been pointed out that the broad trend has been to privilege more confrontational styles of policing as a key corporate strategy to drive down crime. This is highly problematic, for as Darcy (2005:153) observes, 'In the absence of effective dialogue with local communities there is a real risk this form of policing can alienate the communities that most likely need our help.'

The police are a group in society that wields enormous power. What they do has significant and lasting impact on particular groups of young people and their families and communities. How the police use and abuse their power, therefore, is of crucial importance for community relationships as a whole. This again raises many of the issues underpinning any critical analysis of the notion of community policing. In particular, the relationship between young people and the police can be framed in terms of these questions: whether policing is in the interests of young people, whether it is being done in a manner that acknowledges their particular social problems, and whether young people themselves can and should have a say in the nature of the policing that occurs in their midst.

The style of policing, the targets of policing, and the control over policing are crucial issues that must be addressed if tensions and conflicts between young people and police are to be overcome.

STREET LIFE AND DIFFERENTIAL POLICING

Different styles of policing are not mutually exclusive, nor are they socially neutral. Police tend to adopt different methods in their dealings with different groups of people. Since the street is a major place in which young people socialise, young people are frequently targets for particular kinds of police attention. Beyond the contours of the general contact between police and young people—a form of differential policing based upon 'age' and 'generation'—specific population groups of young people tend to be singled out for special measures and special attention.

In Australian society, there is a high level of contact between the police and young people in general. For instance, in a random survey of 383 young people, 80 per cent reported they had been stopped by the police, and 50 percent said they had been escorted back to a police station. Most of the contact occurred in public places, and 70 per cent of the young people reported they had just been 'hanging out' when stopped by the police. Some 37 per cent of the respondents said they were just walking when approached by the police (Alder et al. 1992). Hence, we can extrapolate from this finding that those in Australia aged 15–17 years old experience a lot of interaction with the police.

The police–youth research project included interviews with police officers. They revealed that most of their contact with young people occurred in the early evening shifts, not at night, and that the most frequent location of contact was in malls, shopping centres, and other public spaces. The police interviewed registered considerable concern about the activities of young people. In terms of particular groups of youths, it was reported by the police that they experienced most difficulties with street kids, gangs, and young Aboriginal and Torres Strait Islander people (Alder et al. 1992).

The relationship between the police and young people is frequently marred by tension and conflict. Throughout the 1990s, reports and studies made clear that the issues of harassment, intimidation, and violence lie at the heart of many of the complaints young people make about the police in Australia (Cunneen 1990; Youth Justice Coalition 1990; Alder et al. 1992; Watkins 1992; White & Alder 1994; White et al. 1999; Collins et al. 2000; Cunneen 2001a; Omaji 2003). Conversely, the chronic disrespect for the law and its officials on the part of many young people, and the abuse of police by young people, have also been documented (Alder et al. 1992).

To a certain extent, the issue of police harassment is related to the nature of police work in general. As various reports point out, the use of violence is often seen as a routine part of policing, and any misconduct or overstepping of boundaries in the use of police powers is protected by the police code of silence (Cunneen 1990; Fitzgerald 1989). Media images of the 'tough cop', as well as the age and sex of the officer, also contribute to the adoption of a certain style of policing. A Victorian report (McCulloch & Schetzer 1993:15) noted:

> It is our view that many young people at eighteen and a half (the minimum age for recruitment) are too immature to properly undertake the responsibilities and powers that go with the provision of police uniform and weapons, including guns. It is our perception that this is particularly true of young men who too often bring to the job the desire to test their manhood through physical confrontation with others. The fact that the police force is overwhelmingly male contributes to a culture within the police force whereby physical strength and confrontation is glorified and other perspectives which include alternative methods of conflict resolution are undervalued or dismissed.

A culture of violence involving police and young people is fostered by the actual experience of physical force in their interactions. For example, Alder and others (1992) found that the police have felt there was little respect for them among sizable portions of the youth population. The same study also found that, almost unanimously, police said they had been assaulted and harassed by young people in the course of their work. The nature of the harassment ranged from verbal taunts, being shouted and sworn at, to outright assault, including kicks and punches (Alder et al. 1992). Such reports indicate a high degree of antagonism between police and young people, and 82 per cent of the police reported that they had had to apply force to a young person at some stage. Furthermore, a majority of the police officers interviewed admitted feeling that sometimes too much physical force is used in dealing with young people.

For their part, the young people interviewed in the same study (Alder et al. 1992) reported a high degree of physical and verbal abuse directed at them by the police. They reported that police–youth contact was unfair and often physical. The notion of 'kerbside justice' refers to such things as intimidation, harassment, verbal and physical abuse, and degrading strip searches in public places (see Blagg & Wilkie 1995). How young people respond to specific police intervention, whether involving specific negative incidents or not, is shaped by stories (including urban myths) of the more extreme sorts of police kerbside justice. More generally, in the literature on relations between police and youth, a common theme is 'Why pick on me?' Young people complain of the use of 'name checks', of constantly being stopped and questioned, and of a lack of explanation for such treatment. All these contribute to feelings of frustration and unease in the police–youth relationship. In such circumstances, it is not unusual for emotions to boil over into physical confrontations.

Some groups of young people experience particularly aggressive 'rough treatment'. For example, the 1992 ABC television documentary 'Cop It Sweet' depicted on-the-job racism directed towards young Aboriginal people and people from Asian backgrounds. An earlier report by the HREOC on Aboriginal juveniles and the police found that the majority of Aboriginal juveniles in detention centres in New South Wales, Queensland, and Western Australia had suffered violence at the hands of the police (Cunneen 1990). The study found that, of the juveniles in the study:

- 85 per cent reported being hit, punched, kicked, or slapped by police
- 63 per cent reported being hit with objects (such as police batons, telephone books) by police
- 32 per cent reported police revolvers being drawn and/or fired
- 81 per cent said they had been subjected to racist abuse by police officers.

Clearly, by approaching their work in such an aggressive manner, the police set in train a dynamic of fear, lack of respect, and resistance on the part of many young Aboriginal people. Resentments and negative feelings result, which may fuel continuing conflict and antagonism.

Another occasion for harassment occurs when young people challenge the arbitrary use of police power. Research shows that police tend to treat more favourably those young people who exhibit cooperation and compliance in their dealings (O'Connor & Sweetapple 1988; Alder et al. 1992; O'Connor 1994). Alternatively, some young people who attempt to claim their legal rights are branded as 'troublemakers' or 'smart arses', and consequently suffer. This was certainly so in the case of Joe Dethridge, a 17 year old who had his jaw broken by the sergeant in charge of the Fremantle police station in 1992. Dethridge and a friend had been picked up by two plainclothes police officers for no specific reason other than that of 'hanging around'. Because they challenged the right of the police to intervene without apparent good cause, extra-special treatment was meted out at the police station (White 1993b). Both young men were roughed up, in separate incidents, and Joe Dethridge in particular suffered for months afterwards, through a broken jaw, for confronting the power of the police. Unfortunately, not only is violence part of the police repertoire, but occasionally it is also used to silence the critics of police conduct.

In regard to specific operational processes, we also know that arrest rates, the use of summons, the granting of bail, and the issuing of formal cautions depend heavily on police decisions, and these in turn are greatly influenced by the social background of the young person in question. As we saw in chapter 6, for example, young Aboriginal people are many times more likely than non-Aboriginal young people to be dealt with harshly by the police. The nature of the initial intervention by the police has, of course, major consequences for those caught up in the criminal justice system. Again, Indigenous and ethnic minority young people are systematically disadvantaged by the agents of the state, and this has major ramifications for police and young people alike.

It needs to be highlighted that 'youth' offences are very often precipitated by the intervention of the police in the first place. In the event, very often it is the police themselves who become the 'victim' of the offence (for example 'offensive language' or 'assault police'). Constructing a reason to take young people off the streets, therefore, can be as simple as having the police approach young people in the first instance (see Blagg & Wilkie 1995; Cunneen 2001a; White 2002).

CONCLUSION

The policing of young people involves an intertwining of different images and styles, of different groups of young people, and of different types of police officers. Values such as 'respect for authority' can influence the nature of the police–youth relationship. The ways in which youth collectivities form and take part in the world can be seen as a problem by the formal agencies of social control, especially given that youth offending tends to occur in groups. The creation of a large, visible, youth 'underclass' in the last decade brings with it images of anarchy, desperation, and profound alienation and, correspondingly, political pressure to do something to protect respectable citizens from the perceived threat posed by the dispossessed. Regular moral panics directed at certain groups (ethnic youth gangs) and certain issues (violence, drugs) keep attention on working-class street crime, and not only legitimise but also sustain demand for a strong police presence in the affairs of young people. That the targets of police surveillance and intervention in relation to street crime very often appear to overlap with the targets of counterterrorism, at least in some states, creates a peculiar and potentially very damaging situation for Muslim and 'Middle Eastern' youth in particular. Heavy-handed counter-terrorism measures parallel those of zero tolerance policing, and the negative social consequences are much the same. Community policing ought to occupy a more prominent place in either form of intervention.

This chapter has outlined developments in policing and public space regulation that are by and large premised on the idea of limiting young people's presence in public spaces. These developments have centred on adoption of zero tolerance policing practices, and on a range of legislative initiatives that substantially increase police powers. Where young people have not been directly excluded from public space, attempts have occasionally been made to restrict the kinds of activities in which they might partake.

There are a number of problems and limitations to such law-and-order approaches to policing youth. The main criticisms of this kind of coercive intervention have been summarised as follows (White 1998a):

- Generally speaking, coercive policing strategies emphasise control and containment of young people, rather than addressing the deep structural causes of youthful offending or antisocial behaviour.
- Coercive strategies portray young people generally—and specific groups of disadvantaged young people in particular—as 'outsiders', who are perceived as threats to the community and not as part of the community.
- Such strategies undermine, philosophically and literally, the idea that young people are bona fide rights-holders who, as such, should not be subject to measures that limit their rights and freedoms arbitrarily, regardless of whether any law has been broken and any wrongdoing engaged in.
- Coercive strategies involve the active criminalisation of young people who otherwise may not come into short- or long-term contact with the criminal justice system, and furthermore can exacerbate tensions between youth and other members of the community due to youth perceptions of unfair treatment, excessive restrictions, and unnecessary intervention in their daily affairs.
- The discriminatory application of coercive measures, both geographically in terms of protected places for the privileged, and socially in terms of which groups are targeted for special attention, entrenches major class and ethnic divides, and does little to alleviate core problems of poverty, unemployment, and racism.
- Coercive policing and crime prevention tend to be premised upon varying kinds of social exclusion, a process that intrinsically alienates young

people from decision-making and that can lead to young people being displaced from selected areas and adopting alternative forms of youth lifestyle, some of which may include deviant and antisocial behaviour.

These criticisms should not be read as meaning that any coercive measures whatsoever should never be used. Rather, the point is that as a broad strategy such measures are problematic. In general, the use of law-enforcement measures is both warranted and does have an important, although limited, deterrent effect in preventing further crime (Tonry & Farrington 1995). And, in certain circumstances, 'coercive force' is needed to deal with specific instances of unlawful behaviour. However, juvenile justice intervention that is respectful of young people, and that does not serve to criminalise their activities and very presence in the public domain, demands a different kind of response.

The general social context in which young people are growing up makes it difficult to produce significant reform in the area of police–youth relations without changes to the wider social structure. The history and traditions of policing are bound up with policing the working class (see Farrell 1992), and in particular those sections of the working class identified as the 'criminal classes'. Key targets have always been the youth of these classes. In periods of sustained economic hardship and social upheaval, the primary class role of the police tends to be reasserted, with the focus on containing and managing the effects of economic transformation. Operationally, this is manifested in a major extension of police powers.

Economic recession is associated with survival crime and antisocial behaviour; the police have a significant role to play in the criminalisation of the poor for activities that stem from lack of economic control. Simultaneously, progressive policing reforms are likely to collapse in the face of a conservative backlash—the law-and-order lobby tends to become stronger when the incidence of violent crime and property crime is believed to be high. The role of the police is thus necessarily tied up with structural economic trends and the class-related ebb and flow of electoral politics. Without significant changes in structural features of society, such as a reorientation of economic goals and redistribution of community resources, it is likely that police work will continue to take the form of controlling young people.

10 | Courts and sentencing processes

CHAPTER HIGHLIGHTS

Introduction
The jurisdiction of the children's court
Factors in judicial decision-making
The context of international human rights principles
Understanding the conflicting demands of sentencing
Mandatory sentencing
Guideline judgments
Pre-sentence reports
Drug courts
The utilisation of sentencing options
Young people's experience of the children's court
Conclusion

INTRODUCTION

For many young people, apprehension by police will lead to an appearance in the children's court. We have already discussed in earlier chapters the history of the establishment of separate courts to hear matters involving children (see chapter 1), as well as the types of offences for which young people appear in court (see chapter 3).

In this chapter, we discuss the jurisdiction of the children's courts: which types of offences the court can hear, and other matters about the power of the court. We also look at how the court makes decisions about sentences, which options are available, and which principles are applied. Throughout this chapter, we use the name 'children's court' as a generic term for the specialised court that deals with young people. Most jurisdictions use this name; however, some—such as South Australia (the Youth Court) and the Northern Territory (the Juvenile Court)—use different titles.

THE JURISDICTION OF THE CHILDREN'S COURT

The role of the children's court is to deal with young people in accordance with the special principles and procedures that have been developed as appropriate for this age group. However, the jurisdiction and status of the children's court varies between states and territories. In some states, it is presided over by a magistrate, and in others by a specialist judge from the District Court. Most states have specialist children's courts operating in the cities. Outside these areas, the local magistrate can convene a children's court when necessary.

The children's courts have major jurisdiction over offences committed by young people. These include all summary offences (the less serious offences that are usually heard in a magistrate's court), although traffic offences are usually excluded from the children's court. The hearing in a children's court is summary, that is, before a magistrate and without a jury. The public is excluded from children's courts, and there are prohibitions on publishing the names of young people who go before the courts. For most indictable offences (the more serious offences, such as car theft and break and enter, which are usually heard before a judge and jury in a higher court), the young person can elect to have the matter dealt with by the children's court or in a higher court by a judge and jury. The court itself may decline jurisdiction and refer the case to a higher court. In some jurisdictions, if the young person has been charged jointly with an adult for an offence, the children's court can order that the matter be heard in an adult court. Finally, for serious indictable offences (such as homicide) where the offence might result in a sentence of life imprisonment and there is a prima facie case to answer, the young person will be committed to trial in the Supreme Court. Thus, while the children's court generally deals with offences committed by young people, there is a range of reasons for the matter to be heard in a different court.

In Victoria, Queensland, Western Australia, and South Australia, the children's court is headed by a judge. Other jurisdictions have a children's magistrate or senior children's magistrate. In the jurisdictions where a judge heads the children's court, the judge is able to hear and determine more serious matters than in jurisdictions where a magistrate heads the court. The available maximum penalty is usually greater if the young person is sentenced by a judge rather than a magistrate.

In jurisdictions where the children's court is headed by a judge, the judge also acts as a review court for matters determined by the magistrates. In other states, appeals from decisions by the children's court go to the higher courts.

Criminal responsibility and *doli incapax*

The age of criminal responsibility is an important requirement governing juvenile justice legislation. Under the common law, the age of criminal responsibility is 7 years old. Children younger than this age cannot be charged with a criminal offence. During the course of the twentieth century, most jurisdictions in Australia raised the age of criminal responsibility. For example, in New South Wales the age was raised to 8 years old in the 1930s, and then to 10 years old in the mid-1970s. The age of criminal responsibility is 10 years old in all Australian states.

It should be noted that, whatever age is chosen for the attribution of criminal responsibility, there will be some degree of arbitrariness. Part of the reason for raising the age of criminal responsibility to 10 years old was that few children under this age appeared on criminal matters, and that those who did were better dealt with as welfare or care-and-protection cases. However, because the age is partly arbitrary, it is open to political challenge. During the height of law-and-order campaigns, there have been calls by more extreme groups to lower the age of criminal responsibility to 7 or 8 years old.

Raising the age of criminal responsibility is consistent with what has occurred in many other common law countries. In England and New Zealand, the age of criminal responsibility is 10 years old, and in Canada it is 12 years old (ALRC & HREOC 1997:469). Many European states have an age of criminal responsibility considerably higher than 10 years old. In France, the age is set at 13 years old, and in Norway and Denmark it is 15 years old (ALRC & HREOC 1997:470).

The principle of *doli incapax* is also an important consideration affecting the attribution of criminal responsibility. *Doli incapax* means 'incapable of wrong'. It is a common law principle that a child younger than the age of 14 does not know their criminal conduct is wrong. They are presumed incapable of committing a crime because they lack the necessary criminal intention (*mens rea*). *Doli incapax* applies in all Australian states and territories. The presumption can be rebutted by the prosecution, who must demonstrate that the child knows the criminal act for which she has been charged is a wrong act of some seriousness (rather than mere naughtiness or mischief). Evidence to rebut the presumption,

> May be proved by circumstances attending the act, the manner in which it was done, and evidence to the nature and disposition of the child. Evidence of the child's prior criminal record may be admitted to prove the child's guilty knowledge, if the primary facts are not in dispute. The closer the child is to the age of 10, the stronger must be the evidence to rebut the presumption (Criminal Law Review Division 2000:2).

There have been strong moves in Australia and in England to either abolish *doli incapax* or limit its scope through reducing the age to which it is applicable or reversing the onus of proof. The ALRC and HREOC (1997:471) found that 'the principle of *doli incapax* [is] a practical way of acknowledging young people's developing capacities. It allows for a gradual transition to full criminal responsibility'. The Commission quoted Lord Lowry in a 1996 House of Lords decision: 'the purpose and effect of the presumption is still to protect children between the ages of 10 and 14 from the full force of the criminal law' (1997:471). The principle has the effect of requiring police, prosecutors, and magistrates to stop and assess the degree of responsibility appropriate for each child brought before the court.

In most states of Australia, young people cease to come under the jurisdiction of the children's court once they have reached 18 years of age. In practice, the law normally is that young people can be dealt with in a children's court, providing they were under the age of 18 when they allegedly committed the offence with which they have been charged. In Victoria and Queensland, young people are dealt with by the adult criminal justice system once they turn 17 years old. The CROC requires 18 years old to be the age at which young people become adults for the purposes of the application of the criminal law.

Media identification

It is an offence to publish or broadcast the name or other identifying characteristics of a young person appearing before or convicted by the children's court. This is to avoid future stigmatisation of the young person and to ensure maximum opportunities for personal growth and development. However, there has been increasing political pressure to change this protection that is offered young people. While all states and territories (except the Northern Territory) have a general prohibition on identifying young people, the extent of the prohibition and the circumstances in which publication can occur differ (ALRC 2005:552–3). Dixon (2002) provides an overview of different state provisions on this matter, as well as arguments for and against identification. We use the New South Wales provisions as an example.

In New South Wales, the identification of a young person older than 16 is allowed, if they consent. For young people younger than 16, and unable to consent, the court may allow identification if it is satisfied that this is in the public interest. Amendments introduced in 1999 allow for the identification of young people convicted of serious children's indictable offences in the higher courts, including homicide, rape, malicious wounding, and offences punishable by 25 years or life imprisonment. The court must be satisfied that identification is in the interests of justice and the prejudice to the child does not outweigh those interests. In these cases, consent is not required (NSW Law Reform Commission 2001:73).

Pleading guilty

The children's courts are often seen as the pinnacle of the juvenile justice system. A young person who has been charged with a criminal offence by the police is brought before the court, where their guilt or innocence is established and a penalty is imposed. However, in reality the children's courts play a relatively minor role in testing evidence and in determining the innocence or guilt of the defendant. Most children plead guilty to the offence with which they have been charged, or to a lesser offence after negotiations with the prosecution. Although there are difficulties in obtaining accurate information, Naffine, Wundersitz and Gale (1990) estimated, on South Australian data, that 87 per cent of children's court appearances were guilty pleas. In a further 7 per cent, no plea was entered because the police decided not to proceed with the prosecution and the matter was withdrawn. In 6 per cent of cases, a formal not-guilty plea was lodged and the matter was contested.

It would appear that the South Australian research, although more than a decade old, is generally indicative of children's court appearances, at least in that state. Recent data from the South Australian Youth Court confirm that very few cases result in a young person being found not guilty by the court. Of 2402 cases finalised in the court during 2004, 80.1 per cent resulted in at least one charge being proven, 19.3 per cent resulted in the charges being withdrawn or dismissed, and only 15 finalised cases (0.6 per cent) resulted in an acquittal (Office of Crime Statistics and Research 2005:37). Similar results can be seen in the Western Australian data (Ferrante et al. 2005:109).

The high rate of guilty pleas has important implications for the administration of justice in the children's courts. Naffine and others (1990:196) have stated the position thus:

> If children plead guilty as matter of course, then there is no adjudication and the court's function is simply to decide what to do with offenders. Indeed, with the plea of guilty, the child abandons many of the standard rights and protections implicit in due process ... [the child] fails to take advantage of the presumption of innocence and the right to have the prosecution prove its case beyond reasonable doubt.

With a guilty plea, the young person gives up the right to challenge the prosecution's case and to have a lawyer present a defence and argue their innocence. For the purposes of this discussion, however, the most important point is the role assumed by the court. If young people plead guilty, then the major role of the court is to decide on a penalty. The court is not reviewing evidence and how it was obtained, nor is it playing a significant role in monitoring or remedying any abuses of young people's rights (O'Connor 1994:92–3). The key function of the children's court is to decide on an appropriate penalty for the young person.

FACTORS IN JUDICIAL DECISION-MAKING

How do magistrates and judges make a decision as to a penalty appropriate to the young person before them who has been convicted of an offence? What are the relevant factors to be taken into account, what are the options available, and what external factors affect the court's decision? In the discussion that follows, we consider several areas of importance to sentencing young people:

- the available sentencing options and their hierarchy
- the principles of sentencing
- the international human rights context
- conflicting demands in reaching a sentence
- mandatory sentencing
- guideline judgments
- the role and content of pre-sentence reports
- drug courts.

Sentencing options and hierarchy

Any decision by a children's court on what to do with a young person convicted of an offence is limited by the sentencing options available to the court. These sanctions (or dispositions) vary from one Australian jurisdiction to another. In general, the options available are set out in the legislation that governs juvenile justice in the particular state or territory.

Sentencing hierarchies have also been established in some of the more recent juvenile justice legislation (for example, in New South Wales and Victoria). Such hierarchies set out the available penalties in order of severity. Sentencing hierarchies have been introduced to guide the court in selecting an appropriate penalty and to provide a greater degree of consistency in sentencing. Some legislation (for example, in New South Wales and Victoria) prevents the court from imposing a sentence at one level unless it is satisfied that a sentence at a lower level of the hierarchy is inappropriate. Such requirements have been designed to require magistrates to justify the use of more severe penalties, to promote the use of non-custodial options, and to reinforce the use of detention as a sentence of last resort.

A typical sentencing hierarchy ranges from the most punitive disposition (detention) to the least intrusive, being dismissal with or without conviction. Although the actual sanctions available will vary from one state to another, we can construct a general picture of what is available to the children's courts, and place them within a hierarchy (see Cunneen & White 1995:220–1; ALRC & HREOC 1997:544–5).

The sanctions available to the court, in order of decreasing severity, may include the following:

- *Detention in a youth training or juvenile detention centre*—In some jurisdictions, and in particular types of cases, imprisonment in an adult facility may also be an option. In some jurisdictions, periodic detention, weekend detention, or home detention may also be an option.
- *Suspended detention*—The court makes a detention order that it then suspends, subject to the young person meeting certain requirements

(such as not to offend again). If the young person reoffends, then the original detention order is activated, plus any further sentence for the later offence.

- *Community service order, attendance-centre order and other special orders*— Community service orders and attendance-centre orders usually have maximum hours varying between 100 and 500, depending on jurisdiction. Special orders relate, for example, to orders for people with a mental illness or intellectual disability, or to special orders made by a drug court.
- *Probation (usually up to 2 years) or other supervised order*—These orders are similar to a good behaviour bond, but have additional requirements including supervision and meetings with a probation officer.
- *Fine or compensation and good behaviour bond (or recognisance).*
- *Fine or compensation (with the maximum possible fine limited by the court's jurisdiction).*
- *Referral to a youth-conferencing scheme*—In some jurisdictions, the courts have the power to refer matters back to a conference.
- *Good behaviour bond or recognisance*—These orders require the offender to be of good behaviour for a certain period (usually up to 2 years), but do not involve supervision.
- *Undertaking to observe certain conditions.*
- *Dismissal of charges with or without either a reprimand or a conviction recorded.*

In later chapters, we discuss the more severe sentencing option of incarceration, and various community-based sanctions and restorative justice options in more detail. For the present, it is important to see in general terms the types of penalties that can be applied to a young person who is convicted of an offence.

Sentencing principles

The existence of various sentencing options in itself does not tell us very much about why a particular sanction might or might not be used. How does a magistrate make the decision that the young person before them should receive a community service order or should be sentenced to a period of detention? What are the most important factors to be taken into account: the nature of the specific offence, the prior record of the young person, the protection of society, the prospects of rehabilitation, or the likelihood of reoffending?

The objectives of sentencing are traditionally stated as retribution, deterrence, rehabilitation, and incapacitation (NSW Law Reform Commission 2001:49). There can be obvious tensions as to how these objectives might be met, which we will return to later in the discussion. To begin with, however, there are a number of general principles applicable to the sentencing of young people.

Responsibility refers to the fact that an offender is liable to some form of punishment or sanction for an offence. There may be mitigating factors that reduce the level of responsibility, including factors such as the following:

- *Intent*—For example, was the offence the result of intention or recklessness?
- *Excuse*—For example self-defence, provocation.
- *Impairment*—Mental or physical conditions that might reduce responsibility.
- *Motive*—For example, was the offence an act of maliciousness or an act of conscience?

These mitigating factors are common to both adults and juveniles, and can be taken into account by the magistrate when deciding on an appropriate penalty. However, of particular importance to young people is the notion of reduced responsibility because of age.

It is commonly accepted in sentencing that juveniles are to be treated differently from adults—as having reduced responsibility—because of their immaturity and level of development. It has been regarded as unjust and unrealistic to hold young people to the same standards as adults. Such a view is partly reflected in the different sanctions applied to young people compared with those applied to adults, and in the notion that young people have a particular vulnerability and need for protection.

It is an accepted principle that the severity of the sentence should be commensurate with the seriousness of the offence, that it should possess proportionality. In other words, the sanction applied by the court needs to take account of the seriousness of the crime and the blameworthiness of the offender: that is, the punishment should fit the crime. Such a principle can affect both the upper limit and the lower limit of the punishment, but tends to be concerned with preventing excessive sentences.

The principle of equality refers to consistency in punishment: that is, that like cases are treated alike. Disparity in sentences is seen as undermining a fair and equitable legal system. For example, specialist children's courts in the city may be less likely to impose detention orders than country courts. Other disparities may arise on the basis of race, ethnicity, and gender.

Specificity refers to the precise nature of the sanction. It is accepted that the offender should know precisely the nature of the sentence that is being imposed. Determinacy refers to the duration of the sentence and to the offender knowing the duration in advance.

Sentencers may regard a particular sentence as sending a message to the community concerning the seriousness of an offence and the likely punishment, thus generally deterring other potential offenders. A sentence might also be regarded as designed specifically to deter the particular young person from reoffending. General and specific deterrence are often argued in conjunction with community protection. The view that there is a need to protect the community from particular types of offences may lead to a sentence involving some element of deterrence.

Frugality refers to the principle that the sentence imposed should be the least restrictive that is appropriate. The court should select the least-restrictive sentencing option and time period while taking account of the seriousness of the offence, the role of the young offender, and the offender's age and prior record.

The court should consider the chances of rehabilitation for the offender when determining a sentence. With young people, this normally requires a consideration of their needs in relation to guidance and development.

THE CONTEXT OF INTERNATIONAL HUMAN RIGHTS PRINCIPLES

There are a number of United Nations conventions, guidelines, and rules that are directly relevant to the process of sentencing young offenders. These include the principal conventions outlined in box 4.2 in chapter 4. Of particular importance to our discussion are the Beijing Rules and the CROC. Readers should also refer to the discussion in chapter 4 on the relationship of international obligations to decision-making within Australia.

To fully appreciate the human rights obligations in relation to sentencing, it is first necessary to understand the emphasis placed on diversion of juvenile offenders from the formal justice system. In other words, the context of sentencing children and young people rests on the assumption that there is already in place a significant commitment to, and process for, diverting young people from formal judicial proceedings.

Apart from diversion, there are eleven principles that particularly underpin the sentencing of young people. These include participation, best interests, community protection, rehabilitation, the prohibition on cruel, inhuman, and degrading punishment, the availability of a range of options, the requirement of proportionality, the availability of review, detention as a last resort, detention for the shortest period of time, and freedom from arbitrariness (HREOC 1999).

The principle of diversion

Article 40.3 of the CROC establishes a clear preference for alternative diversionary measures over formal judicial proceedings. Diversion is primarily seen as occurring prior to the formal adjudication of the case. The CROC requires that states promote measures for dealing with young people without resorting to judicial proceedings, providing that human rights and legal safeguards are fully respected.

Rule 11 of the Beijing Rules establishes the need for diversion as follows:

11.1 Consideration shall be given, wherever appropriate, to dealing with juvenile offenders without resorting to formal trial ...

11.2 The police, the prosecution or other agencies dealing with juvenile cases shall be empowered to dispose of such cases, at their discretion, without recourse to formal hearings, in accordance with the criteria laid down for that purpose in the respective legal system and also in accordance with the principles contained in these Rules.

11.3 Any diversion involving referral to appropriate community or other services shall require the consent of the juvenile, or her or his parents or guardian, provided that such decision to refer a case shall be subject to review by a competent authority, upon application.

11.4 In order to facilitate the discretionary disposition of juvenile cases, efforts shall be made to provide for community programs, such as temporary supervision and guidance, restitution, and compensation of victims.

Commentary on the Beijing Rules notes that diversion is commonly practised on a formal and informal basis in many legal systems, and that it may hinder the negative effects of formal proceedings such as the stigma of conviction and sentence. In many situations, non-intervention would be the best response where the offence is not serious, and where other social institutions such as the family or school can react in an appropriate and constructive manner (Detrick 1999).

The principle of participation

There is a requirement that children and young people be given appropriate involvement in proceedings and decisions that affect them (Article 12.1 of the CROC and Beijing Rule 14.2). As the HREOC has stated:

> Involving children in sentencing means giving them a genuine opportunity to express their views freely. This in turn means ensuring that the individual child is able to be fully engaged in the process. This requires the creation of an environment which is not intimidating and using language which is readily understood by the particular individual child (HREOC 1999:1).

The best interests of the child

CROC Article 3.1 requires that in all actions concerning children, whether undertaken by public or private social welfare institutions, courts of law, administrative authorities, or legislative bodies, the best interests of the child shall be a primary consideration.

The CROC does not precisely define a child's best interests. However, there are important indicators of these interests within. These include, first, that the best interests must be determined on the basis of the individual child. Second, it is in the child's best interests to enjoy the rights and freedoms set out in the CROC and in other human rights conventions, treaties, and guidelines. These include the other principles discussed in this section, as well as:

- the provision of conditions under which children can develop their full human potential, with human dignity, and the requirement that treatment be appropriate to the age of the child (for example, children deprived of liberty shall be treated with humanity and respect for the inherent dignity of the human person, and in a manner that takes into account the needs of people of that age)
- the capacity for children to participate and to express their views (if the child is capable of forming a view), including the right of the child to freedom of expression, thought, conscience, and religion (for example, the right to participate and express views in judicial and administrative proceedings)
- the recognition that children require special protection because of their particular vulnerability and stage of maturation (for example, prohibitions on sexual or economic exploitation, or special requirements before the law, such as sentencing dispositions aimed at social integration)
- the recognition that in most circumstances the best interests of the child will be served by remaining with their family, and their family being involved in their development
- the recognition that it is in the best interests of Indigenous children to be raised in the Indigenous community.

Community protection

Human rights law recognises that everyone is entitled to personal security; the safety of the community is a legitimate aim of sentencing. Article 40.1 of the CROC notes that the treatment of the young offender must 'reinforce the child's respect for the human rights and fundamental freedoms of others'.

Rehabilitation

Both the CROC and the Beijing Rules emphasise the importance of rehabilitation. Article 40.1 of the CROC says:

> States recognise the right of every child [who has] infringed the penal law to be treated in a manner ... which takes into account the child's age and the desirability of promoting the child's reintegration and the child's assuming a constructive role in society.

The commentary to Beijing Rule 17 states that 'strictly punitive approaches are not appropriate ... just desert and retributive sanctions ... should always be outweighed by the interest of safeguarding the well-being and the future of the young person'.

The prohibition on cruel, inhuman, or degrading treatment or punishment

Article 37(a) of the CROC states that 'No child shall be subjected to torture or other cruel, inhuman or degrading treatment or punishment. Neither capital punishment nor life imprisonment without possibility of release shall be imposed for offences committed by persons below eighteen years of age.'

Article 37(a) limits the types of punishments that can be imposed as part of a sentence. It is recognised that all punishments contain some element of inhumanity and degradation. However, elements of cruelty, inhumanity, and degradation may be inherent in some types of punishment (for example, corporal punishments) or may arise in the application of particular punishments (for example, the use of mandatory fixed terms of imprisonment can give rise to cruel punishment because of gross disproportionality between the punishment and the offence).

Availability of a range of options

Both the CROC and the Beijing Rules require a range of sentencing options for young people. Article 40.4 of the CROC requires that 'A variety of dispositions, such as care, guidance and supervision orders; counselling; probation; foster care; education and vocational training programs and other alternatives to institutional care shall be available to ensure that children are dealt with in a manner appropriate to their well-being and proportionate both to their circumstances and the offence.'

Beijing Rule 18.1 requires that 'a large variety of disposition measures shall be made available, allowing for flexibility so as to avoid institutionalization to the greatest extent possible.' These measures include care, guidance, and supervision orders; probation; community service orders; financial penalties, compensation, and restitution; treatment orders; orders to participate in group counselling and similar activities; and orders concerning foster care, living communities, or other educational settings.

Commentary on Rule 18.1 notes that the examples have in common a reliance on the community for the effective implementation of alternative sanctions: 'Community-based correction is a traditional measure that has taken on many aspects. On that basis, relevant authorities should be encouraged to offer community-based services.'

The requirement of proportionality

Article 40.4 of the CROC, quoted earlier, establishes the requirement of proportionality: a variety of dispositions allow that children 'are dealt with in a manner appropriate to their well-being and proportionate both to their circumstances and the offence'.

Beijing Rule 5.1 requires that 'the juvenile justice system shall emphasise the well-being of the juvenile and shall ensure that any reaction to juvenile offenders shall always be in proportion to the circumstances of both the offenders and the offence'.

The commentary on Rule 5 notes that the rule refers to two of the most important objectives of juvenile justice. The first objective is the promotion of the wellbeing of the juvenile. The second is the principle of proportionality:

> This principle is well-known as an instrument for curbing punitive sanctions, mostly expressed in terms of just deserts in relation to the gravity of the offence. The response to young offenders should be based on the consideration not only of the gravity of the offence but also of personal circumstances. The individual circumstances of the offender (for example social status, family situation, the harm caused by the offence or other factors affecting personal circumstances) should influence the proportionality of the reactions (for example by having regard to the offender's endeavour to indemnify the victim or to her or his willingness to turn to wholesome and useful life).

By the same token, reactions aiming to ensure the welfare of the young offender may go beyond necessity and therefore infringe upon the fundamental rights of the young individual, as has been observed in some juvenile justice systems. Here, too, the proportionality of the reaction to the circumstances of both the offender and the offence, including the victim, should be safeguarded.

Thus Rule 5 requires 'a fair reaction' in any given case of juvenile crime. The issues combined in the rule may help to stimulate new and innovative types of responses to juvenile crime, as well as requiring vigilance against any undue widening of the net of formal social control over young people.

The availability of review

All young offenders should be accorded the right of appeal against conviction and sentence, as established in Article 40.2(b) of the CROC.

Detention as a last resort

Article 37(b) of the CROC states that the arrest, detention, or imprisonment of a child shall be in conformity with the law, and shall be used only as a measure of last resort and for the shortest period of time. Beijing Rule 17.1, parts (b) and (c), are also relevant:

   (b) Restrictions on the personal liberty of the juvenile shall be imposed only after careful consideration and shall be limited to the possible minimum;

   (c) Deprivation of personal liberty shall not be imposed unless the juvenile is adjudicated of a serious act involving violence against another person or of persistence in committing other serious offences and unless there is no other appropriate response.

Thus, the use of detention should only be used as a measure of last resort. All other lesser options must be considered, and detention should only be imposed for cases of very serious offending.

Detention for the shortest period of time

Both Article 37(b) of the CROC and Beijing Rule 17.1 require that when a detention order is made, it must be for the shortest appropriate period of time. Beijing Rule 19.1 also states that 'the placement of a juvenile in an institution shall always be a disposition of last resort and for the minimum necessary period'.

The commentary on Rule 19 is also instructive:

> Progressive criminology advocates the use of non-institutional over institutional treatment. Little or no difference has been found in terms of the success of institutionalisation as compared to non-institutionalisation. The many adverse influences on an individual that seem unavoidable within any institutional setting evidently cannot be outbalanced by treatment efforts. This is especially the case for juveniles, who are vulnerable to negative influences. Moreover, the negative effects, not only of loss of liberty but also of separation from the usual social environment, are certainly more acute for juveniles than for adults because of their early stage of development.

> Rule 19 aims at restricting institutionalisation in two regards: in quantity (last resort) and in time (minimum necessary period). Rule 19 reflects one of the basic guiding principles ... a juvenile offender should not be incarcerated unless there is no other appropriate response. The rule, therefore, makes the appeal that if a juvenile must be institutionalised, the loss of liberty should be restricted to the least possible degree, with special institutional arrangements for confinement and bearing in mind the differences in kinds of offenders, offences and institutions. In fact, priority should be given to 'open' over 'closed' institutions. Furthermore, any facility should be of a correctional or educational rather than of a prison type.

Ultimately, the court will need to decide what constitutes a 'minimum necessary period'. However, it will be guided by other principles, including proportionality, the need for rehabilitation, community protection, and the best interests of the child.

Freedom from arbitrariness

Article 37(b) of the CROC also requires that no child shall be deprived of its liberty unlawfully or arbitrarily. The two notions of 'arbitrary' and 'unlawful' overlap: 'A sentence which is contrary to law would be arbitrary. But arbitrariness extends much more broadly to sentences which are "unjust", "unreasonable" or "an abuse of power". Arbitrary detention is detention incompatible with the principles of justice or with the dignity of the human person' (HREOC 1999:5).

If basic principles of justice such as proportionality, consistency, and non-discrimination were ignored, then a sentence of detention could be seen as arbitrary. Thus, grossly disproportionate sentences or sentences that reflect adverse discrimination on the basis of race, age, sex, religion, or other status might be seen as arbitrary.

UNDERSTANDING THE CONFLICTING DEMANDS OF SENTENCING

Even a cursory analysis of general sentencing principles and the principles elaborated in human rights standards show the potential difficulties that can be encountered in sentencing practice. How does a court decide what relative weight to place on rehabilitation or deterrence? How does holding young people responsible for their actions sit with notions of reduced responsibility because of age and immaturity? What weight should be given to protecting the community compared to the likelihood of a young person undergoing rehabilitation?

The courts have understood the dilemma of sentencing, and the extent to which it is an 'intuitive exercise'. The High Court noted in *Veen (No. 2)* that:

> Sentencing is not a purely logical exercise, and the troublesome nature of the sentencing discretion arises in large measure from the unavoidable difficulty in giving weight to each of the purposes of punishment. ... The purposes overlap and none of them can be considered in isolation from the others when determining what is an appropriate sentence in a particular case. They are guideposts to the appropriate sentence, but sometimes they point in different directions (*Veen v. The Queen [No. 2] [1988]* 164 CLR 465 at 477).

Generally, juvenile justice legislation in Australia has articulated the sentencing principles applicable to the children's court within the relevant legislation. South Australia was the first state to do this in 1979, and most states now follow this practice. As an example, we list the major sentencing principles from section 150 of the Queensland Juvenile Justice Act of 1992.

In sentencing a child for an offence, the court must have regard to:

- the general principles applying to the sentencing of all persons
- the general principles of juvenile justice
- special considerations (see next paragraph)
- the nature and seriousness of the offence
- the child's previous offending history
- any information about the child that the court considers appropriate, including a pre-sentence report
- any impact of the offence on the victim
- the fitting proportion between the sentence and the offence.

The special considerations referred to in the legislation provide that:

- the child's age is a mitigating factor on any penalty to be imposed
- a non-custodial order is better than detention in promoting the child's reintegration into the community
- rehabilitation of a child is greatly assisted by the child's family and opportunities to engage in educational programs and employment
- a child who has no apparent family support or opportunities to engage in educational programs and employment should not receive a more severe sentence because of the lack of such opportunities
- a detention order should only be imposed as a last resort and for the shortest possible period.

The sentencing principles set out in the Queensland legislation show the incorporation of the general principles referred to previously, as well as attempting to delineate those principles specific to young people.

The ALRC has recommended that national standards for juvenile justice should be developed and that they should include principles for the sentencing of young offenders. According to the Commission, 'the development of national standards for juvenile justice ... is essential to alleviate inequities and injustices in sentencing young offenders' (ALRC & HREOC 1997:538). The sentencing principles identified in the national standards should also be reflected in relevant Commonwealth, state and territory law (ALRC & HREOC 1997:544).

While it is important that such principles are to be found in the legislation, they still tend to be generalised and represent a variety of goals. Their generalised nature limits the assistance they provide in actual sentencing. To illuminate these problems, it is worth considering a specific case that went to the New South Wales Court of Criminal Appeal and that was decided on 22 April 1991 (*R v. GDP* (1991) 53 A Crim R 112).

P was a 15-year-old boy who, with two friends, caused extensive damage to a car yard and construction company in the western suburbs of Sydney, to the value of more than $1.5 million. P was arrested by police and made admissions in two records of interview. P's charge could have been determined in the children's court; however, the court used its discretion to commit P to stand trial in the District Court. P pleaded guilty and was sentenced to 12 months detention. A successful appeal was lodged in the Court of Criminal Appeal and the sentence was reduced to 12 months probation.

Appeal Court Justice Matthews, in her judgment, made a number of points concerning the principles of sentencing young people. She noted that P was a first offender and had received a favourable court report, school report, and psychiatric report. He had rehabilitated himself to a substantial degree since the original offence by not reoffending and by returning to school. Justice Matthews found that the original judge who had imposed the custodial sentence had been wrong on two accounts. First, although the sentence of

12 months detention was within the range of appropriate penalties, given the seriousness of the offence, it did not take into account the youth of the offender or his prospects for rehabilitation. The sentencing judge had stated that the ordinary principles of sentencing applied to young offenders in the same way as they did to adult offenders. Judge Matthews found that this was not the case and that different principles apply in the sentencing of young people. Second, the sentencing judge had failed to distinguish the more minor role played by P in the offences. P had received the same sentence as one co-offender, but had played a substantially lesser role.

Sentencing and case law

In *GDP*, the New South Wales Court of Criminal Appeal followed a line of cases that have consistently held rehabilitation to be the most important consideration in sentencing juveniles. In *Wilcox*, Yeldham J held that 'in the case of a youthful offender … considerations of punishment and of general deterrence of others should and may properly be largely discarded in favour of individual treatment of the offender, directed to rehabilitation' (*R v. Wilcox*, NSW Court of Criminal Appeal, unreported, 15 August 1979, Yeldham J at 3).

In *Pelosi*, Lee CJ stated that 'it is always proper in a court of justice in the case of very young persons [in this case a 17-year-old] to ensure that if rehabilitation is discernible custodial sentences are to be avoided unless circumstances are such that aim cannot be achieved' (*R v. Pelosi*, NSW Court of Criminal Appeal, unreported, 28 September 1988; Lee CJ quoted in Bishop 1992:77).

Other cases since *GDP* have also been significant for upholding the importance of rehabilitation, including *R v. Wilkie* (NSW Court of Criminal Appeal, unreported, 2 July 1992), *R v. Vitros* (NSW Court of Criminal Appeal, unreported, 3 September 1993), and *R v. ALH* (NSW Court of Criminal Appeal, unreported, 26 May 1995). Even when a juvenile is sentenced 'according to law' (that is, in a higher court for a more serious offence), the court is still bound to take account of the different principles relevant to sentencing juveniles (*R v. WKR* (1993) 32 NSWLR 447 per Hunt at 450–1).

Clearly, holding rehabilitation as the primary consideration does not preclude the use of detention as a sentencing option, nor does it preclude any consideration of deterrence. In *R v. XYJ*, Clarke J noted that a concentration on rehabilitation 'is not to say that considerations of general deterrence should be ignored completely when sentencing young offenders. They should not. But they do not have the same importance as they do in sentencing adults' (NSW Court of Criminal Appeal, unreported, 15 June 1992, Clarke J at 7). Wood J noted in *Vitros* that the primary consideration of rehabilitation may have to give way to a sentence of imprisonment that adequately reflects the gravity of the crime in the particular case.

Other Australian courts have followed similar paths in identifying the importance of rehabilitation. In the Northern Territory, in *Nelson v. Chute* (1994) 72 A Crim R 85, Martin J noted the inappropriateness of detention and the generally accepted position that placement in the community with supervision was the preferred option. In *R v. Roy Graham Canfield* (1994), unreported, the Queensland Court of Criminal Appeal quashed a 12-month sentence of detention. Fitzgerald P stated that, when all considerations were taken into account, including the young person's age and previous compliance with a supervisory order, then a custodial sentence was not appropriate.

In South Australia in *Hallam v. O'Dea* (1979) 22 SASR 133, King CJ found that the fundamental principle in adult sentencing of determining a length of imprisonment on the basis of observing a proper proportion between the gravity of the crime and the severity of punishment had no place in sentencing juveniles. Rather, the court's primary focus was to be rehabilitation. In *R v. SV and Nates* (1982) 31 SASR 263, the majority in the Supreme Court held that the principles of general deterrence and retribution have no place in the sentencing of juveniles. The Western Australian Court of Criminal Appeal stated, in *R v. Yorkshire* (No. 7169, 20 June 1988, unreported, quoted in Broadhurst and Loh, 1993:269), that:

> There has been universal acceptance by the courts in England, Australia and elsewhere that there is an essential difference between children and adults when they come before a court exercising criminal jurisdiction. In particular it has been accepted by the courts that the reformation of the (child) offender is always important, if not the dominant consideration, and that any sentences should be tailored with a greater emphasis on the future of the offender.

The discussion of case law shows that there is universal support for the principle of rehabilitation in the sentencing of juveniles. The only difference relates to the extent to which deterrence and retribution might play some role in arriving at a sentence, and whether rehabilitation is the 'primary' consideration or an 'important' consideration. Recognising the importance of rehabilitation as a sentencing principle for juveniles does not preclude the use of incarceration in particular cases.

However, the objective seriousness or gravity of particular crimes may demand the use of imprisonment for the purpose of community protection in particular cases. This principle has been reflected in recent cases of manslaughter by young people arising from attacks of groups of young people on other youth (see *R v. MD, NA, BM, JT* [2005] NSWSC 344; and *R v. CK* [2004] NSWCCA 116), and cases of gang rape by young people (see the case relating to aggravated sexual assault of two sixteen-year-old girls, *R v. AEM Snr; R v. KEM; R v. MM* [2002] NSWCCA 58). In these matters, community protection, denunciation, and general deterrence are important. However, these are clearly only envisaged in particularly serious cases and as a last resort.

MANDATORY SENTENCING

Mandatory detention provisions for young people convicted of certain property offences were introduced in the Northern Territory and Western Australia in 1996. The Northern Territory provisions were repealed in October 2001. The Northern Territory legislation required a magistrate or judge to impose a period of at least 28 days detention for a juvenile (defined as a person between 15 and 17 years of age) who was convicted of certain property offences, and who had at least one prior conviction for a property offence. The offences covered by the legislation included stealing (other than from a shop), criminal damage, receiving stolen property, unlawful entry of a building, unlawful use of a motor vehicle (including being a passenger), robbery, and assault with intent to steal. White-collar crime, such as fraud and embezzlement, was not subject to mandatory sentencing, nor was shoplifting. In Western Australia, an adult or young person convicted for the third time or more for a home burglary was to be sentenced to imprisonment or detention.

Mandatory sentencing regimes in both Western Australia and the Northern Territory have led to grossly unjust outcomes, and have been subject to widespread criticism by judges, lawyers, Indigenous organisations, advocates for young people, religious groups, and international human rights bodies. These criticisms resulted in a Commonwealth inquiry by the Senate Legal and Constitutional References Committee (2000). The Committee's report provides a comprehensive response to the issues.

The mandatory sentencing of juveniles can be criticised for a number of reasons. These issues are discussed here.

Conflict with sentencing principles

There are a number of key contradictions between mandatory sentences of imprisonment and detention, and accepted sentencing principles, as follows:

- *Fairness and proportionality*—Mandatory sentencing infringes principles of fairness and proportionality because it allows no distinction between trivial and serious culpability.
- *Preventive detention*—The common law and the principle of proportionality do not permit preventive detention. Mandatory sentences extend the penalty for a particular crime for the purpose of protecting society from recidivism, and give rise to preventive detention.
- *Cruel and unusual punishment*—A mandatory sentence is not *per se* cruel and unusual, but it may become so because it must be imposed regardless of the circumstances of the offence or the offender. There may be arguments in international law that the gross disproportionality engendered through mandatory sentencing may constitute cruel and inhuman punishment.

- *Undermining the rule of law*—Mandatory sentencing brings about a fundamental change in the roles of parliament and the judiciary—a change that affects the independence of the judiciary and undermines judicial discretion and traditional functions of the court. Mandatory sentencing leads to the relocation of discretion from the judiciary to police and prosecutors. Pretrial decisions by police and prosecutors become a key determinant in the outcome of the case. This is a shift in power from the judiciary to the executive. Under mandatory sentencing, it is prosecutors who decide to invoke such laws against offenders. These decisions are less open to public scrutiny and the safeguard of appeals than judicial decision-making.
- *Age and maturity*—Mandatory sentencing contradicts the common thread that runs through juvenile justice legislative sentencing principles in all Australian jurisdictions, this thread being the need to deal with children in a way appropriate to their age and stage of maturity.
- *Rehabilitation*—Mandatory sentencing is completely out of kilter with the sentencing principles that have been developed by the superior courts in Australia, which establish the principle that special considerations are relevant to sentencing juveniles, and that rehabilitation is seen as the primary consideration when sentencing young people.

Conflict with human rights and international law

Various aspects of international human rights relating to the sentencing of young people have been outlined above. Mandatory sentences of detention breach a number of key sections of the CROC, the International Convention on Civil and Political Rights, and the Convention for the Elimination of All Forms of Racial Discrimination (CERD).

In summary, the conflict with international human rights standards includes the following:

- *The best interests of the child*—Mandatory sentencing fails to allow consideration for the best interests of the individual child when a sentence is formulated.
- *The primacy of rehabilitation*—The prospects of rehabilitation through integration into the community are ignored with mandatory sentences of detention.
- *Proportionality and the need for a wide range of sentencing options*—Mandatory sentencing ignores the requirement of a variety of dispositions and alternatives to institutionalisation to ensure that children are dealt with in a manner appropriate to their wellbeing and proportionate to both their circumstances and the offence.
- *Participation in decisions*—Mandatory sentencing makes irrelevant the requirement that children participate and be given a voice in any decisions that affect them.

- *Imprisonment as a sanction of last resort*—The requirement that children be deprived of their liberty only as a last resort and for the shortest appropriate time is ignored by mandatory sentencing.
- *Prohibition on arbitrary detention*—Mandatory sentences of detention may breach the prohibition on arbitrary detention because arbitrariness can incorporate elements of inappropriateness or injustice. Injustice arises because of gross disproportionality.
- *Prohibition on inhuman and degrading punishment*—Mandatory sentencing can give rise to inhuman treatment through the use of incarceration for trivial offences. In these cases, the gross disproportionality of a sentence can give rise to cruel, inhuman, or degrading punishment.
- *Requirement that sentences be reviewable by a higher or appellate court*—Mandatory sentences by their nature are not reviewable in terms of their severity.
- *Prohibition of discrimination*—Mandatory sentencing has a disproportionate impact on Indigenous young people compared with non-Indigenous young people. For example, Aboriginal juveniles appearing in court are significantly more likely to have a previous offending history and are more likely to be among those with extensive offending histories than are non-Aboriginal people. Thus, mandatory sentencing regimes, although they appear to be racially neutral, are *foreseeably* discriminatory in their impact.

The potential discriminatory impact has been noted by the relevant United Nations committees. These include observations by the Committee on the Rights of the Child, the Committee on the Elimination of Racial Discrimination, and the Human Rights Committee. The comments of these committees show the incompatibility of the mandatory sentencing regimes with Australia's international human rights obligations. The Committee Against Torture was less forthright, but still makes clear its concern with the potential lack of compliance (see Cunneen 2002).

GUIDELINE JUDGMENTS

A recent development in sentencing has been the introduction of guideline judgments in New South Wales. Guideline judgments have been formulated by the New South Wales Court of Criminal Appeal. They are judgments that 'go beyond the facts of a particular case to suggest a sentencing scale, or appropriate sentence for common factual situations' (New South Wales Law Reform Commission 2001:78). Guideline judgments do not bind sentencing judges, but a judge who does not apply a guideline judgment is expected to provide reasons for not doing so. Legislation also allows the attorney-general to request a guideline judgment from the court.

According to the Chief Justice of New South Wales, the purpose of guideline judgments is to foster consistency, to deter potential offenders, and to improve public confidence by bringing sentences into line with 'public expectations' (Spigelman 1999). Not surprisingly there is a perception that guideline judgments will increase the length of sentences.

Guideline judgments have been published for cases involving driving causing grievous bodily harm or death, drug importation, break, enter, and steal, and armed robbery. A guideline judgment has also been published for dealing with guilty pleas. The key issue in relation to juvenile justice is the extent to which guideline judgments apply to juvenile offenders having matters determined in the children's court, and whether they are inconsistent with the importance of considering rehabilitation when sentencing young people.

A recent judgment (*R v. RG*, NSW Supreme Court, unreported, No. 70034/99, 27 October 2000, per Dowd J) found that if a young person was sentenced for an indictable offence under the Children's (Criminal Proceedings) Act, then the sentencing regime proposed by a guideline judgment did not apply. The implication is, however, if a young person is sentenced 'at law' (that is, outside the jurisdiction of the children's court) for a serious indictable offence, then guideline judgments will apply.

PRE-SENTENCE REPORTS

Pre-sentence reports are taken into account by magistrates when they are sentencing young people. These reports have been a feature of the children's courts since they were established, and in many jurisdictions pre-sentence reports are mandatory if the court is considering sentencing a young person to detention. Pre-sentence reports are known under a variety of names, depending on the jurisdiction (social background report, assessment panel report, court report, and so on). Essentially, they are prepared in order to supply social background information on the offender and to assist the court in determining the most appropriate way of dealing with a young person.

There is legislative guidance as to the nature of material in a pre-sentence report, but the extent of guidance varies between states. In Victoria, the legislation refers to information on the circumstances of the offence, any prior offences, family circumstances, education, employment, recreation and leisure activities, and medical and health matters relating to the young person (Freiberg et al. 1988:110). In various jurisdictions, pre-sentence reports have been prepared by assessment panels, police, departmental psychologists, juvenile justice staff, and welfare officers. They have also included reports from probation officers, school, employers, and doctors. The sentencing principles in s. 109 of the *Juvenile Justice Act 1992* (Qld) allow virtually any material to be presented as long as it is deemed relevant by the court.

Research from most states in Australia shows that pre-sentence reports have a significant influence on sentencing decisions. Magistrates in general follow the recommendations put forward in the reports (Freiberg et al. 1988:112–13; Carrington 1993). One particular study conducted in Western Australia in the early 1980s found that 68 per cent of pre-sentence report recommendations were followed in their entirety, and a further 15 per cent were substantially followed. Furthermore, magistrates expressed a desire that pre-sentence reports contain information on possible sentences (Freiberg et al. 1988:113).

The scope of the reports is generally ill-defined, and they can bring before courts information that would otherwise be excluded because of irrelevancy or evidentiary rules (Freiberg et al. 1988:105). Because of this, there has been considerable debate over the information in pre-sentence reports and the effect they have on sentencing. Broadly speaking, pre-sentence reports have been said to contain information that is fundamentally ideological in nature, and rest on particular assumptions concerning the causes of offending. These assumptions work against the interests of Indigenous young people, as well as those from working-class backgrounds and ethnic minority groups. Gender assumptions may work against the interests of young women. Many of the assumptions underlying pre-sentence reports can be understood within a framework of the ideology of cultural deprivation. That is, members of working-class and minority families are assumed to be 'lacking' in comparison to the middle-class norm. For examples of the specific ways in which these assumptions may operate, see Cunneen and White (1995:225–6).

It is apparent that the court puts together a sentence based on an amalgamation of inputs, including the formal requirements of the sentencing hierarchy and sentencing principles, with the information presented in court reports. Such a process is probably more pronounced with use of the more punitive sentencing options such as detention. Clearly, a range of factors is involved, including the nature and seriousness of the offence, prospects for rehabilitation of the defendant; and the defendant's age, prior criminal record, and previous sentences. There is also the influence of other, perhaps less tangible, factors such as conceptions of social normality that find their way into the sentencing process and work to the disadvantage of certain young people. When the court is considering issues such as 'the likelihood of rehabilitation', there is the most room for assumptions about social class and cultural difference to affect decision-making.

Although there have been criticisms of pre-sentence reports, there is also widespread support for their use. Submissions to the ALRC and HREOC's Inquiry into Children in the Legal Process were generally supportive of pre-sentence reports, with some submissions arguing there was insufficient use of them, and one submission from the Australian Association of Social

Workers arguing that they should be provided as a matter of course prior to *any* sentencing decision relating to a young person. The ALRC and HREOC (1997:559) found that there are also some problems associated with reports, these problems being that:

- pre-sentence reports can prolong the process for young people, as the court may need to adjourn for preparation of the report
- the usefulness of the reports is undermined by the constraints on resources of the agencies that produce them
- the reports do not always contain a significant contribution from the young person
- the reports sometimes contain information that the young person was assured would remain confidential.

However, the Commission concluded that reports 'are generally useful when more serious sentences are being considered' (ALRC and HREOC 1997:558). Young people should have a clear understanding of the reporting process, and should be advised of their right not to participate in the preparation of a report if they so choose.

DRUG COURTS

In recent years, there has been an expansion of specialist drug courts to deal with adult offenders in most states of Australia. New South Wales and Western Australia have established youth drug courts to specifically deal with young offenders. The following discussion is based on the procedures introduced for the New South Wales Youth Drug and Alcohol Court (YDAC), whose establishment was recommended by the government-sponsored Drug Summit, held in May 1999.

The New South Wales children's court refers young people to the YDAC, and targets serious injecting drug users, particularly those on remand and young women. Those eligible for the YDAC include young people aged between 14 and 18 years old who have a serious drug or alcohol problem, who have pleaded guilty to an offence over which the children's court has jurisdiction, who are ineligible for a diversionary option under the Young Offenders Act (that is, a warning, caution or conference), who agree to go before the YDAC, and who are likely to be sentenced to detention (NSW Law Reform Commission 2001:33).

Young people who are accepted by the YDAC initially have their case adjourned for 14 days. During this period, they undergo assessment for the development of an individual plan aimed at reducing or eliminating drug and alcohol misuse and associated criminal behaviour. After the plan is developed, the court makes an order requiring the young person to comply with the conditions of the plan, and defers sentencing for 6 months. The young person is allocated a program manager and support worker, and has regular meetings with the YDAC magistrate. Young offenders who successfully complete the program can expect a favourable sentence from the court, such as a suspended sentence or other unsupervised order (NSW Law Reform Commission 2001:33–4). Adequate resourcing, the number of courts available to operate as YDACs, and their geographic location are likely to determine the success or otherwise of the program.

The YDAC has now been evaluated (University of New South Wales 2004). Some 164 referrals were made over a two-year period, and less than half (75) of those referred were accepted as eligible for the program. The evaluation noted that the main problem drug in use by both the referral group and actual participants was heroin (54 per cent of all referrals during the pilot period), followed by amphetamines (15 per cent), cannabis (14 per cent), and alcohol (12 per cent). Of the 75 accepted onto the program, 39 per cent (29) went on to 'graduate' (complete) the program. Those who graduated were less likely to reoffend than those who did not complete the program (University of New South Wales 2004:iii).

THE UTILISATION OF SENTENCING OPTIONS

We have outlined the sentencing options available to the children's court in general terms, and discussed various aspects of sentencing. A key issue that remains to be examined is the actual use of these sentencing options. How often is detention used? What are the most commonly used sentencing dispositions? Table 10.1 shows the court outcomes for New South Wales in 2004.

Table 10.1 shows the utilisation of sentencing options for criminal matters proven before the children's court. The major sentencing category in the children's court data is the use of bonds (31.4 per cent). These may include some supervision requirements (such as reporting to the local juvenile justice officer), or they may be without supervision but make a general requirement of the individual to be of good behaviour, attend school or work, or not associate with certain people).

The next major category is dismissed with a caution (18.3 per cent). The offence categories where dismissals are most frequently used are public order offences and more minor theft offences (NSW Bureau of Crime Statistics and Research 2005a:63–5).

Probation and fines are used in 15.5 per cent and 15.1 per cent of cases respectively. In the majority of probation outcomes, there is supervision ordered. Finally, community service orders and the use of detention each comprise 5.9 per cent and 9.0 per cent of sentencing outcomes respectively.

TABLE 10.1 COURT OUTCOMES FOR PROVEN OFFENCES, NEW SOUTH WALES CHILDREN'S COURT, 2004

COURT OUTCOME	TOTAL	
	N	%
Detention order	496	9.0
Community service order	323	5.9
Probation*	856	15.5
Bond and fine	10	0.2
Fine	834	15.1
Bond*	1736	31.4
Dismissed with caution	1011	18.3
Other proven outcomes	256	4.6
Total proven matters	5522	100.0

* Includes both supervised and unsupervised probation and bonds

Source: New South Wales Bureau of Crime Statistics and Research (2005a:63).

It can be difficult to make comparisons between jurisdictions on children's courts' sentencing outcomes because much depends on the diversionary processes put in place that channel young people out of the court system to begin with. For example, in the Queensland children's courts in 2003–04, some 2.2 per cent of matters resulted in a detention order (compared to New South Wales, where it was 9 per cent of proven matters) (O'Brien 2004:17). This may reflect a less punitive approach in Queensland, but is more likely to reflect the fact that many more matters were diverted from court in New South Wales through the use of youth justice conferencing. In other words, the New South Wales children's courts were dealing with proportionately more serious matters and serious offenders—hence the greater use of detention.

YOUNG PEOPLE'S EXPERIENCE OF THE CHILDREN'S COURT

We have already noted that young people's experience of the children's court is usually that of a defendant who has pleaded guilty to an offence. If young people do not avail themselves of the fundamental right to the presumption of innocence, it is important to ask what level of legal representation they have received. In principle, young people who appear in court have a right to legal representation. In practice, however, this right is limited by the ability to access services, and the quality and availability of those services. Young people are generally represented in court in one of the following ways:

- by a duty solicitor who operates at the particular court
- by a legal aid solicitor or legal aid-funded solicitor
- by a specialist community legal service (for example, the Youth Legal Service, Perth, Youth Advocacy Centre, Brisbane, Shopfront Legal Centre, Sydney) or Aboriginal Legal Service
- by a private solicitor.

O'Connor (1994:88–91) has noted five barriers to accessing appropriate legal representation:

- *The cost of legal representation*—Young people are rarely in a position to afford private representation, and are therefore dependent on the services of legal commissions or community legal centres. Generally, however, the needs of young people are peripheral to such organisations.
- *Young people's lack of legal knowledge*—Although there have been some projects aimed at providing legal education for young people (for example, *Streetwize* comics), the provision of legal education for young people is generally not a high priority.
- *Youth workers' lack of legal knowledge*—Young people are often dependent on youth workers for legal information, and in some cases youth workers are ignorant of legal rights (see also Underwood et al. 1993).
- *Limited availability of services*—Even if young people are aware of their rights, actually accessing services can be difficult, particularly if young people require legal assistance while in police custody.
- *Problems with the way duty-solicitor schemes operate*—Many young people have access to legal services through duty solicitors. We discuss this issue below.

In Queensland, interviews with young people have identified a number of problems with duty-solicitor schemes. Duty solicitors tend to deal with guilty pleas and bail applications. Young people interviewed stated that it was common for them to plead guilty either to 'get things over and done with' or because the duty solicitor had recommended that they do so (Youth Advocacy Centre 1993:38). Young people also identified these major problems: limited time with the duty solicitor; poor communication by the solicitor; and lack of clarity concerning the role of the solicitor. Young people felt they were not properly represented in court (Youth Advocacy Centre 1993:39). The ALRC commented upon the duty solicitor scheme as follows:

> Most young people are represented by duty solicitors attached to the Children's Court ... Currently, duty solicitors often do not have the opportunity to take adequate instructions from children. Generally, the first time they have contact with the child is on the morning of the hearing (ALRC & HREOC 1997:520).

Young people's experience of court processes is shaped by the fact that most young people have pleaded guilty to the offence for which they are appearing. As a result, the court is experienced as an institution that is primarily concerned with sentencing. In a Queensland study, the majority of young people interviewed 'indicated that they believed if they did not plead guilty immediately they ran the risk of being remanded in custody, with the consequent process taking far longer than admitting the crime' (Youth Advocacy Centre 1993:41).

If young people experience court as essentially a system for imposing punishment, then it is important to consider what understanding they have of the court's processes. As we noted previously in this chapter, the CROC and the Beijing Rules require that children and young people be given appropriate involvement in proceedings and decisions that affect them. The ALRC and HREOC (1997: 529) noted the following:

> In New South Wales and Queensland legislation provides that children before the court have the right to participate in decisions that affect them. In the ACT and Victoria courts are required to make sure children understand the nature and purpose of the proceedings. There are no similar provisions in the other States and Territories. Some young people consider that they are not given enough opportunities to talk in their own defence in court. This view is supported by a number of commentators.

Interviews with young people show that the court is seen as an alien world, and that a court appearance is a rapidly conducted and poorly understood process that imposes significant decisions on their lives (Youth Advocacy Centre 1993:41). Young people have indicated that they are unclear about the process that occurs and the meaning of its outcome, in some cases completely misunderstanding the nature of a sanction (O'Connor & Sweetapple 1988).

Given these experiences, it is difficult to see how a court processing from a guilty plea to a sentence can be of benefit to the young person. In the two studies just cited, at least, there appears to be alienation and a poor understanding of what is occurring, even to the point of misunderstanding sentences. Submissions to the ALRC reiterated the point that children are not given an appropriate voice in the sentencing process. The Commission recommended that:

> Duty solicitor schemes should be sufficiently resourced to ensure that children are given timely and appropriate advice on matters relating to sentencing and are assisted to express their views during the sentencing process. This provision should be included in the national standards for juvenile justice (Recommendation 245) (ALRC & HREOC 1997:562).

The Commission also recommended a 24-hour free-call youth legal advice telephone service in each jurisdiction to supplement the demands placed on duty solicitors. The New South Wales Legal Aid Commission has established a Youth Hotline to provide legal advice to young people. The higher courts have ruled that there is a positive obligation on police to make the services known to young people detained in custody. Justice Dowd commented in *R v. Cortez*, in relation to legal representation and the availability of the Legal Aid Hotline, as follows:

> It should also be noted that the obligation to young people includes the obligation to make it known to them that there is a legal hotline available, provided by the Legal Aid Commission; financial provision has been made to enable this to occur at no cost to the young person. ... Young people aged 17 rarely have a solicitor and rarely have a contact number for one available. It is as absurd as suggesting they might contact their architect or their dietary advisor. The whole intention of the hotline is that young people would know that it is free, that is it is available, and would be able to obtain advice there and then. Failure to make it available is a clear breach of the Act and regulations but, more importantly, in breach of the requirement of fairness to the young person (*R V. Cortez*, NSWSC, 2 October 2002 per Dowd J at para 36).

CONCLUSION

We began this chapter by considering the jurisdiction of the children's court, and noting that one of the central features of the courts is that they are essentially mechanisms for imposing penalties rather than determining guilt or innocence. It is therefore critical to assess how the courts go about sentencing and to assess the extent to which they comply with international human rights standards. We did this first by looking at sentencing options and the hierarchy of sentences, and then by discussing sentencing principles and the use of pre-sentence reports. We also noted recent developments in sentencing, including mandatory sentencing, sentencing guidelines, and drug courts.

Most court outcomes involve dismissals, bonds, probation, or fines. However, for some young people the court imposes a custodial sentence. The experiences of incarceration are the subject of the next chapter. Finally, it is important to recognise some of the broader trends that have been evident in the treatment of young people before the courts. While on the one hand human rights standards play an important role in structuring our approach to young people, it is also clear that there has been an increasing tendency toward more punitive approaches to young people and a greater emphasis on individual responsibility and accountability. There has been a diminution of the principle that young people should be treated differently to adults, and we see this in arguments over the retention of *doli incapax*, of publicly naming children and young people, and in a greater preparedness by the courts to place community protection and deterrence above rehabilitation for particular types of juvenile offenders.

11 | Detention and community corrections

INTRODUCTION

Throughout Australia, there are provisions for incarcerating young people in institutions separate from adult offenders. These institutions are variously known as youth training centres, detention centres, juvenile justice centres, and youth residential centres. Apart from rare cases in which young people are sent to adult prisons, a detention order is the most severe of the sentencing options available to the children's court. For this reason, it is necessary to consider in more detail how the use of detention works in practice.

This chapter provides an overview of the extent to which young offenders are placed in juvenile detention, the reasons for use of detention, who is targeted to receive this sanction, and what happens to and with a young person once they become an 'involuntary client' of the criminal justice system. Our concern is not only with the characteristics of detainees, and the service provision available to them while in detention, but is also with the experiences of young inmates and what they face after release from a secure facility. The latter part of the chapter considers the use of 'community corrections' as an alternative to incarceration. This form of punishment is distinguished from other forms of community-based measures, such as juvenile conferencing (where the outcomes vary in relation to the specific dynamics of each session), in that it involves enforced social control over the activities of young people as ordered by the court and as provided in legislation (that is, it is part of the formalised, uniform system of sanctions).

The 'special treatment' of juveniles, due to their age, was historically reflected at the point of sentencing, rather than within the penal system as such (Atkinson 1997). Thus, for example, the First Fleet carried five young convicts younger than 16 years old, including two girls younger than 16 years old. The idea was that diversion from the gallows to a penal colony was appropriate because of the young convicts' tender years (Seymour 1998). As mentioned in chapter 1, within the early colonies there certainly was no compunction about imprisoning young people, and doing so under largely adult conditions of incarceration. Today, there are separate procedures and facilities for dealing with young offenders compared to their adult counterparts. There is also a further separation within the young offending population, on the basis of sex (with separate facilities for boys and girls), and also in some cases on the basis of age (as with provision in Victoria of youth residential centres for those between 10 and 15 years old, and youth training centres for those 15 years or older).

THE USE OF DETENTION

In some jurisdictions, there are certain legislative requirements when the court is considering sentencing a young person to a period of institutionalisation. As we noted in the previous chapter, a pre-sentence report must be considered, unless the jurisdiction has enacted mandatory sentencing in relation to particular offences. Generally speaking, the court must be satisfied that no other sentencing option is appropriate. If the detention order is made, the court must state its reasons for the order in writing. Some jurisdictions also define the purpose of detention in their legislation. For instance, in the *Children (Detention Centres) Act 1987* (NSW), s. 4 stipulates that young people subject to remand or to a detention order should take their place in the community as soon as possible as people who will observe the law, and that 'satisfactory relationships' should be maintained between the young person and their family.

In some cases, the establishment, operation, and procedures relating to detention are spelt out in general juvenile justice legislation. For example, Part 6 of the *Juvenile Justice Act 1992* (Qld) covers:

- the establishment and management of detention centres
- the appointment, functions, and powers of official visitors
- such matters as initial reception, medical treatment, visitors, leave of absence, and transfer to (adult) prison
- complaints and complaint handling
- offences relating to detention centres.

This type of legislation provides a description of the formal aspects of the operation of detention. It does not tell us much about the practices of detention, about who is incarcerated, or about the extent to which detention is utilised. One way of considering the use of detention is to compare the rates of incarceration over time, and between different jurisdictions. It is important to bear in mind that on any one day, more than 700 people are incarcerated in Australian juvenile correction institutions, but this figure also includes a sizable proportion of inmates (approximately 20 per cent in June 1996) who are young adults aged 18 years or older (see Atkinson 1997:403; Keys Young Pty Ltd 1997). For example, there were 211 persons aged 18 years and over in juvenile detention centres around the country on 30 June 2004 (Veld & Taylor, 2005:43). The majority of young people in custody (around 70 per cent) are between 15 and 17 years old (Keys Young Pty Ltd 1997), although the younger age groups (10–14 years old) consist of a disproportionate number of Indigenous young people (Cunneen & McDonald 1997; Harding & Maller 1997; Veld & Taylor, 2005).

The number of juveniles in corrective institutions, and the rate of incarceration of persons aged 10–17 years per 100,000 of the relevant population (that is, the total number of young people in this age group), have varied since the 1980s. For example: 'The number of persons aged 10–17 years held in corrective institutions declined from 1352 in June 1981 until June 1992, when it reached 577. This number increased during the following years and seems to have stabilised around an average 780 persons a year' (Carcarch & Muscat 1999:4). At 30 June 2004, however, only 564 juvenile detainees were recorded (Veld & Taylor, 2005:14). Rates of incarceration follow a similar trend. Explanations for the decline, subsequent rise and then further decline of incarceration rates include changes in the overall youth population size, introduction of greater use of diversionary schemes and intermediate sanctions, changing law-enforcement strategies and priorities, and specific legislative changes affecting how to deal with particular categories of young offenders. The number of young people placed in detention at any time, and the detention rate of young people, require analysis of a wide range of demographic, political, and legal factors.

The rates of youth detention vary considerably between states and territories. Table 11.1 presents statistics on juvenile detention in Australia for 2004, by jurisdiction. The figures tell us that the largest concentration of young people in detention is to be found in New South Wales (198 out of 564). However, the highest rate of incarceration is found in Western Australia (51.9 young people per 100,000 population). In part, this might be attributed to the continued use of mandatory sentencing in that state. For instance, in 1998 the highest rate of incarceration was found in the Northern Territory (103.5 young people per 100,000 population), which was almost double that observed during the same month in 1996 when statistics were collected, and which is largely attributed to the introduction of mandatory sentencing by the Northern Territory government in 1997 (Carcarch & Muscat 1999:6). While Tasmania and the Australian Capital Territory have low numbers of young people in detention (eighteen and sixteen people respectively), the rate of incarceration

TABLE 11.1 PERSONS AGED 10–17 YEARS IN JUVENILE DETENTION BY JURISDICTION IN AUSTRALIA, 30 JUNE 2004

JUVENILE DETENTION	NSW	VIC	QLD	WA	SA	TAS	NT	ACT	AUST
As at 30 June 2004									
No	198	62	91	118	51	18	10	16	564
Rate per 100 000 pop.	27.2	11.7	20.6	51.9	31.5	32.7	39.8	45.1	25.5
Male rate	49.5	21.0	38.3	87.5	56.5	63.7	76.6	82.8	46.0
Female rate	3.7	1.9	1.9	14.4	5.1	0.0	0.0	5.8	4.0
Indigenous rate	372.5	193.7	200.9	654.6	390.0	104.9	74.3	619.6	312.9
Non-Indigenous rate	12.6	9.5	8.7	12.6	19.2	27.3	13.9	31.7	12.2

Source: Data drawn from Veld & Taylor (2005).

is lowest in Victoria (11.7 people compared to the national average of 25.5 people), reflecting a much less punitive social environment than many other states and territories, as well as long-term historical trends associated with Victorian sentencing patterns generally (see Freiberg & Ross 1995).

Figures on juvenile detention for the years 1981 to 2004 show a significant decline in overall numbers nationwide (from 1352 in 1981 to 564 in 2004). For most of this period, the numbers of young people incarcerated declined in all jurisdictions except the two states traditionally associated with low detention rates, Victoria and Tasmania (Veld & Taylor 2005).

Another population group held in detention is child asylum seekers. While not incarcerated due to the interventions of the criminal justice system, or because of the actions of the children and young people themselves, it is notable that in October 2000 there were 300 children in immigration detention centres around Australia (Tashkoff 2000). A year later, there were more than 500 (Everitt 2001). Many of the issues discussed further on—such as service provision, the experiences of incarceration, and specific youth needs—are relevant to this group of detainees. In addition, many child asylum seekers face special challenges due to the circumstances of the flight from their country of origin, the tensions associated with detention conditions, and the uncertainties of the immigration process. While present federal government policy allows greater flexibility for young asylum seekers to be placed into community care, many children and young people remain behind bars nonetheless.

Most young people in detention centres are there because they have been sentenced by the courts. However, one feature of the juvenile justice system is the relatively large number of young people held on remand. These are young people who have been refused bail by the court and who are in custody awaiting the determination of their case. Young people in juvenile corrective institutions are thus classified into two groups according to their legal status: those awaiting court hearings, outcomes or penalty, and sentenced detainees. Significantly, 'the number of persons on remand as a percentage of the total persons held in juvenile corrective institutions has increased from 21.4 per cent during 1981 to 42.6 per cent during 1998' (Carcarch & Muscat 1999:25). Furthermore, other research has shown that the average age of the remand population tends to be lower than that of the young people sentenced to detention, with one-third being younger than 16 years old (Cain 1994c:32). Again, there are variations among the states with regard to the use of remand. As at 30 June 2004, only 46 per cent of those 10–17-year-olds in juvenile detention centres in New South Wales were sentenced persons. This means that more than 50 per cent of detainees were being held on remand. By contrast, Victoria has around 35 per cent of detainees held on remand. It has been suggested that this most probably reflects the diversionary focus of the Victorian juvenile justice system, which aims to reduce instances of custodial remand (Veld & Taylor 2005: 40–2).

Other key characteristics of the young people in detention relate to gender, Indigenous status, and ethnic background. Young male offenders tend to make up the bulk of the incarcerated youth population. As shown in table 11.1, they have much higher participation rates than their female counterparts. It is significant, as well, to note that the contribution of females to the total population of juveniles under detention has substantially declined over the years from 17.2 per cent during June 1981, to 6.3 per cent during June 1998 (Carcach & Muscat 1999:16), to 4.0 per cent in June 2004 (Veld & Taylor 2005). Young Indigenous people continue to be overrepresented in most jurisdictions in the country (Veld & Taylor 2005:31). As at 30 June 2004, they were overrepresented in detention in:

- Western Australia (Indigenous young people were 52 times more likely to be detained per population)
- New South Wales (Indigenous people were 30 times more likely to be detained per population)
- Queensland (Indigenous persons were 23 times more likely to be detained per population)
- South Australia (Indigenous young people were 20 times more likely to be detained per population)
- Victoria (Indigenous young people were 20 times more likely to be detained per population).

While overall rates of detention have been declining in recent years, the Indigenous rate has gone down by only 24 per cent since 1994, compared to a decline of 50 per cent for non-Indigenous young people. Moreover, the ratio of Indigenous over-representation has continued to be relatively stable over this same time period, with Indigenous persons aged 10 to 17 years still 25 times more likely to be in detention (nationally) than non-Indigenous persons of the same age group (Veld & Taylor 2005:23).

Ethnicity is also an important aspect of detention, particularly in New South Wales and Victoria, where significant numbers of young people from non-English-speaking backgrounds (NESBs) are incarcerated. Research in New South Wales, for example, shows that there has been an increase in detention figures for young people of Indo-Chinese, Pacific Islander, and Lebanese background (Cain 1994a; NSW Legislative Council Standing Committee on Social Issues 1995; Gallagher & Poletti 1998). The evidence suggests that minority groups, including Indigenous people, are tending to receive harsher penalties, and also control orders, at a rate higher than Anglo-Australian young people (Cunneen & McDonald 1997; Cunneen 2001a).

Another important issue is the nature of offences for which young people are sentenced to detention. In a review of offences committed by juveniles sentenced to custody drawn from New South Wales, Victoria, and Western Australia, Atkinson (1997) found that, in general, the majority of young offenders in detention had a non-violent offence as their principal offence, mainly relating to theft, break and enter, and other property offences. Furthermore, Atkinson found that girls generally commit less serious offences than boys, including those young female offenders serving time in a detention centre. Finally, many young offenders from minority groups— such as Vietnamese-Australian youth—are overrepresented among drug offenders in detention (Atkinson 1997; see also Mukherjee 1999). The types of offences for which young people are imprisoned raises questions about the appropriateness of the sanction applied and the use of incarceration as a means of 'last resort'.

While overall juvenile detention numbers have stabilised in recent years, and a sizable proportion of those detained are there for non-violent offences, it nevertheless appears that those young people who are incarcerated tend to be those who have committed crimes of a more serious nature, or those who have previously committed crimes of some kind. To put it another way, it is those young people who are deemed to have committed a 'violent' offence (crime against the person) and who are 'habitual' offenders (repeated offending behaviour) who wind up in the detention system. This concentration of 'difficult' cases has a number of implications for service provision and for the capacity of the juvenile corrections system to cater to the needs of the young offenders in its charge. These issues are explored shortly.

In recent years in Australia, there has been considerable controversy concerning these 'serious and repeat offenders' and appropriate policy responses to them. A number of states and territories have introduced specific legislation to deal with repeat offenders, or have special provisions to deal with serious offenders. For example, in Queensland, the legislation has particular provisions for young people convicted of a serious offence (defined as an offence for which an adult would be liable to imprisonment for 14 years or more). In such circumstances, the young person can be sentenced to detention for up to 10 years. In cases of offences that carry life sentences for adults, such as murder or rape, the court can order the detention of the young person for up to 14 years. Recent legislation in the Northern Territory and Western Australia was expressly directed at dealing with repeat offenders through the mechanism of imposing mandatory sentences to detention if the young person has been convicted of a prescribed offence (see chapter 10). More generally, it appears that refining the classification of and responses to specific groups of young offenders represents a form of bifurcation of punishment. This refers to the phenomenon whereby the range of intermediate sanctions (such as juvenile conferencing, community service orders) has been broadened for the majority of offenders, but particularly severe sanctions (such as enforced minimum periods of detention) have simultaneously been introduced for serious and repeat offenders.

There are many problems with legislation and institutional practices that are designed to achieve incapacitation and deterrence. As emphasised in research that looks specifically at the nature of serious and violent juvenile offenders, a 'quick fix' solution to such offending is not possible; rather, a comprehensive strategy must be adopted if the complex reasons for such offending are to be addressed (Loeber & Farrington 1998). Furthermore, it appears that most young people who end up in detention centres are in fact already repeat offenders, irrespective of any specific legislation aimed at incarcerating recidivists (see, for example, Asher 1986; Youth Advocacy Centre 1993; Coumarelos & Weatherburn 1995; Cain 1996). Targeted and punitive responses that focus on certain classes of offenders have been criticised on a number of grounds: that crime is not 'out of control' and does not therefore require such punitive measures, that there is no evidence to suggest such harsh penalties act as either general or specific deterrents, and, as indicated in chapter 10, that mandatory sentences contravene juvenile sentencing principles and human rights, and are also costly in terms of accommodating each juvenile sentenced to a mandatory period of detention.

The issue at hand is not whether serious and repeat young offenders ought to be singled out for specialist intervention of some kind, but whether punitive detention is in fact the most suitable form of intervention. Theories of incapacitation argue that control of delinquency can be achieved by identifying and incarcerating repeat offenders. The argument is that, once chronic offenders are locked up, the juvenile crime rate will be reduced significantly. Considerable criminological research on these issues suggests differently.

For a start, it is difficult to predict who will be a repeat offender (see Lundman 1994). A cohort study by Wolfgang, Figlio, and Sellin (1972) showed that a small group of 6.3 per cent of offenders committed five or more offences, yet the researchers were unable to predict at any stage who, specifically, would become a serious repeat offender. Another US study of a cohort with at least one arrest for a violent crime concluded: 'our research is only one of many studies leading to the same conclusion ... the power to predict is too weak a basis for decision-making' (Hamparian, Schuster, Dinitz & Conrad 1978:133). A similar critique has been mounted against the promises of Australian legislation on repeat offenders. According to Broadhurst and Loh (1993), we know that a few offenders account for a large proportion of offending, but these young people are identified retrospectively, not prospectively. We cannot predict who will be in the high-risk group.

Yet the logic of incapacitation is that, if we want to stop reoffending, then we should incarcerate all first offenders who appear before the court. But this belies the fact that incarceration would be unnecessary for about 70 per cent of these young people, because the data show that, at least until recently, they will not reappear in any case (Coumarelos 1994; Coumarelos & Weatherburn 1995; Cain 1996). We know that the remaining 30 per cent of young offenders will go on to contribute about 62 per cent of all court appearances, but we are unable to predict who the 30 per cent will be on the basis of their first appearances. Perhaps, then, we could contemplate incarcerating all young people who appear a second time. However, only half of those young people will go on to reappear in court for further offences, and in effect, we would be incarcerating double the number of young people than would be necessary otherwise. The same problem remains as we go through the continuum of repeat offenders: the further we go, the fewer potential offences we prevent. Some recent research suggests, however, that with the advent of stronger diversionary measures such as juvenile conferencing, first appearance in court may well indeed be a predictor of future engagement with the criminal justice system (see Chen et al. 2005), and, as we noted in the previous chapter, a larger proportion of court outcomes leading to detention. But does this necessarily translate into support for detention?

Deterrence theorists have argued that incarceration deters further offending, either specifically through direct experience, or generally through knowledge of punitive consequences (specific and general deterrence). However, Thomas and Bishop (1984:1242–3) found no support for the hypothesis that sanctions increase the perception of risk or diminish the likelihood of offending. In Australia, Kraus (1977) used a control group of school attendees and an experimental group of institutional inmates. He found that the use of penalties did not necessarily change offending behaviour, because the offender's fear of being caught and punished was not raised to the same level as that of the non-offender. Rutter and Giller (1983) have also argued that deterrence requires consistency in the detection of the offender and the sentence imposed, in order to have an effect on behaviour. Our earlier discussion in chapter 3 of clear-up rates, apprehension, and unreported crime questions consistency in detection.

Community protection is another reason given for detention. Yet the offences most commonly associated with detention orders are not crimes of violence, but property crimes. This raises the ethical question of whether incarcerating offenders is a suitable response to these types of offences. It also raises questions regarding the link between property crimes, political economy, and social class. Is it the most economically marginalised group of youth who are being sentenced to detention? If we do concentrate on those who have committed violent offences, then does it make sense to put the toughest and most intransigent people all together in the one place? This is a sure recipe for stigmatisation, as well as creating enormous problems from the point of view of detention centre management (see, for example, New South Wales Legislative Council 2005).

Finally, we must consider whether detention actually works in terms of rehabilitation. There have been several empirical studies on aspects of effectiveness. Kraus (1974) examined a group of probationers and a group of juveniles in a detention centre, and generally found greater recidivism after institutionalisation. Another Australian study found that young people who were committed to a detention centre were about four-and-a-half times more likely to be charged with a serious offence once they became adults than young people who were convicted of offences but not committed (Kraus 1981:162). An overseas study by Benda (1987) of status offenders and criminal offenders found that 80 per cent had contact with police after their first release from an institution, and 63 per cent returned to a custodial facility. There have been similar criticisms of the use of remand in custody. Kraus (1978) found that significantly more juveniles reoffended after being remanded in custody. Likewise, Frazier and Cochran (1986) found that young people remanded in custody received more severe judicial outcomes, even with controls for legal and sociodemographic variables. Conversely, when detention has been dispensed with and/or minimised as a sanction, there is evidence that juvenile offenders do not continue their institutional career within criminal justice. For example, in 1969 the head of the Department of Youth Services in Massachusetts, USA, Jerome Miller, transferred all but a handful of young offenders to community-based programs. As Schissel (2002:122–3) observes: 'Subsequent research indicated that within a five-year period the recidivism rate in Massachusetts had dropped and that the number of adults in prison who were alumni of the youth system had dropped dramatically.' This indicates that detention itself is a major source of recidivism.

In summary, evaluations of the effects of detention have not been positive. At best, there seems to be little difference in outcomes in terms of recidivism. And in some cases, it appears that non-custodial options have better results. Incarceration has been criticised on many grounds as being ineffective, criminogenic, stigmatising, expensive, and inhumane. It is also important to consider the effects of gathering often already marginalised young people into segregated groups on an involuntary basis. Such policies are likely to increase resentment and alienation.

EXPERIENCES OF DETENTION AND SERVICE PROVISION

Theoretically, Australian juvenile correction services should be guided by the concerns expressed in the United Nations conventions and protocols that emphasise the special needs and status of children and young people (see chapter 10). How well—if at all—can the Australian juvenile detention systems accommodate or go towards meeting these prescriptions? In part, this depends upon the nature of the client base, and the nature of the services and resources available to that clientele.

The young people in detention are not only distinguishable on the basis offence type and offending record over time. There is also considerable variation among the young people in regard to factors such as gender, ethnicity, Indigenous status, mental illness, experience of abuse, substance use, and so on. The place of state wards in juvenile justice warrants special comment. An astonishing number of state wards end up in detention: '... despite making up only 0.135 per cent of the population, approximately 30 per cent of juvenile offenders have been or are presently in the care of the Minister for Community Services. State wards who have had difficult, troubled childhoods often fall into the juvenile justice system and often have considerable behaviour problems' (NSW Legislative Council 2005:107). From the point of view of service provision, there are a number of serious questions posed by the composition of the detention population. For example, there is bound to be a tension between 'security' and 'service' objectives (which will be considered in greater depth further on). This conflict may well be exacerbated by the entry into the detention context of 'outside' service providers (such as, for example, the YMCA in Victoria, which provides input into recreational programs in juvenile detention centres). Such providers may have quite different agendas and perceptions from the 'insiders' regarding their aims and key priorities.

More generally, in a period of declining fiscal resources (that is, government budget allocations available to public institutions) and escalating costs, it is difficult to envisage that increasing service and funding allocations within a correctional institution will be an easy task. And certain groups require even greater-than-usual staff attention and resources simply because of their unique situations. For instance, the small number of girls in the system has implications for the development of specific programs designed to meet their different needs (see Alder & Baines 1996; Alder 1997; Murray 2000). Likewise, while the number of juvenile sex offenders is small, their demands on professional staff are very great (Reddrop 1998). Most treatment of adolescent sex offenders is provided on an individualised level, with only two states—Victoria and New South Wales—having programs dedicated specifically to such offenders (Grant 2000). The services provided to young people with mental illness and intellectual disability within the juvenile justice system similarly require more attention. A 1988 report on young people with intellectual disabilities in New South Wales, for example, found that more resources were needed for staffing, identification processes, training programs, post-release support services, data collection, information exchange, and so on (NSW Department of Family and Community Services 1988). A subsequent report by the New South Wales Ombudsman in 1996 found that little had been done to recognise and respond to the specific needs of detainees who had physical, intellectual, and learning disabilities and/or brain injury. It was noted that such detainees may comprise between 14 and 20 per cent of the general detainee population, but that the issues identified in 1988 had still not been addressed (NSW Office of the Ombudsman 1996). A health survey of young people in custody in New South Wales carried out in 2003 found that of the 242 participants:

- 88 per cent reported, mild, moderate, or severe symptoms consistent with a clinical disorder
- the three most prevalent disorders were Conduct Disorder, Substance Abuse Disorder and Adjustment Disorder
- 30 per cent reported high or very high psychological distress, implying that they may have a greater than 50 per cent chance of an anxiety or depressive disorder (cited in NSW Legislative Council 2005:103).

The challenge that this poses for service provision is self-evident.

Meanwhile, the issue of drug use and abuse looms large in any program development and service provision. For example, South Australian and New South Wales studies of juveniles in detention have found considerably greater levels of substance use than in other young people of the same age (Howard & Zibert 1990; Copeland & Howard 2001; NSW Juvenile Justice Advisory Council Zoola; Putnins 2001). These studies have found that the young people in detention used drugs due to curiosity, boredom, and a desire to feel good. The studies have also revealed a disturbing lack of access to and use of drug-and-alcohol support services by such young people. Furthermore, the health and wellbeing of young people is directly associated with substance use, prior to and during the process of detention. 'Substance use was strongly associated with both young offender status and the very act of offending, with almost half the offenders reporting using substances at the time of their last offence. High rates of attempted suicide, deliberate self-injury and recent thoughts about suicide were also reported by the detained youths' (Putnins 1995:155). Putnins (1995) also noted that chronic offenders appear to be at greater risk of both substance abuse and suicidal behaviour.

Different population groups respond differently to any program on offer. Substance abuse, for example, is implicated in the majority of young women's offending (among female offenders placed in detention), with particularly high rates of heroin use relative to male offenders. There is also a strong connection between sexual abuse and substance abuse, and this likewise has implications for any treatment program. To date, one of the most successful interventions for young women within a detention-centre setting appears to be the 'Somebody's Daughter' program in Victoria. This is run by women (many of whom are ex-drug users with histories of imprisonment) for young women in detention, and is specifically designed as a multimodal approach within a drug harm-minimisation framework. Arts-based developmental skills include such things as writing, storytelling, movement, presentation, drama, music, and visual arts. The strengths of this approach include an emphasis on the young women choosing when, how often, and how much to participate, making things fun and enjoyable, ensuring flexibility and responsiveness to people and institutional changes, involving active participation, being outcome- and goal-oriented, and having things take place within a safe, non-threatening environment (Coulter 2001). This kind of program, however, does challenge many of the conventional practices and concepts of detention centres and their staff, and this can create tensions and conflicts among all concerned. Moreover, its ultimate success will depend upon how well it articulates with other interventions within detention settings, and the links that are made to outside services and programs.

Issues relating to drugs, abuse, education and vocational needs, psychiatric problems, leisure and recreation, sexuality, and so on demand a high level of professional expertise in addition to the everyday tasks associated with the running of secure facilities. It also has to be remembered that specific difficulties and problems are exacerbated in circumstances where the usual 'pains of imprisonment' obtain (see White & Perrone 2005). These include, among other things, the deprivation of liberty (involving major restrictions on movement, and separation from loved ones), the deprivation of goods and services (involving drastic reduction in availability of material possessions), and the deprivation of autonomy (involving subjection to a vast body of rules, regulations, and commands). Furthermore, the concentration of 'hard cases'—that is, already marginalised young people—into segregated groups tends to influence the institutional dynamic of detention centres in repressive rather than rehabilitative directions. In addition, the periodic escape of young detainees from custody, as happened several times in Tasmania in 1999, or detention centre riots such as occurred at Kariong Juvenile Justice Centre in New South Wales in 2004, are often accompanied by sensationalistic media coverage that invariably places the emphasis on 'security', and thereby reinforces the containment (rather than rehabilitative) rationale of detention centres. This in turn can affect social relationships within juvenile institutions.

Resentment and alienation on the part of the detainees contribute to the 'control' mentality within detention centres, as well as representing a reaction to this institutional imperative. A comprehensive Ombudsman inquiry into juvenile detention centres in New South Wales, for example, found that 'The administration of most centres continues to focus on containment and

compliance rather than on the reintegration of detainees into the community'
(NSW Office of the Ombudsman 1996:iv). This orientation was reflected in
the measures used in the daily management of detainees. Here, the inquiry
(NSW Office of the Ombudsman 1996:xxii) found that:

> Most behaviour management schemes rely on the use of 'points' systems
> which permit detainees increasing levels of privileges. Unfortunately most
> schemes operating within the centres are more linked with control and
> punishment than with encouraging and rewarding detainees to manage
> their own behaviour. The philosophy behind incentive schemes is extremely
> misunderstood ... Many operational staff now consider them to be used to
> deduct points and remove privileges in response to inappropriate behaviour
> and they have become part of most centres' disciplinary system.

The general atmosphere of detention centres, and specific administrative
measures governing institutional life, have a major impact on the experiences
of young detainees. An illustration of a young person's perceptions of
incarceration is provided in this poem by a young detainee in South Australia
(C.D., quoted in Searles & Goodfellow 1994:13).

Hate

I hate being told what to do
I hate being told what food to eat
I hate being told what time to go to bed
I hate being told what channel on TV to watch
I hate being told if I can read at night
or not
I hate being told when I can play sport
what sport
I hate being told what clothes to wear
I hate being asked if I can go to the toilet
I hate being told what I can and can't say
I hate being told to do my work at school
I hate the fact that if you don't do what your told that you get into shit
I hate how the staff always have the last say in everything.

This poem provides a graphic example of the consequences stemming
from institutional practices that do not adequately address the needs of
young offenders and that ignore their basic human rights. The New South
Wales Ombudsman inquiry found 'many shortcomings with the current
operation of juvenile detention centres which impact negatively on the
dignity and rights of detainees, in some cases seriously so', and that 'detainees'
needs and rights are often unrecognised and neglected' (NSW Office of the
Ombudsman 1996:iv). It is not surprising, therefore, that the Youth Justice
Coalition (1990:297) found in its interviews with young people in detention

in New South Wales that detainees saw themselves as being punished. They did not see rehabilitation as the reason for their incarceration. They did view training in skills as useful, but it should be noted that some of these skills were related to crime. Similarly, interviews with young people in detention in Queensland noted that detention did little to assist young people to return to the community with income, housing, or skills. Instead, it seemed to increase a young person's knowledge about crime and established a peer group from within the detention centre that extended to the outside on release: 'you meet others you can do jobs with' (Youth Advocacy Centre 1993:47).

The most negative aspects of detention relate to loss of freedom, isolation, and loss of contact with family and friends. For young people brought up as state wards, the problems may be compounded by the fact that, due to their living circumstances, some of these offenders have very few or no visits from individuals outside the detention centre. Boredom is also seen as an issue in some detention centres. More generally, these criticisms relate to the negative effects of lack of privacy, restriction of creativity, a tense atmosphere, and resentment of a disciplinary regime. In responding to what for many young people is an intimidating and monotonous environment, detainees 'resist' the homogenising order of the detention centre in a variety of ways. For instance, a Queensland study explored how young detainees use and experience their bodies in ways that assert their individuality and limited social power (Ogilvie & Lynch 1999). For example, choice of clothing, hairstyle, body size, necklaces, wristbands, length of fingernails, use of makeup, and so on were actively used by the young people to establish some sense of individual identity, membership of particular ethnic groups, and power and prestige relative to other inmates and detention officers. Manipulation of one's body also extends to self-destructive behaviour: 'The act of cutting could be thought of as attempting to gain a measure of power over one's predicament, of asserting control over one's body. Just as control can be displayed through care of the self, so too can it be seen in self-mutilation' (Ogilvie & Lynch 1999:154). The ways in which young detainees use their bodies, therefore, is reflective of a culture of resistance to the institutionalised authority of the detention centre.

Resistance to authority comes in different forms, and is based upon different responses to diverse aspects of the incarceration experience. Certainly, a big issue is that of the totality of daily routines that structure young people's time, space, activity, and appearance in ways that often exclude young people from having their say, and that reinforce the arbitrariness of decision-making by authority figures. For example, contact between young people who are incarcerated and the outside world has long been recognised as important in preventing further isolation and marginalisation. Yet in practice, contact is often determined by the political whims of senior bureaucrats and politicians. Visiting rights can be restricted, and the number of phone calls reduced. As it stands, there are usually restrictions on the actual days, number, and duration of phone calls and visits. Compounding this, the physical location of centres and their distance from public transport affect the capacity of friends and family to visit detention centres (NSW Office of the Ombudsman 1996). These are important issues for young people who already identify loneliness as a key feature of institutional life. Similarly, the induction process into an institution can be a frightening experience (Youth Justice Coalition 1990:319–20). Being provided with a booklet of twenty or thirty pages is certainly of little assistance to young people in understanding the day-to-day rules and procedures of a particular centre, and does little to reassure them that centre objectives also include rehabilitative goals.

Young people are frequently penalised for trivial offences such as 'abusive, indecent or threatening language' and 'disobeying rules or instructions' in ways that are disproportionate to the nature of the conduct (NSW Office of the Ombudsman 1996). To ensure discipline, most detention centres use cautions, restrictions on sport or recreational activities, and the giving out of extra duties (ALRC & HREOC 1997). The most serious of imposed punishments is that of confinement, although technically it may not be called such. For example, the ALRC and the HREOC (1997) point out that most jurisdictions prohibit the use of isolation as a form of punishment, but permit it for behavioural management, such as when the detainee refuses to participate in a program.

The use of segregation (restricted contact with other detainees) or solitary confinement (isolation) is thus still a feature of detention centres throughout Australia. Rules governing segregation vary from jurisdiction to jurisdiction, but normally stipulate the reasons for segregation and the length of time for which it can be used. From a staff perspective, it is a tool for managing disruptive inmates. But, from the point of view of the young person (Youth Justice Coalition 1990:324), the effect is very different:

> I was there for 12 hours. It's just a little cell, with carpet, a brick bench, with the floor coming up like that. No mattress or pillow or nothing. Just looking at the colour of the brick—makes you, starts to get you crazy after a while ... at night time you think someone's going to come in and shoot you or something—it's just the colour of the wall—it sends you crazy. Then you start to get um ... schizophrenic ... When I was little I got shut in a washing machine. This bloke put me in a washing machine when I was little ...

Other young people in solitary confinement have been described as 'mad' because they 'kicked and screamed' when placed in the holding cells. Given the acute range of potential social, medical, and psychological problems facing young people in detention centres, the use of isolation cells can be highly damaging.

A related issue is the problem of disturbances or riots. Riots have been a feature of the operation of juvenile institutions since the first reformatories were established in the nineteenth century, and they have occurred in both male and female sections of detention centres. We should acknowledge the point of desperation that is reached when prisoners (young or old) decide to rebel in a situation where they are largely without power. Riots are first and foremost rebellions against conditions of incarceration. They usually occur under regimes that manifest petty authoritarianism combined with a lack of programs. Certainly, young people interviewed after one New South Wales disturbance identified boredom, strictness, and poor staff attitudes as central (Youth Justice Coalition 1990:325). Similarly, a major disturbance in Queensland was, according to an official inquiry, partly associated with the failure to provide for the wellbeing and development of the inmates, and with poor staff–inmate relations, including verbal and physical abuse (Ryan & Smith 1994). Problems with staffing, management practices, and lack of adequate programs and services appear to be integral reasons for the riots that have occurred at various times at Kariong Juvenile Justice Centre (NSW Legislative Council 2005).

The range of issues that arises from the administration and regulation of detention centres covers costs, staffing, location, and treatment of young people, as well as the specific services and programs on offer. The costs of incarcerating young people far exceed the costs of the adult system (Youth Justice Coalition 1990), although there is considerable variation within the juvenile justice systems. For instance, smaller detention centres with better staff–inmate ratios are more expensive to run than the average juvenile detention centre, while old-style reformatories with large dormitories, large numbers of young people, few programs, and fewer staff are obviously cheaper to operate. The issue of costs is not insignificant at the beginning of the twenty-first century. Concern about the human rights of incarcerated young people implies greater pressure to find more adequate spaces for them, to build new or redesign existing facilities, to supply adequate numbers of trained professional staff, and to fund services and programs suitable for this population (see ALRC & HREOC 1997).

To take one example of cost pressures, we might consider the matter of food services. Youth detention centres are often notorious for the poor quality of the food provided. The New South Wales Ombudsman inquiry found, for example, that 'There are no regular inspections of kitchens, food storage and preparation. Little effort has been made to ensure the nutritional needs of detainees being met, even though it is recognised that many detainees admitted to detention have a history of poor nutrition and diet' (NSW Office of the Ombudsman 1996:viii). Anecdotal evidence from detention staff, let alone the detainees, often reveals repugnance for the 'mystery meals' served up in their place of work. While the quality of the food will vary from institution to institution, there is no doubt that it will have a major bearing on inmate (and staff) satisfaction and health, as will the variety of food offered within an institution. Increasing attention is being given to the different cultural and ethnic backgrounds of detainees. In New South Wales, for example, 32 per cent of all detainees come from other than Anglo-Australian or Aboriginal cultural backgrounds (NSW Office of the Ombudsman 1996:vi). It is also important to acknowledge that young people may be restricted in what they may eat due to particular religious prescriptions and proscriptions (for example Muslim, Jewish, and Hindu conventions surrounding food preparation and selection). Provision of good, wholesome, and varied food requires money and skill. It is an essential cost of incarcerating young people.

The provision of education, training, and recreational programs is an important part of the rehabilitative project of juvenile detention centres. Yet such programs vary greatly across Australia in terms of quality, design, external community and internal staff involvement, facilities available, and human resources. To some extent, the problems of service provision mirror the difficulties of youth detention centres generally, as demonstrated by the example of the problem of finding appropriate service providers in locations distant from major urban centres. Most jurisdictions have some kind of arrangement in place that allows for Education Department involvement in providing structured educational programs. These are important, especially given that most inmates have had sporadic, limited, and often unhappy experiences with schooling in the first place (Senate Employment, Education and Training References Committee (SEETRC) 1996). There are certainly a number of challenges for educators in a detention complex, relating to the composition of the inmate population, the cultural diversity of detainees, fragmented educational histories, and—last but not least—the fact that the majority of inmates serve sentences of only a few months. The catchcry here is flexibility, for to be successful, educational programs must cater to the special needs of young offenders while simultaneously taking into account the dynamics of forced institutionalisation and institutional life.

The provision of medical services, mental health services, drug and alcohol services, sex offender programs, and so on raises a number of issues pertaining to supervision, care, and specialist intervention. Again, adequate provision costs money. Concerns have also been raised regarding evaluation of the accessibility, appropriateness, and quality of existing programs and supports, and in the implementation and monitoring of Quality of Care Standards nationally (Keys Young Pty Ltd 1997). More generally, the engagement of professionals with a broadly developmental, welfare, and treatment orientation can create internal problems within an institution. As pointed out by the New South Wales Ombudsman inquiry, there is a 'serious division between specialist staff and operational staff in all centres' (1996:xii). The division essentially reflects the difference between 'custodial' and 'welfare' priorities: that is, the relative emphasis each group places on security versus services. Consider, for example, the prescriptions offered by a youth worker who periodically participates in detention programs in New South Wales:

> If a programme seeks to encourage people to respect others, then the programme must respect the participants. If it seeks to encourage self control

then there must be opportunities for this to occur within the programme. If ... choice and decision-making are being developed, then there must be opportunities for these processes within a group. These must be genuinely present and not just expressed verbally (Slattery 2000/2001:57).

These sentiments are expressed in similar programs in other states, such as in the 'Somebody's Daughter' program in Victoria (Coulter 2001). However, these types of intervention may be difficult to implement successfully if adequate protocols are not put in place beforehand. Custodial staff (who are 'permanent' workers with youth detainees) and professional staff (including occasional 'guest' workers) need to be clear about their roles and duties in given situations. Also, the philosophical basis of these kinds of approaches, which emphasise choice, opportunity, and participation, may appear to run counter to a custodial emphasis on security, restriction, and discipline.

The type and style of detention centre interventions pose a number of questions for specialist and operational (that is, custodial) staff alike. For those staff associated with the 'helping professions'—such as social workers, psychologists, and psychiatrists—there are always going to be difficulties and dilemmas in working with 'involuntary clients' who are legally mandated to receive assistance. In addition to working towards the mandated goal of preventing further offending in the future, service providers are influenced by factors such as available resources, the restrictiveness of the young offender's setting, the worker's proficiency in engaging the young offender, and the young offender's willingness and ability to 'become a client in the complete sense of the term and to utilise the services of the correctional worker to address problems and concerns beyond those specified by the mandate' (Borowski 1997:359). Institutional resources, general staff relationships, and professional training specific to the demands and context of juvenile detention centres are all important factors in the nature and quality of the services meant to assist young detainees.

For other staff, the issues are likewise complicated by the multiple demands on the juvenile justice system as a whole. New methods of working with young people—such as 'case management' models that place the focus on the individual detainee to ascertain factors that contribute to their offending behaviour, and that are designed to address their specific needs through development of a defined case plan—have ramifications for the overall management of detention centres, and for the relationship between specialist and operational staff. Importantly, innovative ways of working with young offenders require major shifts in the traditional culture of detention centres (which includes management styles, as well as worker attitudes and practices). This is a significant challenge. But the stakes are high: 'While poorly skilled staff may be able to lock and unlock gates, it takes talented and skilled individuals to be able to interact positively with young offenders, care for their welfare and rights, and also maintain appropriate security and safety for themselves and others' (NSW Office of the Ombudsman 1996:xvii).

The professionalisation of detention management and staff is a vital part of broader institutional reform.

The introduction of new methods of working with young detainees is invariably accompanied by uncertainty, stress, and conflict as old ideas and practices are challenged. An evaluation of a new behaviour-management program in Victoria showed that there were major splits among centre staff regarding the new program (Semmens, Cook & Grimwade 1999). Some believed in security methods that involved being 'hard' on clients, and the active use of isolation. Other staff were open to trying a different approach, such as that involving group work and intensive discussions with the young people, which would diminish the need for harsh punishments. The evaluation research demonstrated that change is possible within detention centres. But such change needs to be managed carefully and to be continuously assessed. Positive change requires different ways of acting and thinking on the part of both staff and detainees. As such, it must be supported institutionally by system managers. To some extent, the impact of the introduction of new methods and philosophies on juvenile corrections can also be quantified (for example, through analysis of incident reports and staff absences, and through staff and/or client surveys that provide indications of the general institutional climate). Evaluation research is essential to ongoing and future program development, especially if staff are to gain the confidence, skills, and commitment necessary to the job.

However, the conditions under which juvenile detention staff work also have a major bearing on potential program development and the realisation of system goals, as articulated in the language of 'case management' and 'rehabilitation'. Staff recruitment has long been a major problem in detention centres, partly because of low pay, poor working conditions, and lack of career structure. In New South Wales, it has been observed that 'in some centres more than 90% of staff are either casual employees or hold temporary appointments' (NSW Office of the Ombudsman 1996:xvi; see also NSW Legislative Council 2005). Poor staff morale, high stress levels, low job satisfaction, and poor communication between different components of the juvenile justice system all contribute to problems within detention centres. With respect to this, improved staff selection, training, and support are necessary, as is the development of better communication channels and training, and education for middle and senior managers within juvenile justice systems (see NSW Office of the Ombudsman 1996). It is also useful to not only develop (and actively monitor) national standards of care and service provision, but, as well, to undertake comparative research across jurisdictions (ALRC & HREOC 1997). Such research can be valuable in highlighting the strengths and weaknesses of existing legislative and policy frameworks guiding detention centre practices (see, for example, Hayter 1994).

What happens within detention centres has a huge impact on the young people sentenced to incarceration. So, too, does what happens to young people once they have been released from the detention centre. We need to consider therefore what is offered to the young person on release. Consider the following points:

- young people in detention centres are likely to have a poor level of education that may not have significantly improved during their time in the detention centre
- young people on release from detention are likely to face employment difficulties even though they want to work
- inadequate income support can be another major problem facing young people when they leave detention, especially if they are under 16 years of age and have to rely on government benefits
- if young people were living marginalised and possibly self-destructive lives prior to detention, there is the issue of how the detention centre experience has affected their self-esteem and social skills
- most young people who have been institutionalised have had problems with substance abuse prior to detention
- young people need accommodation and broad-based personal support services upon their release from detention.

What makes the overall incarceration process even more difficult for the young person is the general lack of resources and strategies in place to ease young people back into mainstream society once their sentence has been served. Here, there are three major issues that warrant much greater attention from juvenile justice systems and administrators, these being the general approach to the pre-release phase of the young person's time in detention, the availability of temporary or staged release, whereby a young offender is gradually integrated back into the community, and the level and type of post-release support that is available to young people once they are released from detention. In a major national review of transitional arrangements and policies for the release of young people from custody to the community, it was observed that there are often problems related to:

- a lack of suitable accommodation for young offenders, particularly for young people who are or have been state wards
- a lack of appropriate community-based mental health services for young people, in particular for those who have an alcohol or other drug problem or a dual diagnosis
- a lack of services for young offenders with an intellectual disability
- difficulties in placing young offenders into the school system
- a lack of appropriate alcohol or other drug services available to young people in the community (Keys Young Pty Ltd 1997).

In addition to active consultation with the young person about their specific needs and wishes, there is a clear need for post-release and transitional arrangements to be well coordinated and to involve a wide range of community, government, and juvenile justice agencies. A collaborative approach to service provision is necessary to meet the multiple needs of young offenders. This pertains to both in-custody service provision, and to post-release service provision.

COMMUNITY CORRECTIONS

Not all serious or repeat offenders are sent to detention centres, or if they are they may not be held for a long period of time. Instead, more and more attention is being given to ways in which to restrict the liberty of young offenders, but within a community rather than an institutional context. The main impetus for the adoption of community corrections as a method of dealing with young people is, at a theoretical level, to prevent stigmatisation as far as possible; and, at a practical level, to manage the overall costs of juvenile punishment by allowing for options that are cheaper than incarceration. Another rationale for keeping young people out of prison is that detention centres are known to function as 'universities of crime', where offenders trade knowledge about criminal techniques and activities, and are socialised into a criminal culture.

The development of community-based corrections has to be seen in the context of wider developments in the field of criminal justice. For example, it is important to acknowledge the proliferation of community-based programs and interventions across areas such as crime prevention, diversion from courts, corrections, and post-release programs (see also chapters 12 and 13). Throughout the history of punishment, there has been a consistent drive to develop modes of punishment that give 'more for less'. In terms of effectiveness and cost–benefit, therefore, if sentences undertaken in the community were seen as effective as those served in prison, then they would be seen as a desirable option. In addition, there has been pressure on modern governments from criminologists and others to take punishment back to the 'community'. The ideas here include a return to other forms of dealing with conflict and punishment (rather than the use of 'total institutions'), and exploring methods of penality that involve members of the community more directly than do present methods.

The combination of these influences serves to provide impetus for the development of *intermediate sanctions*. These kinds of sanctions are seen as a way of achieving multiple objectives, such as:

- reducing the demand for detention centre beds and the costs associated with building, staffing, and maintaining detention centres
- reducing recidivism and providing safety for the public
- providing credible and proportionately scaled punishments that reflect both the nature of the crime and society's denunciation of it.

An underlying principle of 'community' corrections is that a proportion of offenders are best managed in the community, rather than through spending a lot of time in detention centres. This implies that such centres may be inappropriate for certain classes of offender, that such centres may cause more harm than good to specific categories of offenders, and that certain categories of offenders do not pose a particularly bad threat to the security of other members of the community.

Intermediate penalties or sanctions are those that lie between prison and fines. The part of the system that deals with these offenders is known as community corrections, or community-based corrections. In recent years, this area has expanded considerably, both in terms of the number of offenders receiving sentences to be served in the community, and in regard to the number of sentencing options that have been made available to the courts for placing offenders in the community. The express purpose of community-based corrections is to provide control options that offer an alternative to detention centre use. The rationale is to divert offenders from expensive and overcrowded detention centres, while simultaneously protecting the public from further offending, and offering (to some extent) services that may reduce the likelihood of reoffending once the sentence has been completed.

Supervised or monitored orders

Probation is at the least intrusive end of intermediate sanctions. Probation involves supervision of the offender in the community through some kind of periodic reporting to a probation officer, and the development of some sort of relationship between the officer and the offender in which problems are talked over and factors affecting offending behaviour are discussed. An individual placed on probation is ordered by the court to be of good behaviour for the duration of the sentence. Further conditions—such as supervision and regular meetings with a probation officer—generally attach to the order. In practice, the actual levels of supervision and support vary, and are generally poor due to lack of suitable funding, inadequate training of staff, and failure by the court to identify the agency responsible for supervising the offender (ALRC & HREOC 1997). A similar type of scheme is the *recognisance or bond*, whereby the offender is likewise required to be of good behaviour for a specified time, and if they breach the order they may be fined or imprisoned. The court may impose conditions, such as paying compensation to the victim or attending a drug rehabilitation clinic.

A *good behaviour bond* is similar to these measures, but does not have the consequence of imprisonment on breach, or the requirement that the bond be supervised. The conditions of the bond are generally that the offender keep the peace, and be of good behaviour.

Closely related to probationary sentencing options is the *suspended* or *deferred sentence*. The court defers passing a sentence (which might include imprisonment) for a designated period, during which certain conditions may be stipulated. At the end of that period, and with the satisfactory completion of the conditions, the sentence lapses. In New South Wales, deferred sentences are sometimes referred to as 'Griffith Bonds' or 'Griffith Remands,' where the magistrate requests that an offender undertake specified activities during an adjournment of court proceedings, prior to a sentence being imposed. The activities do not constitute part of the formal sentence, but may reduce the sentence that is eventually imposed. Similar procedures have recently been put into place with respect to the operation of youth drug courts.

Another type of diversionary program designed to channel young offenders away from offending behaviour is the *day-in-prison* scheme. Based upon the US 'scared straight' model, this program has been used for young repeat offenders who are assessed as likely to receive a custodial sentence. Operating in several states from time to time over the last decade, the program is aimed at discouraging juveniles from future offending by obliging them to spend a day in prison, during which they are subject to a body search by prison officers, spend time alone in a cell, and attend an encounter session with a panel of prisoners (see Hil & Moyle 1992). Evaluation of such programs in Australia and the USA, however, suggests that they do not affect the rate of recidivism among participants, and moreover traumatise some of the young people involved (Hil & Moyle 1992; O'Malley, Coventry & Walters 1993; Lundman 1994).

Attendance orders, community service orders, and home detention

Community-based programs that stand midway between probation and prison provide more extensive intervention while still keeping juveniles out of detention. A *youth attendance order* (YAO) or *community attendance order* requires the young offender to attend an activity centre with specialist programs as an alternative to detention. Such programs include individual counselling, group work, employment skills, life skills, and specialist drug and alcohol counselling. Offenders can also be placed at an attendance centre in order to undertake a specified amount of unpaid community work. The sanction is punitive in that it deprives the young person of spare time, but it is also meant to provide positive alternatives that may help to rehabilitate the young person.

The biggest questions regarding youth attendance orders, in their various forms and legal frameworks, relate to the issues of eligibility, specific goals, and reduction of the use of custody (Muncie & Coventry 1989). Concern has been expressed over the specific offences and offender groups ('less difficult' rather than persistent and serious offenders; young men rather than young women) that are subject to attendance-centre orders. The quality of the tasks and programs to which a young person may be assigned also needs continual evaluation. Finally, it has been suggested that such orders may actually funnel young offenders towards custody rather than out of it, because the breach of such an order could lead to imprisonment, even though the original offence did not warrant such a response (see Muncie & Coventry 1989). Walters (1996) has argued that the use of such orders in Victoria has had a net-widening effect, and that there are problems in consistency with the administration of community work and breach proceedings.

Closely linked to the attendance-centre order is the more broadly conceived *community service order*. This is a sentencing option that requires young offenders to perform a certain number of hours community work in a designated form and for a designated community organisation (or, in some situations, for the victim). Tasks assigned may include, for example, working in aged people's homes, hospitals, or rehabilitation centres, and, as part of the requirement, the young offender may also have to go to an attendance centre for a specified number of hours each week. Generally, the use of such orders is premised upon work being available in the offender's area, and limits are set on the total number of hours that the young offender is required to put into their community-based work. Not enough work for young offenders and insufficient supervision to ensure compliance have been identified as problems besetting the implementation of such orders (ALRC & HREOC 1997).

As with attendance-centre orders, concern has been raised regarding the purposes and consequences of community service orders. Furthermore, a 1995 study carried out in Victoria on the extent to which community-based correctional programs can successfully reduce repeat offending also considered how program design affected outcomes. In particular, Trotter (1995) found that, as with prisons, community corrections may have a 'contaminating effect' if offenders are put on placement together. In other words, 'offenders who were placed on community worksites with other offenders were more likely to re-offend than offenders who were placed on worksites on their own or with other members of the community' (Trotter 1995:103). The specific features of community corrections therefore require close scrutiny and evaluation if their positive benefits are to be maximised.

The *electronic monitoring* of young offenders and/or *home detention* have been used in a number of jurisdictions. These methods involve the offender wearing an arm or ankle band that is monitored electronically (that is, when they leave the house or certain vicinity the band sets off an alarm at the monitoring station). Young offenders reside at home, and are provided with encouragement to engage in schooling, employment, and rehabilitation activities, while being generally restricted in their movements in the local neighbourhood. An important part of the South Australian project, at least initially, was the allocation of intensive resources and staff into supporting young offenders in the home-detention program. The adoption of a case-management approach, involving a systematic assessment of the needs and problems of each young offender, is now starting to feature more prominently across the community corrections spectrum as well as in some home-detention programs.

Case plans are drawn up with the participation of caseworkers, the young person and their family or significant others, relevant community groups, and government departments. These plans outline both short- and long-term goals, and are intended to provide the young offender with a range of options for employment, skills acquirement, education, and personal development. Importantly, case management is intended to make the caseworker a central player in the rehabilitation process, and also to make caseworkers more accountable for carrying out the specific program order. This has a number of implications for finances, staffing, and resources. It also raises questions regarding how the broad 'control' function of such personnel is to be merged in practice with a more finely mapped 'developmental' role. Again, the actual nature and extent of resources available at a local level determines the amount of assistance and service that can be provided. An evaluation of the use of the 'client service plan' in relation to youth attendance orders in Victoria (Jeffrey 1999) found that the YAO was erratically administered. For example, workers varied greatly in their relationship with young offenders, depending upon subjective factors (that is, some tried to be a 'friend' to the young person, while others adopted a more 'professional' approach) and on how each worker interpreted their role. The study concluded that, while in theory the YAO affords the offender an opportunity to forge links with the community, an integrated, cross-institutional, and holistic approach to addressing multiple-offender needs had yet to be developed (Jeffrey 1999).

Conditional release orders and camps

In addition to measures that put young offenders into community-based institutions as part of a sentence, and that are perceived to be part of a deinstitutionalisation movement away from secure custody, there are programs designed to 'decarcerate' young offenders who have spent some time in detention. These come in various forms, and are subject to varying conditions. *Parole* is where an offender ordered into detention can serve part of the sentence in the community under the supervision of parole officers and under certain restrictive behaviour conditions. Similarly, *day leave* and *special leave* allow individuals to take advantage of educational or work-related activities while still serving a sentence in some type of secure custody. There are also other means to foster young offenders' contact with the outside world.

In some jurisdictions, a *conditional release order* is available for those offenders already in detention who are deemed to be amenable to, and who would benefit from, a community-based program. Essentially, the conditional release order is seen as a transitional phase, wherein the young offender is granted leave from the detention centre in order to begin the process of reintegrating into the community. Offenders are assessed regarding potential danger to the community, or themselves, and then, 'Under close supervision and intensive counselling, conditional release permits the juvenile to live in the general community and participate in community-based educational and vocational programs' (Cain 1994b:31). The intention of such orders is to provide young people with the opportunity to acquire skills and to participate fully in their community.

There are various *camps*, *outdoor*, and *wilderness* programs for young offenders already in detention, and for those deemed to be at risk of detention (see Reddrop 1997). These vary greatly in terms of primary focus, target group, and intended outcomes. Some wilderness programs are intended as early intervention to forestall potential future offending behaviour in certain identified populations of young people, while others are designed to cater specifically for young offenders. In general, evaluation has shown that non-voluntary intensive programs for offenders tend to fail both in prevention and in rehabilitation (Collis & Griffin 1993; Sveen 1993). The camps are oriented towards building self-esteem, cooperative attitudes, and positive problem-solving skills. That is, they are intended to be rehabilitative in nature. After assessing the reasons for the failure of some programs, and analysing the elements of successful wilderness programs, Sveen (1993:19) commented that 'It has been posited that a socially-based community response, a voluntary code of practise, a focus on maturation levels, and a recognition of experiential learning; rather than a segregated, legally-imposed and coerced homogeneity, will achieve positive behavioural changes with our youth.' In a review of literature and case studies of outdoor programs for young offenders in Australia, Reddrop (1997) concluded that the majority of such programs had not been evaluated in a formal manner, although anecdotal evidence suggested either positive results or little or no change among participants. The specific features and dynamics of different kinds of camps are considered essential to evaluate in determining whether they reduce recidivism rates for young offenders or contribute to positive youth development in other ways.

A possible exception to these general findings regards programs designed specifically for young Aboriginal offenders. For example, the Lake Jasper Project in Western Australia was designed for young Aboriginal offenders as an alternative to custody, and incorporated principles of the Royal Commission into Aboriginal Deaths in Custody regarding the use of extended family members to act as mentors and to teach young people about their heritage and culture. Such camps are culturally specific and community sensitive. Another example of this approach is the scheme run by the Tasmanian Aboriginal Centre on Lungtalananna (Clarke Island). The experience is designed to encourage young Indigenous offenders to 'fend for themselves' by contributing to all of the things on the island that are necessary for everybody to survive. A crucial aspect of the project is to connect the young people with their family and history, and their culture and traditions. In this way, the young people involved come to see themselves differently by gaining a better understanding of their unique history, and the experience is meant to provide them with a different basis for operating in the general community when they go back into it (Mansell 2000). For further discussion of Indigenous-operated community-based programs, see Urbis Keys Young (2001).

Another type of camp—which was promoted in Western Australia in the early 1990s as an alternative to conventional detention—is the *boot camp*. This kind of camp is clearly punitive in orientation, and costs as much as or more than programs such as the Lake Jasper Project. Boot camps have operated in the USA for a number of years, and research evidence indicates that they do not significantly affect post-release criminality. Boot camps are actually more likely to increase rather than decrease prison populations and total correctional costs, and such camps neither reduce repeat offending nor reduce the number of young people in detention (Parent 1994). The Western Australian boot camp was intended to provide young offenders with a 'short, sharp shock', and to instil self-discipline and control (see Indermaur & White 1994). It was to involve a rigorous program of early-morning rising and hard physical labour. Four months attendance at a boot camp was meant to reduce an offender's overall time in detention, and to be followed by an intensive supervision program in the community. The boot camp idea failed in the Western Australian context due to a number of factors, such as remoteness of the site, costs, and concerns over appropriateness depending upon the background of the offender. The idea was also in direct contradiction to the established evidence that close family and community contact are integral to any kind of rehabilitation.

Another kind of outback or wilderness camp is that intended for offenders *after release*, and which aims to develop the offender's skills, knowledge, and confidence. Such camps are few and far between, and are generally run by non-government agencies such as the Brosnan Centre in Victoria. The idea behind such programs is to provide young offenders with an opportunity to develop their personal and practical skills in order to improve their employment prospects. Such programs tend to be located in rural or outback areas, detaching the young person for a week or two from the social and economic context within which the offending behaviour occurred. The emphasis is on personal development, improved health, physical and emotional wellbeing, and learning important social and vocational skills. The key problem with such programs—in addition to the perennial issues of resources, funding, and staffing—is that when a young person returns to their previous environment, and even though they might have changed and developed in some personal way, the general social conditions within which they operate remain the same.

Generally speaking, the use of probation, community service orders, conditional release, and various types of wilderness programs or camps has tended to focus on the twin issues of controlling offenders and treating individuals. In some cases, the emphasis is simply on how best to punish the young offender at the community level (broadly defined to include boot camps); in others, the emphasis is on rehabilitation strategies. The key questions regarding each of the available alternatives are:

- to what extent do they prevent recidivism or repeat offending?
- how successful are they in reintegrating the young person into the community, and—given the community the young person might come from—is this always desirable?
- do programs centring on individual attributes and based on case management principles address the structural causes of the offending behaviour?
- do the competing aims of punishment—including, for example, treatment, retribution, community protection, and deterrence—actually preclude the possibility of a coherent and positive response on the part of the state and community to the young offender?

In other words, we still need to know whether the shift towards community-based strategies and programs really makes a difference in terms of dealing adequately with youth crime and with young people who offend. Further to this, we can ask whether 'alternatives' to imprisonment (such as fines, probation, and parole orders, community service orders, home detention, and suspended sentences) are merely being used as alternatives to one another rather than as measures that genuinely reduce the flow of offenders into prisons or reduce the amount of time offenders spend inside. If community-based sanctions are really alternatives to the use of imprisonment, then we would need to compare, over time, the proportion of sentenced offenders sent to prison relative to those on intermediate sanctions. One way in which to do this would be to consider the percentage of sentences imposed across the different types of dispositions available to the courts. The key questions here concern which sanctions are being used by the courts, and how and if the patterns of specific use are changing over time. However, even though incarceration may not be used to the same degree as a court disposition relative to other sanctions, nevertheless the overall imprisonment rate could still continue to grow. If so, this might be due to increased numbers of people going through the sanctions process as a whole (number of offenders sentenced), or to the fact that only the most serious offenders are being imprisoned, but for longer periods of time (leading to an overall increase in the number of people in detention).

Another issue to consider is the patterns of use of community-based sanctions over time, and how these may in effect be increasing the total number of people under some kind of system control. Any growth in the use of community-based sanctions generally (including juvenile conferencing) raises major questions about the quality and quantity of programs, and the training and coordination of staff to administer them. In looking at the relationship between custodial and community-based sanctions, it is also important to consider the potential impact of the latter on the former. In other words, there is a danger that with some of the non-custodial measures towards the upper end of the hierarchy of penalties, the inevitable proportion of failures will actually boost detention numbers. To put it differently, a breach of conditions of a very strict order will almost certainly result in a period of imprisonment. A breach of a less strict order, however, may well result in the offender being given a second or even third chance in the community. There are two issues in particular that need to be addressed regarding the effectiveness of intermediate sanctions. First, such sanctions are effective if they are used in the way for which they are designed: that is, if they are used only for offenders who would otherwise receive only short sentences of imprisonment. Second, they are not effective if they are used for everyone but the original target group, that is, they tend to draw offenders 'up' from less intrusive sanctions lower down in the hierarchy.

CONCLUSION

The use of detention is meant to be a 'last resort' measure, to be applied to only the most serious and persistent of young offenders. The profile of the juveniles who end up in detention indicates that they are among the most vulnerable, socially disadvantaged people in Australian society. How best to deal with these young offenders is thus ultimately a matter of how best to deal with social disadvantage generally and at the level of specific individuals.

The detention of young offenders is driven by several competing rationales, including deterrence, retribution, community safety, and rehabilitation. The relative emphasis placed upon these will shape the overall direction of detention centre policy (and sentencing legislation), and have a major impact on the nature of the incarceration experience. Similarly, the political context within which juvenile detention is discussed and debated has significant implications for the allocation of resources to, and within, the correctional system. Media stories about detention escapes, for example, tend to reinforce the public focus on 'security' issues, often at the expense of 'service' issues. Political and media attention that emphasises the incapacitation of young offenders under the rubric of 'community protection' provides encouragement for institutional approaches geared towards control and containment, and punishment and inmate management. This can place professionals within the juvenile justice system in an invidious position, especially if rehabilitation and restorative justice ideals are subordinated to custodial imperatives rather than being seen as intertwined with them.

Alternatively, and as indicated in this chapter, the actual experiences of detainees prior to and during detention suggests that the needs and rights of young people ought to be of foremost concern in developing strategies to deal with young offenders. State intervention in the lives of young people is increasingly being evaluated by all levels of government in terms of human rights instruments such as the United Nations Convention on the Rights of the Child. Accordingly, it is essential to construct policy and legislation in the area of detention from a starting point that respects, maintains, and promotes the dignity and wellbeing of each young person. One implication of this is that enhanced service provision, increased multi-agency collaboration, and the professionalisation of detention centre staff be seen as core rather than peripheral concerns in the development of juvenile justice policy.

The value of juvenile detention centres, in both fiscal and human terms, is highly questionable. If they are to remain as a 'necessary evil', then it is vital that such institutions be operated in ways that enhance the life prospects of the young people inside them. This is a difficult, complicated, and costly exercise. But if we are to prevent recidivism on the one hand, and to positively shape the young person's opportunities on the other, then the price must be paid. To do otherwise is to abrogate the social responsibilities that go hand in hand with the use of coercive state power.

One of the justifications of punishment is that it will deter the individual offender from committing offences in the future. Another aspect of punishment, however, is that the system, by its very functioning, ought not to increase the chances of future offending. If we are to evaluate the changing face of corrections, we have to appreciate that part of the impetus for change stems from concerns about dealing with recidivism. In particular, questions can be asked regarding where the key causal factors lie when it comes to explaining reoffending behaviour. If the system itself is implicated as a causal factor in why some offenders move into a criminal career, then this has obvious consequences for how the system should be organised or modified; hence, increasing concern with the use of intermediate sanctions as an alternative to detention. But, even here, it is important to be aware of how program design, implementation strategy, and available resources are central to the success or otherwise of a particular sanction.

The post-release transition (whether from detention or from a community-based program) is vitally important in shaping the immediate and longer-term prospects of young offenders, especially those who have had extensive contact with the juvenile justice system for a reasonably long period of time.

If 'corrections' as such generally do not appear to be preventing crime, including individual reoffending, then there will be pressure to change aspects of existing practice. To some extent, this failure of corrections is reflected in other types of community-based programs that attempt to prevent crime before it occurs, or to deal with offenders in ways that focus on repairing social harm rather than punishment *per se*. These approaches are the concern of the next two chapters.

12 | Youth crime prevention

CHAPTER HIGHLIGHTS

Introduction
Social institutions and young people
Models of youth crime prevention
Social crime prevention in Australia
Pathways to prevention
A crime prevention framework
Conclusion

INTRODUCTION

Crime prevention involves a wide range of models and techniques, variously aimed at reducing opportunities for crime, enhancing social opportunities for individuals and groups, and facilitating social empowerment and institutional change (see Iadicola 1986; White 1996e; O'Malley & Sutton 1997). Specific crime prevention measures might include, for example, attempts to modify the physical environment (such as improved street lighting), situational prevention dealing with specific problem areas or issues (such as the use of anti-theft tags in shops), increasing surveillance in particular locations (such as Neighbourhood Watch), and holding sporting or social events for local youth (such as Blue Light Discos). The specific approaches to crime prevention vary greatly, reflecting political differences in orientation (from conservative to radical) and differences in practical application (see, for example, Geason & Wilson 1989; Clarke 1992; Felson 1994; Semmens 1990; White & Perrone 2005; O'Malley & Sutton 1997). Our present concern is not to map out the crime prevention field as such, but to indicate the most prominent approaches specifically referred to in relation to young people and children.

In media terms, coercive methods based on law-and-order commonsense constitute the most prominent form of 'crime prevention'. However, as this chapter demonstrates, this kind of approach is not the only option available to policymakers and criminal justice officials. Indeed, there is considerable support among some political leaders, bureaucrats, criminologists, and community agencies for what can be described as 'social development' approaches to crime prevention. At the level of practice, it is not unusual to find elements of the law-and-order approach sitting beside a social development approach.

One aim of this chapter, therefore, is to map out three broad models of youth crime prevention. In particular, the concern is to highlight the nature of and differences between 'coercive', 'developmental', and 'accommodating' approaches to dealing with young people. In doing so, the chapter outlines the key concepts, main institutional players, primary methods and techniques, and substantive criticisms of these three perspectives, and provides examples from Australia and internationally of social developmental types of approaches to youth crime prevention.

Sutton (1994) points out that crime prevention is 'a diffuse set of theories and practices' that can refer to quite different types of intervention at different points in the web of the criminal justice system, and in some instances to initiatives not based in criminal justice. For present purposes, 'crime prevention' will be used to refer solely to those types of programs and interventions that attempt to stop offending behaviour before it begins. We do not use the term to refer to attempts to change behaviour after the fact (for example, individual deterrence through youth conferencing or other means), or to models of general deterrence associated with regimes of punishment (for example, specific sentencing options and laws) that are oriented to the convicted offender.

Before discussing the main features of the particular crime prevention typology presented further on, several other preliminary points need to be made. First, the three approaches (coercive, developmental, accommodating) have been constructed here as 'ideal types', in that each presents an exaggerated view of particular clusters of ideas and techniques. The actual practices of police, justice officials, and others involved in crime prevention are often more complicated than suggested by such models, and may involve a wide range and diverse combinations of techniques and ideas. Second, the three approaches are not necessarily mutually exclusive, in that they can and do to some degree coexist in any particular jurisdictional setting.

The weight given to any one model in practice, however, does have major social implications. That is, the *overall strategic orientation* of youth crime prevention has major ramifications for the position and experiences of young people in society. The philosophical basis of intervention and the particular mix of programs is crucial in whether or not a strategy will act so as to best protect the rights of children while simultaneously making a concrete and positive difference in addressing the causes of juvenile offending.

SOCIAL INSTITUTIONS AND YOUNG PEOPLE

There are large numbers of social institutions, community organisations, and community action groups involved in juvenile justice (see chapter 4). These range from state agencies such as the police, courts, and corrections, through to non-government bodies such as community legal centres, prisoners' rights groups, and victims' groups (White & Perrone 2005). Various agencies and institutions play a number of different roles in relation to criminal justice issues and practices, covering both broad welfare and educational concerns (such as schools, welfare agencies, and the like), and more directly regulatory and coercive concerns (such as private security guards and justice department officials).

If we are to assess adequately the nature of diverse youth crime prevention approaches, we need first to discuss the institutional setting for much of the activity related to crime prevention. A distinction can be drawn between *particular institutions* (which have specific structural imperatives to perform certain social roles), and *particular crime prevention approaches* (which are evident in each institutional sphere, regardless of the dominant functional imperative of the institution). As will be suggested below, the institutional rationale of any particular agency or organisation will have a major influence on the type of approach adopted in youth crime prevention. Acknowledging this is essential to any discussion of possible reform or program initiatives, and especially in regard to changes in institutional practices within the different social spheres.

Broadly stated, there are three main types of institutions that predominate in the lives of young people: coercive, developmental, and commercial (see box 12.1). These can initially be described in terms of core operational imperatives, that is, their guiding rationale.

Coercive institutions

Coercive institutions are those designed primarily to enforce rules, regulations, and laws of some kind. Ultimately, they operate on the basis of violence or the threat of violence, and their agents are generally seen as legitimate wielders of coercion in the enforcement of particular kinds of behaviour and codes of conduct. Such institutions include the police, private security guards, the courts, corrections, transit police, and welfare workers engaged in administering control and protection orders.

By their very nature, coercive institutions are involved in the negative labelling of young people (Polk 1997b). That is, the impact of these institutions on young people is by and large one that constructs an 'illegitimate identity' for those caught up in the net of social control (Polk & Kobrin 1973). Furthermore, much of the work of these institutions is meant to separate certain groups of young people from the rest of society by excluding them from particular physical sites or by containing them in secure facilities. The activities of coercive institutions are thus often premised upon ensuring a *disconnection* between some young people and other people and/or institutions, including their peers.

BOX 12.1 SOCIAL INSTITUTIONS AND YOUNG PEOPLE

COERCIVE INSTITUTIONS
- designed to enforce rules, regulations, and laws
- operate on a basis of coercion or violence
- include police, private security guards, courts, and corrections
- impart negative labels to young people
- disconnect and separate young people from the community
- deny usual freedoms.

DEVELOPMENTAL INSTITUTIONS
- designed to enhance development, opportunity, and potential
- operate on a basis of resources, skills, and knowledge
- include schools, family, work, recreation, and social work
- have power to confer positive and negative labels on young people
- sources of institutional connection and social inclusion
- flexible in meeting young people's needs.

COMMERCIAL INSTITUTIONS
- designed to make a profit
- operate on basis of buyer—seller commercial nexus
- include shopping centres and commercial leisure outlets
- have ability to confer positive and negative images of young people
- important places for social connection and social activity
- main focus is on customer needs, including those of young people.

The main purpose of coercive institutions is to meet broad system needs by symbolically and practically constructing boundaries between what is 'acceptable' behaviour and what is not, and between who is deemed to be 'conformist' and who is 'deviant'. The overall orientation is one that is 'society-centred' insofar as the stress is on rule maintenance and upholding conventional social interaction. The point of intervention is to curtail perceived deviant or criminal activity. This often involves the denial of usual freedoms or the detainment of young people against their will.

Developmental institutions

Developmental institutions are those designed first and foremost to assist young people on the basis of developmental potential, work opportunities, and social functioning. They operate to provide young people with resources, skills, and knowledge that they can use to more fully integrate into mainstream social life. Such institutions include the family, school, work, recreation- and leisure-based organisations, social workers, and youth and community workers.

Developmental institutions vary in practice, but one outstanding feature is that they have the power to confer positive as well as negative social labels (Polk 1997b). They thus embody both negative and positive social aspects (for example success at school versus alienation, family as safe haven versus place of child abuse, wages for work versus exploited labour). In a similar vein, while developmental institutions may involve some degree of compulsion (such as compulsory schooling), they nevertheless can be seen as operating mainly through 'consent' rather than 'coercion'. That is, contact with such institutions is generally seen as desirable and of benefit to the person who engages with them. It is assumed there will be social benefits and rewards for participants (for example, certificates, knowledge, wages).

Developmental institutions are often an important point and source of social connection for young people, both in terms of peer group relationships and with regard to active participation in other mainstream social institutions (in that there is an intersection of participation in the family, at school, and in work). To put it differently, positive participation in any one developmental institution usually implies that a young person is simultaneously nested in a web of supportive relationships involving more than one such institution.

The main purpose of developmental institutions is to meet system needs for well-socialised, work-ready, healthy young people. The services and benefits provided are 'youth-centred', as part of the process of working towards the achievement of wider social aims. This includes encouraging and developing acceptable behaviour among young people. One institutional feature of most developmental institutions today is a concern to be as flexible as possible in meeting young people's needs.

Commercial institutions

Commercial institutions are those that are designed first and foremost to make a profit. The overriding purpose of the commercial enterprise is to bring buyers and sellers together in the cash nexus. Commercial institutions operate so as to entice patrons and customers to buy certain goods and services. Such institutions include shopping centres, malls, specific retail outlets, fast-food shops, restaurants, video-game arcades, and commercial providers of sport and leisure activities.

As with developmental institutions, commercial institutions have the capacity to apply positive and negative social labels to young people. Through participation with such institutions, young people may develop particular forms of 'consumer-related identity'. Alternatively, as non-consumers they may be labelled 'troublemakers' or 'undesirables'. Given the physical location and the diverse congregations of people who engage with them, young people see commercial institutions as important places for social connection, employment opportunities and social activity.

The main purpose of such institutions is business. They are 'money-centred', and the reason for being of any such institution is to produce and sell enough goods and services to make a profit. The main focus of attention is on business—and customer—needs. Young people are variously perceived either as direct customers or as potential threats to the commercial trading process.

MODELS OF YOUTH CRIME PREVENTION

Each of the three types of social institutions described occupies an important place in young people's lives. For example, young people have extensive contact with the police, with teachers, and with shopkeepers. The relationships that young people have with the agents of these institutions are crucial to any discussion of youth crime prevention. Bearing in mind the main institutional imperatives across the three areas, we turn now to consider three approaches to crime prevention, each of which has implications for how the agents within the different social institutions might perform their tasks (see box 12.2). A major concern is discerning how different intervention strategies might be operationalised within the context of the diverse institutional settings.

Before discussing how different intervention strategies might be operationalised, it is important to comment briefly on the use of terminology in the broad area of youth crime prevention. It needs to be clarified that the substantive content and philosophical orientation of specific approaches vary considerably, even when similar labels are used to describe particular programs and interventions (see Tonry & Farrington 1995; O'Malley & Sutton 1997). For example, a 'developmental' approach may be designed to target specific individuals so that their presumed 'faults' or 'deficits' can be addressed (Tonry & Farrington 1995). Alternatively, what is meant by 'developmental' may refer to assisting whole communities to use their own resources to improve their social and economic conditions (Lincoln & Wilson 1994b). The precise meaning of the term is given by the specific nature of the program or intervention strategy in question.

In a similar vein, there has been some debate over whether 'crime prevention' is necessarily in conflict with the idea of 'social development' (see Hil 1996; Hill & Sutton 1996). For example, it has been noted that crime prevention, in some of its definitions, is mainly oriented towards rectifying the troublesome behaviour of young people, rather than fostering positive institutional change (Coventry, Muncie & Walters 1992). Insofar as crime prevention is conceived in this way, it can be seen to be tied to a controlling and behavioural-modification agenda.

BOX 12.2 MODELS OF YOUTH CRIME PREVENTION

COERCIVE APPROACHES
- emphasis is on crime control
- key concepts are deterrence, opportunity reduction, and exclusion of troublemakers
- main players are police, security guards, and transit police
- young people are seen as a problem or threat
- key methods are heavy street policing and youth curfews
- key problems are offence displacement, denial of youth rights, and stigmatisation of young people.

DEVELOPMENTAL APPROACHES
- emphasis is on dealing with social problems
- key concepts are youth participation, opportunity enhancement, and inclusion of all young people
- main players are schools, local councils, parents, and young people
- young people are seen as part of the community and as part of the solution
- key methods are developing positive options in school, work, and leisure
- key problems are lack of resources, multi-agency coordination, and getting youth to take action.

ACCOMMODATING APPROACHES
- emphasis is on dealing with immediate conflicts
- key concepts are negotiation, stakeholder interaction, and multi-agency cooperation
- main players are shopkeepers, local councils, police, and young people
- young people are seen as legitimate stakeholders and users of public space
- key methods are open lines of communication, use of youth advocates, and provision of youth services
- key problems are the issue of 'community' spaces and private interests, and the commercialisation of leisure.

However, crime prevention—as defined in a more holistic and broadly social-developmental sense—has also been used to challenge more traditional 'law-and-order' discourses that attempt to impose various forms of coercive social control on young people (see Sutton 1994, 2000). In this context, the principles of youth crime prevention are entirely consistent with progressive practices and interventions that are based on addressing structural issues of unemployment and inequality, and that recognise the importance of community consultation and youth participation. For present purposes, and as reflected below, social development and crime prevention are seen as compatible and interlinked concepts.

Coercive approaches to crime prevention

A broad survey of youth crime prevention strategies here and overseas indicates that in many places the favoured approach is to use coercion or the threat of unpleasant sanctions as the principal way to 'keep young people in line' (Loader 1996; Males 1996; Schissel 1997). The privileged position of *coercive* measures is reinforced by a combination of 'law-and-order' rhetoric and media hype, situational crime prevention strategies that are oriented first and foremost to crime control (rather than community building), and a casual dismissal of any notion that young people have the same basic civil and human rights as other members of the population (see White 1998a; Davis 1994; Jeffs & Smith 1996; United States National Crime Prevention Council 1996).

Given that the law-enforcement approach to crime prevention has been described in our chapter on police and young people (see chapter 9), it will not be discussed further (see also box 12.2). Suffice to say coercive measures have been shown to have only modest effects on crime reduction (Tonry & Farrington 1995), and in some cases they exacerbate or create social problems in their own right (due to the resistance of young people to such measures). Coercive approaches can be criticised on a number of grounds beyond those relating to crime prevention *per se* (White 1998a). For example, they use coercion as a means of first rather than last resort, which is contrary to major international human rights instruments (namely the United Nations Convention on the Rights of the Child). Such strategies involve the active stigmatisation and criminalisation of children and young people who may normally have had little to do with the formal justice system; and they can make worse police—youth relations due to youth perceptions of unfair treatment, excessive restrictions, and unnecessary intervention in their daily affairs. Broad and drastic 'street cleaning' measures can also displace youth crime—and congregations of young people—into other city areas.

Developmental approaches to crime prevention

Developmental approaches can be characterised as approaches directed at enhancing the opportunities of young people through encouraging their participation in activities that reflect youth interests and needs. The guiding idea is that young people be given some ownership of the solutions to youth problems, and that various people and agencies at a local level should work together to advocate for the wider involvement and participation of all young people, including the most marginalised (Polk 1997b). In this perspective, it is important to involve young people in any crime prevention strategy, and to see them as part of the community, not merely as threats to it.

The key organising concept of the developmental approach is that of dealing with social problems. Emphasis is placed on enhancing youth opportunities, diversion from potential criminal behaviour and bad peer influences, and reforming institutional processes that disadvantage and marginalise young people. The core idea behind such an approach is to provide space for young people to develop a greater sense of competence, usefulness, belongingness, and power or potency (Polk & Kobrin 1973). To assist the development of young people requires that analysis and strategic action be undertaken to improve the performance of social institutions in working with young people.

The primary institutions associated with this approach are public bodies such as schools, welfare and health authorities, and local councils. The main players are social workers, youth and community workers, teachers, parents, police youth liaison officers, and employers. Police and security guards generally play an auxiliary role, providing links and referrals to appropriate agencies as required.

The methods of developmental crime prevention revolve around *problem-solving*. This translates at an operational level into strategies designed to improve the access of young people to 'legitimate identities' in school, work, and politics; and to reduce their access to 'illegitimate identities' associated with the formal institutions of criminal justice, such as police arrest, court, and juvenile justice sanctions (Polk & Kobrin 1973). The developmental approach generally tries to involve a more holistic approach to youth needs and issues, and thus often incorporates multi-agency collaboration into its framework. This means that youth and community workers, local councils, the police, and other interested parties attempt to work in partnership to provide young people with positive options in relation to work, education, and leisure pursuits.

An emphasis is placed on encouraging positive and empowering peer relationships among young people, and in bringing young people directly into institutional decision-making processes. A central concern of this approach is to open up lines of communication between various parties, including young people themselves, and thereby to foster a sense of community and solidarity through honest and open dialogue across a range of social and legal issues.

One of the biggest problems with the adoption of these kinds of approaches is the lack of adequate community investment in developmental institutions generally (for example, the education sector, welfare services, and health and community services), which in turn makes interagency collaborative work difficult from a resources point of view. Government cutbacks in needed public services, changes to rules guiding service provision and benefit allocation for young people, and the dearth of concerted state action on issues such as unemployment, restrict the ability of people at the local level to 'solve' problems that have their source in wider political—economic transformations and national policy development. Specific institutions, such as the police, can likewise be evaluated from the perspective of internal allocation of resources (for example, education and training packages) and staffing (for example, the number and training of youth liaison personnel) in the area of police—youth relations.

Conceptually, there exist difficulties over how certain preferred methods are to be interpreted in practice (see Stokes & Tyler 1997). For example, multi-agency collaboration often begs the question of who is to coordinate the process, and which criteria are to be used for evaluating the purposes and performance indicators of such cooperation (Hughes 1996). The issue of accountability looms large here, particularly given the different institutional sectors that may be represented in any such collaborative effort. It is worth reiterating that the different institutional sectors in a collaborative relationship often have very different core imperatives. This can lead to significant differences in outlook and intervention preferences.

Problems may also arise from how the term 'developmental' is construed. Tonry and Farrington (1995), for example, distinguish between 'developmental prevention', 'community prevention', and 'situational prevention'. The first refers to interventions designed to prevent the development of criminal potential in individuals, the second to strategies designed to change the social conditions that influence offending in residential communities, and the third to measures designed to prevent the occurrence of crimes through opportunity reduction and increasing risks. In fact, there is considerable overlap between all three approaches. The best type of social-developmental crime prevention is one that incorporates all three in a coherent fashion.

However, if it is interpreted in narrow individualistic terms, the core problem of a developmental approach may simply mean attention to the presumed 'deficits' and 'at-risk' behaviours of selected young people. How the problem is conceptualised has major implications for the kind of intervention strategy adopted. Rather than focusing on the ways in which institutions marginalise young people (such as through an analysis of how schooling processes alienate some young people), or emphasising the existing strengths of young people (that is, through reinforcing their sense of power, competency, belonging, and usefulness), some psychological-based concepts of development concentrate on how to *change* the young person through therapy, remedial education, or treatment.

Other modes of intervention stress the importance of wider institutional change and better institutional provision for young people, as illustrated in discussions of 'prosocial' and 'antisocial' paths within different institutional spheres (see Catalano & Hawkins 1996). Instead of seeing a developmental project as something done to, or for, young people, this broadly developmental approach emphasises the role of young people as direct participants and decision-makers. It makes the link between individual circumstances and community social life, and suggests how to improve both.

Accommodating approaches to crime prevention

An *accommodating* approach is not concerned with coercion or developmental concerns *per se*. The accommodating approach arises out of conflicts experienced at a practical level in youth—adult interactions. In this sense, the accommodating perspective basically originated as a reaction to a social problem, rather than being institutionally tied to wider communal projects such as law enforcement or socialisation processes.

The key concept of the accommodating approach is that of *negotiation*. The approach is premised on the idea that there may be diverse and competing perspectives regarding how certain publicly accessible resources are or ought to be used. Recognition of the specific needs and desires of different parties is then linked to the importance of public participation in any decisions that affect the concerned parties. From a crime prevention perspective, the accommodating approach attempts to use participatory methods as a means to reduce youth crime, antisocial behaviour, and fear of crime in particular settings and locales.

The primary institutions involved in these kinds of approaches are shopping centre managers, developers, commercial sport-and-recreational outlets, retailers, and local councils. Business proprietors, youth and community workers, architects, social planners, and town planners are the central players, with police, welfare, and justice officials also having advisory and minor intervention roles (usually oriented towards supporting any rules of behaviour and diversionary procedures that may be negotiated among the parties).

The main method of the accommodating approach is that of direct interaction between interested parties. Young people are considered as legitimate 'stakeholders' who, ideally, should have a say in any consultative process. As with the developmental approach, much consideration is given to problem-solving and to multi-agency collaboration. Importantly, the approach is based on the idea that young people have legitimate concerns, particularly over how they are treated in public spaces such as shopping centres and the street, and that they should be involved in negotiating outcomes beneficial to all parties in some way. Rather than attempting to exclude young people—whether as users of certain public spaces, as active participants in community life, or as rights-holders—this approach is based on the notion of social inclusion. In some instances, the approach may also be linked directly to developmental strategies insofar as provision of youth services and youth-friendly spaces can be an outcome of the negotiation process.

There are a growing number of crime prevention initiatives relating to shopping centres that do not rely extensively or exclusively on coercive tactics (such as banning young people from the centre). Basically these interventions are premised on the adoption of youth-friendly approaches. These approaches generally include active dialogue between interested parties, including youth advocates and young people directly, support for youth services and youth workers, and the reliance upon low-key inclusive management procedures (see Crane & Marston 1999; Crane 2000; White, Kosky & Kosky 2001). For instance, in Bribane, the Myer Centre Youth Protocol was developed in 1998 as a means of dealing with any potential problems that might arise from young people's use of the Centre. The protocol was developed as a collaborative effort involving a local government authority, a major retail centre and the youth sector. Some of the principles underpinning the protocol include: transparency and accountability; health and safety; access and equity; involvement of young people; minimally intrusive security provision; customer service; and redress in the case of complaints (Crane & Marston, 1999). In New South Wales, a guide has been developed that provides a step-by-step outline how to devise an agreement (protocol) between key people involved in managing, maintaining security, accessing or using a shopping centre. The guide is intended to assist people at the local level to develop a protocol that best suits the specific needs of their particular community and particular shopping centre (NSW Shopping Centre Protocol Project 2005).

Accommodating approaches thus explicitly recognise the importance of involving the private commercial sector in non-coercive forms of youth crime prevention. They also take into account that much police—youth contact, and conflict, occurs in the precincts of shopping centres and malls, and that a large proportion of young offending involves shoplifting offences. Not surprisingly, such approaches therefore tend to be dominated by commercial imperatives. There are a number of questions that arise from the tension between a 'commercial' and a 'community' rationale for specific youth crime prevention schemes (see White, Murray & Robins 1996). For example, at a practical level, protocols need to be developed that spell out the lines of accountability and responsibility when youth-intervention projects are funded collaboratively by commercial enterprises, local governments, and the community sector.

In many cases, the accommodating approach takes place in the context of privately owned public space. Given this, it is important to explore the implications of the approach for the possible transformation of such space from use for relatively narrow commercial purposes to broader communal objectives and purposes. This raises issues of how best to extend public access, public control, and public ownership over community spaces, regardless of whether the current managers are state governments, local councils, or private companies. It also alerts us to the social implications of constructing crime prevention approaches that do not challenge the commercial imperatives and setting of many youth activities. For instance, the approach may simply reinforce the profit imperative of commercial enterprise by orienting youth activity towards what is offered on a commercial basis (for example, video games). Especially given the concerns of developmental approaches to widen the intellectual, physical, spiritual, political, and community horizons of young people, major questions can be asked regarding the social significance of consumer-oriented commercial settings in their lives.

SOCIAL CRIME PREVENTION IN AUSTRALIA

Crime prevention policies and programs along broadly social developmental lines have begun to feature prominently in Australia in recent years. For example, a proposal for a criminal justice strategy for Tasmania called 'Crime Prevention Through Community Enhancement' was prepared in June 1995. The key rationale behind the strategy is that an effective crime prevention strategy will:

- assist communities to fully understand the picture of crime in Australia today, through community safety surveys and information provision
- empower community-based and community-driven crime prevention and community safety solutions
- foster a comprehensive approach to short- and long-term crime prevention and community safety, by assisting with practical local projects to make communities safer, and by addressing the risk factors of crime.

From this perspective, it is essential that decision-making processes at the heart of the strategy be community-based (Tasmanian Inter-Departmental Committee on Public Safety and the Response to Crime 1995; see also Brown & Polk 1996). This implies that participation must be integral to the model, that progress will thereby be slow and inconsistent, and that the final result will differ from place to place, depending on local circumstances.

From the point of view of youth crime prevention as defined in this chapter (meaning that which is in place prior to any actual offending behaviour for which a young person might be apprehended), the Tasmanian proposal's discussion of 'community enhancement initiatives' is most relevant. The intention of this approach is to bring about community integration and enhancement by focusing prevention on widening the opportunities for a wide range of community residents to participate in mainstream activities. This could be achieved through a number of types of community bodies, such as:

- community consultation teams that are organised to bring youth and adult perspectives and skills together to provide advice on community problems
- community action planning teams, where young people and adults work together to develop action plans for solving visible community problems
- community action teams, where young people and adults come together, often over a short period of time, to take action to solve a particular community problem
- community service teams that are organised to provide some form of short- or long-range service within the community (for example, tutoring, performance arts)
- specific programs of youth and resident participation and involvement that are designed to increase access to, and involvement within, existing community and work organisations.

The model ultimately places responsibility for the basic work of crime prevention on community-based and community-driven initiatives. For the model to be implemented fully, it requires political and funding support at the state level, active collaboration between criminal justice agencies and local-level community bodies, and a commitment overall to a social-development model of crime prevention. The fate of the proposal in the Tasmanian context ultimately hinges upon these vital ingredients.

Another example of a social-development approach that incorporates some of the elements of the projects and policies considered so far is found in New South Wales. As part of the provisions of the *Children (Protection and Parental Responsibility) Act 1997* (NSW), there is reference to 'local crime prevention plans'. These plans are designed to encourage local councils to develop community-based measures to reduce crime. If a local crime prevention plan is approved, or is proposed to be submitted for approval, by the Attorney-General as a 'safer community compact', the Department can offer financial assistance to the council (Luker 1997).

A local crime prevention plan includes provisions relating to:

• Aboriginal community development
• NESB community development
• crime prevention
• drug and alcohol management
• open-space planning and management
• parental education and family-support programs
• youth-development strategies
• consultation
• arrangements for reporting and coordination
• other matters.

When making a decision to approve a local crime prevention plan as a safer community compact, the Attorney-General must consider:

• whether the plan was prepared in accordance with specific guidelines
• whether the plan is appropriate for the extent and nature of crime in the area
• the council has adequately consulted with the local community, including young people and the Aboriginal community
• the likely effect of the plan on crime and the local community, including young people and the Aboriginal community
• any other matter considered relevant.

More recently, in 2004 the New South Wales government introduced the Community Solutions and Crime Prevention Strategy, which focuses on the development of local crime prevention plans. Specific programs as part of the local strategy may receive funding assistance from the government. Many of these are aimed at young people, such as improving school attendance and

retention, and providing recreational facilities (see www.communitybuilders.
nsw.gov.au/solutions/overview.html).

PATHWAYS TO PREVENTION

Perhaps the most influential model of crime prevention in Australia in recent
years is that put forward by the Developmental Crime Prevention Consortium
(1999) in a report prepared for National Crime Prevention. Titled 'Pathways
to Prevention: Developmental and Early Intervention Approaches to Crime in
Australia', the report emphasises the complexity of the causes of offensive and
antisocial behaviour, and the complexity of the responses required to address
them. The consortium (see Developmental Crime Prevention Consortium
1999:100) emphasises the importance of 'the targeting of multiple risk and
protective factors at multiple levels (the individual, the family, the immediate
social group, and the larger community) and at multiple life phases and
transition points in an individual's development'. Schematically, this approach
can be summarised as in the following two sections.

Multiple factors at multiple levels

Risk factors include factors that increase the likelihood of an offence occurring
or being repeated. These factors might include such things as individual
characteristics (for example, a child's impulsivity), the family (for example, a
parent's harsh discipline or weak supervision), the social group (for example,
peers that encourage or tolerate the occurrence of crime), and the community
(for example, a community that is disorganised and that offers few alternatives
to crime as a source of money or activity).

Protective factors include factors that reduce the impact of an unavoidable
negative event, that help individuals avoid or resist temptations to break
the law, that reduce the chances of people starting on a path likely to lead
to breaches of the law, and that promote an alternative pathway. Again,
these factors might include such things as responding to the needs of the
individual (such as through active promotion of self-esteem), enhancing
family relationships (such as through advice and information), fostering
positive social group activity (for example, sport) and community building
(for example, facilities and social structures that support involvement and
attachment).

Multiple life phases and transition points

Pathways—Developmental perspectives view life as a progression through
various stages and transition points. These include, for example, the movement
of a child from the family as the prime setting for their activity, through early
education, primary school, high school and adolescence, and adult life.

Positive experiences in each setting and at each transition point will foster prosocial behaviour.

Vulnerabilities—At each life stage or transition point, there is the risk of possible negative experiences that may put individuals on an at-risk pathway. Such experiences might include, for example, the experience of school failure, alienation, becoming involved with an antisocial peer group, and unemployment. It is recognised in this perspective that while behaviour can be changed more easily in the young than in the old, later transition points are also sensitive times, and it is important to structure intervention to diminish the risk of movement into harmful paths at these times as well.

The crux of the developmental crime prevention approach described here is that crime is seen to be a consequence of cumulative risks and combinations of factors, and that these vary over the life course. To respond adequately to potential and actual offending behaviour, it is recommended that action be taken across a range of institutional and relationship domains, such as family, school, and community. As the Consortium members (Developmental Crime Prevention Consortium 1999:100) put it:

> This necessarily entails a whole of community intervention model that incorporates a range of programs and services, rather than an intervention built around a single program. It also entails a process of 'community building' that helps to create an inclusive, 'child friendly' or 'family supportive' environment that promotes the normal, prosocial development of children.

In designing youth crime prevention interventions, it is recommended that a wide range of community members, institutions, and services be involved. These include, among others, children and young people, parents and carers, other family members, neighbours and friends, schools, housing providers, leisure and recreation services, health services and general practitioners, drug and alcohol services, community services, non-government organisations, the police, employers, trade unions, the media, and so on.

One practical attempt to implement this kind of intervention model is the 'Communities That Care' prevention strategy, trialled in Victoria in 1999 (Toumbourou 1999). First developed in the USA, the intention of this program is to coordinate local community efforts from the point of view of a risk-focused approach to prevention. This has involved the development and administration of a youth survey to measure risk and protective factors among young people across the areas of community, school, family, and peer-individual. The idea is that data generated from such surveys will provide baseline information that will inform specific service interventions and community mobilisations.

Recent developments in Australia parallel work that has been done on youth crime prevention overseas in places such as Canada (National Crime Prevention Council 1996), the United Kingdom (Utting 1996; Crawford 1998) and the USA (United States Coordinating Council on Juvenile Justice and Delinquency Prevention 1996; Krisberg 2005). In particular, the emphasis on assessment of the broad range of risk and protective factors present in local environments, and the adoption of positive whole-of-community approaches, are central

The barriers to such an approach are familiar across jurisdictions as well. As identified by the National Crime Prevention Council of Canada, some of these include not enough early intervention, the inappropriate use of the justice system to deal with health and social problems, too little follow-up and follow-through in programming, the fragmented and territorial nature of programs, the racist and classist nature of the youth justice system, too little evaluation of existing programs, the impact of cuts to social and health programs on crime causation, the problem of short-term funding and lack of continuity in service provision, and misinformation about young people and youth crime—all of which reduce the effectiveness of policies and programs (National Crime Prevention Council 1996).

Social development crime prevention may have support politically in some communities and in specific jurisdictions. However, the place of and resources given to such approaches relative to the more coercive law-and-order approaches have a major bearing on their potential success and effectiveness. Moreover, it is essential that specific programs and approaches be evaluated if we are to adequately gauge the strengths and limitations of social development models in specific localities.

A CRIME PREVENTION FRAMEWORK

It is easy to be cynical in the area of youth crime prevention. Superficially, it would appear that 'nothing works' when it comes to preventing youth crime. Certainly, the use of punitive measures against offenders has not worked (McGuire 1995; Krisberg 2005), and the use of coercive measures to 'clean up the streets' has had modest success at best. While politically popular, a law-and-order approach has generally proven to be unsatisfactory when it comes to getting results, as well as most damaging for those individuals and groups who have been the targets of such campaigns. It some cases, those campaigns have unnecessarily increased the fear of crime without doing anything to reassure the community that crimes are being dealt with adequately at a concrete level. Coercive action does have a place in law enforcement and crime prevention, but it needs to be specifically targeted (such as with violence reduction in particular localities at particular times), and it should not undermine or dominate other crime prevention strategic alternatives.

There is evidence that social development approaches to crime prevention are effective to some degree in preventing youth crime and antisocial behaviour. From the literature cited earlier, it would appear that the following elements are important components of a successful youth crime prevention framework:

- the adoption of a broad *social development* approach, which incorporates measures designed to enhance the opportunities of young people, and which allows them to take part in the negotiations and decisions that affect them and others around them

- the creation of a *constellation of programs and activities* to cater to a wide variety of interests, needs, and situations, and which includes programs that are well targeted at specific problems
- the importance of *community ownership*, which takes into account local conditions, and which allows the direct and active involvement of local young people and other members of the community
- the necessity of adopting a *holistic approach* to youth issues, which recognises the intersection of family, school, employment, recreation, and other issues in creating 'risk' situations
- the importance of *multi-agency involvement*, including the involvement of young people, so that a wide range of skills, knowledge, and resources can be drawn upon in addressing complex problems
- the necessity of *research and auditing processes* in order to determine levels and types of need, sources of conflict, and potential avenues for action
- the importance of *evaluation* of existing projects and programs, and the need for greater information about the effectiveness of different kinds of interventions
- the necessity of being *flexible in approach* so that programs can be changed or modified as required, and so that through ongoing evaluation, better targeting and better outcomes can be achieved.

Fundamentally, if crime prevention strategies are to work, and better relationships between young people and other stakeholders are to occur, then certain baseline human rights need to be acknowledged. Human rights are rights that are meant to prevail regardless of the behaviour of particular individuals and whether or not they are acting responsibly. That is, these rights refer to the *conduct of institutions*, in the sense that, while some limitation of rights may be warranted or legally justified in the case of specific transgressions of state laws by individuals (for example, particular young offenders), institutions must not take away these rights from whole classes of people (for example, young people as a group). More positively, governments are obliged to uphold certain rights that have been deemed to be universal—that is, applicable to everyone simply by virtue of their status as human beings.

It is useful in this regard to cite relevant articles from the United Nations Convention on the Rights of the Child. These sections provide a clear indication of the responsibilities of government in ensuring the overall wellbeing of children and young people:

> The States Parties to the present Convention shall respect and ensure the rights set forth in this Convention to each child within their jurisdiction without discrimination of any kind, irrespective of the child's or his or her

parent's or legal guardian's race, colour, sex, language, religion, political or other opinion, national, ethnic or social origin, property, disability, birth or other status.

Article 2

States Parties recognise the rights of the child to freedom of association and to freedom of peaceful assembly.

Article 15

States Parties recognise the right of the child to rest and leisure, to engage in play and recreational activities appropriate to the age of the child and to participate freely in cultural life and the arts.

Article 31

While one may question the practical enforcement of United Nations Human Rights Conventions, they do nevertheless provide an important internationally accepted *legal and moral framework* upon which to base our actions. This legal and ethical structure should underpin any dealings with, and provisions for, young people. Taken together, the quoted articles highlight important considerations, such as how well—or if—governments are ensuring adequate public amenities for young people in general, and for specific categories of young people (such as young women, ethnic minority young people, and especially Indigenous young people) in particular. Acknowledgment of the rights, worth, and dignity of each human should be integral to how youth issues are dealt with, and to the role that young people themselves play in social life generally.

There are a number of commonalities that many young people appear to share. Lack of adequate resources, a dearth of youth-friendly amenities, constant harassment from authority figures, fear of becoming a victim, and exclusion from decision-making processes constitute a recipe for resentment, frustration, alienation, and retaliation. If the social environment is unpleasant, then it is no wonder that this will be reflected in the perceptions of crime (for example, fear of crime) and the realities of crime (for example, vandalism, disrespect for authority).

As has been well documented in the youth crime prevention literature, the provision of legitimate activities for young people is a vital ingredient in successful crime prevention. This requires that governments, communities, and commercial enterprises make it a priority to provide resources and facilities for young people, in the interests of the social good. The benefits of such provisions are not solely for young people: they encompass values and outcomes relating to community solidarity, personal safety, public order, and commercial gain.

While the principle of respect for the rights of young people and the recognition of youth needs provide the strategic base for improving existing relationships, these need to be translated into concrete measures at a practical level. General prescriptions in this area include (White 1998b; 1999a):

- provision of a *diverse range of options* for young people—meaning that young people need to be provided with facilities and spaces that are multi-functional or that offer a range of uses, and that do not become the exclusive domain of any one group of young people (for example, skateboard ramps tend to have limited, but nevertheless important, appeal to a small proportion of young people)

- provision of *youth outreach services* so young people can connect with youth advocates, adult mentors, and service providers where they hang out, rather than having to go to specific fixed locations, and that assistance in the form of welfare, counselling, health, and legal support—as well as someone to mediate between groups of young people, and between young people and authority figures—is available

- provision of *youth-oriented public transport services* to ensure that public transportation is available and matches the entertainment needs of young people (as in the case of cinema end-times), that special services be available for weekend late-night travel or special events (for example, concerts or sports carnivals), and that public transport personnel are adequately prepared to deal with, and are respectful of, young users of public transportation

- provision of spaces and facilities that take into account the *social differences between young people*, and that thereby offer flexible usages, meaning that smaller, publicly visible spaces and larger-sized spaces can be combined to provide different groups (such as young women and young men) with places within which they can feel comfortable and safe, yet still part of a general congregation of people; or that different age groups be provided with specific types of amenities in line with their particular interests (for example, games parlours, café-style shops)

- the need to adopt a *range of communication strategies* in order to cater for the needs of different groups of young people—meaning varying the methods of consultation and information provision to suit the distinctive style of any particular groups (for example language, single-sex groups, use of youth advocates, links to wider community and family networks)

- the guaranteeing of *safe, confidential methods of consultation*—meaning that certain issues (for example, those relating to illegal drugs) and conflicts (for example, those relating to racism or sexual harassment) that have a big impact on how public spaces are used, must be able to be conveyed and discussed in ways that allow for voices that otherwise may be silenced, to be heard

- allowing for *formal and informal means of participation*—meaning setting up 'youth councils' or similar types of participatory bodies (as part of local councils, local youth services, or site-management committees), as well as ongoing grassroots consultation (through forums, use of advocates, surveys, and so on) with young people who may not wish to become active, who may not feel able to articulate their ideas, or who may be prevented for social and economic reasons from participating in more structured bodies

- development of *competencies* in young people so as to ensure better use of resources and facilities—meaning that in some cases young people need to be shown how to use facilities, or to learn certain skills, in order to maximise their use of and interest in what is on offer (for example, sports, computers)

- development of *clear guidelines and codes of conduct involving young people themselves*—meaning that young people participate directly in establishing boundaries of acceptable or unacceptable behaviour in particular kinds of public spaces (for example, shopping centres, city skating zones) as appropriate, and that there be effective and fair application of rules, and defined avenues of appeal when rules have apparently been breached

- provision of some spaces for the *exclusive use* of certain groups of young people—meaning that some young people (such as young women, Indigenous young people, and ethnic minority young people) have access to spaces, perhaps at designated times, on an exclusive basis in order to reflect their specific needs and interests, as well as safety concerns

- undertaking of *proactive campaigns* that attempt to break down social stereotypes and barriers that may be limiting or oppressive to certain groups of young—meaning carrying out activities such as youth reconciliation projects for young people from diverse cultural and ethnic backgrounds in order to foster better relationships between different groups of young people who use public space.

The development of specific projects or programs needs to take into account these kinds of concerns, especially given the common problems faced by many young people. However, there are particular groups and particular issues that warrant separate and further attention. This is most evident in the case of young women, ethnic minority young people, and Indigenous young people. Here, the key problems tend to revolve around two major issues that, while alluded to above, deserve further discussion.

First, there is the issue of whether to construct some spaces and activities as *exclusive to certain groups*, given their particular needs and histories, or whether to attempt to integrate each group into the mainstream of public-space life. The answer is that it is possible to do both, particularly if there are mixed opinions among the young people themselves as to what they prefer. For example, it is important to ensure that consultation processes be as inclusive as possible, and public space areas and activities as diverse as possible, in order to cater to multiple uses and groups. Simultaneously, it may be appropriate to set aside certain spaces (such as women-only rooms in a drop-in centre, Indigenous cultural centres, ethnic minority meeting places) for the use of particular groups and/or certain times for the use of some facilities or amenities (such as hours for exclusive swimming-pool use for some young people, which might, for example, fit the cultural and safety requirements of some women). Building a skateboard ramp is rarely seen in terms of social exclusivity; nor should providing separate spaces for other groups be seen as such.

These concerns also have a number of program and design implications. For example, young women need to have input into the kinds of activities that might appeal specifically to them as a group, rather than having things done *for* them. Many youth services and activities are very male-oriented, for instance being centred on computer games and sports activities. In addition to encouragement of and facilities for female sports, such as netball, it is essential to plan for non-sports activities as well. With respect to the design of public spaces, creative thought needs to go into how best to design 'small' spaces that are user-friendly for groups of friends, but that nevertheless allow for visual contact with larger congregations of people in public places. This would allow the possibility of both 'passive' security (through open-plan construction) and scope for intimate gatherings (through the privacy afforded by sectioned-off areas in a larger public area).

Second, although it is important to meet the needs of particular 'special population' groups, such as young women or Indigenous people, it is equally important to engage in *proactive campaigns* that attempt to break down social prejudices that may fuel conflicts between different groups of young people.

The marginalised position of Indigenous people in Australia, for example, is in many cases compounded by deeply ingrained and widely shared negative stereotypes, and there are many instances of racist attitudes and behaviour being directed at Aboriginal and Torres Strait Islander people, not only by authority figures such as the police and security guards, but also by other young people, their parents, and members of their wider community. A 'youth reconciliation' project undertaken in Adelaide provides one example of what such a proactive campaign might look like (City of Adelaide 1997). In this instance, the project was devised to overcome some of the problems relating to tensions between different ethnic and/or racial groups in the inner city, and to counter racist attacks on particular groups (especially 'Asians' and Indigenous people). The aim of the project was to promote better relations between young people of diverse cultural backgrounds by applying concepts of reconciliation and anti-racism. Similar attempts to challenge racism and cultural misunderstandings in Melbourne and Brisbane have used performance drama as the medium for the message (Rodd 1995; Seeto 1995).

The place of Indigenous young people in society generally, and in relation to the criminal justice system, deserves special mention. Public-space issues in particular are heavily overlaid with problems stemming from colonialism and invasion. While the matter of separate spaces should not be seen in terms of an either/or proposition (as already discussed), the regulation of public space is a slightly different issue. Given the historical relationship between the police and Indigenous young people (see Cunneen 1994, 2001a; and chapter 6), and given the recommendations of the Royal Commission into Aboriginal Deaths in Custody on the importance of self-determination in Indigenous affairs (Johnston 1991), it seems reasonable that special protocols continue to be developed, and resourced, in relation to the social regulation of Indigenous young people. In particular, the use of Indigenous police officers, advocates, community justice panel members, night and youth patrols, and other appropriate people in devising ways to diffuse problems before they arise, and also to solve them when they do, is essential (see, for example, Blagg & Valuri 2004).

The implementation of specific strategies, however, should be undertaken with full regard to the importance of community decision-making input into the process. As indicated in the Stolen Generations report, this requires sensitivity to local community circumstances, as well as reliance upon sustained negotiations between relevant parties:

> Before informed decisions can be made there needs to be proper negotiation between government and Indigenous communities and organisations relating to self-determination in juvenile justice, welfare and adoption matters. Communities must be in a position to make choices about what they see as suitable long-term solutions to particular issues (NISATSIC 1997:577).

The precise measures to be adopted should be the result of direct negotiation with the immediate communities concerned. This includes discussion of the appointment conditions of Indigenous police and other community officials, as well as broad policy and program matters.

The situation of ethnic minority young people also deserves particular consideration. As indicated in chapter 7, there is a wide range of issues pertaining specifically to ethnic minority youth, and especially to those from other than English-speaking backgrounds. It is clear that greater consultation is needed with these young people, and their families and communities. Furthermore, the development of appropriate youth-related and other community services likewise demands further attention. An issue that deserves much greater attention, as well, is how to devise suitable crime prevention measures in a climate of suspicion and hostility, one that is heightened by particular kinds of counterterrorism rhetoric and state intervention. In some cases, the targets of certain types of law enforcement (e.g., anti-gang strategies) and of counter terrorism (e.g., active surveillance, home searches) appear to overlap or be the same (that is, young men of 'Middle Eastern' background). Coercive forms of crime prevention, and coercive forms of counter-terrorist action, may in fact exacerbate existing social tensions and further alienate precisely those young people who yearn to belong and contribute. Crime prevention in relation to ethnic minority youth has to be extremely sensitive to the wider social, political and security environment within which these young people are growing up. If we, as a society, get it wrong, the consequences will extend far beyond the young people themselves.

CONCLUSION

This chapter has provided an overview of three broad approaches to youth crime prevention. It is important in any such discussion to distinguish the diverse and distinctive operational logic of different social institutions (coercion, development, and commercial imperatives), and the ways in which different crime prevention approaches have relevance and specific applications within the context of each of these institutional spheres (coercive, developmental, and accommodating measures). In analysing the pros and cons of each crime prevention perspective, it is essential to appreciate the limits and possibilities of institutional support for the adoption of a particular approach, and the conflicts and debates within different institutional settings on crime prevention matters. Crime prevention cannot be divorced from broader social policy and social justice issues. As such, interventions by criminologists and others in the area are always subject to diverse interpretations and selective program choices on the part of governments (see Sutton 2000; White 2001).

This chapter also reviewed examples of social-developmental approaches to crime prevention. The hallmark of such approaches is a high degree of community involvement, participation, and ownership over the crime prevention process. Such approaches stress the need for multi-dimensional and holistic ways of working at the local community level. They also acknowledge the crucial role of young people themselves in the crime prevention process.

As mentioned earlier, the approaches identified in this chapter are not mutually exclusive. However, the overall direction of youth intervention is dictated by the particular approach adopted as the main organising philosophy of crime prevention. With respect to this, and in the light of the very difficult social, economic, and political climate within which many young people are trying to make ends meet and make sense of their world (see White & Wyn 2004), it is preferable to adopt approaches to crime prevention that do the least amount of harm to young people. Regardless of existing conceptual difficulties and practical limitations, it is clear that the developmental and accommodating approaches offer the most constructive avenues for positive and socially inclusive forms of youth crime prevention.

To summarise, 'coercive' forms of crime prevention are detrimental to the best interests of children and young people for a number of reasons. In many instances, the use of coercion is unnecessary, unduly penalising of all young people, and ultimately socially discriminatory. It may well be that coercive measures need to be used in particular circumstances to protect and defend people and property from actual instances of criminal behaviour; however, the adoption of coercion as a strategy and as the main plank of juvenile crime prevention carries with it major problems from the point of view of youth rights and the causes of youth crime.

Conversely, the developmental and accommodating approaches offer a more youth-friendly perspective on crime prevention, and are premised upon the inclusion of young people as legitimate participants in decision-making and mainstream institutional processes. While tactically the use of coercion may have its place in specific instances of juvenile crime control, crime prevention is best dealt with through strategic measures that address youth concerns and youth needs directly, and in a positive and constructive manner. In these approaches, the emphasis is on diverting young people away from negative, antisocial, or criminal behaviour; on enhancing their leisure, employment, and educational opportunities; and on providing a social environment that is inclusive of young people.

13 | Restorative justice and juvenile conferencing

CHAPTER HIGHLIGHTS

Introduction
The origins of restorative justice
Practical forms of restorative justice
Diversion and juvenile conferencing in Australia
Police cautions
Juvenile conferencing
Strengths and limitations of restorative justice
Social justice and community wellbeing
Conclusion

INTRODUCTION

How the state and members of the community respond to young offenders is shaped by our images of the 'typical' young offender, the types of measures popularised in the mass media, and theories (popular and academic) regarding the central causes or reasons for offending. Responses to young offenders are also influenced by international conventions and human rights considerations. Since the early 1990s, a new way of thinking about juvenile offenders and how to deal with them has emerged and captured the imagination of many people associated with the juvenile justice system. This new approach to the issues is premised upon radically diverting young people away from the traditional pathways of the juvenile justice system.

In practice, once a young person has been drawn into the formal processes of the criminal justice system, there are several institutional approaches that might be adopted in regard to their offending behaviour. The usual debate here is over a perceived split between a 'justice' approach and a 'welfare' approach (see chapter 10). This divide has now been supplemented by reference to a third path: that of 'restorative justice' (see Bazemore 1991). Box 13.1 provides a summary of the three approaches.

331

BOX 13.1 THREE WAYS TO RESPOND TO YOUNG OFFENDERS

PUNISHMENT APPROACHES

Regimentation

Responsibility

Retribution

For example: Tougher sentences, greater use of incarceration, boot camps, stricter regimes of discipline, parental fines.

WELFARE APPROACHES

Rehabilitation

Resocialisation

Remedial treatment

For example: Therapeutic services, remedial education, wilderness camps, individualised treatment, community-based programs.

RESTORATIVE APPROACHES

Reconciliation

Reparation

Reintegration

For example: Family group conferences, direct work experience, victim-reparation schemes, youth development programs.

Generally speaking, the first approach in box 13.1 emphasises such things as juveniles' 'responsibility' for their actions, as well as punishment, control-oriented objectives, and a focus on what the offender has actually done wrong. Juvenile justice is thus *something that is done to you*. Often this involves the use of incarceration in a detention centre, or stringent penalties of some other kind. The idea is to get 'tough' on the young offender, and to punish that offender for what he or she has done.

The second approach in Box 13.1 places the emphasis on the offender, and favours greater use of community-based sanctions, individual treatment services, and attempts to resocialise or address the 'deficits' within the young person that are seen to be associated with the commission of crime. In this case, juvenile justice is *something that is done for you*. The point of this kind of intervention is rehabilitation, taking into account the vulnerability and special needs of young people. Most juvenile justice systems around the country embody elements drawn from the justice and welfare models.

The third approach in box 13.1 has gained popularity in recent years, and emphasises 'restorative justice'. This type of approach wishes to maintain a relationship of respect with the offender while simultaneously making amends for the harm caused. In its more developed form, this approach attempts to weigh up the specific requirements of each case of offending, and to variably respond to each offender in terms of personal accountability, the development of individual competencies, and the need for community-based incapacitation (Bazemore 1991; Bilchik 1998). Here, juvenile justice is *something that is done by you*.

The aim of this chapter is to explore the dynamics and nature of 'restorative justice' as it has developed in Australia. The chapter begins by discussing the origins and theoretical basis of restorative justice. It then describes the ways in which restorative justice approaches have been institutionalised, in terms of the various models and forms restorative justice takes at a practical level. The limitations and potential of restorative justice in addressing issues of juvenile offending are explored in the final part of the chapter.

The most popular example of the restorative justice approach in the Australian and New Zealand context is the family group conference (or juvenile conferencing) model. This type of intervention is based on the idea of bringing the young offender, the victim, and their respective families and friends together in a meeting chaired by an appropriate independent adult (juvenile justice worker or police officer). Collectively, the group goes through the reasons for the crime, the harms suffered, and the best ways to resolve the issues. Usually, some kind of apology is made by the offender to the victim, and often the offender has to repair the damage they have caused in some way (through undertaking community work, or mowing the lawns of the victim for a month).

The restorative approach would appear to have the greatest potential to effect positive change in the young offender's behaviour and attitudes. This is because it does not exclude young people from the community (or, conversely, expose them to a school of crime, as in the case of detention centres), nor does it pathologise young offenders by placing most attention on their faults and weaknesses. The restorative perspective is driven by the idea that the offender deserves respect and dignity (they are a person), and that they already have basic competencies and capacities that need to be developed further if they are not to reoffend. In this framework, the emphasis is on what the young person could do, rather than what they *should* do. What is important is that young offenders achieve things at a concrete level, for themselves, including making reparation to their victims. In the end, the point of dealing with young offenders in particular ways is to reinforce the notion that they have done something wrong, to repair the damage done as far as possible, and to open the door for their reintegration into the mainstream of society. The key way to stop reoffending, however, is to prevent it from happening in the first place.

THE ORIGINS OF RESTORATIVE JUSTICE

The idea of 'restorative justice' has been embraced in many jurisdictions around the world since the early 1990s, particularly in relation to juvenile justice (Braithwaite 1999; Bazemore & Walgrave 1999a; McLaughlin et al. 2003). Restorative justice refers to an emphasis on dealing with offenders by focusing on repairing harm, and in so doing involving victims and communities—as well as offenders—in the reparation process.

The appeal of this approach to criminal justice has many and varied origins. Culturally, it has been linked to Indigenous methods of dispute resolution that emphasise whole-of-community approaches to criminal and deviant behaviour, as in the case of Maori people in New Zealand and Indigenous people in Canada (see, for example, Maxwell & Morris 1994; Stuart 1997). It is also tied to particular religions and religious prescripts among communities such as the Mennonites (see Zehr 1990) or more broadly Canada's Church Council on Justice and Corrections (1996). Here, acts of social transgression are viewed as disrupting the basic harmony and peace of communities; the point of intervention being to restore peace and the boundaries of good behaviour. The restorative justice approach is also associated with particular political ideals and theoretical models, especially that of 'republican justice' (see Braithwaite & Pettit 1990). The basic concept of the republican justice model is that of personal dominion, conceptualised as 'republican liberty' involving institutions of civil society and the state in guaranteeing maximum freedom—now and into the future—for offenders, victims, and community members. Across these cultural, spiritual, and political domains, there is broad agreement that 'justice' should be about incorporating directly all those affected by crime and incivility into a positive process of reconciliation and reparation.

The 'restorative lens'

When discussing broad system orientations and imperatives, a distinction is often made between 'retributive' and 'restorative' justice, although the terminology varies depending on the writer (see, for example, Zehr, 1990; Braithwaite & Pettit 1990). The weaknesses and limitations of retributive justice are generally juxtaposed with the strengths and opportunities of restorative justice (see Zehr 1990; Bazemore & Umbreit 1995). The former is deemed to be backward-looking and grounded in the past, the latter progressive and looking to the future. The retributive justice perspective is seen as being guided by notions of blame, guilt, individual responsibility, and punishment for past harms. The restorative justice perspective is informed by concepts such as those of harm reparation, social restoration, community harmony, and problem-solving. A retributive system of justice is essentially punitive in nature, with the key focus on using punishment as a means to deter future crime and to provide 'just deserts' for any harm committed. A restorative approach—or, as it is sometimes referred to, 'republican justice'—is concerned with promoting harmonious relationships by means of restitution, reparation, and reconciliation involving offenders, victims, and the wider community.

One of the most influential perspectives in the area of restorative justice is that based on biblical traditions and Judaeo-Christian principles. For example, Zehr (1990) opens his book on restorative justice with a quote from the Jerusalem Bible:

Psalm 103
Yahweh [God] is tender and compassionate,
Slow to anger, most loving;
His indignation does not last forever,
His resentment exists a short time only;
He never treats us, never punishes us,
As our guilt and our sins deserve.

The message being conveyed here and throughout Zehr's work is that crime must be understood as particular readings of the Bible understand it: that is, with a clear orientation towards forgiveness and problem-solving. It is time, Zehr argues, to adopt a different lens, and thus to view the issues in a very different way.

Zehr posits two contrasting lenses in regard to conceptions of justice. These are (Zehr 1990: 181):

- *retributive justice*, where crime is a violation of the state, defined by law-breaking and guilt; justice determines blame and administers pain in a contest between the offender and the state directed by systematic rules
- *restorative justice*, where crime is a violation of people and relationships. It creates obligations to make things right. Justice involves the victim, the offender, and the community in a search for solutions that promote repair, reconciliation, and reassurance.

In developing alternative principles of justice and intervention, this approach to restorative justice stresses the *moral framework* that should guide decisions and actions over crime: that is, what ought to be the norm in how we respond to the majority of 'ordinary' offences. It also points to the actual experiences of people, both victims and offenders (and those around them), and the considerable damage and lack of satisfaction associated with conventional forms of punishment and retribution. Ultimately, the goal of intervention is seen as building positive social relationships, and the mission is to reflect Judaeo-Christian beliefs and practices as part of this process: 'The Bible holds out for us a vision of how people ought to live together, in a state of shalom, of right relationship' (Zehr 1990:185).

Translated into specific assumptions and principles, the restorative lens advocated here is one based upon three interrelated propositions (Zehr & Mika 1998):

- *Crime is fundamentally a violation of people and interpersonal relationships.* The key issue is that victims and the community have been harmed and are in need of restoration. Importantly, victims, offenders, and affected communities are seen as the key stakeholders in justice, and as such ought to be directly involved in the justice process.
- *Violations create obligations and liabilities.* It is felt that the offender's obligation is to make things right as much as possible for the harm they have caused. However, it is also argued that the community's obligations

extend to victims and to offenders, and to the general welfare of its members. Obligations are thus both individual and collective in nature.

- *Restorative justice seeks to heal and put right the wrong.* The starting point for justice is victims' need for information, validation, vindication, restitution, testimony, safety, and support. The process of justice ought to maximise the opportunities for exchange of information, participation, dialogue, and mutual consent between victim and offender, and the justice process ought to belong to the community. The offenders' needs and competencies also are to be addressed. In the end, justice needs to be mindful of the outcomes— intended and unintended—of its responses to crime and victimisation.

The basis for restorative justice in this framework is religious belief and principles. That is, from the point of view of particular faith communities, issues of crime and justice ought to be driven by particular moral precepts that are meant to guide how members of communities relate to one another generally, as well as in specific instances of social harm.

Republican theory

Other approaches to restorative justice may likewise be built upon certain ethical principles, but they are grounded less in religious traditions than in political theory. The most influential of these, particularly in the Australian setting, is the *republican theory* of criminal justice. While bearing many similarities to faith-driven models, it nevertheless proceeds from a secular conceptual base. The republican theory of criminal justice offers a perspective on juvenile justice that attempts to combine elements of strain theory and labelling (among other theoretical approaches) through a series of practical institutional measures. It is argued that the key to crime control is 'reintegrative shaming'. Before discussing what this means, it is useful to sketch out some of the details of the normative bases of republican theory as a whole.

The core concept of this theory is the notion of republican liberty, or 'dominion'. This refers to a form of liberty where non-interference in our lives by other people (including state officials) is protected by law and general community norms, but so too is interventionist state policy that secures equality of liberty prospects for all. According to the authors of republican theory, Braithwaite and Pettit (1990), the prime goal of any society should be to maximise the enjoyment of dominion (personal liberty).

In this framework, crime is seen as the *denial of dominion*. This is so at three different levels.

- Crime is a negative challenge to the dominion status of the person who is the victim: that is, a threat to or disregard of the dominion of an individual attacks the status of that individual as someone who holds a protected dominion in society. If someone commits a crime against an individual, the criminal act asserts the vulnerability of the victim to the will of the criminal, nullifying the protected status of the victim.

- If successful, the criminal attempt not only disregards the victim's dominion status, but also directly undermines, diminishes, and perhaps even destroys, the individual's dominion. For example, kidnapping or murdering someone destroys that person's dominion, while stealing someone's property diminishes the property owner's dominion by undermining certain exercises of choice they might have otherwise pursued.
- Every crime also represents communal evil. That is, not only does a crime affect the dominion status of the individual victim, but it endangers the community's dominion generally. This is because the fear of crime, or lack of action taken to assist the victim, can have the impact of reducing the liberty of those who fear possible victimisation themselves.

If every act of crime represents damage of some kind to dominion, then the task of the criminal justice system is to promote dominion by rectifying or remedying the damage caused by the crime. What should the courts do in response to the convicted offender? Theoretically, in sentencing the convicted offender there are three considerations that need to be taken into account: recognising the evil on the part of the offender, recompensing the victim for the harm suffered by them, and reassuring the community as a means to restore confidence in collective dominion.

The focus of republican theory is on *restoring dominion* for the victim, for the community, and—importantly—for the offender as well. In other words, republican theory is based upon an equilibrium model in which the needs of victim, offender, and community are considered. Republican responses to crime, therefore, include the following three elements (see Braithwaite & Pettit 1990; Pettit & Braithwaite 1993):

- *Recognition*—The offender must recognise the personal liberty of the victim in order to restore the dominion status of the victim. In order to do this, the offender must withdraw the implicit claim that the victim did not enjoy the dominion that was challenged by the crime. This can be achieved through some type of symbolic measure: for example, an apology on the part of the offender for their behaviour, a commitment not to reoffend, and/or reconciliation with the victim.
- *Recompense*—In order to restore the victim's former dominion (which might not have been simply disregarded, but which might have been destroyed or diminished), there must be some form of recompense for the damage done to that dominion. This can be achieved through a range of substantive measures, such as restitution to the victim of whatever was lost in the commission of an offence, compensation where restitution is not possible, and reparation where restitution or compensation is not possible (for example, compensation could be made to those close to and dependent upon a victim of murder).

- *Reassurance*—General reassurance must be given to the community at large of a kind that will undo the negative impact of the crime on its members' collective and personal enjoyment of dominion. This means that there has to be some guarantee that the community will be protected from future acts. For example, through a process of reprobation, the criminal justice system should expose offenders in a constructive way to community disapproval, and reintegrate the victim and the offender back into community life.

In the specific area of juvenile justice, Braithwaite (1989) argues that the restoration of dominion can be achieved through a process of 'shame and reintegration'. It is argued that we need to distinguish between stigmatisation, which increases the risk of reoffending by the shamed actor, and reintegrative shaming, in which disapproval is extended but a relationship of respect is maintained with the offender.

Stigmatisation is disrespectful of the offender. It is a humiliating form of shaming, where the offender is branded an evil person and cast out of the community in a permanent or open-ended fashion. *Reintegrative shaming*, by contrast, seeks to shame the evil deed, but sees the offender in a respectable light. The shaming is finite and the offender is given the opportunity to re-enter society by recognising their wrongdoing, apologising for their actions, and repenting. In this way, shame is seen as a useful means of combating crime, as long as it is not applied in a stigmatising manner.

Braithwaite (1989) argues that we need in society a culture in which we promote a *self-sanctioning conscience*. That is, if certain norms and values are generally accepted and widely promoted, individuals will not engage in certain activities because their conscience will prevent them from doing so. Thus, the theory looks both to external processes of shaming (through the criminal justice system), and to internal mechanisms of shaming (by way of socialisation through the family, media, and schooling).

An important feature of republican theory is the way in which it attempts to combine many elements of the different theories of juvenile offending within criminology. Thus, for example, republican theory tries to explain crime in terms of conditions affecting the individual and those occurring at a societal level. Crime is seen to stem from a combination of individual factors (such as being unemployed, male, unmarried, and/or a young person), social processes (such as stigmatisation and/or criminal subcultural formation), and institutional structures (such as blocked legitimate opportunities and/or presence of illegitimate opportunities).

A reintegrative shaming strategy works—or at least works effectively—only under certain conditions. These relate to the degree of *interdependency* (attachment to parents, school, neighbours, employer) experienced by the individual, and the degree of *communitarianism* (the extent and depth of interdependent social networks) at the level of society as a whole. As Braithwaite (1989:101) explains it: 'Interdependent persons are more susceptible to shaming. More importantly, societies in which individuals are subject to extensive interdependencies are more likely to be communitarian, and shaming is much more widespread and potent in communitarian societies. Urbanization and high residential mobility are societal characteristics which undermine communitarianism.'

While republican theory acknowledges the importance of economic variables (such as a lack of opportunities for employment) and cultural variables (such as stigmatisation) in the construction of criminality, the main practical thrust of the theory is on the reintegrative shaming process.

In summary, republican theory, as it relates to juvenile justice policy, is framed in terms of responding to crime (rather than crime prevention *per se*), and doing so in a manner that distinguishes between reintegrative shaming and stigmatisation. The aim of any resulting policy is to reintegrate the victim and offender into the society (and hence to restore dominion). Such policy is thus aimed at reinforcing communal disapproval of the criminal act, while acknowledging and valuing the individual offender.

PRACTICAL FORMS OF RESTORATIVE JUSTICE

In abstract terms, clear differences can be drawn between a system of justice based primarily on the concept of retribution, and one based on restoration. This is recognised in most of the literature dealing with restorative justice (see, for example, Zehr 1990; Bazemore & Umbreit 1995). There are nevertheless different analytical emphases within the broad restorative justice literature, with some writers placing greater importance than others on community, some putting the victim at the centre of the criminal justice process, and others paying most attention to how best to respond to the offender (Church Council on Justice and Corrections 1996; Bazemore 1997). Different approaches thus emphasise different objectives. These include victim restoration, shaming and denouncing offenders, citizen involvement, through to community empowerment (Bazemore 1997).

There is, then, a range of specific models and institutional approaches to restorative justice, which includes, for instance, family group conferencing through to circle sentencing and victim-offender mediation programs (Bazemore 1997; Braithwaite 1999). Some approaches are based on moral categories such as reintegrative shaming, where the aim is to shame the offence while offering forgiveness to the offender (Braithwaite 1989). Others are based upon the strategic assessment of offenders and events (such as the balanced restorative approach), in which the aim is to design interventions that best address issues of offender accountability, competency development, and community safety (Bazemore 1991; Bilchik 1998). Some approaches focus almost exclusively on meeting victim needs (usually through some method of restitution or compensation involving the offender), while others place emphasis on widespread community engagement in dealing with underlying problems and issues, of which specific offending is but one manifestation.

339

Some of the different practical approaches to restorative justice may be summarised as follows (see also Bazemore 1997; Bilchik 1998; Braithwaite 1999).

- *Victim–offender mediation and dialogue*, in which victim restoration is highly important, along with active victim involvement, protection of the victim, and meeting of victim needs. It involves a process, under the guidance of a trained mediator, in which victims and offenders meet in a safe and structured setting to discuss the nature of the harm committed. An important component of the process is for the offender to be held directly accountable for their behaviour and to provide assistance to the victim in an agreed manner.

- *Family group conferencing*, in which victim restoration is highly valued, and where the offender's actions are denounced through reintegrative shaming. Affected community members are encouraged to participate (including especially the friends and family of the victims and offenders). The purpose of the meeting is to discuss how the crime has affected the various parties, and to decide as a group how the offender may repair the harm.

- *Circle sentencing or peacemaking circles*, in which citizen involvement and sharing of power, as well as community empowerment, are highly regarded. This involves creating a respectful space (literally, a circle of concerned people) in which consensus decisions can be made on an appropriate disposition or outcome that addresses the concerns of all parties. Emphasis is placed on speaking from the heart, in an effort to find the best way to assist in healing all affected parties and preventing future occurrences.

- *Reparative probation*, in which the main concern is with victim restoration and community empowerment through offenders undertaking tasks that directly benefit victims and communities. The young person works in the community to perform personal services (such as house painting) for victims and/or community services. For the latter, often the community service project is oriented towards enhancing conditions for disadvantaged or less fortunate people within particular communities.

- *Balanced restorative*, in which victims are afforded services and opportunities for involvement and input, offenders are given the opportunity to increase their skills and capacities, and connections can be forged between different community members. It involves assessing offenders from the point of view of ensuring community safety, allowing offenders accountability for their actions, and enhancing offenders' competency development while they are in the criminal justice system.

Under the restorative justice umbrella, there are differences between those who see restorative justice as, essentially, a form of diversion from the formal criminal justice system, and those who view it as a potential alternative to that system and thus as something that could supplant the existing system completely (see Bazemore & Walgrave 1999b). Whatever the specific differences, it appears that the central thread underlying restorative justice is the spirit within which 'justice' is undertaken: that is, the intent and outcomes of the process are meant to be primarily oriented towards repairing harm caused by a crime, and this means working to heal victims, offenders, and communities that have been directly injured by the crime (Zehr & Mika 1998; Bazemore & Walgrave 1999b).

The restorative justice approach constitutes another 'add-on' to systems that have developed, usually in an ad hoc manner, in ways that to varying degrees include elements associated with classical (for example 'justice') and positivist (for example 'treatment') understandings of crime and criminality. Historically, the development of criminal justice systems has been marked essentially by the simultaneous incorporation of apparently contradictory sentencing principles (such as retribution versus rehabilitation) and conflicting institutional responses (such as punishment versus treatment). Community service, for example, can be associated with rehabilitation objectives or with restorative justice objectives (see Walgrave 1999). The specific content of the practice will therefore vary according to the philosophical framework informing its implementation.

DIVERSION AND JUVENILE CONFERENCING IN AUSTRALIA

The favoured model of restorative justice in the Australian context is that of juvenile conferencing, a form of conferencing heavily influenced by the family group conferences first trialled in New Zealand in the 1980s. Before discussing juvenile conferencing as such, it is useful to review the philosophy and history of 'diversion', since the introduction of conferencing is in many ways associated with this concept (see, for example, Chan 2005).

Young people who offend, and who are apprehended for (allegedly) doing so, are subject to a range of state sanctions. They may have to attend court, and may be sentenced to a wide range of dispositions. However, not all young people end up in court, and of those who do, not all have the case adjudicated or decided upon in the formal court setting.

This is where 'diversion' is employed as a key concept within the juvenile justice system. The term generally refers to instances where young people are turned away from the more formal processes, procedures, and sanctions of the criminal justice system. The rationale for diversion is twofold. First, from an interactionist perspective, concerns have long been raised regarding the harmful effects of the stigmatisation that may accompany the formal court and detention process. Young people are seen to be particularly vulnerable to the social effects of negative labelling, and if labelled 'bad' or 'criminal' by the courts, may take on the behaviours and attitudes described by the label (see chapter 2). Labelling is seen to be harsh and unforgiving, affecting the opportunities and life chances of young people beyond the period of sanction. The second rationale for diversion comes from considering the needs of the victim and the offender. The republican perspective, for instance, argues that young people know they have done wrong—that they have harmed another human being in some way—but that they should be encouraged to make the situation right again through discussions with the victim. The method here is reintegrative shaming, a process that expresses reprobation for the act, not the actor, and that ultimately restores 'dominion' to the victim and the offender. For young offenders, this theory suggests that the most positive and constructive approach is one that brings victim and offender together, under particular conditions, and that allows some kind of reconciliation and restitution to occur.

Actual program developments tend to reflect varying emphases on these two rationales. Diversion in a strong or traditional sense means to divert the young person from the system as a whole. At a policy level, this is manifest in statements that see diversion as a form of non-intervention, or at best minimal intervention. The nature of diversionary processes is complex, however, and involves assessment of different types of diversionary intervention. For instance, any analysis of diversion needs to take into account the following sorts of considerations.

- The different points within the criminal justice system at which diversion may occur—such as police contact, pre-court meetings, and court-ordered alternatives to detention—must be considered. The first two points refer to diversion from formal systems of court adjudication, the latter to diversion from incarceration.
- Diversion may be reserved for certain types of offences, such as minor infringements or first-time offending, and particular types of offenders, such as those who have had little or no prior contact with the criminal justice system. Serious and repeat offenders may not be diverted from the formal systems of criminal justice.
- Regardless of the seriousness or triviality of the offence, or the background of individual offenders, there are some cases in which diversion is simply not allowed. This was the case, for example, with mandatory sentencing for certain prescribed property offences in the Northern Territory in the late 1990s. Regardless of circumstances, judges and magistrates were not given discretionary latitude to divert young people from the penalties mandated by law.
- Diversionary measures may be set out formally in legislation, they may stem from organisational initiatives (such as police guidelines encouraging the use of informal means of conflict resolution), or they may be linked to particular pilot projects (such as the targeted use of juvenile conferencing in particular geographical locations).

The use of diversion is certainly not new to the criminal justice system, and whereas policy prescriptions such as zero tolerance policing (see chapter 9) tend to undermine its use, these may be offset by legislation that guides the use of police discretion in favour of the use of diversionary measures (Chan, 2005).

POLICE CAUTIONS

The use of an *informal* police caution is one example of the practical application of diversion. This is where a police officer advises a young person directly, and on the spot, that they have done or are doing something wrong and will suffer bad consequences if they persist in the offending behaviour. In other words, an informal police caution usually consists of police on the beat telling young people to move on or to desist from certain behaviours. Police take no further action, providing the young person heeds the caution.

Similarly, a *formal* police caution usually aims to divert the young person from the formal court system. This process involves an admission by the juvenile and a warning from the police officer, often in the presence of the young person's family. This normally takes place at the police station, and is officially recorded. No further action is taken, although a caution having been issued is likely to affect later police interactions with the young person.

There have been important legal and administrative differences between the states in relation to police cautions. For example, in some states cautioning programs are the result of administrative policy decisions, whereas in others the rules guiding the cautioning program are stipulated in legislation that sets out the purpose of the caution and the procedures involved. The actual use of the formal police caution, in terms of frequency, also varies considerably between jurisdictions.

A further type of police caution involves a much higher degree of police intervention and youth engagement with criminal justice officials. An example is an experiment undertaken in 1991 in Wagga Wagga, New South Wales (O'Connell 1993). This was a cautioning program initiated by the police, which directly involved the young offender and their family (and significant others), and the victim and their family, with the police officer taking an active part in discussions. This style of police cautioning makes use of models of conflict resolution that emphasise victim–offender relations. It incorporates many of the philosophical principles of the republican theory and the New Zealand family group conference experience. Most juvenile conferencing in Australia is now incorporated into relevant juvenile justice legislation, and most favours non-police-run conference models (Daly & Hayes 2001). A notable exception, however, is Tasmania, where there exist police-run 'cautioning' conferences and juvenile conferencing undertaken by the Department of Health and Human Services.

From the point of view of diversion, a significant question is whether the use of such schemes as the Wagga Wagga experiment or Tasmania's police-run cautioning conferences represents anything other than a major increase in state intervention. The crucial area of change is that more cases can be dealt with on a more informal basis, without referral to courts or legal assistance. Hence, it is diversion *to* other parts of the criminal justice system, rather than diversion *from* the system itself. It is also an intensification of state intrusion, insofar as immediate imposition of penalty is now possible at the very earliest stages of the process. Importantly, in many jurisdictions the prime referring bodies for conferencing, whether this be police-run or not, are the police as well as the courts. The police therefore have great input into the manner in which young people will be treated, and where within the criminal justice system they will be dealt with. A recent evaluation of police practices in New South Wales, however, indicated that where legislation clearly sets out the procedures, conditions and target offences for diversionary options, then the groundwork exists for a substantial increase in warnings and cautions of a non-conference nature (Chan, 2005). From an implementation point of view, a lot depends upon how police discretion is regulated at the gate-keeping level, and how 'diversion' itself as a concept is interpreted by police agencies.

JUVENILE CONFERENCING

Dealing with juveniles charged with minor offences has generally been framed in terms of finding ways to divert them from formal court proceedings and sanctions. In most Australian jurisdictions, there has been a notable increase since the early 1990s in the role and powers of the police in relation to referring young people to court alternatives. In addition to police cautionary measures, the main method of diversion has been through the use of juvenile conferencing.

For many years, some states had panel systems as an alternative to court. For example, in South Australia the majority of matters used to go before a Children's Aid Panel rather than the children's court. In more than 80 per cent of the matters before the Aid Panel, the child was warned and counselled (Cunneen & Morrow 1994). Recent changes to young offender legislation in most states, however, have seen the panels superseded by juvenile conferencing. These forms of intervention are much more intensive in nature than the previous panels, and involve a larger number of people in their operation. The introduction of these particular alternatives reflects a major shift in thinking, away from a narrowly defined concern about the negative effects of labelling young offenders, towards making them responsible for their actions within a wider communal framework.

The impetus for adopting juvenile conferencing for dealing with young offenders stems from varying pressures, depending upon jurisdiction. In some cases, it has been linked to grassroots developments among Indigenous people (Morris & Maxwell 1993; Maxwell & Morris 1994; but see also Tauri 1999 for a different view), in other cases to police initiatives (O'Connell 1993), and, more generally, to new thinking at a theoretical level about juvenile justice (Braithwaite 1989, 1993). Certainly, the rhetoric of this approach has caught on in most jurisdictions within Australia, although it is highly questionable whether the philosophical basis of the model is necessarily being adhered to in practical programs.

In terms of actual program development, the leading example of juvenile conferencing was provided by New Zealand's family group conference model. The approach to juvenile justice adopted in New Zealand in the late 1980s emphasised the need to keep children and young people with their families and in their communities. The model emphasises the following key elements (see Maxwell & Morris 1994:15–17):

- *Justice*—Making young offenders accountable for their offences, and doing so in the legal context of proportionality of punishment and respect for due process.
- *Diversion, decarceration, and destigmatisation*—A means of avoiding the negative labelling of young people.
- *Enhancing wellbeing and strengthening families*—Providing support for young people and their families.
- *Victim involvement, mediation, reparation, and reconciliation*—Reflecting wider trends to cater better for the needs of victims and to see 'justice' in terms of conflict resolution.
- *Family participation and consensus decision-making*—To ensure people are empowered by the process itself.
- *Cultural appropriateness*—Services and procedures are to be appropriate to the background of the people involved.

The practical elements of the family group conference model have been described as follows (Braithwaite 1993:40):

- convene a conference of the offender, the people who are most supportive of the offender (usually the family), the victim, and people to support the victim
- give all the participants an opportunity to explain how the offence affected their lives and to put forward proposals for a plan of action
- after the offender and the offender's family have listened to the other speakers, empower them to propose plans until they come up with one that is agreeable to all participants in the conference (including the police)
- monitor the plan's implementation, particularly those elements involving compensation to victims, and community work.

In Australia, all states and territories have now implemented some form of conferencing, although most jurisdictions refer to these forums as juvenile conferencing, rather than family group conferences. The intended outcome of the conferences is that the young offender is expected to complete some kind of agreement or undertaking; thus: 'The sanctions or reparations that are part of agreements include verbal and written apologies, paying some form of monetary compensation, working for the victim or doing other community work, and attending counselling sessions, among others' (Daly & Hayes 2001:2). The form of the conference is basically the same, although there are jurisdictional differences in terms of the kinds of offences that are conferenced, the volume of activity that is engaged in through conferencing, the upper limit on conference outcomes, the statutory basis for conferencing, and the organisational placement or administration of the conferencing process. Evaluation research that has been carried out to date indicates that 'conferences are perceived as fair and participants are satisfied with the process and outcomes' (Daly & Hayes 2001:6; see also Strang 2001; Chan, 2005).

Programs and strategies designed to divert the young offender from formal court proceedings are generally characterised by a degree of informalism in terms of their structures, operations, and records. From a theoretical perspective, the trend towards informalism and community-based programs has been conceptualised as an expansion of regulation. While superficially power is transferred to the community level, and into the hands of members of the community, the overall tendency is for the state to retain control over the process and for social control to be maintained in fairly conventional ways. For example, Cohen (1985:44) argues that such moves, while defended on the basis of being less intrusive and less coercive than formal court-based systems, serve as a form of net-widening. Specifically, Cohen argues that we need to evaluate the impact of apparently benign community-based programs such as those just described. Accordingly, we need to enquire into the size of the net that is being constructed to process the young offender, and ask whether those now in the net would have been processed previously (is the net wider?). We need to examine the level of intervention, and ask whether it is more intense than in the past (is the net denser?). And finally, we need to evaluate whether the new agencies and strategies are supplementing rather than replacing the original, formal mechanisms of social control (is the net different?).

In practical terms, there are likewise a number of issues that continue to require attention and further debate. For example, concerns have been raised regarding the systematic denial of young people's legal rights due to the informal nature of some community-based schemes and the prior guilty plea demanded of young people (Warner 1994). More generally, evaluations of previous diversionary programs have tended to be mixed: net-widening was seen as a persistent problem, and there were gender discrepancies in the use of such mechanisms (see Alder & Polk 1985). Similarly, the use of diversionary measures has tended to be biased against Aboriginal and Torres Strait Islander people, who are quickly drawn deeper and deeper into the criminal justice system, with fewer diversionary options (Cunneen 1997; Blagg, 1997, 1998). Thus, community-based programs may not only be unequal in application to specific groups of young people, but they may also serve to channel young people into a system that they might otherwise have avoided (see chapter 6). On the other hand, systematic evaluation of developments in New South Wales show that increased diversion in recent years has not resulted in net-widening, and that the Young Offenders Act, while not overcoming existing inequalities and disparities in treatment, has fostered increased diversion for Indigenous young people (Chan, 2005). In the longer term, this may lead to a reduction in the over-representation of Indigenous youth among those arrested and brought before the courts.

STRENGTHS AND LIMITATIONS OF RESTORATIVE JUSTICE

Theoretically, restorative justice promises a more constructive, positive approach to criminal justice than retributive or therapeutic approaches. Punitive responses have not taken into account specific offender circumstances and how these shape offending behaviour. At a systemic level, punitive responses have proved to:

- be costly
- damage offenders' life chances once a sanction has been applied
- do little to prevent recidivism
- fail to act as a general deterrent, or to address the fundamental causes of crime.

The sooner a young person comes into contact with the more formal parts of the criminal justice system, the more likely they are to reoffend and to re-enter that system. As recent research demonstrates, a high proportion of young people making their first appearance in a children's court continue their offending into adulthood, particularly if their first court appearance occurred when they were young (Chen et al. 2005).

Welfare responses, on the other hand, have been criticised for their lack of attention to victim needs, for viewing offenders in deficit terms, for their patronising 'expert' attitudes towards 'clients', for their failure to link efforts to change offender lives to efforts to transform social contexts, and for inadequate transitional arrangements between treatment and non-treatment phases (see Cunneen & White 1995; Walgrave 1999). Such approaches have also been criticised for apparent inconsistencies in the treatment of offenders. Some young people, for example, were subjected to long periods of treatment (including incarceration) if perceived not to be responding to the assistance provided, while others experienced only short periods of treatment if they showed the right signs and demonstrated a positive response to the 'expert' intervention. In either case, the treatment response was not seen to be appropriate to the situation.

Restorative justice, with its emphasis on repairing harm, emphasises reintegrative and developmental principles. It offers the hope that opportunities will be enhanced for victims, offenders, and their immediate communities, with the direct participation of all concerned in this process. The most detailed and sophisticated example of restorative justice is probably the balanced restorative approach (see Bilchik 1998), although considerable institutional resources have also been put into juvenile conferencing, especially in places such as Australia (Braithwaite 1999; Daly 2000). The benefits of restorative justice can be seen in terms of its emphasis on 'active agency' (young people doing things for themselves), cost-effectiveness (compared with detention or imprisonment), victim recognition and engagement (often through face-to-face meetings with offenders), and community benefit (through participation and through community service). While it can be argued that juvenile conferencing actually incorporates elements of retributive justice, rehabilitative justice and restorative justice, at least at the experiential level (see Daly 2002), there is nevertheless a distinctiveness in orientation that marks this approach off from others within the field.

Compared with previous theoretical approaches to offending, restorative justice appears to offer a practically effective, philosophically attractive, and financially prudent method of doing justice. It is peacemaking in orientation, rather than punishment-based. It is socially inclusive rather than reliant upon experts and officials. It attempts to provide a symbolic and practical solution to actual harms, rather than a response to violation of laws (that represent, in abstract, acts against the state). Victims and community, as well as offenders, are central to resolving issues of harm, rather than peripheral to the processes of criminal justice. At the level of sentiment and utopian vision, restorative justice does indeed have a powerful emotional appeal. This has drawn the critical attention of those who question its basic propositions about justice, its reliance on 'good news' stories, and its apparent optimism that even the most heinous of crimes can be dealt with in a restorative manner (Acorn 2004). Even supporters of the broad thrust of restorative justice have asked hard questions about the prominent myths that feature in advocates' stories and claims (Daly 2002). What is being done to whom, why, and with what consequences, remain central questions for sceptic and supporter alike.

In most cases, restorative justice approaches have been designed as a form of diversionary measure (primarily used at the front end of the traditional criminal justice system), or integrated as a specific form of response applicable or appropriate only for particular types of offenders. For example, most serious and repeat juvenile offenders are not 'invited' to take part in juvenile conferencing in Australia. One result of this is that Indigenous young people are—due to their early and repeated contacts with the criminal justice system—less likely than non-Indigenous young people to be referred to conferences (Cunneen 1997; see also Harding & Maller 1997), although a systemic emphasis on diversion as a key juvenile justice principle has been shown to dramatically reduce the number of first-time Indigenous offenders having to appear before the children's court (Chan 2005). The manner in which restorative justice has been adopted has tended to reflect institutional pressures (to cut costs), electoral considerations (the appeal of 'new' thinking), and administrative considerations ('Nothing works, but this might'). It is rare to see restorative justice appropriated as a general philosophical ideal; and even rarer therefore to see it as a systemic alternative intended to replace the existing system.

Partly due to the diversity of opinion, values, and models that reside under the restorative justice tag, there has been a tendency for specific forms of restorative justice to be implemented in a manner that actively reproduces the dominant forms of social control. For example, juvenile conferencing may be used solely for first-time offenders and/or trivial offences (as a means of diversion at the 'soft' end of the juvenile justice spectrum), and therefore as a filter that reinforces the logic and necessity of the 'hard' end of the system (the 'real justice' of retribution and punishment). The former thus may well help to legitimise the latter, rather than constitute a challenge to it. Substantial variations in the introduction of restorative justice are apparent across diverse jurisdictions, if we compare legislative, administrative, and operational frameworks (Daly & Hayes 2001; see also Chan 2005). In almost all cases, however, restorative justice has been blended into existing institutional patterns, as part of the continuing hybridisation of criminal justice. How this 'blending' occurs is important, of course, as it makes a major difference in terms of overall system orientation. The degree of expansion of restorative justice into the criminal justice system, for example, to include more serious kinds of offences and offenders with extensive criminal records, could provide one indication of potential systemic change.

The ALRC and HREOC (1997:482) found that all models of youth conferencing in Australia have been the subject of criticism, and recommended that national standards for juvenile justice should provide best-practice guidelines for conferencing (Recommendation 200). They found that standards should include the following (ALRC and HREOC 1997:482–3):

- the desirability of diversionary schemes being administered by someone independent of law-enforcement bodies, such as a judicial officer, youth worker, or community-based lawyer
- the need to monitor penalties agreed to in conferences, to ensure that they are not significantly more punitive than those a court would impose as appropriate to the offence
- the need to ensure that young people do not get a criminal record as a result of participating in conferencing
- the need to monitor conferencing proceedings, to ensure that they do not operate in a manner oppressive or intimidating to the young person
- the need to ensure the child's access to legal advice prior to the agreement to participate in a conference
- the need to determine whether it is preferable for schemes to have a legislative basis, so that the process is more accountable and less ad hoc
- the need to monitor the overall effect of conferencing schemes to ensure they do not draw greater numbers of young people into the criminal justice system or escalate children's degree of involvement with the system.

Youth conferences have also been introduced in the school setting in Queensland, New South Wales, and the Australian Capital Territory (see Strang 2001; Strang & Braithwaite 2001). As with criminal justice conferences, a number of difficult practical issues have been identified in relation to the use of conferences in this setting. For example, the traditional management and disciplinary culture of many schools (with an emphasis on punishment and behavioural control) have inhibited successful implementation of conferencing strategies (which emphasise restorative justice in pursuit of a supportive school environment) (Cameron & Thorsborne 2001). On the other hand, the relationship between school disciplinary practices—in particular, suspensions and expulsions—and youth justice conferencing outside the school has placed some young people in double jeopardy. That is, in some cases young people are being doubly punished: once by the school, and again by the juvenile justice system (see Scher & Payne 1999). In either instance, it is recommended that professional, administrative, and legal guidelines be put into effect in order to ensure that young people's rights are protected, and that conferencing processes reflect a restorative outcome (see Scher & Payne 1999; Cameron & Thorsborne 2001).

In addition to specific legal and criminological concerns about how youth conferencing ought to be undertaken, attention has been directed to how conferencing often embodies a narrow rather than expansive version of restorative justice. Within restorative justice frameworks, the idea of social harm is generally conceptualised in immediate, direct, and individualistic terms (and hence often ignores the broader social processes underpinning—and patterns of—both offending and victimisation). One consequence of this is that the emphasis on repairing harm tends to be restricted to the immediate violations and immediate victim concerns, thereby ignoring communal objectives and collective needs in framing reparation processes. Thus, the heart of the matter remains that of changing the offender—albeit with their involvement—rather than transforming communities and building progressive social alliances that might change the conditions under which offending takes place. The distinction between 'restorative justice' and 'community justice' has been described in the following terms (Crawford & Clear 2001:129):

> While restorative justice is about cases, community justice is about places ...
> A restorative justice program 'works' when key constituents experience a restorative process and end up feeling restored by it. Community justice programs 'work' when the quality of life in a given place improves.

Most discussions of restorative justice tend to concentrate on 'cases' within existing criminal justice systems, and to evaluate practice in relation to traditional criminal justice objectives (such as reducing juvenile reoffending). Conversely, 'community empowerment', which connotes a concern to intervene in and perhaps to transform community relations, does not feature strongly in some of the more popular restorative justice models, such as family group conferences and juvenile conferencing (see Bazemore 1997).

SOCIAL JUSTICE AND COMMUNITY WELLBEING

There is a sense in which the basic principles and practices of restorative justice can be thought of as prefiguring the changes required for creating a just and equal society (see Walgrave & Bazemore 1999). The key challenge is how to engage in 'restorative social justice' (White 2000) by shifting the focus of intervention much more directly onto the tasks of community-building. For example, the guiding concepts might be solidarity, compensation, and community empowerment (see White 2003).

Solidarity implies that the politically and socially weak members of a group need to be included rather than excluded, in the sense that tasks are to be performed for and by them, and emotional support is to be given to them. Offenders and victims need to be offered solidarity, a voice in what affects them, and support in the healing process.

Compensation refers to the idea that weakness, on the part of the victims and the offenders, ought to be compensated. We need to address the social disadvantages of people who offend, and the social harms experienced by those who are victimised. The process of repairing harm has to be reconceptualised as social rather than solely individual in nature. This involves state-provided resources as well as input from individuals and groups.

Community empowerment is about enhancing the welfare and prospects of collectivities, of which individuals are integral members. The point of intervention is to change the material conditions and circumstances of neighbourhoods and family networks, with the active involvement of local people.

Conceptually, the general contours of a restorative social justice model, as a specifically juvenile justice model of intervention, can be organised around four general themes (White 2003), which are:

- an emphasis on social inclusion in any process involving young offenders, victims, and potential offenders
- responsive practices that are based upon communal objectives
- the formation of communities of support
- enhancement of community resources.

Social inclusion

What the restorative social justice approach implies is that any strategy of reform and positive change must be premised upon the ideas of social inclusion and community engagement. This means that victims (and offenders) have a right to be heard and to be compensated, but does not mean that victims should necessarily become part of a punishment process *per se*. Such a principle also implies that young offenders ought to be viewed as part of communities, not simply as individuals. Repairing social harm should not be seen as a 'micro' event, involving only the immediate affected parties: it is indicative of much broader social processes, in which both victim and offender are implicated. A central idea relating to social inclusion is to bring into any decision-making process a wide range of interested parties. These ought to include young people, as well as authority figures.

Communal objectives

We know that substantive inequalities restrict individual choice and freedom, and narrow the scope for the expression of positive agency in an environment hostile to working-class, Indigenous, and ethnic minority youth. Any response to specific offending should take this as its starting point. In programmatic terms, this means that communal objectives, rather than individual incentives or punishments, should form the framework for reparation. That is, the expression of 'taking responsibility' and the performance of certain tasks on the young offender's part should bear a direct relation to what the community needs in order to break the cycle of violence and crime. This is too important to be left solely to criminal justice administrators, victims, and immediate family members. Thus, social inclusion means, among other things, taking into account the specific needs and wishes of particular communities. This requires a sense of what is happening at the local level, and which groups or individuals can most benefit from the assistance provided by young people.

Communities of support

The building of communities of support is an essential part of transforming the conditions that give rise to criminality and criminalisation. Crime is not reducible to the individual: it is a social phenomenon. Concentrating solely on the individual offender, or specific incidents of harm, belies the necessity for widespread changes in particular locales. An important task in dealing with young offenders is to use the opportunity of intervention in order to rebuild communities, and as part of this to foster the ideas of solidarity and cooperation. Reintegration, to be meaningful, must involve the nesting of the young offender in a web of familiar, prosocial relationships oriented towards community improvement. Victims, likewise, need access to such relationships, with similar objectives. This is especially so given that victims are generally members of the same neighbourhood or community.

Community resources

The enhancement of community resources is a crucial aspect of any anti-crime and social justice strategy. In this regard, in addition to political campaigns for greater assistance in the redevelopment of local neighbourhoods, creative thinking has to go into how best to use existing community resources in the here and now. The mapping of assets, capacities and skills of residents, associations, and institutions can provide some indication of the strengths that can be built upon. There is also much scope for the alternative use of existing resources: for example, schools should be used as multi-purpose community resources, and not be treated as age-specific or function-limited. Developing a variety of physical sites for connecting people is an important component in rekindling community pride and neighbourhood spirit. These also provide avenues for the provision of programs and services (such as mentor schemes), which are particularly important in ensuring that young offenders have the chance to participate in communal life.

The development of restorative community justice ultimately rests upon the type of intervention strategy chosen, and the interest, professionalism, and enthusiasm of the service providers who oversee the intervention process. Depending upon individual circumstances and specific situations, different types of intervention will be appropriate in relation to specific kinds of clients. However, the weight given to each form of intervention will very much shape the allocation of resources, staff time and energy being put into specific measures. There is considerable scope to develop further a restorative social justice style of intervention (see Bilchik 1998; White 2003). To do so, however, implies serious consideration of the preferred roles and activities of juvenile justice workers, whether in government or non-government sectors.

CONCLUSION

This chapter has provided an outline of restorative justice principles and juvenile conferencing practices. Philosophically, restorative justice offers a major change of lens from retributive views on criminal justice. As such, restorative justice can be seen at one level as a major challenge to more conservative 'law-and-order' types of approaches that emphasise punishment and coercive means of dealing with young offenders. Nevertheless, questions can be asked regarding how restorative principles can be integrated into existing systems in ways that modify or transform the operation of these systems as a whole. The precise institutional weight given to restorative justice is hugely important in terms of the overall direction and orientation of juvenile justice, from the point of police contact through to the use of detention centres.

In its practical forms, restorative justice also places great faith in community-based and community-oriented solutions to youthful offending. That is, it encourages greater public participation in addressing victim concerns and needs, and takes into account the context and conditions under which certain types of youth offending occur. It is an active model of justice, yet concerns have been raised about the potential net-widening effect of early intervention forms of juvenile conferencing (especially in respect to relatively minor or first offences). One might also wonder about the potential negative impact of conferencing on those young people who may not have the family or friendship resources to respond adequately to the emotional and resource demands of conference processes and agreements.

Yet another practical problem relates to the fact that most young people are members of peer networks of some kind. There have been cases, for example, where an individual offender has attended a conference, has been publicly shamed during the conference process, and has agreed to make recompense to the victim. The offender's friends, however—some of whom have attended the conference—have ended up taking revenge on the victim (outside the conference, at a later date, and through violent means) for the perceived humiliation the offender suffered at the conference. Sometimes it is easy to forget that important affective ties bind individual young people into affinity groups. This has implications not only for the manner in which offending occurs (that is, in groups) but also for how specific incidents might be responded to by the criminal justice system. Individualised justice, whether in the form of conferences or otherwise, does not adequately address the collective nature of much offending behaviour.

Finally, while the restorative justice framework provides a vital starting point for juvenile justice reform, much more needs to be done to explore conceptually and practically the links between restorative justice and social justice. Given the disadvantaged backgrounds and circumstances of most officially designated young offenders, these are not trivial issues. They go to the heart of the criminal justice system and societal relationships generally. Unless the responses to youthful offending begin to address wider structural issues of (among others) unemployment, poverty, and homelessness, it is hard to see what, in fact, is being 'restored' for the offender. Victims and offenders need to be nurtured and respected as human beings. Being held accountable or being encouraged to participate are not sufficient in themselves to rectify unpleasant situations and environments that generate much of the pressure or impetus to offend in the first place. Social empowerment and community development objectives remain as pertinent as ever in any discussion of juvenile justice reform and innovative practice, including restorative justice.

BIBLIOGRAPHY

Access to Justice Advisory Committee (1994) *Access to Justice: An Action Plan*, Australian Government Publishing Service, Canberra.

Acorn, A. (2004) *Compulsory Compassion: A Critique of Restorative Justice*, UBC Press, Vancouver.

Adelaide, City (1997) *OutaSpace Youth Speak: Views and Proposals from a Forum on Young People's Access to Public Space in the City of Adelaide*, City of Adelaide.

Alder, C. (1984) 'Gender Bias in Juvenile Diversion', *Crime and Delinquency*, 30(3) July.

—— (1985) 'Theories of Female Delinquency', in Borowski, A. & Murray, J. (eds) *Juvenile Delinquency in Australia*, Methuen, Sydney.

—— (1986) '"Unemployed Women Have Got It Heaps Worse": Exploring the Implications of Female Youth Unemployment', *Australian and New Zealand Journal of Criminology*, 19(3): 210–24.

—— (1991) 'Victims of Violence: The Case of Homeless Youth', *Australian and New Zealand Journal of Criminology*, 24(1): 1–14.

—— (1993) 'Services for Young Women: Future Directions', in Atkinson, L. & Gerull, S.-A. (eds) *National Conference on Juvenile Justice: Conference Proceedings*, Australian Institute of Criminology, Canberra.

—— (1994) 'The Policing of Young Women', in White, R. & Alder, C. (eds) *The Police and Young People in Australia*, Cambridge University Press, Melbourne.

—— (1997) 'Theories of Female Delinquency', in Borowski, A. & O'Connor, I. (eds) *Juvenile Crime, Justice and Corrections*, Longman, Melbourne.

—— (1998) 'Young Women and Juvenile Justice: Objectives, Frameworks and Strategies', in Alder, C. (ed.) *Juvenile Crime and Juvenile Justice*, Australian Institute of Criminology Research and Public Policy Series No. 14, Australian Institute of Criminology, Canberra.

—— & Polk, K. (1985) 'Diversion Programmes', in Borowski, A. & Murray, J. (eds) *Juvenile Delinquency in Australia*, Methuen, Melbourne.

—— (2001) *Child Victims of Homicide*, Cambridge University Press, Melbourne.

Alder, C., O'Connor, I., Warner, K. & White, R. (1992) *Perceptions of the Treatment of Juveniles in the Legal System*, National Youth Affairs Research Scheme, National Clearinghouse for Youth Studies, Hobart.

Alder, C. & Baines, M. (eds) (1996) *And When She was Bad? Working with Young Women in Juvenile Justice and Related Areas*, National Clearinghouse for Youth Studies, Hobart.

Allen, J. (1990) '"The Wild Ones": The Disavowal of Men in Criminology', in Graycar, R. (ed.) *Dissenting Opinions*, Allen & Unwin, Sydney.

Alston, P., Parker, S. & Seymour, J. (eds) (1992) *Children, Rights and the Law*, Clarendon Press, Oxford.

Asher, G. (1986) *Custody and Control: The Social Worlds of Imprisoned Youth*, Allen & Unwin, Sydney.

Atkinson, L. (1997) 'Juvenile Correctional Institutions', in Borowski, A. & O'Connor, I. (eds) *Juvenile Crime, Justice and Corrections*, Longman, Melbourne.

Attwood, B. (1989) *The Making of the Aborigines*, Allen & Unwin, Sydney.

Aumair, M. & Warren, I. (1994) 'Characteristics of Juvenile Gangs in Melbourne', *Youth Studies Australia*, 13(2): 40–4.

Australian Bureau of Statistics (2003) *Crime and Safety*, Australia, 4509.0, Australian Bureau of Statistics, Sydney.

—— (2004) *Crime and Safety*, New South Wales, 4509.1, Australian Bureau of Statistics, Sydney.

—— and National Youth Affairs Research Scheme (1993) *Australia's Young People*, Commonwealth of Australia, Canberra.

Australian Council of Social Services (1992) 'A Day of Action on Unemployment', special insert, *Social Welfare Impact*, 22(4).

—— (2001) *Breaching the Safety Net: The harsh impact of social security penalties*, ACOSS, Sydney.

Australian Institute of Criminology (2004) *Australian Crime: Facts and Figures*, AIC, Canberra.

Australian Institute of Health and Welfare (1996) *Australia's Health*, AIHW, Canberra.

Australian Law Reform Commission (1992) *Multiculturalism and the Law* (Report No. 57), Commonwealth of Australia, Sydney.

—— (2005) *Sentencing Federal Offenders*, Discussion Paper 70, Commonwealth of Australia, Sydney.

—— (ALRC) and Human Rights and Equal Opportunity Commission (HREOC) (1997) *Seen and Heard: Priority for Children in the Legal Process*, Australian Law Reform Commission Report No 84, Sydney.

Baker, J. (1998) *Juvenile in Crime—Part 1: Participation Rates and Risk Factors*. NSW Bureau of Crime Statistics and Research, Attorney-General's Department, Sydney.

Bargen, J. (1994) 'In Need of Care: Delinquent Young Women in a Delinquent System', in Atkinson, L. & Gerull, S.-A. (eds) *National Conference on Juvenile Detention: Conference Proceedings*, Australian Institute of Criminology, Canberra.

Bartemucci, M. (1996) 'Aboriginal Young Women: New Challenges' in Alder, C. & Baines, M. (eds) *And When She was Bad? Working with Young Women in Juvenile Justice and Related Areas*, National Clearinghouse for Youth Studies, Hobart.

Bayley, D. (1999) *Capacity-building in Law Enforcement, Trends and Issues in Crime and Criminal Justice*, No.123, Australian Institute of Criminology, Canberra.

Bazemore, G. (1991) 'Beyond Punishment, Surveillance and Traditional Treatment: Themes for a new mission in U.S. Juvenile Justice', in Hackler, J. (ed.) *Official Responses to Problem Juveniles: Some International Reflections*, Onati International Institute for the Sociology of Law, Onati, Spain.

—— (1997) 'The "Community" in Community Justice: Issues, Themes, and Questions for the New Neighbourhood Sanctioning Models', *Justice System Journal*, 19(2): 193–227.

—— & Umbreit, M. (1995) 'Rethinking the Sanctioning Function in Juvenile Court: Retributive or Restorative Responses to Youth Crime', *Crime & Delinquency*, 41(3): 296–316.

Bazemore, G. & Walgrave, L. (1999a) 'Restorative Juvenile Justice: In Search of Fundamentals and an Outline for Systemic Reform', in Bazemore, G. & Walgrave, L. (eds) *Restorative Juvenile Justice: Repairing the Harm of Youth Crime*, Criminal Justice Press, Monsey, New York.

—— (eds) (1999b) *Restorative Juvenile Justice: Repairing the Harm of Youth Crime*, Criminal Justice Press, Monsey, New York.

Becker, H. (1963) *Outsiders: Studies in the Sociology of Deviance*, Free Press, New York.

Beikoff, L. (1996) 'Queensland's Juvenile Justice System: Equity, Access and Justice for Young Women?', Alder, C. & Baines, M. (eds) *And When She was Bad? Working with Young Women in Juvenile Justice and Related Areas*, National Clearinghouse for Youth Studies, Hobart.

Benda, B. (1987) 'Comparison Rates of Recidivism Among Status Offenders and Delinquents', *Adolescence*, 37(5): 31–4.

Berger, P. & Luckmann, T. (1971) *The Social Construction of Reality*, Allen Lane, London.

Bernard, T. J. (1992) *The Cycle of Juvenile Justice*, Oxford University Press, New York.

Bessant, J. & Hil, R. (eds) (1997) *Youth, Crime and the Media*, National Clearinghouse for Youth Studies, Hobart.

Beyer, L., Reid, G. & Crofts, N. (2001) 'Ethnic Based Differences in Drug Offending', *Australian and New Zealand Journal of Criminology*, 34(2): 169–81.

Bhathal, A. (1998) 'Culturally Accessible Justice or Cultural Curse? Family Group Conferencing and Vietnamese Juvenile Offending', Master's thesis, School of Law and Legal Studies, La Trobe University, Melbourne.

Bilchik, S. (1996) *Curfew: An Answer to Juvenile Delinquency and Victimization?* Office of Juvenile Justice and Delinquency Prevention, Washington, DC.

—— (1998) *Guide for Implementing the Balanced and Restorative Justice Model*, Office of Juvenile Justice and Delinquency Prevention, Washington, DC.

Biondo, S. & Palmer, D. (1993) *Federation of Community Legal Centres Report into Mistreatment by Police*, 1991–92, FCLC, Melbourne.

Bird, G. (1988) *The Process of Law in Australia: Intercultural perspectives*, Butterworths, Sydney.

Bishop, S. (1992) 'Rehabilitation the Primary Aim', *Law Society Journal*, May 1992, 76–7.

Blacktown Youth Services Association (1997) *Not Just Buses and Trains: Young People and Public Transport Interchanges in the Blacktown Local Government Area* [information pamphlet], Blacktown Youth Services Association, Sydney.

—— and Holroyd/Parramatta Migrant Services (1992) *NESB Youth Needs in Blacktown and Parramatta: Strategic Plan Summary*, Blacktown Youth Services Association, Blacktown.

Blagg, H. (1997) 'A Just Measure of Shame? Aboriginal Youth and Conferencing in Australia', *British Journal of Criminology*, 37(4): 481–506.

—— (1998) 'Restorative Visions and Restorative Justice Practices: Conferencing, Ceremony and Reconciliation in Australia', *Current Issues in Criminal Justice*, 10(1): 5–14.

—— & Valuri, G. (2004) 'Self-policing and Community Safety: The Work of Aboriginal Community Patrols in Australia', *Current Issues in Criminal Justice*, 15(3): 205–19.

Blagg, H. & Wilkie, M. (1995) *Young People and Police Powers*, The Australian Youth Foundation, Sydney.

Borowski, A. (1997) 'Working with Juvenile Offenders in Correctional Settings: Practice with the Involuntary Client', in Borowski, A. & O'Connor, I. (eds) *Juvenile Crime, Justice & Corrections*, Longman, Melbourne.

Bottomley, K. & Coleman, C. (1981) *Understanding Crime Rates*, Gower, [publisher], Aldershot.

Bowlby, J. (1947) *Forty-Four Juvenile Thieves: Their Character and Home Life*, Bailliere, Tindall, & Cox, London.

—— (1952) *Maternal Care and Mental Health*, World Health Organisation, Geneva.

Brady, M. (1985) 'Aboriginal Youth and the Juvenile Justice System', in Borowski, A. & Murray, J. (eds) *Juvenile Delinquency in Australia*, Methuen, Sydney.

Braithwaite, J. (1989). *Crime, Shame and Reintegration*, Cambridge University Press, Cambridge.

—— (1993) 'Juvenile Offending: New Theory and Practice', in Atkinson, L. & Gerull, S.-A. (eds) *National Conference on Juvenile Justice: Conference Proceedings*, Australian Institute of Criminology, Canberra.

—— (1999) 'Restorative Justice: Assessing Optimistic and Pessimistic Accounts', in Tonry, M. (ed.) *Crime and Justice: A Review of Research*, Vol. 25, University of Chicago Press, Chicago: 1–127.

Braithwaite, J. & Chappell, D. (1994) 'The Job Compact and Crime: Submission to the Committee on Employment Opportunities', *Current Issues in Criminal Justice*, 5(3): 295–300.

Braithwaite, J. & Pettit, P. (1990) *Not Just Deserts: A Republican Theory of Criminal Justice*, Clarendon Press, Oxford.

Brake, M. (1985) *Comparative Youth Culture*, Routledge & Kegan Paul, London.

Broadhurst, R. & Loh, N. (1993) 'Selective Incapacitation and the Phantom of Deterrence', in Harding, R. (ed.) *Juvenile Repeat Offenders*, Crime Research Centre, University of Western Australia, Perth.

Brook, J. & Kohen, J. (1991) *The Parramatta Native Institution and the Black Town*, UNSW Press, Sydney.

Brown, M. & Polk, K. (1996) 'Taking Fear of Crime Seriously: The Tasmanian Approach to Community Crime Prevention', *Crime & Delinquency*, 42(3): 398–420.

Bruce, J. (1997) 'Crime Prevention is a Suburban Shopping Centre: An Analysis of Young People's Use of the Chadstone Shopping Centre', Honours thesis, Department of Criminology, University of Melbourne.

Buchanan, C. & Hartley, P. (1992) *Criminal Choice: The Economic Theory of Crime and its Implications for Crime Control*, Centre for Independent Studies, Sydney.

Burley, J. (1995) 'Issues of Access and Equity: Barriers to reform', *Criminology Australia*, 6(4): 15–19.

Buttrum, K. (1998) 'Juvenile Justice: What works and what doesn't', in Alder, C. (ed.) *Juvenile Crime and Juvenile Justice*, Australian Institute of Criminology Research and Public Policy Series No. 14, Australian Institute of Criminology, Canberra.

Byrne, J. (1995) 'Youth Service', Footscray Drug & Safer Community Forum Proceedings, Melbourne, 13 September.

Cain, Maureen (1989) 'Introduction: Feminists Transgress Criminology', in Cain, M. (ed.) *Growing Up Good*, Sage, London.

Cain, Michael (1994a) *Juveniles in Detention. Special Needs Groups: Young Women, Aboriginal and Indo-Chinese Detainees*, Information and Evaluation Series No. 3, Department of Juvenile Justice, Sydney.

—— (1994b) 'Diversion from Custody and Rehabilitation of Juvenile Detainees: Management Philosophies of the NSW Department of Juvenile Justice', *Youth Studies Australia*, 13(1): 29–35.

—— (1994c) 'A Profile of Juveniles in NSW Juvenile Justice Centres', in Atkinson, L. & Gerull, S.-A. (eds) *National Conference on Juvenile Justice: Conference Proceedings*, Australian Institute of Criminology, Canberra.

—— (1996) *Recidivism of Juvenile Offenders in New South Wales*, NSW Department of Juvenile Justice, Sydney.

Cameron, L. & Thorsborne, M. (2001) 'Restorative Justice and School Discipline: Mutually Exclusive?', in Strang, H. & Braithwaite, J. (eds) *Restorative Justice and Civil Society*, Cambridge University Press, Cambridge.

Campbell, I. (1997) 'Beyond Unemployment: The Challenge of Increased Precarious Employment', *Just Policy*, No. 11: 4–20.

Carcach, C. & Leverett, S. (1999) *Recidivism Among Juvenile Offenders: An Analysis of Times to Reappearance in Court*, Research and Public Policy Series No. 17, Australian Institute of Criminology, Canberra.

Carcach, C. & Muscat, G. (1999) *Juveniles in Australian Corrective Institutions 1981–1998*, Research and Public Policy Series No. 20, Australian Institute of Criminology, Canberra.

Carlen, P. (1992) 'Women, Crime, Feminism and Realism', in Lowman, J. & MacLean, B. (eds) *Realist Criminology: Crime control and policing in the 1990s*, University of Toronto Press, Toronto.

Carrington, K. (1993) *Offending Girls*, Allen & Unwin, Sydney.

—— (2006) 'Does Feminism Spoil Girls? Explanations for Rises in Female Delinquency', *Australian and New Zealand Journal of Criminology*, 39(1).

Carter, J. (ed.) (1991) *Measuring Child Poverty*, Brotherhood of St Laurence, Melbourne.

Casburn, M. (1979) *Girls Will be Girls*, Explorations in Feminism, Willow Run Research Center, London.

Castles, S., Kalantzis, M., Cope, B. & Morrissey, M. (1990) *Mistaken Identity: Multiculturalism and the Demise of Nationalism in Australia*, Pluto Press, Sydney.

Catalano, R. & Hawkins, J. (1996) 'The Social Development Model: A Theory of Antisocial Behavior', in Hawkins, J. (ed.) *Delinquency and Crime: Current Theories*, Cambridge University Press, New York.

Centre for Labour Studies (1997) *Regional Youth Unemployment Profile—1988–96*, Vol. 1, No. 1, Centre for Labour Studies, University of Adelaide, Adelaide.

Challenger, D. (1997) 'The Launceston Mall', Corporate Security and Loss Prevention Paper, Coles Myer Limited, Coles Myer, Launceston.

Chan, C. & Cunneen, C. (2000) *Evaluation of the Implementation of the New South Wales Police Service Aboriginal Strategic Plan*, Institute of Criminology, Sydney.

Chan, J. (1994) 'Policing Youth in "Ethnic" Communities: Is Community Policing the Answer?', in White R. & Alder C. (eds) *The Police and Young People in Australia*, Cambridge University Press, Melbourne.

—— (1996) 'Police Racism: Experiences and reforms', in Vasta, E. & Castles, S. (eds) *The Teeth Are Smiling: The Persistence of Racism in Multicultural Australia*, Allen & Unwin, Sydney.

—— (1997) *Changing Police Culture: Policing in a Multicultural Society*, Cambridge University Press, Melbourne.

—— (ed) (2005) *Reshaping Juvenile Justice: The NSW Young Offenders Act 1997*, Sydney Institute of Criminology, Sydney.

Chatterton, P. & Hollands, R. (2003) *Urban Nightscapes: Youth cultures, pleasure spaces and corporate power*, Routledge, London.

Chen, S., Matruglio, T., Weatherburn, D. & Hua, J. (2005) 'The Transition from Juvenile to Adult Criminal Careers', *Contemporary Issues in Crime and Justice*, No.86, NSW Bureau of Crime Statistics and Research, Sydney.

Chesney-Lind, M. (1974) 'Juvenile Delinquency and the Sexualisation of Female Crime', *Psychology Today*, July: 4–7.

Chesney-Lind, M. & Shelden, R. (1992) Girls, *Delinquency and Juvenile Justice*, Brooks/Cole Publishing, Belmont.

Chisholm, R. (1988) 'Towards an Aboriginal Child Placement Principle: A View from New South Wales', in Morse, B. & Woodman, G. (eds) *Indigenous Law and the State*, Foris Publications, Dordrecht.

Church Council on Justice and Corrections (1996) *Satisfying Justice: Safe Community Options that Attempt to Repair Harm from Crime and Reduce the Use or Length of Imprisonment*, Church Council on Justice and Corrections, Ottawa.

Cicourel, A. (1976) *The Social Organisation of Juvenile Justice*, Heinemann, London.

Clancey, G. & Kirwin, D. (1996) 'Young Women in Custody: The Yasmar Experience', in Alder, C. & Baines, M. (eds) (1996) *And When She was Bad? Working with Young Women in Juvenile Justice and Related Areas*, National Clearinghouse for Youth Studies, Hobart.

Clarke, J. (1985) 'Whose Justice? The Politics of Juvenile Control', *International Journal of the Sociology of Law*, 13: 407–21.

——, Hall, S., Jefferson, T. & Roberts, B. (1976) 'Subcultures, Cultures and Class: A Theoretical Overview', in Hall, S. & Jefferson, T. (eds) *Resistance Through Rituals: Youth Subcultures in Post-War Britain*, Hutchinson, London.

Clarke, R. (ed.) (1992) *Situational Crime Prevention: Successful Case Studies*, Harrow & Heston, New York.

Clinard, B. (1974) *The Sociology of Deviant Behaviour*, Holt, Rinehart & Winston, New York.

Cloward, R. & Ohlin, L. (1960) *Delinquency and Opportunity: A Theory of Delinquent Gangs*, Free Press, Chicago.

Cohen, A. (1955) *Delinquent Boys: The Culture of the Gang*, Free Press, Chicago.

Cohen, P. (1979) 'Policing the Working-Class City', in Fine et al. (eds) *Capitalism and the Rule of Law*, Hutchinson, London.

Cohen, S. (1973) *Folk Devils and Moral Panics*, Paladin, London.

—— (1979) 'The Punitive City: Notes on the Dispersal of Social Control', *Contemporary Crises*, 3: 339–63.

—— (1985) *Visions of Social Control: Crime, Punishment and Classification*, Polity Press, Cambridge.

Collier, R. (1998) *Masculinities, Crime and Criminality*, Sage, London.

Collins, J., Noble, G., Poynting, S. & Tabar, P. (2000) *Kebabs, Kids, Cops and Crime: Youth, Ethnicity and Crime*, Pluto Press, Sydney.

Collis, M. & Griffin, M. (1993) 'Developing a Course for Young Offenders', *Youth Studies Australia*, 12(3): 25–8.

Community Services Commission (1996) *The Drift of Children in Care into the Juvenile Justice System*, Community Services Commission, Sydney.

Comstock, G. D. (1991) *Violence Against Lesbians and Gay Men*, Columbia University Press, New York.

Connell, R. W. (1987) *Gender and Power*, Allen & Unwin, Sydney.

—— (1995) *Masculinities*, Allen & Unwin, Sydney.

—— (2000) *The Men and the Boys*, Allen & Unwin, Sydney.

Conway, E. (1992) 'Digging into Disorder: Some Initial Reflections on the Tyneside Riots', *Youth and Policy*, 37: 4–14.

Copeland, J. & Howard, J. (1997) 'Substance Abuse and Juvenile Crime', in Borowski, A. & O'Connor, I. (eds) *Juvenile Crime, Justice and Corrections*, Longman, Melbourne.

—— (2001) 'Alcohol and Other Drug Issues amongst New South Wales Juvenile Detainees', paper presented at Australia's First Forensic Psychology Conference, Sydney, 7–11 February 2001.

Coulter, K. (2001) 'Drug Harm Minimisation, Creating Change: The role of the Arts as a program response in the "Rehabilitation" of Young Female Serious Offenders in Detention.' Bachelor of Arts (Honours) thesis, Department of Criminology, University of Melbourne.

Coumarelos, C. (1994) *Juvenile Offending: Predicting Persistence and Determining Cost-Effectiveness of Interventions*, NSW Bureau of Crime Statistics and Research, Sydney.

Coumarelos, C. & Weatherburn, D. (1995) 'Targeting Intervention Strategies to Reduce Juvenile Recidivism', *Australian and New Zealand Journal of Criminology*, 28(1): 55–72.

Coventry, G., Muncie, J., & Walters, R. (1992) *Rethinking Social Policy for Young People and Crime Prevention*, Discussion Paper No. 1, National Centre for Socio-Legal Studies, La Trobe University, Melbourne.

Coventry, G. & Polk, K. (1985) 'Theoretical Perspectives on Juvenile Delinquency', in Borowski, A. & Murray, J. (eds) *Juvenile Delinquency in Australia*, Methuen, Sydney.

Cowlishaw, G. (1988) *Black, White or Brindle*, Cambridge University Press, Cambridge.

Cozens, M. (1993) 'Ensuring Detention is a Last Resort for Young Women', paper presented to Youth 93: The Regeneration Conference, Hobart, 3–5 November 1993.

Crane, P. (1993) 'The United Nations and Juvenile Justice: An Overview', *Transitions*, 3(3): 41–7.

—— (2000) 'Young People and Public Space: Developing Inclusive Policy and Practice', *Scottish Youth Issues Journal*, 1(1): 105–24.

—— & Heywood, P. with Earl, G., Egginton, A. & Gleeson, J. (1997) *Young People and Major Centres: The Development of Principles for Design, Planning and Management guidelines in Brisbane City*, Brisbane City Council.

Crane, P. & Marston, G. (1999) *The Myer Centre Youth Protocol: A Summary*, Brisbane City Council, Brisbane.

Crawford, A. (1998) *Crime Prevention & Community Safety: Politics, Policies & Practices*, Longman, London.

—— & Clear, T. (2001) 'Community Justice: Transforming Communities through Restorative Justice?', in Bazemore, G. & Schift, M. (eds) *Restorative Community Justice*, Anderson Publishing, Cincinnati.

Criminal Law Review Division (2000) *A Review of the Law on the Age of Criminal Responsibility of Children*, NSW Attorney-General's Department, Sydney.

Cunneen, C. (1985) 'Working Class Boys and Crime: Theorising the Class/Gender Mix', in Patton, P. & Poole, R. (eds) *War/Masculinity*, Intervention Publications, Sydney.

—— (1990) *A Study of Aboriginal Juveniles and Police Violence*, Human Rights and Equal Opportunity Commission, Sydney.

—— (1993) 'Juvenile Justice Compromise in NSW', *Alternative Law Journal*, 18(4): 186–7.

—— (1994) 'Enforcing Genocide? Aboriginal Young People and the Police', in White, R. & Alder, C. (eds) *The Police and Young People in Australia*, Cambridge University Press, Melbourne.

—— (1995) 'Ethnic Minority Youth and Juvenile Justice: Beyond the Stereotype of Ethnic Gangs', in Guerra, C. & White, R. (eds) *Ethnic Minority Youth in Australia: Challenges and Myths*, National Clearinghouse for Youth Studies, Hobart.

—— (1997) 'Community Conferencing and the Fiction of Indigenous Control', *Australian and New Zealand Journal of Criminology*, 30(3): 292–311.

—— (1999) 'Zero Tolerance Policing and the Experience of New York City', *Current Issues in Criminal Justice*, 10(3): 299–313.

—— (2001a) *Conflict, Politics and Crime. Aboriginal Communities and the Police*, Allen & Unwin, Sydney.

—— (2001b) 'Reparations, Human Rights and the Challenge of Confronting a Recalcitrant Government', *Third World Legal Studies Journal*, Special Volume on Reconstruction and Reparations in International Law, Volume 2000/2001.

—— (2002) 'Mandatory Sentencing and Human Rights', *Current Issues in Criminal Justice*, 13(3): 322–7.

—— (2005) *Evaluation of the Queensland Aboriginal and Torres Strait Islander Justice Agreement*, Institute of Criminology, University of Sydney, Sydney.

——, Findlay, M., Lynch, R. & Tupper, V. (1989) *Dynamics of Collective Conflict. Riots at the Bathurst Motorcycle Races*, Law Book Company, North Ryde.

Cunneen, C., Fraser, D. & Tomsen, S. (1997) 'Introduction: Defining the Issues', in Cunneen, C., Fraser, D. & Tomsen, S. (eds) *Faces of Hate: Hate Crime in Australia*, Hawkins Press, Sydney.

Cunneen, C. & Kerley, K. (1995) 'Indigenous Women and Criminal Justice: Some Comments on the Australian Situation', in Hazlehurst, K. (ed.) *Perceptions of Justice: Issues in Indigenous and Community Empowerment*, Avebury, Aldershot.

Cunneen, C. & Libesman, T. (2001) 'Cultural Rights, Human Rights and the Contemporary Removal of Aboriginal and Torres Strait Islander Children from their Families', in Garkawe, S., Kelly, L. & Fisher, W. (eds) *Indigenous Human Rights*, Sydney Institute of Criminology, Sydney.

Cunneen, C. & Luke, G. (2006) *Evaluation of the Aboriginal Over-Representation Strategy*, Report to the NSW Department of Juvenile Justice, Sydney.

Cunneen, C. & McDonald, D. (1997) *Keeping Aboriginal and Torres Strait Islander People Out of Custody: An Evaluation of the Implementation of the Recommendations of the Royal Commission into Aboriginal Deaths in Custody*, Aboriginal and Torres Strait Islander Commission, Canberra.

Cunneen, C. & Morrow, J. (1994) 'Alternative Penal Sanctions', in Tay, A. & Leung, C. (eds) *Australian Law and Legal Thinking in the 1990s*, Faculty of Law, University of Sydney, Sydney.

Cunneen, C. & Robb, T. (1987) *Criminal Justice in North-west New South Wales*, NSW Bureau of Crime Statistics and Research, Sydney.

Cunneen, C. & White, R. (1995) *Juvenile Justice: An Australian Perspective*, Oxford University Press, Melbourne.

Daly, K. (2000) 'Restorative Justice in Diverse and Unequal Societies', *Law in Context*, 17(1): 167–90.

—— (2002) 'Restorative Justice: the Real Story', *Punishment and Society*, 4(1): 55–79.

Daly, K. & Hayes, H. (2001) *Restorative Justice and Conferencing in Australia*, Trends and Issues in Crime and Criminal Justice, No. 186, Australian Institute of Criminology, Canberra.

Daniel, A. & Cornwall, J. (1993) *A Lost Generation?* Australian Youth Foundation, Sydney.

Darcy, D. (2005) 'Policing the Socially Disadvantaged, the Value of Rekindling Community Policing in Woolloomooloo – A Police Commander's perspective', *Current Issues in Criminal Justice*, 17(1): 144–53.

Datesman, S. & Scarpitti, F. (1980) 'Unequal Protection for Males and Females in the Juvenile Court', in Datesman, S. & Scarpitti, F. (eds) *Women, Crime and Justice*, Oxford University Press, Oxford.

Davies, J. (1995) Less Mickey Mouse, More Dirty Harry: Property, Policing and the Postmodern Metropolis', *Polemic*, 5(2): 63–9.

Davis, M. (1994). *Beyond Bladerunner: Urban Control and the Ecology of Fear*, Open Magazine Pamphlet Series No. 23, Westfield, New Jersey.

Dennison, S., Stewart, A. & Hurren, E. (2006) 'Police Cautioning in Queensland: The Impact on Juvenile Offending Pathways', *Trends and Issues* No 306, Australian Institute of Criminology, Canberra.

Department of Aboriginal and Torres Strait Islander Policy and Development (DATSIPD) (1999) *Local Justices Initiatives Program. Interim Assessment of the Community Justice Groups*, Queensland Government, Brisbane.

Detrick, S. (1999) *A Commentary on the United Nations Convention on the Rights of the Child*, Martinus Nijhoff, The Hague.

Developmental Crime Prevention Consortium (1999) *Pathways to Prevention: Developmental and Early Intervention Approaches to Crime in Australia*, National Crime Prevention, Attorney-General's Department, Canberra.

Devery, C. (1991) *Disadvantage and Crime in New South Wales*, NSW Bureau of Crime Statistics, Sydney.

Dixon, D. (1998) 'Broken Windows, Zero Tolerance, and the New York Miracle', *Current Issues in Criminal Justice*, 10(1): 96–106.

Dixon, N. (2002) *Naming Juvenile Offenders – Juvenile Justice Amendment Bill 2002 (QLD)*, Research Brief No 22, Queensland Parliamentary Library, Brisbane.

Doan, V. (1995) 'Indo-Chinese Youth: Issues of culture and justice', in Guerra, C. & White, R. (eds) *Ethnic Minority Youth in Australia*, National Clearinghouse for Youth Studies, Hobart.

Dodson, M. (1993) *First Report Aboriginal and Torres Strait Islander Social Justice Commission*, Australian Government Publishing Service, Canberra.

—— (1995) Aboriginal and Torres Strait Islander Social Justice Commissioner Third Report, Australian Government Publishing Service, Canberra.

—— (1996) *Aboriginal and Torres Strait Islander Social Justice Commissioner Fourth Report*, Australian Government Publishing Service, Canberra.

Donzelot, J. (1979) *The Policing of Families*, Hutchinson, London.

Downes, D. (1966) *The Delinquent Solution*, Routledge & Kegan Paul, London.

Drugs and Crime Prevention Committee (1997) *Victorian Government's Drug Reform Strategy: Turning the Tide*, Victorian Government Printer, Melbourne.

D'Souza, N. (1990) 'Aboriginal Children and the Juvenile Justice System', *Aboriginal Law Bulletin*, 2(44): 4–5.

Dusseldorp Skills Forum (1998) *Australia's Youth: Reality and Risk*, Dusseldorp Skills Forum & Others, Sydney.

Easteal, P. (1989) *Vietnamese Refugees: Crime Rates of Minors and Youths in NSW*, Australian Institute of Criminology, Canberra.

—— (1997) 'Migrant Youth and Juvenile Justice', in Borowski, A. & O'Connor, I. (eds) *Juvenile Crime, Justice and Corrections*, Longman, Melbourne.

Edwards, C. & Read, P. (1988) *The Lost Children*, Doubleday, Moorebank.

Edwards, J., Oakley, R. & Carey, S. (1987) 'Street Life, Ethnicity and Social Policy', in Gaskell, G. & Benewick, R. (eds) *The Crowd in Contemporary Britain*, Sage, London.

Eisenstein, H. (1984) *Contemporary Feminist Thought*, Unwin Paperbacks, London.

Empey, L. (1982) *American Delinquency: Its Meaning and Construction*, Dorsey Press, Chicago.

Ericson, R., Baranek, P. & Chan, J. (1991). *Representing Order: Crime, law and justice in the news media*, University of Toronto Press, Toronto.

Ethnic Affairs Commission of NSW (1986) *Not a Single Problem: Not a Single Solution*, Ethnic Affairs Commission of NSW, Sydney.

Everitt, J. (2001) 'Mandatory Immigration Detention: Where are children's rights?', *Rights Now* (National Children's and Youth Law Centre), December: 3–4.

Eysenck, H. (1984) 'Crime and Personality', in Muller, D., Blackman, D. & Chapman, A. (eds) *Psychology and Law*, John Wiley & Sons, New York.

Farrell, A. (1992) *Crime, Class and Corruption: The Politics of the Police*, Bookmarks, London.

Farrington, D. (1996) 'The Development of Offending and Antisocial Behavior from Childhood to Adulthood', in Cordella, P. & Siegel, L. (eds) *Readings in Contemporary Criminological Theory*, Northeastern University Press, Boston.

Fasher, A. M., Dunbar, N., Rothenbury, B. A., Bebb, D. K. & Young, S. J. W. (1997) 'The Health of a Group of Young Australians in a New South Wales Juvenile Justice Detention Centre: A Pilot Study', *Journal of Paediatrics and Child Health*, 35(5): 426–9.

Federation of Ethnic Communities' Councils of Australia (FECCA) (1991) *Background Paper on Ethnic Youth*, paper prepared for FECCA's Multicultural Youth Conference, Sydney.

Felson, M. (1994) *Crime and Everyday Life: Insights and Implications for Society*, Pine Forge Press, London.

Ferdinand, T. N. (1989) 'Juvenile Delinquency or Juvenile Justice: Which Came First?', *Criminology*, 27(1): 79–106.

Ferrante, A., Loh, N., Maller, M. Valuri, G. & Fernandez, J. (2005) *Crime and Justice Statistics for Western Australia: 2004*, Crime Research Centre, Crawley.

Finnane, M. (1994) 'Larrikins, Delinquents and Cops: Police and Young People in Australian History', in White, R. & Alder, C. (eds) *The Police and Young People in Australia*, Cambridge University Press, Melbourne.

Fishbein, D. (1990) 'Biological Perspectives in Criminology', *Criminology*, 28(1): 27–72.

Fitzgerald, G. (1989) *Report of the Commission of Possible Illegal Activities and Associated Police Misconduct*, Queensland Government Printer, Brisbane.

Fitzgerald, J. (2000) *Knife Offences and Policing*, Crime and Justice Statistics, Bureau Brief No. 8, June 2000, New South Wales Bureau of Crime Statistics and Research, Sydney.

Floro, A. (2001) 'The Class that Won', *Rights Now*, National Children's and Youth Law Centre, Sydney, March 2001, 6–7.

Foote, P. (1993) 'Like, I'll tell you what happened from experience ... Perspectives on Italo-Australian youth gangs in Adelaide', in White, R. (ed.) *Youth Subcultures: Theory, History and the Australian Experience*, National Clearinghouse for Youth Studies, Hobart.

Forrester, L. (1999) 'Street Machiners and "Showing Off"', in White, R. (ed.) *Australian Youth Subcultures: On the Margins and In the Mainstream*, National Clearinghouse for Youth Studies, Hobart.

Foster, J. (1995) 'Informal Social Control and Community Crime Prevention', *British Journal of Criminology*, 35(4): 563–83.

Foucault, M. (1977) *Discipline and Punish: The Birth of the Prison*, Penguin, Harmondsworth.

Frazier, C. & Cochran, J. (1986) 'Detention of Juveniles: Its Effects on Subsequent Juvenile Court Processing', *Youth and Society*, 17(1): 286–305.

Freeman, K. (1996) *Young People and Crime*, Crime and Justice Bulletin No. 32, NSW Bureau of Crime Statistics and Research, Sydney.

Freiberg, A., Fox, R. & Hogan, M. (1988) *Sentencing Young Offenders*, Australian Law Reform Commission, Sentencing Research Paper 11, Sydney.

Freiberg, A. & Ross, S. (1995) 'Change and Stability in Sentencing: A Victorian study', *Law in Context*, 13(2): 107–42.

Furlong, A. & Cartmel, F. (1997) *Young People and Social Change*, Open University Press, Buckingham.

Gale, F., Bailey-Harris, R. & Wundersitz, J. (1990) *Aboriginal Youth and the Criminal Justice System*, Cambridge University Press, Cambridge.

Gallagher, P. & Poletti, P. (1998) *Sentencing Disparity and the Ethnicity of Juvenile Offenders*, Judicial Commission of NSW, Sydney.

Gallagher, P., Poletti, P. & MacKinnell, I. (1997) *Sentencing Disparity and the Gender of Juvenile Offenders*, Judicial Commission of NSW, Sydney.

Garland, D. (1985) *Punishment and Welfare: A History of Penal Sanctions*, Gower, Aldershot.

Gay Men and Lesbians Against Discrimination (GLAD) (1994) *Not a Day Goes By*, GLAD, Melbourne.

Geason, S. & Wilson, P. (1989) *Designing Out Crime: Crime Prevention Through Environmental Design*, Australian Institute of Criminology, Canberra.

Gelsthorpe, L. & Morris, A. (eds) (1990) *Feminist Perspectives in Criminology*, Open University Press, Milton Keynes.

Ghys, P. (1994) 'Aboriginals and the Juvenile Justice System. The Victorian Koori Justice Project', paper presented to the Australian Institute of Criminology, Aboriginal Justice Issues II Conference, Townsville, 14–17 June 1994.

Gibbons, D. (1977) *Society, Crime and Criminal Careers*, Prentice-Hall, Englewood Cliffs, NJ.

—— (1979) *The Criminological Enterprise: Theories and Perspectives*, Prentice-Hall, Englewood Cliffs, NJ.

Gillis, J. R. (1975) 'The Evolution of Juvenile Delinquency in England 1890–1914', *Past and Present*, 65: 96–126.

—— (1981) *Youth and History*, Academic Press, New York.

Gliksman, M. & Chen, J. (2001) 'Research Note: Changes in the Juvenile Crime Incidence Rate by Gender in New South Wales, Australia, 1991/2 to 1996/7', *Australia and New Zealand Journal of Criminology*, 34(3): 302–9.

Goodall, H. (1982) 'A History of Aboriginal Communities in NSW, 1909–1939', PhD thesis, University of Sydney, Sydney.

—— (1990) 'Saving the Children', *Aboriginal Law Bulletin*, 2(44): 6–9.

Goode, E. & Ben-Yehuda, N. (1994) 'Moral Panics: An Introduction', in Goode, E. & Ben-Yehuda, N. (eds) *Moral Panics: The Social Constructing of Deviance*, Blackwell, Oxford.

Gottfredson, M. & Hirschi, T. (1990) *A General Theory of Crime*, Stanford University Press, Stanford.

Grabosky, P. (1999) *Zero Tolerance Policing*, Trends and Issues in Crime and Criminal Justice, No. 102, Australian Institute of Criminology, Canberra.

—— & Wilson, P. (1989) *Journalism and Justice: How crime is reported*, Pluto Press, Sydney.

Grant, A. (2000) *The Historical Development of Treatment for Adolescent Sex Offenders*, Trends and Issues in Crime and Criminal Justice No. 145, Australian Institute of Criminology, Canberra.

Graycar, A. & Jamrozik, A. (1989) *How Australians Live: Social Policy in Theory and Practice*, Macmillan, Melbourne.

Gregory, R. & Hunter, B. (1995) *The Macro Economy and the Growth of Ghettos and Urban Poverty in Australia*, Discussion Paper No. 325, Centre for Economic Policy Research, Australian National University, Canberra.

Gregory, R. & Sheehan, P. (1998) 'Poverty and the Collapse of Full Employment', in Fincher, R. & Nieuwenhuysen, J. (eds) *Australian Poverty: Then and Now*, Melbourne University Press, Melbourne.

Grunseit, A., Weatherburn, D. & Donnelly, N. (2005) *School Violence and Its Antecedents: Interviews with High School Students*, NSW Bureau of Crime Statistics and Research, Sydney.

Guerra, C. & White, R. (eds) (1995) *Ethnic Minority Youth in Australia: Challenges and Myths*, National Clearinghouse for Youth Studies, Hobart.

Haebich, A. (2001) *For Their Own Good: Aborigines and Government in the South-West of Western Australia 1900–1940*, University of Western Australia Press, Perth.

Hage, G. (1998) *White Nation: Fantasies of White Supremacy in a Multicultural Society*, Pluto Press and Commerford & Miller Publishers, Sydney.

Hall, S. & Jefferson, T. (eds) (1976) *Resistance Through Rituals: Youth Subcultures in Post-War Britain*, Hutchinson, London.

——, Critcher, C. & Roberts, B. (1978) *Policing the Crisis: Mugging, the State, and Law and Order*, Macmillan, London.

Hamparian, D., Schuster, R., Dinitz, S. & Conrad, J. (1978) *The Violent Few: A Study of Dangerous Juvenile Offenders*, Lexington Books, Lexington.

Hancock, L. (1980) 'The Myth that Females are Treated More Leniently than Males in the Juvenile Justice System', *Australian and New Zealand Journal of Sociology*, 63: 4–13.

Hancock, L. & Chesney-Lind, M. (1982) 'Female Status Offenders and Justice Reforms: An International Perspective', *Australian and New Zealand Journal of Criminology*, 15(2): 109–23.

—— (1985) 'Juvenile Justice Legislation and Gender Discrimination', in Borowski, A. and Murray, J. (eds) *Juvenile Delinquency in Australia*, Methuen, Sydney.

Harding, R. & Maller, R. (1997) 'An Improved Methodology for Analyzing Age-Arrest Profiles: Application to a Western Australian Offender Population', *Journal of Quantitative Criminology*, 13(4): 349–72.

Harris, M. (2004) 'From Australian Courts to Aboriginal Courts in Australia–Bridging the Gap?', *Current Issues in Criminal Justice*, 16(1), July 2004.

Harris, R. & Webb, D. (1987) *Welfare, Power and Juvenile Justice*, Tavistock, London.

Hassan, R. (1996) *Social Factors in Suicide in Australia*, Trends and Issues in Crime and Criminal Justice, No. 52, Australian Institute of Criminology, Canberra.

Hayes, H. and Daly, K (2004) 'Conferencing and Re-offending in Queensland' *Australian and New Zealand Journal of Criminology*, 37(2): 167–91.

Hayter, C. (1994) *Youth Detention Centres: Policy and Legislation Comparative Research*, National Children's and Youth Law Centre, Sydney.

Hayward, K. (2002) 'The Vilification and Pleasures of Youthful Transgression', in Muncie, J., Hughes, G., & McLaughlin, E. (eds) *Youth Justice: Critical Readings*, Sage, London.

Healey, K. (ed.) (1996) *Youth Gangs*, Spinney Press, Sydney.

Hebdige, D. (1979) *Subculture: The meaning of style*, Methuen, London.

Hennessy, N. (1999) *Review of the Gate Keeping Role in the Young Offenders Act 1997* (NSW), Youth Justice Advisory Committee, Sydney.

Herek, G.M. & Berrill, K.T. (eds) (1992) *Hate Crimes: Confronting Violence Against Lesbians and Gay Men*, Sage, London.

Heywood, P. & Crane, P. with A. Egginton & J. Gleeson (1998) *Out and About: In or Out? Better Outcomes from Young People's Use of Public and Community Space in the City of Brisbane* (3 vols), Community Development Team West, Brisbane City Council, Brisbane.

Higgins, M. & Vinson, T. (1998) 'Social Disadvantage and Regional Youth Unemployment', *Uniya Brief Research Report*, No. 1, Uniya Jesuit Social Justice Centre, Sydney.

Hil, R. (1996) 'Crime Prevention and the Technologies of Social Order—A response to Philip Hill and Adam Sutton', *Just Policy*, No. 6: 59–62.

—— & Moyle, P. (1992) 'A Day in Prison: A Solution to Reducing Juvenile Recidivism Rates?', *Alternative Law Journal*, 17(5): 224–7.

Hill, P. & Sutton, A. (1996) 'Crime Prevention: Not just Neighbourhood Watch and street lighting', *Just Policy*, No. 6: 54–8.

Hirschfield, A. & Bowers, K. (1997) 'The Effect of Social Cohesion on Levels of Recorded Crime in Disadvantaged Areas', *Urban Studies*, 34(8): 1274–302.

Hirschi, T. (1969) *Causes of Delinquency*, University of California Press, Berkeley and Los Angeles.

Hirschi, T. & Gottfredson, M. (1983) 'Age and the Explanation of Crime', *American Journal of Sociology*, 89(3): 552–84.

Hogg, R. & Brown, D. (1998) *Rethinking Law and Order*, Pluto Press, Sydney.

Hogg, R. & Golder, H. (1987) 'Policing Sydney in the Late Nineteenth Century', in Finnane, M. (ed.) *Policing in Australia: Historical Perspectives*, UNSW Press, Sydney.

Hollands, R. (1995) *Friday Night, Saturday Night: Youth Cultural Identification in the Post-Industrial City*, Department of Social Policy, University of Newcastle, Newcastle Upon Tyne.

Howard, J. & Zibert, E. (1990) 'Curious, Bored and Wanting to Feel Good: The Drug Use of Detained Young Offenders', *Drug and Alcohol Review*, 9: 225–31.

Howe, A. (1990) 'Sweet Dreams: Deinstitutionalising Young Women' in Graycar, R. (ed.) *Dissenting Opinions*, Allen & Unwin, Sydney.

Hughes, G. (1996). 'Strategies of Multi-Agency Crime Prevention and Community Safety in Contemporary Britain', *Studies on Crime & Crime Prevention*, 5(2): 221–44.

Human Rights and Equal Opportunity Commission (HREOC) (1991) *Racist Violence: Report of the National Inquiry into Racist Violence in Australia*, Australian Government Publishing Service, Canberra.

—— (1993a) *National Inquiry into the Human Rights of People with Mental Illness*, Australian Government Publishing Service, Canberra.

—— (1993b) *State of the Nation Report on People of Non-English Speaking Background*, Australian Government Publishing Service, Canberra.

—— (1999) *Sentencing Juvenile Offenders*, Human Rights Brief No. 2, Human Rights and Equal Opportunity Commission, Sydney.

—— (2004) *Ismae – Listen: National Consultations on Eliminating Prejudice Against Arab and Muslim Australians*, Human Rights and Equal Opportunity Commission, Sydney.

Humphries, S. (1981) *Hooligans or Rebels?* Basil Blackwell, Oxford.

Hunter, B. (1998) 'Addressing Youth Unemployment: Re-Examining Social and Locational Disadvantage within Australian Cities', *Urban Policy and Research*, 16(1): 47–58.

Hutchings, S. (1995) 'The Great Shoe Store Robbery', in Cowlinshaw, G. & Morris, B. (eds) *Racism Today*, Australian Institute of Aboriginal and Torres Strait Islander Studies Press, Canberra.

Iadicola, P. (1986) 'Community Crime Control Strategies', *Crime and Social Justice*, 25: 140–65.

Indermaur, D. & White, R. (1994) 'Juvenile Rights Given the Boot in Western Australia', *Civil Liberty*, 10(2): 12–14.

Jaggs, D. (1986) *Neglected and Criminal: Foundations of Child Welfare Legislation in Victoria*, Phillip Institute of Technology, Melbourne.

Jakubowicz, A. (1989) 'Social Justice and the Politics of Multiculturalism in Australia', *Social Justice*, 16(3): 69–86.

James, S. (1994) 'Contemporary Programs with Young People: Beyond Traditional Law Enforcement?', in White, R. & Alder, C. (eds) *The Police and Young People in Australia*, Cambridge University Press, Melbourne.

—— & Polk, K. (1989) 'Policing Youth: Themes and Directions', in Chappell, D. & Wilson, P. (eds) *Australian Policing: Contemporary Issues*, Butterworths, Sydney.

Jamrozik, A. (1984) 'Community Resources as a Component of the Social Wage: Implications for Youth Services', paper presented at a conference on community-based care, Adelaide.

—— (1987) 'Winners and Losers in the Welfare State: Recent Trends and Pointers to the Future', in Saunders, P. & Jamrozik, A. (eds) *Social Welfare in the Late 1980s: Reform, Progress or Retreat?* Social Welfare Research Centre, UNSW press, Sydney.

—— (1998) 'Transformation in the Youth Labour Market: An Empirical Examination 1945–1996', in Bessant, J. and Cook, S. (eds) *Against the Odds: Young People and Work*, Australian Clearinghouse for Youth Studies, Hobart.

Jamrozik, A., Boland, C. & Urquhart, R. (1995) *Social Change and Cultural Transformation in Australia*, Cambridge University Press, Melbourne.

Jefferson, T. (1996) 'Introduction', *British Journal of Criminology*, Special Issue on Masculinity and Crime, 36(3): 337–47.

Jeffrey, M. (1999) Growing Out of Crime? Young Men and the Victorian Youth Attendance Order, Master's thesis, Department of Criminology, University of Melbourne, Melbourne.

Jeffs, T. & Smith, M. (1996) '"Getting the Dirtbags off the Streets": Curfews and Other Solutions to Juvenile Crime', *Youth and Policy*, No. 53: 1–14.

Johnston, E. (1991) *National Report*, 5 vols, *Royal Commission into Aboriginal Deaths in Custody*, Australian Government Publishing Service, Canberra.

Jones, A. & Symth, P. (1999) 'Social Exclusion: A New Framework for Social Policy Analysis?', *Just Policy*, 17: 11–20.

Junger-Tas, J. (1994) 'Delinquency in Thirteen Western Countries: Some Preliminary Conclusions', in Junger-Tas, J., Terlouw, G.-J. & Klein, M. (eds) *Delinquency Behavior Among Young People in the Western World: First Results of the International Self-Report Delinquency Study*, Kugler Publications, Amsterdam.

Juvenile Justice Branch (1998) *Juvenile Offending and Recidivism in Queensland*, Department of Families, Youth and Community Care, Brisbane.

Kelly, L. & Oxley, E. (1999) 'A Dingo in Sheep's Clothing?' *Indigenous Law Bulletin*, 4(18).

Kersten, J. (1989) 'The Institutional Control of Boys and Girls', in Cain, M. (ed.) *Growing Up Good*, Sage, London.

Keys Young Pty Ltd (1997) *Juvenile Justice Services and Transition Arrangements*, A Report to the National Youth Affairs Research Scheme, National Clearinghouse for Youth Studies, Hobart.

Kraus, J. (1974) 'A Comparison of Corrective Effects of Probation and Detention on Male Juvenile Offenders', *British Journal of Criminology*, 8(1): 49–62.

—— (1977) 'Do Existing Penal Measures Reform Juvenile Offenders?', *Australian and New Zealand Journal of Criminology*, 10(3): 217–22.

—— (1978) 'Remand in Custody as a Deterrent in the Juvenile Jurisdiction', *British Journal of Criminology*, 18(3): 285–92.

—— (1981) 'On the Adult Criminality of Male Juvenile Delinquents', *Australian and New Zealand Journal Of Criminology*, 14(2): 157.

—— & Bowmaker, S. (1982) 'How Delinquent are the Delinquents? A Study of Self-reported Offences', *Australian and New Zealand Journal of Criminology*, 15(2): 163–9.

Krisberg, B. (2005) *Juvenile Justice: Redeeming Our Children*, Sage, Thousand Oaks.

Lamb, S. (1994) 'Dropping out of school in Australia: Recent Trends in Participation and Outcomes', *Youth and Society*, 26(2): 194–222.

Landt, J. & Scott, P. (1998) 'Youth Incomes', in Australia's Youth: Reality and Risk, Dusseldorp Skills Forum and Others, Sydney.

Lee, M. (2005) '"Fields of Fire": Crime, Dissent and Social Isolation in South-Western Sydney', in Julian, R., Rottier, R. & White, R. (eds) *TASA Conference Proceedings*, University of Tasmania, Hobart.

Lesbian and Gay Anti-Violence Project (1992) *The Off Our Backs Report: A Study into Anti-Lesbian Violence*, Gay and Lesbian Rights Lobby, Sydney.

Lincoln, R. & Wilson, P. (1994b) Questioning Crime Prevention: Towards a Social Development Approach, *Transitions*, 3(3): 7–11.

Loader, I. (1996) *Youth, Policing and Democracy*, Macmillan, London.

Loeber, R. & Farrington, D. (eds) (1998) *Serious & Violent Juvenile Offenders: Risk Factors and Successful Interventions*, Sage, Thousand Oaks.

Luke, G. (1988) 'Gaol as a Last Resort: The Situation for Juveniles', in Findlay, M. & Hogg, R. (eds) *Understanding Crime and Criminal Justice*, Law Book Company, Sydney.

Luke, G. & Cunneen, C. (1995) *Aboriginal Over-Representation and Discretionary Decisions in the NSW Juvenile Justice System*, Juvenile Justice Advisory Council of New South Wales, Sydney.

Luke, G. & Lind, B. (2002) *Reducing Juvenile Crime: Conferencing versus Court*, NSW Bureau of Crime Statistics and Research, Sydney.

Luker, T. (1997) *Juvenile Justice: Recent debates in the law*, Legal Information Access Centre, Sydney.

Lundman, R. (1994) *Prevention and Control of Juvenile Delinquency*, Oxford University Press, Oxford.

Lynch, M., Buckman, J. and Krenske, L. (2003) *Youth Justice: criminal Trajectories*, Research and Issues Paper No 4 July 2003, Crime and Misconduct Commission, Brisbane.

Lyons, E. (1995) 'New Clients, Old Problems: Vietnamese young people's experiences with police', in Guerra, C. & White, R. (eds) *Ethnic Minority Youth in Australia*, National Clearinghouse for Youth Studies, Hobart.

Mackay, M. (1996) 'Aboriginal Juveniles and the Criminal Justice System: The Case of Victoria', *Children Australia*, 21(3): 11–22.

Maher, L., Dixon, D., Swift, W. & Nguyen, T. (1997) *Anh Hai: Young Asian Background People's Perceptions and Experiences of Policing*, University of New South Wales Faculty of Law Research Monograph Series, Sydney.

Maher, L., Nguyen, T. & Le, T. (1999) 'Wall of Silence: Stories of Cabramatta Street Youth' in White, R. (ed.) *Australian Youth Subcultures: On the Margins and In the Mainstream*, National Clearinghouse for Youth Studies, Hobart.

Males, M. (1996) *The Scapegoat Generation: America's War on Adolescents*, Common Courage Press, Maine.

Mansell, M. (2000) 'Alternatives to Imprisonment', in Massina, M. & White, R. (eds) *Beyond Imprisonment: Conference Proceedings*, Tasmanian Council of Social Services and Criminology Research Unit, University of Tasmania, Hobart.

Marchetti, E., & Daly, K. (2004) 'Indigenous Courts and Justice Practices in Australia', *Trends and Issues No 277*, Australian Institute of Criminology, Canberra.

Markus, A. (1990) *Governing Savages*, Allen & Unwin, Sydney.

Marshall, J. (1999) *Zero Tolerance Policing*, Information Bulletin No. 9, Office of Crime Statistics, Attorney-General's Department, Adelaide.

Mason, G. (1997) 'Sexuality and Violence: Questions of Difference' in Cunneen, C., Fraser, D. & Tomsen, S. (eds) *Faces of Hate: Hate Crime in Australia*, Hawkins Press, Sydney.

Matza, D. (1964) *Delinquency and Drift*, John Wiley & Sons, New York.

Maunders, D. (1984) *Keeping Them off the Streets: A History of Voluntary Youth Organisations in Australia 1850–1980*, Phillip Institute of Technology, Melbourne.

Maxwell, G. & Morris, A. (1994) 'The New Zealand Model of Family Group Conferences', in Alder, C. & Wundersitz, J. (eds) *Family Conferencing and Juvenile Justice*, Australian Institute of Criminology, Canberra.

May, M. (1981) 'Innocence and Experience: The Evolution of the Concept of Juvenile Delinquency in the Mid-Nineteenth Century', in Dale, R. (ed.), *Education and the State*, vol. 2, Falmer Press, Lewes.

Mayhew, P. (2003) 'Counting the Costs of Crime in Australia', *Trends and Issues*, No 247, Australian Institute of Criminology, Canberra.

McCulloch, J. & Schetzer, L. (1993) *Brute Force: The Need for Affirmative Action in the Victoria Police Force*, Federation of Community Legal Centres (Victoria), Melbourne.

McGuire, J. (1995) 'Reviewing "What Works": Past, Present and Future', in McGuire, J. (ed.) *What Works: Reducing Reoffending—Guidelines from Research and Practice*, John Wiley & Sons, London.

McLaren, K. (2000) *Tough Is Not Enough—Getting Smart About Youth Crime: A Review of Research on What Works to Reduce Offending by Young People*, Ministry of Youth Affairs, Wellington.

McLaughlin, E., Fergusson, R., Hughes, G. & Westmarland, L. (2003) (eds) *Restorative Justice: Critical Issues*, Sage, London.

McNamara, L. (2002) *Regulating Racism: Racial Vilification Laws in Australia*, Sydney Institute of Criminology Monograph Series No.16, Sydney.

McRobbie, A. & Garber, J. (1976) 'Girls and Subcultures', in Hall, S. & Jefferson, T. (eds) *Resistance through Rituals: Youth Subcultures in Post-War Britain*, Hutchinson, London.

Merton, R. (1957) *Social Theory and Social Structure*, Free Press, New York.

Messerschmidt, J. (1993) *Masculinities and Crime*, Rowan & Littlefield, Maryland.

Meucci, S. & Redmon, J. (1997) 'Safe Spaces: California Children Enter a Policy Debate', *Social Justice*, 24(3): 139–51.

Miles, S., Cliff, D. & Burr, V. (1998) '"Fitting In and Sticking Out": Consumption, Consumer Meanings and the Construction of Young People's Identities', *Journal of Youth Studies*, 1(1): 81–96.

Miller, J.B. (1958) 'Lower Class Culture as a Milieu of Gang Delinquency', *Journal of Social Issues*, 14:3.

Miller, L. (1983) *Runaway Girls: Uncontrollable or Unsupported*, Marrickville Legal Centre, Sydney.

Milne, C. & Munro, L. Jnr (1981) 'Who is Unresponsive: Negative Assessments of Aboriginal Children', Discussion Paper No. 1, Aboriginal Children's Research Project, Family and Children's Services Agency, Sydney.

Moffatt, S., Weatherburn, D. and Donnelly, N. (2005) 'What Caused the Recent Drop in Property Crime?' *Crime and Justice Bulletin* No 85, NSW Bureau of Crime Statistics and Research, Sydney.

Moffitt, T. (1996) 'The Neuropsychology of Conduct Disorder', in Cordella, P. & Siegel, L. (eds) *Readings in Contemporary Criminological Theory*, Northeastern University Press, Boston.

Moore, E. (1994) 'Alternatives to Secure Detention for Girls', in Atkinson, L. & Gerull, S.-A. (eds) *National Conference on Juvenile Detention: Conference Proceedings*, Australian Institute of Criminology, Canberra.

Morgan, F. (1993) 'Contact with the Justice System over the Juvenile Years', in Atkinson, L. & Gerull, S.-A. (eds) *National Conference on Juvenile Justice: Conference Proceedings*, Australian Institute of Criminology, Canberra.

Morris, A. (1987) *Women, Crime and Criminal Justice*, Basil Blackwell, Oxford.

—— & Giller, H. (1987) *Understanding Juvenile Justice*, Croom Helm, London.

Morris, A. & Maxwell, G. (1993) 'Juvenile Justice in New Zealand: A New Paradigm', *Australian and New Zealand Journal of Criminology*, 26(1): 72–90.

Morris, L. & Irwin, S. (1992) 'Employment Histories and the Concept of the Underclass', *Sociology: The Journal of the British Sociological Association*, 26(3): 401–20.

Moss, I. (1993) *State of the Nation: A Report on People of Non-English-Speaking Backgrounds* (Human Rights and Equal Opportunity Commission), Australian Government Publishing Service, Canberra.

Moynihan, J. & Coleman, C. (1996) 'Unemployment and Crime', *New Law Journal*, 27 September: 1382–4.

Mukherjee, S.K. (1983) *Age and Crime*, Australian Institute of Criminology, Canberra.

—— (1985) 'Juvenile Delinquency: Dimensions of the Problem', in Borowski, A. & Murray, J. (eds) *Juvenile Delinquency in Australia*, Methuen, North Ryde.

—— (1997a) 'The Dimensions of Juvenile Crime' in Borowski, A. & O'Connor, I. (eds) *Juvenile Crime, Justice and Corrections*, Longman, Sydney.

—— (1999) *Ethnicity and Crime*, Trends and Issues in Crime and Criminal Justice No.117, Australian Institute of Criminology, Canberra.

Mukherjee, S. K., Carcach, C. & Higgins, K. (1997) *Juvenile Crime and Justice: Australia 1997*, Australian Institute of Criminology, Canberra.

Muncie, J. (2002) 'Policy Transfers and What Works: Some Reflections on Comparative Youth Justice', *Youth Justice*, 1(3): 27–35.

—— (2004) *Youth and Crime* (2nd edn), Sage, London.

Muncie, J. & Coventry, G. (1989) 'Punishment in the Community and the Victorian Youth Attendance Order: A Look into the Future', *Australian and New Zealand Journal of Criminology*, 22(2): 179–90.

Murray, G. (1995) 'The Authoritarian Exclusion of Young People from the Public Domain—Prevention or Provocation?', paper presented at the Youth and Community Preventing Crime Conference, Brisbane, 27–28 September.

—— (2000) 'A Review of a Young Women's Project: What about the Girls!', *Rights Now*, National Children's and Youth Law Centre, Sydney.

Naffine, N. (1987) *Female Crime: The Construction of Women in Criminology*, Allen & Unwin, Sydney.

—— (1990) *Law and the Sexes: Explorations in Feminist Jurisprudence*, Allen & Unwin, Sydney.

—— (1993) 'Philosophies of Juvenile Justice', in Gale, F., Naffine, N. & Wundersitz, J. (eds) *Juvenile Justice: Debating the Issues*, Allen & Unwin, Sydney.

—— (1997) *Feminism and Criminology*, Allen & Unwin, Sydney.

—— & Gale, F. (1989) 'Testing the Nexus: Gender, Crime and Unemployment', *British Journal of Criminology*, 29:144.

Naffine, N., Wundersitz, J. & Gale, F. (1990) 'Back to Justice for Juveniles: The Rhetoric or Reality of Law Reform', *Australian and New Zealand Journal of Criminology*, 23(3): 192–205.

National Children's Youth and Law Centre (1995) *Australian Children's Charter*, National Children's and Youth Law Centre, Sydney.

—— and Defence for Children International (2005) *The Non-Government Report on the Implementation of the United Nations Convention on the Rights of the Child in Australia*, National Children's Youth and Law Centre, Kensington.

National Crime Prevention (Australia) (1999) *Pathways to Prevention. Developmental and Early Intervention Approaches to Crime in Australia*, National Crime Prevention, Commonwealth Attorney-General's Department, Canberra.

National Crime Prevention Council (Canada) (1996) *Mobilizing Political Will and Community Responsibility to Prevent Youth Crime*, National Crime Prevention Council, Ottawa.

National Inquiry into the Separation of Aboriginal and Torres Strait Islander Children and Their Families (NISATSIC) (1997) *Bringing Them Home*, Commonwealth of Australia, Canberra.

National Motor Vehicle Theft Reduction Council (2006) *Theft Watch No. 18*, Melbourne.

National Police Ethnic Advisory Bureau (1997) *Descriptions of Persons Issued by Police to the Media: National Guidelines*, National Police Ethnic Advisory Bureau, Melbourne.

National Youth Affairs Research Scheme/Australian Bureau of Statistics (NYARS/ABS) (1993) *Australia's Young People: A Statistical Profile*, National Clearinghouse for Youth Studies, Hobart.

Nava, M. (1984) 'Youth Service Provision, Social Order and the Question of Girls', in McRobbie, A. & Nava, M. (eds) *Gender and Generation*, Macmillan, London.

Nettler, G. (1984) *Explaining Crime*, McGraw-Hill, New York.

New South Wales AJAC (2000) *Discussion Paper on Circle Sentencing*, <www.lawlink. nsw.gov.au/ajac.nsf/pages/circle>, accessed 30 September 2001.

New South Wales Bureau of Crime Statistics and Research (2004) *Who are the Offenders?*, [publisher], Sydney.

—— (2005a) *NSW Criminal Courts Statistics* 2004, [publisher], Sydney.

—— (2005b) Recorded Crime Statistics 2004, [publisher], Sydney.

New South Wales Crime Prevention Division (1999) *Juvenile Crime in New South Wales. A Review of the Literature*, Attorney-General's Department, Sydney.

New South Wales Department of Family and Community Services (1988) *Report from the Working Party on Services to Young People with Intellectual Disabilities in the Juvenile Justice System*, NSW Department of Family and Community Services, Sydney.

New South Wales Department of Juvenile Justice (1999) *Annual Report 1998–99*, NSW Department of Juvenile Justice, Sydney.

—— (2000) *Annual Children's Court Statistics Criminal Matters 1999–2000*, NSW Department of Juvenile Justice, Sydney.

—— (2000) *Girls' and Young Women's Action Plan 2002–2004*, NSW Department of Juvenile Justice, Sydney.

—— (2003) *Young People in Custody Health Survey 2003. Key Findings Report*, available online at <www.djj.nsw.gov.au/pdf/publications/2003YoungPeopleInCustody.pdf>.

—— (2005) *Annual Report 2004–05*, NSW Department of Juvenile Justice, Sydney.

New South Wales Juvenile Justice Advisory Council (1993) *Green Paper Future Directions for Juvenile Justice in NSW*, Juvenile Justice Advisory Council, Sydney.

—— (2001a) *Report from the Mental Health Working Party*, Juvenile Justice Advisory Council, Sydney.

—— (2001b) *Report from the Young Women's Working Party*, Juvenile Justice Advisory Council, Sydney.

New South Wales Law Reform Commission (1996) *People With an Intellectual Disability and the Criminal Justice System*, Report No. 80, Law Reform Commission, Sydney.

—— (2001) *Sentencing Young Offenders*, Issues Paper No. 19, Law Reform Commission, Sydney.

New South Wales Legislative Council (2005) *Report of the Inquiry into Juvenile Offenders*, Select Committee on Juvenile Offenders, Parliament, Sydney.

New South Wales Office of the Ombudsman (1994) *Race Relations and Our Police*, Office of the Ombudsman, Sydney.

—— (1996) *Report of the Inquiry into Juvenile Detention Centres*, Office of the Ombudsman, Sydney.

—— (1999) *Policing Public Safety*, Office of the Ombudsman, Sydney.

—— (2000) *Police and Public Safety Act*, Office of the Ombudsman, Sydney.

New South Wales Shopping Centre Protocol Project (2005) *Creating the Dialogue: A guide to developing a local youth shopping centre protocol*, New South Wales Attorney General's Crime Prevention Division, Sydney.

New South Wales Standing Committee on Social Issues (1992) *Juvenile Justice in New South Wales*, *Report No. 4*, Parliament of New South Wales, Legislative Council, Sydney.

—— (1995) *A Report into Youth Violence in New South Wales*, Legislative Council, Parliament of New South Wales, Sydney.

—— (1996) *Inquiry into Children's Advocacy*, *Report No. 10*, Parliament of New South Wales, Legislative Council, Sydney.

New Zealand Ministry of Justice & the Ministry of Social Development (2002) *Youth Offending Strategy*, Ministry of Justice and Ministry of Social Development, Wellington.

Noble, G., Poynting, S. & Tabar, P. (1999) 'Lebanese Youth and Social Identity', in White, R. (ed.) *Australian Youth Subcultures: On the Margins and In the Mainstream*, National Clearinghouse for Youth Studies, Hobart.

O'Brien, K.J. (2004) *Childrens Court of Queensland 11th Annual Report, 2003–2004*, Childrens Court of Queensland, Brisbane.

O'Connell, T. (1993) 'Wagga Wagga Juvenile Cautioning Program: "It May Be The Way To Go!"', in Atkinson, L. & Gerull, S.-A. (eds) *National Conference on Juvenile Justice: Conference Proceedings*, Australian Institute of Criminology, Canberra.

O'Connor, I. (1994) 'Young People and their Rights', in White, R. & Alder, C. (eds) *The Police and Young People in Australia*, Cambridge University Press, Melbourne.

—— (1998) 'Models of Juvenile Justice', in Alder, C. (ed.) *Juvenile Crime and Juvenile Justice*, Research and Public Policy Series No 14, Australian Institute of Criminology, Canberra.

—— & Sweetapple, P. (1988) *Children in Justice*, Longman Cheshire, Melbourne.

O'Grady, C. (1992) 'A Rising Star in the Prosecution of Juveniles in Victoria', *Youth Studies Australia*, 11(4): 35–40.

O'Malley, P. (1999) 'Volatile and Contradictory Punishment', *Theoretical Criminology*, 3(2), May 1999, 175–96.

——, Coventry, G. & Walters, R. (1993) 'Victoria's "Day in Prison Program"': An Evaluation and Critique', *Australian and New Zealand Journal of Criminology*, 26(2): 171–83.

O'Malley, P. & Sutton, A. (eds) (1997) *Crime Prevention in Australia: Issues in Policy & Research*, Federation Press, Sydney.

O'Neill, S. & Bathgate, J. (1993) *Policing Strategies in Aboriginal and Non-English Speaking Background Communities*, Northern Territory Police, Winnellie, Northern Territory.

Office of Crime Statistics and Research (2005) *Crime and Justice in South Australia, 2004. Juvenile Justice*, Office of Crime Statistics and Research, South Australian Attorney-General's Department, Adelaide.

Office of Juvenile Justice and Delinquency Prevention (2000) *OJJDP Statistical Briefing Book*, Office of Juvenile Justice and Delinquency Prevention, US Department of Justice, Washington, DC, at <http://ojjdb.ncjrs.org/ojstatbb/html/qa253.html>, accessed 10 January 2002.

Ogilvie, E. (1996) 'Masculine Obsessions: An Examination of Criminology, Criminality and Gender', *Australian and New Zealand Journal of Criminology*, 29(3): 205–27.

—— & Lynch, M. (1999) 'A Culture of Resistance: Adolescents in Detention', in White R. (ed.) *Australian Youth Subcultures: On the Margins and In the Mainstream*, National Clearinghouse for Youth Studies, Hobart.

Ogilvie, E., Lynch, M. & Bell, S. (2000) *Gender and Official Statistics: The Juvenile Justice System in Queensland, 1998–1999*, Trends and Issues No. 162, Australian Institute of Criminology, Canberra.

Omaji, P. (2003) *Responding to Youth Crime: Towards Radical Criminal Justice Partnerships*, Hawkins Press, Sydney.

Palmer, D. (1997) 'When Tolerance is Zero', *Alternative Law Journal*, 22(5): 232–6.

Parent, D. (1994) 'Boot Camps Failing to Achieve Goals', *Overcrowded Times*, 5(4): 8–11.

Parker, H., Casburn, M. & Turnbull, D. (1981) *Receiving Juvenile Justice*, Basil Blackwell, Oxford.

Pascoe, T. (2005) 'The Youth Justice System and the Youth Murri Court', paper presented at *Our Shared Future Conference*, Brisbane Youth Detention Centre, 7 June 2005.

Pearson, G. (1983) *Hooligan: A History of Respectable Fears*, Macmillan, London.

Pe-Pua R. (1996) *'We're Just Like Other Kids!': Street-frequenting Youth of Non-English-speaking Background*, Bureau of Immigration, Multicultural and Population Research, Melbourne.

—— (1999) 'Youth and Ethnicity: Images and Constructions' in White, R. (ed.) *Australian Youth Subcultures: On the Margins and In the Mainstream*, Australian Clearinghouse for Youth Studies, Hobart.

Perrone S. & White R. (2000) *Young People and Gangs*, Trends and Issues in Crime and Criminal Justice, No. 167, Australian Institute of Criminology, Canberra.

Pettit, P. & Braithwaite, J. (1993) 'Not Just Deserts, Even in Sentencing', *Current Issues in Criminal Justice*, 4(3): 225–39.

Pitts, J. (1988) *The Politics of Juvenile Crime*, Sage, London.

Pixley, J. (1993) *Citizenship and Employment: Investigating Post-Industrial Options*, Cambridge University Press, Melbourne.

Platt, A. (1977) *The Child Savers*, University of Chicago Press, Chicago.

Plummer, K. (1979) 'Misunderstanding Labelling Perspectives', in Downes, D. & Rock, P. (eds) *Deviant Interpretations*, Martin Robertson, Oxford.

Polk, K. (1997a) 'The Coming Crisis of Abandoned Youth: A look at the future of juvenile justice in Australia', in Borowski, A. and O'Connor, I. (eds) *Juvenile Crime, Justice and Corrections*, Longman, Melbourne.

—— (1997b) 'A Community and Youth Development Approach to Youth Crime Prevention', in O'Malley, P. & Sutton, A. (eds) *Crime Prevention in Australia: Issues in Policy & Research*, Federation Press, Sydney.

—— & Kobrin, S. (1973) *Delinquency Prevention Through Youth Development*, US Department of Health, Education and Welfare, Washington.

Polk, K. & White, R. (1999) 'Economic Adversity and Criminal Behaviour: Rethinking Youth Unemployment and Crime', *Australian and New Zealand Journal of Criminology*, 32(3): 284–302.

Potas, I., Vining, A. & Wilson, P. (1990) *Young People and Crime: Costs and Prevention*, Australian Institute of Criminology, Canberra.

Poynting, S. (1999) 'When "Zero Tolerance" Looks Like Racial Intolerance: "Lebanese Youth Gangs", Discrimination and Resistance', *Current Issues in Criminal Justice*, 11(1): 74–8.

——, Noble, G. & Tabar, P. (2001) 'Middle Eastern Appearances: "Ethnic Gangs", Moral Panic and Media Framing', *Australian and New Zealand Journal of Criminology*, 34(1): 67–90.

—— & Collins, J. (2004) *Bin Laden in the Suburbs: Criminalising the Arab Other*, Sydney Institute of Criminology, Sydney.

Pratt, J. (1989) 'Corporatism: The Third Model of Juvenile Justice', *British Journal of Criminology*, 29(3): 236–54.

Premier's Department (Queensland) (1999) *Tough on the Causes of Crime: Towards a Queensland Crime Prevention Strategy Discussion Paper*, Queensland Government, Brisbane.

Presdee, M. (2001) *Cultural Criminology and the Carnival of Crime*, Routledge, London.

Pusey, M. (2003) *The Experience of Middle Australia: The Troubling Experience of Economic Reform*, Cambridge University Press, Cambridge.

—— (2004) *The Changing Relationship Between The Generations ... it could even be good news?* Bob White Memorial Lecture, No.3, School of Sociology & Social Work, University of Tasmania, Hobart.

Putnins, A. (1995) 'Recent Drug Use and Suicidal Behaviour among Young Offenders', *Drug and Alcohol Review*, 14: 151–8.

—— (2001) *Substance Use by South Australian Young Offenders*, Information Bulletin No. 19, Office of Crime Statistics, Attorney-General's Department, Adelaide.

Race Discrimination Commissioner (1995) *State of the Nation*, Human Rights and Equal Opportunity Commission, Sydney.

Read, P. (1982) *The Stolen Generations*, NSW Ministry of Aboriginal Affairs, Sydney.

Reddrop, S. (1997) *Outdoor Programs for Young Offenders in Detention: An Overview*, National Clearinghouse for Youth Studies, Hobart.

—— (1998) 'Outdoor Programs for Serious Young Offenders', Master's thesis, Department of Criminology, University of Melbourne, Melbourne.

Redhead, S. (1997) *Subculture to Clubcultures: An Introduction to Popular Cultural Studies*, Blackwell, Oxford.

Reiss, A. (1986) 'Why Are Communities Important in Understanding Crime?', in Reiss, A. & Tonry, M. (eds) *Communities and Crime*, University of Chicago Press, Chicago.

Rodd, H. (1995) 'Collectively Reshaping Lives: The experience of growing up "ethnic" in Melbourne's west', in Guerra, C. & White, R. (eds) *Ethnic Minority Youth in Australia*, National Clearinghouse for Youth Studies, Hobart.

Rodger, J. (1992) 'The Welfare State and Social Closure: Social Division and the "Underclass"', *Critical Social Policy*, 35: 45–63.

Rose, N. (1989) *Governing the Soul: The Shaping of the Private Self*, Routledge, London.

Rubington, E. & Weinberg, M. (eds) (1978) *Deviance: The Interactionist Perspective*, Macmillan, New York.

Rutherford, A. (1986) *Growing Out of Crime*, Penguin, Harmondsworth.

Rutter, M. & Giller, M. (1983) *Juvenile Delinquency: Trends and Perspectives*, Penguin, Harmondsworth.

Ryan, M. & Smith, D. (1994) *Investigation of the Circumstances Surrounding Incidents at Westbrook Youth Detention Centre*, Department of Family Services and Aboriginal and Islander Affairs, Brisbane.

Salmelainen, P. (1995) *The Correlates of Offending Frequency: A Study of Juvenile Theft Offenders in Detention*, NSW Bureau of Crime Statistics and Research, Sydney.

Sampson, R. (1991) 'Linking the Micro- and Macro-Level Dimensions of Community Social Organisation', *Social Forces*, 70(1): 43–64.

—— (1993) 'The Community Context of Violent Crime', in Wilson, W. (ed.) *Sociology and the Public Agenda*, Sage, Newbury Park.

Sampson, R., Raudenbush, S. & Earls, F. (1997) 'Neighborhoods and Violent Crime: A Multilevel Study of Collective Efficacy', *Science*, 277:918–24.

Sandercock, L. (1997) 'From Main Street to Fortress: The future of malls as public spaces—or "shut up and shop"', *Just Policy*, (9): 27–34.

Sandor, D. & White, R. (1993) 'Police Powers Extended', *Alternative Law Journal*, 18(6): 299–300.

Sansom, B. & Baines, P. (1988) 'Aboriginal Child Placement in the Urban Context', in Morse, B. & Woodman, G. (eds) *Indigenous Law and the State*, Foris Publications, Dordrecht.

Sarri, R. (1983) 'Gender Issues in Juvenile Justice', *Crime and Delinquency*, 29(3): 381.

Saville, L. (1993) 'Future Directions for Girls in Custody', in Atkinson, L. & Gerull, S.-A. (eds) *National Conference on Juvenile Justice: Conference Proceedings*, Australian Institute of Criminology, Canberra.

Scher, I. & Payne, J. (1999) 'School Discipline and Youth Justice Conferencing', Discussion Paper 002/99, National Children's and Youth Law Centre, Sydney.

Schissel, B. (1993) *Social Dimensions of Canadian Youth Justice*, Oxford University Press, Toronto.

—— (1997) *Blaming Children: Youth Crime, Moral Panics and the Politics of Hate*, Fernwood Publishing, Halifax.

—— (2002) 'Youth Crime, Youth Justice, and the Politics of Marginalization', in Schissel, B. & Brooks, C. (eds) *Marginality and Condemnation: An Introduction to Critical Criminology*, Fernwood Publishing, Halifax.

Schlossman, S. & Wallace, S. (1978) 'The Crime of Precocious Sexuality: Female Juvenile Delinquency in the Progressive Era', *Harvard Educational Review*, 48(1): 65–94.

Schulte, C., Mouzos, J. & Makkai, T. (2005) *Drug Use Monitoring in Australia, 2004 Annual Report on Drug Use Among Police Detainees*, Australian Institute of Criminology, Canberra.

Scraton, P. & Chadwick, K. (1991) 'The Theoretical and Political Priorities of Critical Criminology', in Stenson, K. & Cowell, D. (eds) *The Politics of Crime Control*, Sage, London.

Searles, M. & Goodfellow, G. (eds) (1994) *Heroes and Villains: An Anthology of Poems by Young People in Detention*, South Australian Youth Participation Arts Project, Adelaide.

Seeto, F. (1995) 'Not Pretending, Acting: Young people of non-English-speaking background using drama to create change', in Guerra, C. & White, R. (eds) *Ethnic Minority Youth in Australia*, National Clearinghouse for Youth Studies, Hobart.

Segal, L. (1990) *Slow Motion: Changing Masculinities, Changing Men*, Virago Press, London.

Semmens, B., Cook, S. & Grimwade, C. (1999) *Evaluation of the Behaviour Management Program at the Melbourne Juvenile Justice Centre*, Working Paper 20, Youth Research Centre, University of Melbourne.

Semmens, R. (1990) 'Individual Control or Social Development', *Youth Studies*, 9(3): 23–9.

Senate Community Affairs References Committee (2004) *Forgotten Australians. A Report on Australians Who Experienced Institutional or Out-of-Home Care*, Commonwealth of Australia, Canberra.

Senate Community Affairs References Committee (2004) *A Hand Up Not A Hand Out: Renewing the Fight Against Poverty, Report on Poverty and Financial Hardship*, Senate Printing Unit, Parliament House, Canberra.

Senate Employment, Education and Training References Committee (1996) *Report of the Inquiry into Education and Training in Correctional Facilities*, Australian Government Publishing Service, Canberra.

Senate Legal and Constitutional References Committee (2000) *Inquiry into the Human Rights (Mandatory Sentencing of Juvenile Offenders) Bill 1999*, Commonwealth of Australia, Canberra.

Sercombe, H. (1993) 'Easy Pickings: The Children's Court and the Economy of News Production', paper presented to Youth 93: The Regeneration Conference, Hobart, 3–5 November.

—— (1995) 'The Face of the Criminal is Aboriginal', in Bessant, J., Carrington, K. & Cook, S. (eds) *Cultures of Crime and Violence: The Australian Experience*, La Trobe University Press, Melbourne.

—— (1997) 'Clearing the Streets: Youth curfews and social order', *Just Policy*, (10): 14–19.

Seymour, J. (1988) *Dealing With Young Offenders*, Law Book Company, Sydney.

Shacklady-Smith, L. (1978) 'Sexist Assumptions and Female Delinquency: An Empirical Investigation', in Smart, C. & Smart, B. (eds) *Women, Sexuality and Social Control*, Routledge & Kegan Paul, London.

Shaw, C. & McKay, H. (1942) *Juvenile Delinquency and Urban Areas*, Chicago University Press, Chicago.

Simpson, B. & Simpson, C. (1993) 'The Use of Curfews to Control Juvenile Offending in Australia: Managing Crime or Wasting Time?', *Current Issues in Criminal Justice*, 5(2): 184–99.

Skrzypiec, G. and Wundersitz, J. (2005) *Young People Born 1984. Extent of Involvement with the Juvenile Justice System*, Office of Crime Statistics and Research, Adelaide.

Slattery, P. (2000/2001) 'Kids locked up', *Education Links*, (61/62): 56–60.

Smart, C. (1976) Women, *Crime and Criminology: A Feminist Critique*, Routledge & Kegan Paul, London.

Smith, G. (1975) 'Kids and Coppers', *Australian and New Zealand Journal of Criminology*, 8(2): 221–230.

Sparkes, R. F., Genn, H. G. & Dodd, D. J. (1977) *Surveying Victims*, Wiley, London.

Spigelman, J. (1999) 'Sentencing Guideline Judgments', *Australian Law Journal*, 73: 876–81.

Spitzer, S. (1975) 'Toward a Marxian Theory of Deviance', *Social Problems*, 22: 638–51.

Spoehr, J. (1997) 'Alternatives to Despair—Reflections on the youth employment policy debate', *Australian Options*, (9): 2–6.

Stokes, H. & Tyler, D. (1997) *Rethinking Inter-Agency Collaboration and Young People*, Language Australia and the Youth Research Centre, Melbourne University Press, Melbourne.

Stokes, I. (1992) 'Juvenile Justice in Tasmania', *Criminology Australia*, 4(1): 11–13.

Strang, H. (2001) *Restorative Justice Programs in Australia, A Report to the Criminology Research Council*, Australian Institute of Criminology, Canberra.

Strang, H. & Braithwaite, J. (eds) (2001) *Restorative Justice and Civil Society*, Cambridge University Press, Cambridge.

Stratton, J. (1992) *The Young Ones: Working Class Culture, Consumption and the Category of Youth*, Black Swan Press, Perth.

Stuart, B. (1997) *Building Community Justice Partnerships: Community Peacemaking Circles*, Aboriginal Justice Section, Department of Justice of Canada, Ottawa.

Sumner, C. (1990) 'Foucault, Gender and the Censure of Deviance', in Gelsthorpe, L. & Morris, A. (eds) *Feminist Perspectives in Criminology*, Open University Press, Milton Keynes.

Sutherland, E. & Cressy, D. (1974) *Criminology*, Lippincott Company, New York.

Sutton, A. (1994) 'Crime Prevention: Promise or Threat?', *Australian and New Zealand Journal of Criminology*, 27(1): 5–20.

—— (2000) 'Crime Prevention: A Viable Alternative to the Justice System?', in Chappell, D. & Wilson, P. (eds) *Crime and the Criminal Justice System in Australia: 2000 and Beyond*, Butterworths, Sydney.

Sveen, R. (1993) 'Travelling in the Wilderness: Experiential Learning and Youth-at-Risk', *Youth Studies Australia*, 12(3): 14–20.

Sweet, R. (1998) 'Youth: The Rhetoric and the Reality of the 1990s', in *Australia's Youth: Reality and Risk*, Dusseldorp Skills Forum and Others, Sydney.

Sykes, G. & Matza, D. (1957) 'Techniques of Neutralization: A Theory of Delinquency', *American Sociological Review*, 22: 664–70.

Szukalska, A. & Robinson, A. (2000) *Distributional Analysis of Youth Allowance*, Discussion Paper No. 49, National Centre for Social and Economic Modelling, Canberra.

Tait, D. (1994) 'Cautions and Appearances: Statistics About Youth and Police', in White, R. and Alder, C. (eds) *The Police and Young People in Australia*, Cambridge University Press, Melbourne.

Tame, C. (1991) 'Freedom, Responsibility and Justice: The Criminology of the "New Right"', in Stenson, K. and Cowell, D. (eds) *The Politics of Crime Control*, Sage, London.

Tashkoff, S. (2000) 'Children as Asylum Seekers in Australia', *Rights Now* (December: 7–8). National Children's and Youth Law Centre, Sydney.

Tasmanian Inter-Departmental Committee on Public Safety and the Response to Crime (1995) *Crime Prevention Through Community Enhancement: A Proposal for a Criminal Justice Strategy for Tasmania*, Government of Tasmania, Hobart.

Tauri, J. (1999) 'Explaining Recent Innovations in New Zealand's Criminal Justice System: Empowering Maori or Biculturalising the State', *Australian and New Zealand Journal of Criminology*, 32(2): 153–67.

Taylor, N. & Bareja, M. (2005) *2002 National Police Custody Survey*, Australian Institute of Criminology, Canberra.

Thomas, C. & Bishop, D. (1984) 'The Effect of Formal and Informal Sanctions on Delinquency: A Longitudinal Comparison of Labelling and Deterrence Theories', *Journal of Criminal Law and Criminology*, 75(4): 1222–45.

Tomsen, S. (1996) 'Ruling Men? Some Comments on Masculinity and Juvenile Justice', *Australian and New Zealand Journal of Criminology*, 29(2): 191–4.

—— (1997) 'Sexual Identity and Victimhood in Gay-Hate Murder Trials' in Cunneen, C., Fraser, D. & Tomsen, S. (eds) *Faces of Hate: Hate Crime in Australia*, Hawkins Press, Sydney.

Tomsen, S. & Mason, G. (2001) 'Engendering Homophobia: Violence, Sexuality and Gender Conformity', *Journal of Sociology*, 37(3): 265–81.

Tonry, M. & Farrington, D. (1995) 'Strategic Approaches to Crime Prevention', in Tonry, M. & Farrington, D. (eds) *Building a Safer Society: Strategic Approaches to Crime Prevention*, University of Chicago Press, Chicago.

Toumbourou, J. (1999) *Implementing Communities that Care in Australia: A Community Mobilisation Approach to Crime Prevention*, Trends and Issues in Crime and Criminal Justice, No. 122, Australian Institute of Criminology, Canberra.

Tressider, J., Macaskill, P., Bennett, D. & Nutbeam, D. (1997) 'Health Risks and Behaviour of Out-of-School 16-year-olds in New South Wales', *Australian and New Zealand Journal of Public Health*, 21(2): 168–74.

Trimboli, L. (2000) *An Evaluation of the New South Wales Youth Justice Conferencing Scheme*, NSW Bureau of Crime Statistics and Research, Sydney.

Trotter, C. (1995) *The Supervision of Offenders—What Works? A Study undertaken in community based corrections, Victoria*, Social Work Department, Monash University, Melbourne.

Tucker, M. (1977) *If Everyone Cared*, Ure Smith, Sydney.

Underwood, R., White, R. & Omelczuk, S. (1993) *Young People, Youth Services and Legal Issues*, Edith Cowan University, Joondalup.

United States Coordinating Council on Juvenile Justice and Delinquency Prevention (1996) *Combating Violence and Delinquency: The National Juvenile Justice Action Plan*, OJJDP, Washington, DC.

United States National Crime Prevention Council (1996) *Working with Local Laws to Reduce Crime*, NCPC, Washington, DC.

University of New South Wales Evaluation Consortium (2004) *Evaluation of the New South Wales Youth Drug Court Pilot Program*, Social Policy Research Centre, University of New South Wales, Sydney.

Urbis Keys Young (2001) *Aboriginal Child Welfare and Juvenile Justice Good Practice Project*, Urbis Keys Young, Sydney.

Utting, D. (1996) *Reducing Criminality Among Young People: A Sample of Relevant Programs in the United Kingdom*, Home Office Research Study 161, Home Office, London.

Van Krieken, R. (1991) *Children and the State*, Allen & Unwin, Sydney.

Veld, M. and Taylor, N. (2005), *Statistics On Juvenile Detention in Australia 1981–2004*, Technical and Background Paper No 18, Australian Institute of Criminology, Canberra.

Victorian Multicultural Commission (2000) *Multicultural Perspectives of Crime and Safety*, VMC, Melbourne.

Vinson, T. (2004) *Community Adversity and Resilience: The Distribution of Social Disadvantage in Victoria and New South Wales and the Mediating Role of Social Cohesion*, The Ignatius Centre for social policy and research, Jesuit Social Services, Melbourne.

Vinson, T., Abela, M. & Hutka, R. (1997) *Making Ends Meet: A Study of Unemployed Young People Living in Sydney*, Uniya Research Report No.1, Uniya Jesuit Social Justice Centre, Sydney.

Walgrave, L. (1999) 'Community Service as a Cornerstone of a Systemic Restorative Response to (Juvenile) Crime', in Bazemore, G. & Walgrave, L. (eds) *Restorative Juvenile Justice: Repairing the Harm of Youth Crime*, Criminal Justice Press, Monsey, New York.

—— & Bazemore, G. (1999) 'Reflections on the Future of Restorative Justice for Juveniles', in Bazemore, G. & Walgrave, L. (eds) *Restorative Juvenile Justice: Repairing the Harm of Youth Crime*, Criminal Justice Press, Monsey, New York.

Walker, J. (1992) *Estimates of the Cost of Crime in Australia*, Trends and Issues in Crime and Criminal Justice, No. 39, Australian Institute of Criminology, Canberra.

Walker, L. (1999) 'Hydraulic sexuality and hegemonic masculinity: Young working-class men and car culture' in White, R. (ed.) *Australian Youth Subcultures: On the Margins and In the Mainstream*, Australian Clearinghouse for Youth Studies, Hobart.

Walters, R. (1996) 'Alternatives to Youth Imprisonment: Evaluating the Victorian Youth Attendance Order', *Australian and New Zealand Journal of Criminology*, 29(2): 166–81.

Walton, P. (1993) 'Youth Subcultures, Deviancy and the Media', in White, R. (ed.) *Youth Subcultures: Theory, History and the Australian Experience*, National Clearinghouse for Youth Studies, Hobart.

Warner, C. (1982) 'A Study of Self-reported Crime of a Group of Male and Female High School Students', *Australian and New Zealand Journal of Criminology*, 15: 255–73.

—— (1994) 'The Legal Framework of Juvenile Justice', in White, R. and Alder, C. (eds) *The Police and Young People in Australia*, Cambridge University Press, Melbourne.

Watkins, J. (1992) *Youth and the Law*, Discussion Paper No. 3, Select Committee into Youth Affairs, Western Australian Government Printer, Perth.

Watson, L. (1989) 'Our Children: Part of the Past, Present, and Providing a Vision for the Future. A Murri Perspective', *Australian Child and Family Welfare*, August.

Watts, R. (1987) *The Foundations of the National Welfare State*, Allen & Unwin, Sydney.

—— (1996) 'Unemployment, the Underclass and Crime in Australia: A Critique', *Australian and New Zealand Journal of Criminology*, 29(1): 1–19.

Weatherburn, D. (1992) *Economic Adversity and Crime*, Trends and Issues in Crime and Criminal Justice, No. 40, Australian Institute of Criminology, Canberra.

—— & Lind, B. (1998) *Poverty, Parenting, Peers and Crime-Prone Neighbourhoods*, Trends and Issues in Crime and Criminal Justice, No. 85, Australian Institute of Criminology, Canberra.

—— (2001) *Delinquent-Prone Communities*, Cambridge Studies in Criminology, Cambridge University Press, Cambridge.

West, D. (1982) *Delinquency: Its Roots, Careers and Prospects*, Heinemann, London.

White, R. (1989) 'Making Ends Meet: Young People, Work and the Criminal Economy', *Australian and New Zealand Journal of Criminology*, 22(2): 136–50.

—— (1990) *No Space of Their Own: Young People and Social Control in Australia*, Cambridge University Press, Melbourne.

—— (1992) 'Tough Laws for Hard-Core Politicians', *Alternative Law Journal*, 17(2): 58–60.

—— (ed) (1993a) *Youth Subcultures: Theory, History and the Australian Experience*, National Clearinghouse for Youth Studies, Hobart.

—— (1993b) 'Police Vidiots', *Alternative Law Journal*, 18(3): 109–12.

—— (1994) 'Young People, Unemployment and Health', in Waddell, C. & Petersen, A. (eds) *Just Health: Inequality in Illness, Care and Prevention*, Churchill Livingstone, Melbourne.

—— (1996a) 'No-Go in the Fortress City: Young people, inequality and space', *Urban Policy and Research*, 14(1): 37–50.

—— (1996b) 'The Poverty of the Welfare State: Managing An Underclass', in James, P. (ed.) *The State in Question: Transformations of the Australian State*, Allen & Unwin, Sydney.

—— (1996c) 'Schooling with a Future?', *Just Policy*, No. 5: 44–50.

—— (1996d) 'Racism, Policing and Ethnic Youth Gangs', *Current Issues in Criminal Justice* 7(3): 302–13.

—— (1996e) 'Situating Crime Prevention: Models, Methods and Political Perspectives', *Crime Prevention Studies*, (5): 97–113.

—— (1997) 'Young People, Waged Work and Exploitation', *Journal of Australian Political Economy*, (40): 61–79.

—— (1997/98) 'Violence and Masculinity: The Construction of Criminality', *Arena Magazine*, December–January: 41–4.

—— (1998a) 'Curtailing Youth: A Critique of Coercive Crime Prevention', *Crime Prevention Studies*, (9): 93–113.

—— (1998b) *Public Space for Young People: A Guide to Creative Projects and Positive Strategies*, Australian Youth Foundation and the National Campaign Against Violence and Crime, Sydney.

—— (1999a) *Hanging Out: Negotiating Young People's Use of Public Space*, National Crime Prevention, Attorney-General's Department, Canberra.

—— (1999b) (ed.) *Australian Youth Subcultures: On the Margins and In the Mainstream*, Australian Clearinghouse for Youth Studies, Hobart.

—— (2000) 'Social Justice, Community Building and Restorative Strategies', *Contemporary Justice Review*, 3(1): 55–72.

—— (2001) 'Criminology for Sale: Institutional Change and Intellectual Field', *Current Issues in Criminal Justice*, 13(2): 127–42.

—— (2002) 'Indigenous Young Australians, Criminal Justice and Offensive Language', *Journal of Youth Studies*, 5(1): 21–34.

—— (2003) 'Communities, Conferences and Restorative Social Justice', *Criminal Justice*, 3(2): 139–160.

—— (2006) Youth Gang Research in Australia, in J. Short & L. Hughes (eds), *Studying Youth Gangs*, AltaMira Press, Walnut Creek, California.

—— & Alder, C. (eds) (1994) *The Police and Young People in Australia*, Cambridge University Press, Melbourne.

White, R. & Cunneen, C. (2006) 'Social Class, Youth Crime and Justice', in Goldson, B. & Muncie, J. (eds) *Youth Crime and Justice: Critical Issues*, Sage, London.

White, R. & Haines, F. (2004) *Crime and Criminology*, Oxford University Press, Melbourne.

White, R., Kosky, B. & Kosky, M. (2001) *MCS Shopping Centre Youth Project: A Youth-Friendly Approach to Shopping Centre Management*, Australian Clearinghouse for Youth Studies, Hobart.

White, R. & Mason, R. (2006) 'Youth Gangs and Youth Violence: Charting the Key Dimensions', *Australian and New Zealand Journal of Criminology*, 39(1): 54–70.

White, R., Murray, G. & Robins, N. (1996) *Negotiating Youth-Specific Public Space: A guide for youth & community workers, town planners and local councils*, Department of Training and Education Co-ordination, Sydney.

White, R. & Perrone, S. (2005) *Crime and Social Control: An Introduction*, Oxford University Press, Melbourne.

——, Guerra, C. & Lampugnani R. (1999) *Ethnic Youth Gangs in Australia: Do They Exist?* [Seven reports—Vietnamese, Latin American, Turkish, Somalian, Pacific Islander, Anglo-Australian, Summary], Australian Multicultural Foundation, Melbourne.

White, R. & van der Velden, J. (1996) 'Class and Criminality', *Social Justice*, 22(1): 51–74.

White, R. with Aumair, M., Harris, A. & McDonnell, L. (1997). *Any Which Way You Can: Youth livelihoods, community resources and crime*, Australian Youth Foundation, Sydney.

White, R. & Wyn, J. (2004) *Youth and Society: Exploring the Social Dynamics of Youth Experience*, Oxford University Press, Melbourne.

Willis, S. (1980) 'Made To Be Moral—At Parramatta Girls' School, 1898–1923', in Roe, J. (ed.) *Twentieth Century Sydney*, Hale & Iremonger, Sydney.

Wilson, P. & Lincoln, R. (1992) 'Young People, Economic Crisis, Social Control and Crime', *Current Issues in Criminal Justice*, 4(2): 110–16.

Wolfgang, M. E., Figlio, R. M. & Sellin, T. (1972) *Delinquency in a Birth Cohort*, University of Chicago Press, Chicago.

Women's Co-ordination Unit (1986) *Girls at Risk Report*, Women's Co-ordination Unit, NSW Premier's Office, Sydney.

Wooden, M. (1996) 'The Youth Labour Market: Characteristics and Trends', *Australian Bulletin of Labour*, 22(2): 137–60.

Wootten, H. (1989) *Report of the Inquiry into the Death of Malcolm Charles Smith*, Royal Commission into Aboriginal Deaths in Custody, Australian Government Publishing Service, Canberra.

—— (1991) *Regional Report of Inquiry in New South Wales, Victoria and Tasmania*, Royal Commission into Aboriginal Deaths in Custody, Australian Government Publishing Service, Canberra.

Wortley, S. (1999) 'A Northern Taboo: Research on Race, Crime and Criminal Justice in Canada', *Canadian Journal of Criminology*, 41(2): 261–74.

Wundersitz, J. (1993) 'Some Statistics on Youth Offending', in Gale, F., Naffine, N. & Wundersitz, J. (eds) *Juvenile Justice: Debating the Issues*, Allen & Unwin, Sydney.

Wundersitz, J., Naffine, N. & Gale, F. (1988) 'Chivalry, Justice or Paternalism? The Female Offender in the Juvenile Justice System', *Australian and New Zealand Journal of Criminology*, 24(3): 359–76.

Wyn, J. & White, R. (1997) *Rethinking Youth*, Allen & Unwin, Sydney.

Yasmar Juvenile Justice Centre (1994) *Mission and the Philosophy, Objectives and Key Outcomes for the Young Women in Custody Program*, Yasmar Juvenile Justice Centre, Sydney.

Young, J. (1971) 'The Role of the Police as Amplifiers of Deviancy, Negotiators of Reality and Translators of Fantasy: Some Consequences of Our Present System of Drug Control as Seen in Notting Hill', in Cohen, S. (ed.) *Images of Deviance*, Penguin, Harmondsworth.

—— (1981) 'Thinking Seriously About Crime: Some Models of Criminology', in Fitzgerald, M., McLennon, G. & Pawson, J. (eds) *Crime and Society: Readings in History and Theory*, Routledge & Kegan Paul, London.

Youth Action and Policy Association NSW (1997) *No Standing: Young People and Community Space Project Research Report*, YAPA, Sydney.

Youth Advocacy Centre (1993) *Juvenile Justice: Rhetoric or Reality?*, Youth Advocacy Centre, Brisbane.

Youth Justice Coalition (1990) *Kids in Justice. A Blueprint for the 90s*, Youth Justice Coalition, Sydney.

Youth Justice Coalition of NSW (1994) *Nobody Listens: The Experience of Contact between Young People and Police*, Youth Justice Coalition of NSW, Western Sydney Juvenile Justice Interest Group, and the Youth Action and Policy Association (NSW), Sydney.

Zehr, H. (1990) *Changing Lens: A New Focus for Crime and Justice*, Herald Press, Scottdale, Pennsylvania.

Zehr, H. & Mika, H. (1998) 'Fundamental Concepts of Restorative Justice', *Contemporary Justice Review*, 1(1): 47–56.

Zelinka, S. (1995) 'Ethnic Minority Young People', in Guerra, C. & White, R. (eds) *Ethnic Minority Youth in Australia*, National Clearinghouse for Youth Studies, Hobart.

INDEX

Birmingham Centre for Contemporary
  Cultural Studies (BCCS)   41
Blagg, H.   225
Blue Light discos   239
bodily samples   231
bonds   253, 271, 297
    see also diversion; good behaviour
      bonds
boot camps   302
boredom   289
Bowlby, John   214
Braithwaite, J.   77, 336–9, 345
Brisbane Youth Murri Court   168
budgets and resources, for detention
  centres   285
bureaus of crime statistics   98
burglary   57, 151

Cabramatta   178
camps   301–4
Canada   14, 17, 48, 321, 334
    sentencing circles   167
car stealing   56–7, 62, 64
Carpenter, Mary   9, 11
Carr, Bob   236
Carrington, K.   200, 202
case management   293
case planning   102, 300
    cautions   90, 155–6, 230–1, 271,
      343–4
    see also diversion
child labour   5–6
Child Welfare Act 1947 (WA)   235–6
Child Welfare Act 1960 (Tas)   107
child welfare system   5, 7–8
Children and Young Person's Act 1989
  (Vic)   107
children, best interests of and
  sentencing   256–7
Children (Care and Protection) Act 1987
  (NSW)   107
Children (Criminal Proceedings) Act 1987
  (NSW)   107
Children (Detention Centres Act) 1987
  (NSW)   277
*Children (Protection and Parental
  Responsibility) Act 1997* (NSW)
  55–6, 104, 236, 319

children's courts   13–15
    contact with   66–7
    Indigenous youth and   160–3
    judicial therapy   16–17
    utilization of sentencing options
      by   271–2
    welfare and criminal role   15
    welfare model of   107–9
    young people's experiences of   272–5
    see also juvenile courts; juvenile justice
church and Aboriginal people   144
circle sentencing   167–8, 340
city spaces and consumption   127–8,
  228–30, 310–11
Clarke, J.   263
class
    Australian society   117
    classical theory overlooks   30
    feminism and   204
    juvenile justice and   111
    multifactorial explanations of
      offending and   46, 73–4
    people and police   21, 245
    see also underclass; working class
classical theory   27–30, 106
coercive approaches to crime
  prevention   312, 313
coercive institutions   308–9
Collier, R.   216
commercial institutions   310–11
Commonwealth government   98–9
    see also state
communal objectives   352
communitarianism   338
Communities That Care prevention strategy   321
community
    corrections   296–304
    crime and   131–8, 236
    enhancement   318–19
    fear and policing of young people
      226, 236
    input, crime prevention   104, 316–20
    justice   350
    justice groups   165–6
    legal centres   100
    policing   239–41
    protection   257, 284